T0140519

Communications
in Computer and Information Science

2040

Rationale

The CCIS series is devoted to the publication of proceedings of computer science conferences. Its aim is to efficiently disseminate original research results in informatics in printed and electronic form. While the focus is on publication of peer-reviewed full papers presenting mature work, inclusion of reviewed short papers reporting on work in progress is welcome, too. Besides globally relevant meetings with internationally representative program committees guaranteeing a strict peer-reviewing and paper selection process, conferences run by societies or of high regional or national relevance are also considered for publication.

Topics

The topical scope of CCIS spans the entire spectrum of informatics ranging from foundational topics in the theory of computing to information and communications science and technology and a broad variety of interdisciplinary application fields.

Information for Volume Editors and Authors

Publication in CCIS is free of charge. No royalties are paid, however, we offer registered conference participants temporary free access to the online version of the conference proceedings on SpringerLink (http://link.springer.com) by means of an http referrer from the conference website and/or a number of complimentary printed copies, as specified in the official acceptance email of the event.

CCIS proceedings can be published in time for distribution at conferences or as post-proceedings, and delivered in the form of printed books and/or electronically as USBs and/or e-content licenses for accessing proceedings at SpringerLink. Furthermore, CCIS proceedings are included in the CCIS electronic book series hosted in the SpringerLink digital library at http://link.springer.com/bookseries/7899. Conferences publishing in CCIS are allowed to use Online Conference Service (OCS) for managing the whole proceedings lifecycle (from submission and reviewing to preparing for publication) free of charge.

Publication process

The language of publication is exclusively English. Authors publishing in CCIS have to sign the Springer CCIS copyright transfer form, however, they are free to use their material published in CCIS for substantially changed, more elaborate subsequent publications elsewhere. For the preparation of the camera-ready papers/files, authors have to strictly adhere to the Springer CCIS Authors' Instructions and are strongly encouraged to use the CCIS LaTeX style files or templates.

Abstracting/Indexing

CCIS is abstracted/indexed in DBLP, Google Scholar, EI-Compendex, Mathematical Reviews, SCImago, Scopus. CCIS volumes are also submitted for the inclusion in ISI Proceedings.

How to start

To start the evaluation of your proposal for inclusion in the CCIS series, please send an e-mail to ccis@springer.com.

Sridaran Rajagopal · Kalpesh Popat ·
Divyakant Meva · Sunil Bajeja
Editors

Advancements in Smart Computing and Information Security

Second International Conference, ASCIS 2023
Rajkot, India, December 7–9, 2023
Revised Selected Papers, Part IV

Springer

Editors
Sridaran Rajagopal (iD)
Marwadi University
Rajkot, Gujarat, India

Kalpesh Popat (iD)
Marwadi University
Rajkot, Gujarat, India

Divyakant Meva (iD)
Marwadi University
Rajkot, Gujarat, India

Sunil Bajeja (iD)
Marwadi University
Rajkot, Gujarat, India

ISSN 1865-0929 ISSN 1865-0937 (electronic)
Communications in Computer and Information Science
ISBN 978-3-031-59106-8 ISBN 978-3-031-59107-5 (eBook)
https://doi.org/10.1007/978-3-031-59107-5

Preface

In continuation of the successful introduction of the ASCIS series during 2022, we feel extremely happy and privileged to roll out the 2nd season: the International Conference on Advancements in Smart Computing & Information Security (ASCIS 2023). The conference was conducted during 7–9 December 2023, wherein leading researchers, academicians and industrialists participated from various countries across the globe. Eminent experts from Academia and Industry, including researchers in the top 2% of global scientific researchers from the Stanford list and industry were among our general co-chairs, program chairs and track chairs. ASCIS 2023 welcomed experts from top-ranked Indian Institutes such as IITs and NITs and reputable foreign universities. The members of the Advisory, Program and Branding & Outreach committees ensured the quality of the submissions and contributed majorly to the overall success of the conference.

Altogether, we received 432 technical papers under the 5 tracks, viz. AI & ML, Cyber Security, Computer Networks, Smart Computing and Inter-disciplinary Computer Applications, out of which we shortlisted 127 papers (29%) for Springer CCIS. There were 91 long papers (≥ 12 pages) and 36 short papers (< 12 pages). This year each paper underwent 4 technical reviews and the review process was also strengthened compared to last year. Thanks go to the staff of Springer CCIS for their consistent guidance and for supporting us for the second time.

The technical papers presented across the various application domains included healthcare, agriculture, automobile, civil and mechanical engineering, pharma, cybercrime, and sports. We appreciate all the enthusiastic authors who submitted their innovative research works as technical papers.

Some of the reputed global and national experts included Venkat Rayapati, Cyber Forza Inc, USA; H.R. Mohan, IEEE Computer Society, India; Deepak Jain, Dalian University of Technology, China; Ishu Gupta, International Institute of Information Technology, Bengaluru, India; Shamala Subramanian, University Putra Malaysia, Malaysia; Krishna Kumar, Keisoku Engineering System Co., Ltd., Japan; Sheng-Lung Peng, National Taipei University of Business, Taiwan; Sonali Agarwal, IIIT Allahabad, India; Sharad Raghavendra, Virginia Tech, USA; and Mahesh Ramachandran, Larsen & Toubro, India, who participated in ASCIS and gave the keynote addresses.

Our sincere thanks go to the esteemed sponsors, including the Science and Engineering Research Board (SERB), Coursera, D-Link, Stelcore, and Samatrix.

We believe that this collection will be highly useful for researchers and practitioners of AI & ML and their allied domains.

December 2023

Sridaran Rajagopal
Kalpesh Popat
Divyakant Meva
Sunil Bajeja

Organization

General Chair

R. Sridaran   Marwadi University, India

Program Committee Chairs

R. Sridaran   Marwadi University, India
Kalpesh Popat   Marwadi University, India
Divyakant Meva   Marwadi University, India
Sunil Bajeja   Marwadi University, India

Steering Committee

Ketanbhai Marwadi	Marwadi University, India
Jitubhai Chandarana	Marwadi University, India
Sandeep Sancheti	Marwadi University, India
R. B. Jadeja	Marwadi University, India
Lalitkumar Avasthi	NIT Hamirpur, India
H. R. Mohan	The Hindu/ICT Consultant, India
Sudeep Tanvar	Nirma University, India
R. Sridaran	Marwadi University, India
Naresh Jadeja	Marwadi University, India
Ankur Dumka	Women Institute of Technology, India
Ashwin Dobariya	Marwadi University, India
Shamala Subramanyam	Universiti Putra Malaysia, Malaysia
Oscar Castillo	Tijuana Institute of Technology, Mexico
Pascal Lorenz	University of Haute Alsace, France
Alvaro Rocha	University of Lisbon, Portugal
Shubhra Sankar Ray	Indian Statistical Institute, India
Kalpdrum Passi	Laurentian University, Canada
Varatharajan Ramachandran	Bharath University, India
Shruti Patil	Symbiosis Institute of Technology, India
Silvia Priscila	Bharath Institute of Higher Education and Research, India
Rajesh Kaluri	Vellore Institute of Technology, India

Suraiya Jabin	Jamia Millia Islamia University, India
Madhu Shukla	Marwadi University, India
Vijay Katkar	Annasaheb Dange College of Engineering and Technology, India
Pankaj Mudholkar	Marwadi University, India
Dimple Thakar	Marwadi University, India
Hardik Dhulia	Marwadi University, India
Jaypalsinh Gohil	Marwadi University, India
Sriram Padmanabhan	Marwadi University, India
Devang Patel	Marwadi University, India
Thangraj	Madurai Kamraj University, India
T. Devi	Bharathiar University, India
Padmavathi	Avinashilingam Institute for Home Science and Higher Education for Women, India
Vishal Jain	Sharda University, India
Banoth Rajkumar	University of Texas, USA
D. C. Jinwala	Sardar Vallabhbhai National Institute of Technology, India
R. Balasubhramanyam	Indian Institute of Technology, Roorkee, India
Umesh Bellur	Indian Institute of Technology, Bombay, India
Rajkumar Buyya	University of Melbourne, Australia
Valentina Emilia Balas	Aurel Vlaicu University of Arad/Academy of Romanian Scientists, Romania
Vincenzo Piuri	University of Milan, Italy
Xavier Fernando	Toronto Metropolitan University, Canada
Rodina Ahmad	University of Malaya, Malaysia
Xiao-zhigao	University of Eastern Finland, Finland
Tianhua Xu	University of Warwick, UK
Sheng-Lung Peng	National Taipei University of Business, Taiwan
Vijay Singh Rathore	Jaipur Engineering College & Research Center, India
C. K. Kumbharana	Saurashtra University, India
Parag Rughani	National Forensic Sciences University, India
Durgesh Mishra	Sri Aurobindo Institute of Technology, Indore, India
Vipin Tyagi	Jaypee University of Engineering and Technology, Guna, India
Hardik Joshi	Gujarat University, India
P. V. Virparia	Sardar Patel University, India
Priyanka Sharma	Rashtriya Raksha University, India
Uma Dulhare	MJCET, India
Chhagan Lal	Delft University of Technology, The Netherlands
Deepakkumar Panda	Cranfield University, UK

Shukor Sanim Mohd. Fauzi   Universiti Teknologi MARA, Malaysia
Sridhar Krishnan   Toronto Metropolitan University, Canada
Brajendra Panda   University of Arkansas, USA
Anand Nayyar   Duy Tan University, Vietnam
Monika Bansal   SSD Women's Institute of Technology, India
Ajay Kumar   KIET Group of Institutions, India

Technical Program Committee Chairs

AI & ML Track

Priti Sajja   Sardar Patel University, India
Kumar Rajamani   KLA Tencor, India
Sonali Agarwal   IIIT Allahabad, India

Cyber Security Track

Sudeep Tanwar   Nirma University, India
Padmavathi Ganpathi   Avinashilingam Institute for Home Science and
                                     Higher Education for Women, India
Vipin Tyagi   Jaypee University, India

Smart Computing Track

Jatinderkumar R. Saini   Symbiosis Institute of Computer Studies, India
Rajesh Kaluri   Vellor Institute of Technology, India
Shriram Kris Vasudevan   Intel Corporation, India

Computer Networks Track

Shamala Subramaniam   University Putra Malaysia, Malaysia
Atul Gonsai   Saurashtra University, India
Vijay Katkar   Annasaheb Dange College of Engineering and
                                     Technology, India

Interdisciplinary Computer Applications Track

Shobhit Patel   Marwadi University, India
Simar Preet Singh   Bennett University, India
Manvinder Singh Pahwa   Marwadi University, India

Additional Reviewers

A. Maheswary
A. P. Nirmala
A. Yovan Felix
Abhay Bhadauria
Abhilasha Vyas
Abhinav Tomar
Abhishek Sharma
Aditi Sharma
Ahmed BaniMustafa
Ajay Kumar
Ajay Kushwaha
Ajaykumar Patel
Ajita Deshmukh
Akash Saxena
Akshara Dave
Alvaro Rocha
Amanpreet Kaur
Amit Gupta
Amita Sharma
Amrinder Kaur
Amrita Kumari
Amutha S.
Anamika Rana
Anand Nayyar
Anandkumar Ramakrishnan
Anbmumani K.
Angelina R.
Anilkumar Suthar
Anitha K.
Ankit Didwania
Ankit Faldu
Ankit Shah
Ankur Goel
Anubhav Kumar Prasad
Anurag Vijay Agrawal
Anvip Deora
Anwar Basha H.
Arcangelo Castiglione
Arun Adiththan
Arun Raj Lakshminarayanan
Aruna Pavate
Asha V.
Ashish Kumar

Ashish Saini
Ashwin Makwana
Ashwin R. Dobariya
Ashwin Raiyani
Asmita Manna
Avinash Sharma
Avnip Deora
Ayush Somani
B. Suresh Kumar
B. Surendiran
Balraj Verma
Bandu Meshram
Banoth Rajkumar
Bharanidharan G.
Bharat Pahadiya
Bhavana Kaushik
Biswaranjan Mishra
B. J. D. Kalyani
Brajendra Panda
Brijesh Jajal
Budesh Kanwer
C. K. Kumbharana
C. P. Chandran
C. Prema
Chandra J.
Chandra Mohan
Charu Gupta
Chetan Dudhagara
Chhagan Lal
Chintan Thacker
Chintan Patel
D. C. Jinwala
Dafni Rose
Darshita Pathak
Daxa Vekariya
Deepak Kumar Verma
Deepakkumar Panda
Delecta Jenifer R.
Dhanamma Jagli
Dhruba Bhattacharyya
Dimple Thakar
Dipak Ramolia
Dipti Chauhan

Dipti Domadia
Disha Parekh
Disha Shah
Divya R.
Divya Didwania
Dviyanshu Chandra
Durgesh Mishra
Dushyantsinh Rathod
E. Karthikeyan
Deepak Tiwari
G. Charles Babu
G. Kavitha
G. Mahalakshmi
Galiveeti Poornima
Gaurav Agarwal
Gaurav Kumar Ameta
Goi Bok Min
Gulfarida Tulemissova
Gunjan Agarwal
Hardik Joshi
Hardik Patel
Hardik Molia
Hari Kumar Palani
Harish Kundra
Harshal Salunkhe
Hemant Ingale
Hemraj Lamkuche
Himanshu Maniar
Himanshu Rai
Ipseeta Nanda
J. Ramkumar
Jaimin Undavia
Jasminder Kaur Sandhu
Jatinderkumar Saini
Jay Dave
Jay Kumar Jain
Jayant Nandwalkar
Jayashree Nair
Jaydeep Ramani
Jaydeep Ramani
Jaykumar Dave
Jaypalsinh Gohil
Jignesh Doshi
Jinal Tailor
Jonnadula Narasimharao

Jose M. Molina
Juhi Singh
Juliet Rozario
Jyothi Balreddygari
Jyoti Khubchandani
Jyoti Kharade
Jyotsna Amin
K. Priya
K. Vallidevi
Kailash Patidar
Kajal Patel
Kalpdrum Passi
Kamal Batta
Kamal Saluja
Kamal Sutaria
Kannadhasan Suriyan
Kapil Joshi
Karuna Nidhi Pandagre
Karthik B.
Karthikeyan R.
Kavipriya P.
Kavitha Ganesh
Kaviyarasi R.
Kedir Lemma Arega
Keerti Jain
Keyurkumar Patel
Khaled Kamel
Krupa Mehta
Kruti Sutaria
Kumuthini C.
Lata Suresh
Lataben Gadhavi
Latchoumy P.
Lilly Florence M.
Lipsa Das
Lokesh Gagnani
M. Vinoth Kumar
M. Mohamed Iqbal
M. N. Hoda
Madhu Kirola
Madhu Shukla
Mahalakshmi G.
Malarkodi K. P.
Mahesh Shirole
Mallika Ravi Bhatt

Manisha Rawat

Manohar N.

Manoj Patil

Maruthamuthu R.

Mastan Vali Shaik

Maulik Trivedi

Maulika Patel

Meet Patel

Megha Jain

Mohamed Mosbah

Mohammed Wajid Khan

Mohan Subramani

Mohit Tiwari

Monika Arora

Monika Bansal

Monther Tarawneh

Mythili Shanmugam

N. Rajendran

N. Noor Alleema

Nabeena Ameen

Nagappan Govindarajan

Nagaraju Kilari

Nageswari D.

Narayan Joshi

Naresh Kumar

Navnish Goel

Nebojsa Bacanin

Neeraj Kumar Pandey

Neerja Kumari

Neeru Sharma

Neha Parashar

Neha Sharma

Neha Soni

Nethmini Thilakshi Weerawarna

Nidhi Chaudhry

Nilesh Patil

Nilesh Sabnis

Nirav Bhatt

Nirav Mehta

Nisha Khurana

Noel E. Estrella

Oscar Castillo

P. Rizwan Ahmed

P. Latchoumy

P. V. Virparia

Padma Selvaraj

Padmavathi

Pankaj Chawla

Parag Rughani

Parth Gautam

Parvathaneni Naga Srinivasu

Parwinder Kaur

Pascal Lorenz

Pathan Mohd Shafi

Patil Rahul Ashokrao

Payal Khubchandani

Poornima Vijaykumar

Pradip Jawandhiya

Pragadesawaran S.

Prashant Pittalia

Praveen Kumar

Pravesh Kumar Bansal

Preethi Sambandam Raju

Premkumar Borugadda

Priteshkumar Prajapati

Priya Chandran

Priya K.

Priyanka Sharma

Priyanka Suyal

Purnendu Bikash Acharjee

Pushparaj

Qixia Zhang

R. Balasubhramanyam

R. Senthil Kumar

R. Saranya

R. Sujithra Kanmani

Rachit Garg

Radha B.

Raghu N.

Rajan Patel

Rajasekaran Selvaraju

Rajender Kumar

Rajesh Bansode

Rajesh Kaluri

Raji C. G.

Rajib Biswas

Rajiv Iyer

Rajkumar Buyya

Rajkumar R.

Rakesh Kumar Yadav

Ramesh T. Prajapati
Ramveer Singh
Rashmi Soni
Ravendra Ratan Singh Jandail
Ravi Khatri
Ravirajsinh S. Vaghela
Rekha Rani
Renjith V. Ravi
Richa Adlakha
Rinkoo Bhatia
Ripal Ranpara
Ritesh Patel
Ritu Bhargava
Rodina Ahmad
Rohit Goyal
Rohit Kanauzia
Rujuta Shah
Rupali Atul Mahajan
Rupesh Kumar Jindal
Rushikumar Raval
Rutvi Shah
S. Sriranjani Mokshagundam
S. Jafar Ali Ibrahim
S. Balambigai
S. Kannadhasan
S. Muthakshi
S. Sharanyaa
S. Silvia Priscila
Safvan Vahora
Saifullah Khalid
Sailesh Iyer
Samir Patel
Samir Malakar
Samriti Mahajan
Sandeep Mathur
Sandip Sapan Chandra
Sandip T. Shingade
Sangeet Saha
Santosh Kumar Shukla
Sarita Vitthal Balshetwar
Saswati Mahapatra
Satvik Khara
Shadab Siddiqui
Shahera Patel
Shaik Khaja Mohiddin

Shailaja Jayashankar
Shamala Subramaniam
Shanti Verma
Sheikh Fahad Ahmad
Sheng-Lung Peng
Shilpa
Shruti Jain
Shruti Patil
Shubhra Sankar Ray
Shukor Sanim Mohd. Fauzi
Sonali Mishra
Sreejith Vignesh B. P.
Sridhar Krishnan
Subhadeep Chakraborty
Subramanian Karthikeyan
Sudhanshu Maurya
Suhasini Vijaykumar
Sumit Mittal
Sunil Bhirud
Sunil Gautam
Sunil Gupta
Sunil Kumar
Sunil Saxena
Suraiya Jabin
Surendra Rahamatkar
Swamydoss D.
Swarnlata Dakua
Sweeti Sah
Swetta Kukreja
T. S. Murugesh
T. Devi
T. Sathish Kumar
T. Buvaneswari
Tanmay Kasbe
Tejavath Balakrishna
Thangraj
Thirumurugan Shanmugam
Tianhua Xu
Tushar Jaware
U. Surya Kameswari
Uma Dulhare
Umang Thakkar
Umesh Bellur
V. Asha
V. Ajitha

V. S. D. Rekha
Vaibhav Gandhi
Valentina Emilia Balas
Varatharajan Ramachandran
Varinder Singh Rana
Varun Chand H.
Vatsal Shah
Vijay D. Katkar
Vijay Singh Rathore
Vikas Tripathi
Vincenzo Piuri
Vineet Kumar Singh
Vinjamuri Snch Dattu
Vinod L. Desai

Vinoth Kumar M.
Vinothina V.
Vipin Sharma
Vipin Tyagi
Vipul A. Shah
Vishal Bharti
Viswan Vimbi
Xavier Fernando
Xiao-Zhi Gao
Yogendra Kumar
Yogesh Kumar
Yogesh R. Ghodasara
Yugendra D. Chincholkar

Abstract of Keynotes

Generative AI vs Chat GPT vs Cognitive AI Impact on Cyber Security Real World Applications

Venkat Rayapati

Cyber Forza, Inc., USA

This presentation provides an overview of Generative AI vs Chat GPT vs Cognitive AI impact on the real-world Cyber Security Applications. State-Sponsored Cyber Attacks against India went up by 278% between 2021 and September 2023. Cyber security is a real challenge for the whole world, India is a major target about 15% of the total cyberattacks have been observed in 2023. This presentation covers brief summary of the cyberattacks and the impact. Artificial Intelligence (AI) will be used for certain behavioral analytics, predictive analytics, and risk reduction analytics purpose.

Generative AI and Open AI current applications used in the industry, they do not have direct impact on security. Chat GPT and Open AI current applications in the industry, how they will influence cyber security impact analysis provided. Cognitive AI methods and applications importance for the overall cyber risk reduction addressed.

Generative AI or Chat GPT or Cognitive AI are all fundamentally dependent on certain Open AI Algorithms, libraries, API's, which further refines application domain and efficacy. Cyber criminals can modify malware code to evade detection. ML is ideal for anti-malware protection, since it can draw on data from previously detected malware to detect new variants. This works even when dangerous code is hidden within innocent code. AI-powered network monitoring tools can track user behavior, detect anomalies, and react accordingly. A simple case study is presented to demonstrated the effective of the current AI versus feature needs of AI. The dangers of AI in Cyberattack space is highlighted with an example. Recommendations provided for the over all real time cyber security risk reduction.

Empowering Smart Computing Through the Power of Light

Shamala Subramaniam

Universiti Putra Malaysia

The paradigms which govern technology and civilization is constantly emerging with innovations and transforming the definition of norms. These require pre-requisites encompassing the pillars which constitute the Industry 4.0, 5.0 and the subsequent revolutions. It is require discussing the ability to harness the wide spectrum of rich resources and discover the profound impact that the technology transformation is having on industry innovation, exploring the challenges and opportunities that this presents, and consider the significant implications.

Subsequently, leveraging co-existence strategies to address particularly, the Internet of Things (IoT) and the Internet of Everything (IoE) as a driving force behind further densification. The LiFi technology, which stands for light fidelity role in addressing the challenges emerging from densification and as a factor to optimize co-existences and interdisciplinary dimensions. It is require discussing the significant and high impact of the correlation between sports and technology encompassing creative LiFi solutions in this area. The realization of an idea is largely attributed to the ability of a researcher to deploy strategies to evaluate and gauge the actual performance of this idea. The substantial research findings in the area of Access Point Assignment (APA) algorithms in a hybrid LiFi – WiFi network require to be discussed. A Multi-criteria Decision-Making (MCDM) problem is formulated to determine a network-level selection for each user over a period of time The decision problem is modelled as a hierarchy that fragments a problem into a hierarchy of simple and small sub problems, and the selection of the AP network among various alternatives is a considered as an MCDM problem. The result of this research empowers the APA for hybrid LiFi networks with a new perspective.

Optimal Transport Algorithms with Machine Learning Applications

Sharath Raghavendra

Virginia Tech, USA

Optimal Transport distance is a metric to measure similarity between probability distributions and has been extensively studied in economics and statistics since the 18th century. Here we introduce the optimal transport problem and present several of its modern applications in data analytics and machine learning. It is also require to address algorithmic challenges related to scalability and robustness and present partial solutions towards overcoming these challenges.

Some Research Issues on Cyber Security

Sheng-Lung Peng

National Taipei University of Business, Taiwan

Recently, a cyber security model M is defined by a three-tuple $M = (T, C, P)$, where $T = (V, E)$ is a tree rooted at r having n non-root vertices, C is a multiset of penetration costs $c_1, \ldots, c_n \in Z^+$, and P is a multiset of prizes $p_1, \ldots, p_n \in Z^+$. The attack always begins at the root r and the root always has prize 0. A security system (T, c, p) with respect to a cyber security model $M = (T, C, P)$ is given by two bijections $c : E(T) \rightarrow C$ and $p : V(T) \backslash \{r\} \rightarrow P$. A system attack in (T, c, p) is given by a subtree T' of T that contains the root r of T. The cost of a system attack T' with respect to (T, c, p) is given by the cost $cst(c, p, T') = \Sigma_{e \in E(T')} c(e)$. The prize of a system attack T' with respect to (T, c, p) is given by the prize $pr(c, p, T') = \Sigma_{u \in V(T')} p(u)$. For a given budget $B \in Z^+$ the maximum prize $pr^*(c, p, B)$ with respect to B is defined by $pr^*(c, p, B) = \max\{pr(c, p, T') | \text{for all } T' \subseteq T, \text{ where } cst(c, p, T') \leq B\}$. A system attack T' whose prize is maximum with respect to a given budget B is called an optimal attack. In this talk, we first introduce the defined cyber security problem. We then propose some extended models for future research.

Smart Infrastructure and Smart Agriculture- Japan Use Cases

Krishna Kumar

Vice President - Corporate Strategy, Keisoku Engineering System Co., Ltd., Tokyo, Japan

To understand the smart infrastructure and smart agriculture and its key aspects it is require to discuss the use cases of advanced countries. This explores the burgeoning landscape of smart computing applications in Japan, where the pressing challenges of population decline and an aging society have accelerated the adoption of intelligent systems. It also delves into the diverse applications of information and communication technologies (ICT) in pivotal sectors such as Agriculture, Infrastructure, Mobility, Energy, and Safety. By seamlessly integrating Artificial Intelligence (AI), Internet of Things (IoT), Big Data, and Computer Vision, Japan is witnessing a transformative wave of smart computing solutions aimed at enhancing efficiency and reducing time, cost, and labor.

Unveiling the Dynamics of Spontaneous Micro and Macro Facial Expressions

Deepak Jain

Dalian University of technology, Dalian, China

Facial expressions serve as a fundamental channel for human communication, conveying a rich spectrum of emotions and social cues. This study delves into the intricate realm of spontaneous facial expressions, examining both micro and macro expressions to unravel the nuanced dynamics underlying human nonverbal communication. Employing advanced facial recognition technologies and nuanced observational methods, we explore the spontaneous micro expressions that manifest in fleeting moments, lasting mere fractions of a second, as well as the more extended macro expressions that reveal deeper emotional states.

The research investigates the physiological and psychological mechanisms governing the generation of spontaneous facial expressions, shedding light on the spontaneous nature of these expressions and their significance in interpersonal dynamics. By employing cutting-edge techniques, including high-speed imaging and machine learning algorithms, we aim to discern subtle nuances in facial movements that often elude conscious awareness.

Furthermore, the study explores the cross-cultural universality of spontaneous facial expressions, examining how cultural and individual differences may influence the interpretation and recognition of micro and macro expressions. Understanding the universality and cultural variability of these expressions is crucial for developing more inclusive and accurate models of nonverbal communication.

Insights gained from this research have implications for fields such as psychology, human-computer interaction, and artificial intelligence, where a nuanced understanding of facial expressions can enhance emotional intelligence, interpersonal communication, and the design of empathetic technologies. The exploration of spontaneous micro and macro facial expressions opens new avenues for comprehending the subtleties of human emotion, enriching our understanding of the intricate tapestry of nonverbal communication.

AI Advancements in Biomedical Image Processing: Challenges, Innovations, and Insights

Sonali Agarwal

Indian Institute of Information Technology, Allahabad, India

With the rapid development of Artificial Intelligence (AI), biomedical image processing has made remarkable progress in disease diagnosis, segmentation, and classification tasks, establishing itself as a key research area in both medicine and academia. Gaining insights into the use of deep learning for tasks such as identifying diseases in various imaging modalities, localizing anatomical features, and precisely segmenting target regions is important.

Deep learning models are data-hungry, but challenges arise due to the limited availability of biomedical data, data security concerns, and high data acquisition costs. To address these issues, exploring the emerging technology of self-supervised learning is important, as it enhances feature representation capture and result generation. While AI shows great potential in medical image analysis, it struggles with effectively handling multimodal data. Moreover, exploring the complexities of learning and diagnosing diseases in heterogeneous environments with limited multimodal images is essential.

Methods to enhance the interpretability of AI models include providing visual explanations with class activation maps and uncertainty maps, which offer transparency and rationale for model predictions. Conducting a SWOT analysis is crucial to evaluate the current state of AI methods, taking into account their strengths, weaknesses, opportunities, and threats in clinical implementation.

Emerging Technologies and Models for Data Protection and Resource Management in Cloud Environments

Ishu Gupta

Ramanujan Faculty Fellow, IIIT-B, Bangalore, India

Cloud environments have emanated as an essential benchmark for storage, sharing, and computation facilities through the internet that is extensively utilized in online transactions, research, academia, business, marketing, etc. It offers liberty to pay-as-per-use sculpture and ubiquitous computing amenities to every user and acts as a backbone for emerging technologies such as Cyber-Physical Systems (CPS), Internet of Things (IoT), and Big Data, etc. in the field of engineering sciences and technology that is the future of human society. These technologies are increasingly supported by Artificial Intelligence (AI) and Machine Learning (ML) to furnish advanced capabilities to the world. Despite numerous benefits offered by the cloud environments, it also faces several inevitable challenges including data security, privacy, data leakage, upcoming workload prediction, load balancing, resource management, etc.

The data sets generated by various organizations are uploaded to the cloud for storage and analysis due to their tremendous characteristics such as low maintenance cost, intrinsic resource sharing, etc., and shared among various stakeholders for its utilities. However, it exposes the data's privacy at risk, because the entities involved in communication can misuse or leak the data. Consequently, data security and privacy have emerged as leading challenges in cloud environments. The predicted workload information is crucial for effective resource management and load balancing that leads to reducing the cost associated with cloud services. However, the resource demands can vary significantly over time, making accurate workload estimation challenging. This talk will explore mitigation strategies for these challenges and highlight various technologies, including Quantum Machine Learning (QML), which is emerging as a prominent solution in the field of AI and ML to address these issues.

Artificial Intelligence and Jobs of the Future 2030

T. Devi

Bharathiar University, Coimbatore, India

The industrial revolutions Industry 4.0 and Industry 5.0 are changing the world around us. Artificial Intelligence and Machine Learning are the tools of Industry 4.0. Improved collaboration is seen between smart systems and humans, which merges the critical and cognitive thinking abilities of humans with the highly accurate and fast industrial automation. Artificial Intelligence (AI) is a pivotal tool of Industry 4.0 in transforming the future through intelligent computational systems. AI automates repetitive learning and discovery through data. Instead of automating manual tasks, AI performs frequent, high-volume, computerized tasks reliably and without fatigue. For this type of automation, human inquiry is still essential to set up the system and ask the right questions. AI adds intelligence to existing products. Automation, conversational platforms, bots, and smart machines can be combined with large amounts of data to improve many technologies.

To prepare the future pillars of our Globe to face the Volatile, Uncertain, Complex and Ambiguous (VUCA) world, and to help the academic community, Universities are revising the curricula to match with Industry 4.0. Towards this and to provide knowledge resources such as books, the author had co-edited five books titled Artificial Intelligence Theory, Models, and Applications, Big Data Applications in Industry 4.0, Industry 4.0 Technologies for Education Transformative Technologies and Applications, Innovating with Augmented Reality Applications in Education and Industry, Securing IoT in Industry 4.0 Applications with Blockchain.

Jobs of the Future 2030: Prominent sectors that will have more jobs in 2030 are Healthcare, Education, Information Technology, Digital Marketing, Automation, Manufacturing, and Logistics. The jobs in these sectors would include: Healthcare - Medical: doctors, nurses, pharmacists, drug developers - demand for better medicine and treatments are ever increasing; Education – Teachers (School, College), Other education professionals, Education support workers; Information Technology Specialists: Artificial Intelligence, Internet of Things (IoT), Data Analytics, Augmented Reality Computer Specialists; Digital Marketing; Automation Specialists: Drone pilots; Manufacturing: Automation using Robots and Artificial Intelligence; Logistics: as Globalisation will lead to more Global trade; and Restaurant Cooks

Artificial Intelligence Jobs in Future 2030: Automation and artificial intelligence will drive the world. Cars that drive themselves, machines that read X-rays and algorithms that respond to customer-service inquiries are new forms of automation. Automation can be applied more in sectors such as Pharmaceuticals (research and development, Marketing (consumer Marketing) Digital Marketing, Automotive (redesign and new development), and Oil and Gas.

New Age Cyber Risks Due to AI Intervention

Ram Kumar G.

Information Security and Risk Leader, Nissan Motor Corporation, Bangalore, India

Artificial Intelligence especially the generative variant is reshaping the world. Generative Artificial Intelligence (Gen AI) tool like ChatGPT - the new AI chatbot can hold entire conversations, speaking in the style of someone else, and play out nearly any imaginary scenario an user can ask it for.

Ever since its release late 2022, Generative AI tool ChatGPT has stormed the tech world with its amazing capabilities leveraging on generative Artificial Intelligence. While everyone is aware and excited about the immense potential and utility of such AI platform, it is important to understand the security and data privacy risks they pose.

With the corporate sector embracing generative AI tools for their benefit, there have been widespread concerns among security executives about the malicious usage of new age technology like Gen AI. Media reports highlighting cyber security risks of using Gen AI from real world incidents has only added to the apprehension among business executives about the blind adoption of such innovative tools without adequate safeguards about usage.

While the focus is on the cyber security and privacy risks arising from use of generative AI, it is also to be noted that AI tools can be used for defending against cyber threats and risks. Gen AI helps to enhance security and reduce risks which help in:

1. Detecting security vulnerabilities
2. Generating security code
3. Integration with SIEM/SOAR to improve SOC effectiveness
4. Enhancing email security
5. Improving identity and access management

In conclusion, it is critical for everyone to realize the security implications of cutting edge technology like Gen AI and make conscious decision to adopt safety precautions while using them. It will do a world of good for securing sensitive data including IP and protecting against AI-triggered phishing or malware attacks against businesses.

Challenges of 5G in Combat Networks

Col Mahesh Ramachandran

L&T, New Delhi, India

While 5G technology promises to change the rules of telecommunication in terms of high data rates, accurate location services, security and SWaP (Size, Weight and Power), it is by no means a 'One size fits All' solution for all applications - especially combat networks which have their unique requirements and challenges. This is because technology that works in commercial static networks cannot be simply replicated and rolled out in tactical networks due to the huge challenges imposed by terrain, mobility, electronic/cyber-attacks, SWaP, EMI/EMC (Electromagnetic Interference/Electromagnetic Compatibility) and country specific encryption requirements.

Mission criticality through Quality of Service (QOS), Quality of User Experience (QOE), redundancy and reliability is of utmost importance to voice, video, data and application services, including GIS in Combat Networks. The issue is further exacerbated, given the practical constraints in placing the nodes at the optimum locations due to reasons of terrain, enemy threat and operational plans. The infrastructure provisioning has to be done with optimization of size, weight and power while reducing the electronic signature to a minimum.

Notwithstanding the fact that concurrent "Releases" approach used by 3GPP provides developers with a secure foundation for implementing features at a particular time and then enables the inclusion of new capabilities in subsequent releases, besides also enabling the features to be updated in a same release as technology advances over time, it is an irony that the new versions of 3GPP releases only have a minimal impact on tactical combat networks in terms of efficiency and speeds. In other words the high data rates, enhanced security and other features of new releases do not address the challenges of combat networks due to the uniqueness of such networks. This paper analyses the peculiar communication requirements of Tactical combat networks and the challenges of adapting 5g technologies for such networks.

Dark Side of Artificial Intelligence

H. R. Mohan

ICT Consultant, Chair - Events, IEEE CS Madras, Chennai, India

While the potential of AI to transform our world is tremendous, the risks associated with it's ethical norms, safety, privacy, security, bias and consequences of the use of bad data, unpredictability, wrong decision making, weaponizaton, inequality, accessibility, misinformation, deep fakes, regulation, legality, societal impact, transparency, account-ability, explainability, reliability, environmental impact, geopolitical issues and human rights are quite significant, complex, fast-evolving and turning to be real. The unintended consequences of GenAI can cause disruptions globally with high stakes in all sectors of economy. This presentation on Dark Side of AI will elaborate on these risks associated with AI and the need for the global cooperation in its use and regulation.

Blockchain Integrated Security Solution for Internet of Drones (IoD)

Sudhanshu Maurya

Symbiosis International (Deemed University) Pune, India

The rising reception of drones across different areas, including regular citizen and military applications, requires the improvement of cutting-edge insight, unwavering quality, and security for these automated airborne vehicles. This work proposes a blockchain-based security answer for the 'Multitude of Drones'; current circumstance, planning to guarantee the mystery, unwavering quality, and protection of information move. The proposed technique considers consistent check and enrolment of drones, approval of administrators, sending and withdrawal of drones, information assortment from drones, and secure stockpiling and recovery of information in a blockchain-based framework. The assessment of the proposed strategy on reproduced drones exhibits its viability in giving prevalent information stockpiling security and keeping up with the classification and genuineness of communicated information. The use of blockchain innovation offers various benefits in the drone climate. Blockchain's decentralized nature guarantees that all exchanges and information trades are recorded across various frameworks, making it almost unthinkable for unapproved gatherings to adjust or erase data. Moreover, blockchain's innate encryption instruments give an extra layer of safety, defending information from potential digital dangers.

Besides, blockchain innovation can work with the making of a dependable and secure correspondence network for drones, assisting with forestalling unapproved access and impedance. By making a straightforward and unalterable record of all drone exercises, blockchain can likewise aid responsibility and administrative consistency. By consolidating blockchain innovation, this examination means adding to the advancement of more brilliant, more private, and safer drones. This could make ready for their extended use from here on out, in applications going from conveyance and observation to catastrophe reaction and ecological checking. The combination of blockchain into drone tasks addresses a huge forward-moving step chasing dependable and secure automated flying frameworks.

Generative Intelligence: A Catalyst for Safeguarding Society in the Age of GenAI

K. Vallidevi

VIT, Chennai, India

Generative Adversarial Networks (GANs) which is a subset of Generative AI (GenAI), can be used as a catalyst for fraud detection and prevention to shape the safety of the society in a better way. Though it is definitely a double edged sword, it could be efficiently used for proactively detecting fraudulent activities. GenAI plays a major role in video analytics for proactively detecting frauds by employing various techniques like Behavioural Analysis, Anomaly Detection and so on. By simulating fraudulent activities and generating synthetic data will help in detecting criminal activities in a proactive manner. Through this method, the intelligent system could analyse the various patterns involved in fraudulent activities and could identify them when such systems are used in real-time CCTV footage monitoring.

There are several use-cases for using Gen-AI in Proactive Policing.

1) Applying a face mask to the person's image
2) Removing face mask in the masked face image by generating the covered part of the face corresponding to rest of the face part with multiple outputs,
3) Checking similarity between resultant images and input images given by user,
4) Querying a person's availability in group image and
5) Face aging module where a person of any age is given along with the desired age number, where it generates the face image of the required age of a person. The found similar person can be checked for his outlook on various angles, by rotating the person's face. Face generation algorithms are prone to generate differentiating outputs when compared with the ground truth image'.

As these algorithms generate only single output, there is a high scope these outputs not being closely matched with the original image. Hence, a new technique of multiple diverse output images being generated, increases the probability of achieving the highest similarity with the original image. Masking the face is attained by using Dlib library while the rendering of the face is achieved by using Generative Adversarial Networks (GAN). GANs, comprising a generator and discriminator, are trained to create synthetic facial images with accurately generated masked regions. The generator network learns to produce realistic facial features, including accurately placed and shaped masks, while the discriminator distinguishes between authentic and generated images.

Contents – Part IV

Interdisciplinary Computer
Applications

Automatic Plant Watering System for Smart Water Management

Mukund Kulkarni, Kaushalya Thopate$^{(\boxtimes)}$, Aaditya Deshpande,
Jidnyasa Anil Dadmal, Bhumika Chule, and Pritam Tushar Bhamare

Vishwakarma Institute of Technology, 666, Upper Indira Nagar, Bibwewadi, Pune,
Maharashtra 411037, India
{mukund.kulkarni,kaushalya.thopate,aadityadeshpande21,
jidnyasa.dadmal21,bhumika.chule21,pritam.bhamare21}@vit.edu

Abstract. The research paper presents a groundbreaking contribution by introducing the "Advanced Irrigation System" to tackle the pressing issue of optimizing water and power usage in agriculture. This innovative solution encompasses several key features, including an automated water-pump operation system, a farmer-friendly interface via a mobile application, and seamless integration with Google Assistant for remote control. The proposed system addresses a crucial challenge faced by the agricultural sector, where efficient resource management is paramount. Traditional water-pump operating systems lack the sophistication needed to optimize water and power consumption, leading to inefficiencies and environmental concerns. Recognizing these limitations, the research paper puts forth the "Advanced Irrigation System" as a viable and practical solution. The heart of the system lies in its automated water-pump operations. By intelligently toggling the water pump on and off based on crop types and their specific moisture requirements, the system eliminates the need for constant manual oversight. This not only ensures that crops receive the optimal amount of water for growth but also minimizes water wastage, contributing to sustainable agricultural practices. Furthermore, the system introduces a farmer interface through a mobile application, presented in their regional language for user convenience. This interface empowers farmers with real-time information on crucial environmental factors such as humidity, temperature, and soil moisture. Armed with this data, farmers can make informed decisions about irrigation, fostering precision agriculture and resource-efficient farming practices. The integration of Google Assistant adds an additional layer of accessibility and user-friendliness to the system. Through voice commands, farmers can remotely operate the water pump, offering a hands-free solution that is not only convenient but also practical in scenarios where manual intervention may be challenging.

Keywords: Automatic plant watering · Node-MCU ESP8266 · Feedback control

1 Introduction

Plants provide numerous benefits by purifying the air and creating oxygen, but modern lifestyles and limited space have led to container gardening. Automated plant watering systems can solve the problem of forgetting to water plants and conserve water resources

S. Rajagopal et al (Eds.): ASCIS 2023, CCIS 2040, pp. 3–15, 2024.
https://doi.org/10.1007/978-3-031-59107-5_1

in agriculture [1]. Advanced technology has made life easier by automating tasks that once required human labor. The autonomous plant watering system uses sensor technology to monitor soil moisture and prevent plant decay, benefiting millions of people [2]. An automated system for watering plants measures and estimates the existing plant before supplying the water the plant needs. It maintains plant health while reducing excessive water use [3]. This paper discusses an automated plant watering system that conserves manpower, time, and water, with precise outcomes displayed on the receiver's LCD, but the delay in receiving information from the transmitter can be prevented with a better transceiver [4]. An automatic watering system that controls water flow based on soil moisture levels, which is cost-effective for growers with limited resources and has produced good results [5]. An initiative that conserves water, increases crop yield, and is affordable for low-income farmers is expected to improve their livelihoods and boost food security, demonstrating how innovation can advance sustainability and agriculture [6]. An autonomous watering system utilizing an Arduino board and soil moisture sensor was developed to hydrate plants when the soil gets dry, leading to more productive crop yields and less labor in agriculture. The system's efficiency was tested over time using soil samples to ensure crop health and water consumption tracking for different crop types [7]. Using a rain-gun irrigation system, GSM-based automated irrigation control. Android is a software stack used for mobile devices, which consists of a file system, middleware, and essential programs. The tools and APIs needed to begin creating Java apps for the Android operating system are included in the Android SDK. Mobile devices, which meet a broad range of human demands, have almost completely taken over our life. This service gives an irrigated control system solution using the GPRS functionality of a smartphone. This technique was not economic sustainable and only covered a tiny area of agricultural land [8]. The turf maintenance team frequently uses portable measurement tools to get soil information. Yet, over time, manually gathered data is not reliable. In addition to the fact that it takes time to fully cover a whole field, you must gather enough samples to make up for this discrepancy [9]. Online moisture measurements that provide continuous readings can help food processing and manufacturing plants save money. Because subsequently raw materials often get weighed, it is crucial to understand how much moisture remains in the food item as it bakes. Companies typically employ a kind of sensor for moisture that can rapidly determine the moisture content in manufacturing raw materials; this ends up in significant reductions in costs for the purchasing plant. These immediate readings can reduce the cost of research, logistics, and shipment [10].

2   Literature Review

The system described in the paper, which transmits data wirelessly via a ZigBee module, uses an Arduino Uno board, the sensor for soil moisture, and a DS18B20 temperature sensor. The project attempts to solve the shortcomings of current soil monitoring systems, which are costly, intricate, and challenging to maintain. The device is a good and dependable solution for small-scale agriculture and research purposes because the studies show its capacity to assess soil moisture and temperature precisely. Future research, according to the authors, might increase the ZigBee module's range and create a mobile app for real-time soil parameter monitoring [11]. An inexpensive capacitive soil moisture sensor for smart agriculture built on an Arduino platform is described in the study along with a calibration procedure. The limits of traditional sensors were determined after the authors reviewed the literature on the various soil moisture sensors currently in use. The suggested sensor has two electrodes that use the capacitance. For estimating the soil's moisture content. The calibration approach that has been suggested by the authors increases the accuracy of the sensor's readings, according to trials that were done to test the sensor's functionality. For applications involving small-scale agriculture, the paper contends that the inexpensive sensor may be a practical substitute for costly and power-guzzling conventional Sensors [12]. The study suggests an inexpensive and effective irrigation system for smart agriculture using an Arduino Uno chip and a soil moisture sensor. The proposed method is found to use less water and keep the soil's moisture content at ideal levels when performance is compared to that of a standard irrigation system. The created technology, according to the authors, is a good substitute for traditional irrigation systems in applications involving small-scale agricultural. Future work could concentrate on improving the system's usefulness by incorporating extra sensors and creating a mobile application for remote monitoring and control of the system [13]. The proposed use of an Arduino system in the study for greenhouse monitoring and control addresses the limitations seen in traditional systems. By leveraging a diverse array of sensors, the system aims to precisely measure and regulate crucial environmental variables such as temperature, humidity, and light intensity. This comprehensive approach ensures a more efficient and responsive management of greenhouse conditions, potentially leading to improved crop yields and resource utilization. The study's detailed examination of conventional shortcomings and the provided system architecture underscores a commitment to advancing agricultural technology for enhanced sustainability and productivity. The outcomes show that the system can successfully control the greenhouse's environment, giving it a dependable and affordable solution for small-scale greenhouse farming. The authors propose that future work might concentrate on creating a smartphone application for remote system monitoring and control [14]. The paper introduces an innovative approach by suggesting an Arduino-based system for soil moisture measurement. The proposed system utilizes Arduino technology, showcasing its adaptability and versatility. The authors review the limitations of traditional soil moisture sensors and present the proposed system's design, which utilizes a capacitive soil moisture sensor, an Arduino Uno board, and a wireless communication module to transmit the data to a remote server. The results demonstrate the system's ability to accurately measure soil moisture, making it a reliable and cost-effective alternative for small-scale agriculture applications. The study suggests that future work could focus on improving the range of the wireless communication module and integrating additional sensors to monitor other soil parameters [15]. This study suggests a low-cost soil moisture sensor design that communicates via the SDI-12 protocol and using a frequency-domain measurement technique. The sensor's performance was tested by the authors, who also compared it to a widely available commercial soil moisture sensor [16]. The findings demonstrated that, for a fraction of the price of commercial sensors, the proposed sensor had comparable accuracy [17]. According to the study's findings, the created sensor provides a practical and affordable replacement for traditional soil moisture sensors in small-scale agricultural applications [18]. Future research, according to the authors, might concentrate on enhancing the sensor's robustness and incorporating more sensors to track different soil properties [19]. The study suggests an agricultural monitoring system based on Arduino that makes use of a mobile app to track and manage various environmental variables influencing plant growth, such as temperature, humidity, and soil moisture [20].

3   Methodology

The design and implementation of the Automatic Water Management System epitomize a meticulous integration of hardware and software components. The system's design focused on leveraging the Nodemcu ESP8266 microcontroller for data processing, coupled with strategically chosen sensors, a relay module, and an LCD screen. The synergy between these elements facilitated the real-time monitoring of soil moisture levels and precise control of the water pump. Implementation involved meticulous circuitry connections, ensuring seamless communication between components. Arduino code was meticulously crafted and uploaded to the microcontroller, orchestrating the system's functionality. The design intricacies and precise implementation underscore the system's robustness, enabling it to adapt to varying plant species' needs and environmental conditions (Table 1).

Table 1. Components used to implements the idea

Component	Quantity	Description
Nodemcu ESP8266	1	Microcontroller with Wi-Fi connectivity
Soil moisture sensor	1	Detects soil moisture levels
Relay module	1	Controls the water pump
LCD screen	1	Displays moisture levels and system information
I2C module	1	Enables communication between components
Jumper wires	-	Wiring connections
Breadboard	1	Platform for prototyping circuits
Mini water pump	1	Provides water to plants
Mini water pipe	1	Conveys water from pump to the plant pot
3.9 V battery clip	1	Powers the system
4.9 V Battery	1	Power source for the water pump

This table provides an exhaustive list of the components meticulously chosen and integrated into the 'Automatic Water Management System.' The selection criteria were based on the system's design requirements, aiming for reliability, accuracy, and adaptability. Each component serves a crucial role in ensuring the system's efficiency and functionality.

The components range from the Nodemcu ESP8266 microcontroller responsible for data processing and control to the soil moisture sensors that form the core of moisture level monitoring. Additionally, the relay module, LCD screen, and other peripherals contribute to the system's overall functionality and user interface. This comprehensive list demonstrates the diverse set of hardware utilized, reflecting a strategic amalgamation aimed at addressing the limitations observed in existing water management systems.

The meticulous selection and integration of these components represent a pivotal phase in the system: development, ensuring a robust and efficient solution to cater to diverse plant species and environmental conditions.

Design and Construction of the Automatic Plant Watering System: The first step in the methodology is to design and construct the automatic plant watering system. This includes selecting the necessary components such as a microcontroller, sensors, water pump, and tubing. The microcontroller will be programmed to read the soil moisture level and control the water pump accordingly. The sensors will be used to measure the soil moisture level, and the water pump will be used to water the plants when the soil moisture level drops below a certain threshold.

Integration of the Blynk Application: The next step is to integrate the Blynk application with the automatic plant watering system. Blynk is a mobile application that allows users to control and monitor IoT devices. The Blynk app will be used to remotely monitor the soil moisture level and control the watering of the plants.

Testing and Validation of the System: Once the system has been designed and constructed, it will be tested to ensure that it is functioning properly. The system will be tested using a variety of plants with different watering requirements to ensure that it can adapt to different plant species and environmental conditions.

Data Collection and Analysis: Data will be collected from the sensors and the Blynk application to evaluate the performance of the system. The data will be analyzed to determine if the system is providing the necessary amount of water to the plants and if the Blynk application is working properly.

Hardware Required

1. Nodemcu ESP8266 × 1
2. Soil moisture sensor × 1
3. Relay module × 1
4. LCD screen × 1
5. I2C module × 1
6. Jumper wires
7. Breadboard × 1
8. Mini water pump × 1
9. Mini water pipe × 1
10. 3.9 v battery clip × 1
11. 4.9 v Battery × 1.

Connections/Construction

1. Connect the VCC and GND pins of the soil moisture sensor to the VCC and GND rails on the breadboard, respectively as shown in Figs. 1 and 2.
2. Take part in the A0 pin and the SIG the pin for the soil moisture detector on the Node-MCU ESP8266.
3. Connect the VCC and I2C module GND pins ought to be linked to the breadboard's VCC and GND rails, accordingly.
4. Connect the SDA and SCL pins of the I2C module to the corresponding pins (D2 and D1, respectively) on the Node-MCU ESP8266.
5. Connect the VCC and GND Associate the relay module's pins to the breadboard's GND and VCC rails, respectively.
6. Connect the IN pin of the relay module to pin D0 on the Node-MCU ESP8266.
7. Connect the VCC and GND pins of the LCD screen to the VCC and GND rails on the breadboard, respectively.
8. Connect the SDA and SCL pins of the LCD screen to the corresponding pins on the I2C module.
9. Connect the positive and negative terminals of the mini water pump to the normally open (NO) and common (COM) pins, respectively, on the relay module.
10. Using the battery clip, attach the positive connection on the 4.9 V batteries to the breadboard's VCC rail.
11. Connect the negative terminal of the 4.9 V battery to the GND rail on the breadboard.
12. Connect the positive terminal of the mini water pump to the positive terminal of the 4.9 V battery.
13. Connect one end of the mini water pipe to the outlet of the mini water pump.
14. Connect the other end of the mini water pipe to the plant pot. Once all the connections have been made, upload the Arduino code to the Node-MCU ESP8266. The code should read the moisture level from the sensor for soil moisture and turn on the pump through the relay module when the moisture level falls below a certain threshold. The LCD screen should display the moisture level and other information.

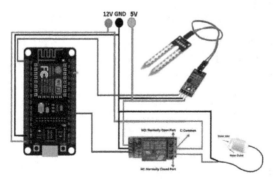

Fig. 1. Circuit diagram

Figure 1 illustrates the interconnected components of a smart automatic plant watering system. Key elements include the NodeMCU ESP8266, soil moisture sensor, relay module, LCD screen, I2C module, mini water pump, and associated components such as jumper wires, breadboard, mini water pipe, 3.9 V battery clip, and a 4.9 V battery. Soil moisture sensor calibration equation: A linear regression equation can be used to equate the readings from a soil moisture detector to the moisture content of the soil. The equation can be of the form

$$y = mx + c$$

where Y is the soil moisture content, X is the sensor reading, m is the slope of the line, and b is the y-intercept. Watering frequency equation: The frequency of watering can be determined by dividing the daily water requirement of the plant by the capacity of the water storage tank. The equation can be of the form

$$F = R/T$$

where F is the frequency of watering, R is the daily water requirement of the plant, and T is the capacity of the water storage tank.

Watering Duration Equation: The duration of watering can be established by dividing the necessary water's volume by the water pump's flow rate. The formula for an expression can be

$$D = V/O$$

where D is the duration of watering, V is the required amount of water, and Q is the flow rate of the water pump. Pump power consumption equation: The power consumption of the water pump can be determined by multiplying the voltage, current, and power factor of the pump. The equation can be of the form

$$P = VI\cos\alpha$$

where P stands for power utilisation, V for voltage, I for current, and α for power factor.

The sensor that detects soil moisture gauges the amount of moisture in the soil and sends the analog signal to the Node-MCU ESP8266. The Node-MCU ESP8266 reads the analog signal from the soil moisture sensor and converts it to a digital value using the built-in ADC (analog-to-digital converter). The Node-MCU ESP8266 compares the digital value with a preset threshold value. If the moisture content is below the cutoff, it sends a signal to the relay module to on the mini water pump. The relay module switches on the mini water pump, which pumps water through the mini water pipe to the plant pot, thus watering the plant. The LCD screen displays the moisture level and other information such as the current status of the watering system. The system continues to monitor the moisture level in the soil and turns off the water pump when the moisture level reaches the desired level. This process is repeated by the system on a regular basis, guaranteeing the plant gets the right quantity water when it requires it.

4   Results

The study's results affirm the effective implementation of the suggested smart automatic plant watering system. Through real-time monitoring facilitated by the Blynk interface, the system successfully gauges and manages essential factors such as moisture, humidity, and temperature. This integration reflects a notable advancement in plant care, as it ensures a responsive and automated approach to maintaining optimal environmental conditions for plant growth. The emphasis on real-time monitoring underscores the system's ability to adapt dynamically, fostering an environment conducive to efficient and thriving plant growth. Overall, the demonstrated success of this technology points towards the potential for enhanced precision and convenience in plant care practices.

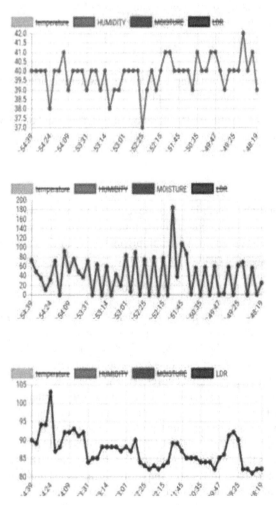

Fig. 2. Graphs of Humidity, moisture and LDR respectively

Figure 2 showcases dynamic graphs depicting the temporal evolution of key environmental parameters—humidity, soil moisture, and Light Dependent Resistor (LDR)—in the context of a smart automatic plant watering system. These real-time data representations enable precise monitoring, facilitating optimal plant care and irrigation management over time.

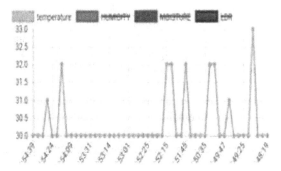

Fig. 3. Graphs of Temperature vs Time

Figure 3 showcases dynamic graphs depicting the temporal evolution of key environmental parameter-Temperature vs Time.

Overall, the system automates the process of plant watering, ensuring that the lacking the need for human intervention, the plant receives an appropriate quantity of water at the proper time.

I. APPLICATIONS

I. Agriculture

For agricultural applications, measuring soil moisture is crucial for farmers to effectively manage their irrigation systems.

Understanding the necessary levels of soil moisture allows producers to employ fewer water supplies for the fields while improving crop output and quality.

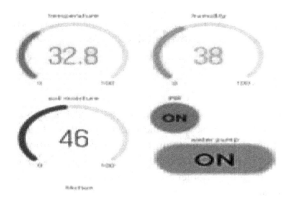

Fig. 4. Blynk interface of Humidity, moisture and Temperature respectively

Figure 4 illustrates a Blynk interface displaying real-time data of moisture, humidity, and temperature in the smart automatic plant watering system. This graphical representation enhances user interaction, allowing seamless monitoring of environmental conditions for informed decision-making in plant care and irrigation management.

II. IRRIGATION FOR LANDSCAPING

Soil moisture sensors that are connected to an irrigation controls are used for residential lawns and landscaping in urban and suburban areas. A simple irrigation clock becomes a "smart" irrigation controller when a soil moisture sensor is added, stopping irrigation cycles when the soil is already wet. To improve the effectiveness of their irrigation systems and reduce overwatering and fertiliser and other chemical leaking into the soil, golf courses use soil moisture monitors.

III. RESEARCH

Soil moisture sensors are used in numerous research applications, including soil respiration measurements, environmental science studies of solute transport, and planning for irrigation in horticulture and agriculture. Plants can be checked to see if they have enough moisture for survival using relatively cheap, straightforward technologies that don't need a power source.

IV. FOOD- RELATED BUSINESSES

Food production and processing facilities can save a lot of money by using via the internet moisture measurements that provide real-time readings. Knowing how much moisture is present in the food as it bakes is essential because raw materials are frequently measured by weight.

V. MEASUREMENTS

Companies typically employ a particular kind of moisture detection device that can quickly assess the amount of moisture in a manufacturer's raw materials, conserving a buying plant a sizable sum of money in the process. The analysis, shipping, and delivery costs can all be reduced as a result of these instant measurements.

VI. TURF MAINTENANCE

You can minimise variations in quality across the field while simultaneously enhancing turf quality. You can modify the field hardness to reduce injuries, avoid fertiliser leaching, use fewer water additives, and surfactants by using precise and up-to-date soil data.

You can safely reduce water use due to the fact that you constantly understand the precise soil moisture level. As the efficiency of the maintenance work rises, you can switch from reactive repair to proactive turf development.

5 Future Scope

The automatic plant watering system has great potential for future development and expansion. One possible future scope is the integration of weather forecasting, which can optimize water usage according to upcoming weather conditions. This will further improve the efficiency of the system and reduce water usage, making it more sustainable and environmentally friendly. Another potential future scope is expanding the system for larger applications, such as commercial farming, landscaping, and greenhouse farming. This will require designing the system to accommodate larger areas and multiple plants.

A mobile app integration can also be implemented to provide instantaneous updates on soil moisture levels, water usage, and plant health. This will enable users to remotely monitor and control the system from their smartphones, providing convenience and flexibility. Machine learning algorithms can also be incorporated into the system to optimize the watering process and improve plant growth. The algorithms can analyze the data obtained from the sensors to provide insights and recommendations for improving the system's performance. Furthermore, integrating the automatic plant watering system with smart irrigation systems that use real-time data and weather forecasting can result in more sustainable and efficient irrigation practices.

Advantages and Disadvantages

Advantages of this project include the automation of plant watering, which saves time and effort for gardeners and farmers. The use of a soil moisture sensor ensures that plants receive the appropriate amount of water, preventing overwatering and conserving water. The system can also be set up to water plants at specific intervals, ensuring consistent watering. Additionally, the system allows for remote monitoring and control, which can be useful for people who travel frequently or have multiple plants to water.

Disadvantages of this project could include the initial cost of setting up the system, which may be prohibitive for some individuals. Additionally, the system may require maintenance and calibration to ensure that it is functioning properly, which could be a potential hassle for some users. The system also relies on electricity and may be vulnerable to power outages, which could result in plants not being watered properly. Finally, some individuals may prefer the tactile experience of manually watering plants and may find that this system takes away from the personal connection with their plants.

6 Conclusion

In conclusion, the automatic plant watering system is a highly effective solution for maintaining plant health and reducing water usage. By utilizing the soil moisture sensor and microcontroller, the system can accurately monitor soil moisture levels and water the plants accordingly. The integration of the relay module, mini water pump, and battery clip enables the system to operate automatically and without the need for human intervention.

This project provides a cost-effective and eco-friendly solution for plant care and irrigation, and has great potential for future development and expansion. With the implementation of future scope ideas such as integration with weather forecasting, expansion for larger applications, mobile app integration, implementation of machine learning, and integration with smart irrigation systems, the automatic plant watering system can become even more efficient, sustainable, and adaptable to different scenarios.

Overall, this project demonstrates the practical application of technology in agriculture and highlights the potential for innovative solutions in addressing environmental challenges. By providing a low-cost and easy-to-implement solution, this project can contribute to promoting sustainable agriculture practices and fostering a greener future.

References

1. Thopate, K., Bhatlawande, S., Shilaskar, S.: Smart pumping system using energy efficiency control algorithm. Int. J. Recent Innov. Trends Comput. Commun. **11**(8), 14–20 (2023)
2. Thopate, K., et al.: Keyless security: the smart solution for home with a smart door lock. Int. J. Recent Innov. Trends Comput. Commun. **11**(8s), 170–174 (2023)
3. Thopate, K., Shilaskar, S., Bhatlawande, S.: An internet of things based solar power monitoring system using node MCU. Int. J. Recent Innov. Trends Comput. Commun. **11**(10s), 708–714 (2023)
4. Ganesh, R., Yadav, M.R., Gupta, A., Thopate, K., Ishrat, M., Lohani, M.: Prediction of residual energy in batteries using CNN-BiGRU and attention mechanism model. In: 2023 International Conference on Sustainable Computing and Smart Systems (ICSCSS), Coimbatore, India, pp. 547–552 (2023)
5. Shifa, T.K.: Moisture sensing automatic plant watering system using Arduino Uno. Am. J. Eng. Res. (AJER) **7**, 326–330 (2018)
6. Gutierrez, J., Villa-Medina, J.F., Nieto-Garibay, A., Porta-Gandara, M.A.: Automated irrigation system using a wireless sensor network and GPRS module. IEEE Trans. Instrum. Measure. **63**(1), 166–176 (2014)
7. Devika, S.V., Khamaruddin, S., Khamurunnisa, S., Thota, J., Shaikh, K.: Arduino based automatic plant watering system. Int. J. Adv. Res. Comput. Sci. Softw. Eng. **10**(10), 449–456 (2014)
8. Archana, P., Priya, R.: Design and implementation of automatic plant watering system. Int. J. Adv. Eng. Glob. Technol. **4**(1), 1567–1570 (2016)
9. Devika, C.M., Bose, K., Vijayalakshmi, S.: Automatic plant irrigation system using Arduino. In: IEEE International Conference on Technology (ICST), Auckland, New Zealand, December 2015 (2015)
10. Alex, G., Janakiranimathi, M.: Solar based plant irrigation system. In: 2016 2nd International Conference on Advances in Electrical, Electronics, Information, Communication and Bio-Informatics (AEEICB), Chennai, Tamil Nadu. IEEE (2016)
11. Jain, P., Kumar, P., Palwalia, D.K.: Irrigation management system with micro-controller application. In: 2017 1st International Conference on Electronics, Materials Engineering and Nano-Technology (IEMENTech), Rajasthan, India. IEEE (2017)
12. Divani, D., Patil, P., Punjabi, S.K.: Automated plant watering system. In: 2016 International Conference on Computation of Power, Energy Information and Communication (ICCPEIC), Navi Mumbai, India. IEEE (2016)
13. Namala, K.K., Krishna Kanth Prabhu, A.V., Math, A., Kumari, A., Kulkarni, S.: Smart irrigation with embedded system. In: 2016 IEEE Bombay Section Symposium (IBSS), Kalaburagi, India. IEEE (2016)
14. Miskam, M.A., Sidek, O., Rahim, I.A., Omar, M.Q., Ishak, M.Z.: Fully automatic water irrigation and drainage system for paddy rice cropping in Malaysia. In: 2013 IEEE 3rd International Conference on System Engineering and Technology, Shah Alam, Malaysia (2013)
15. Zhao, Y., Zhang, J., Guan, J., Yin, W.: Study on precision water-saving irrigation automatic control system by plant physiology. In: 2009 4th IEEE Conference on Industrial Electronics and Applications, Beijing, China (2009)
16. Đuzić, N., Đumić, D.: Automatic plant watering system via soil moisture sensing by means of suitable electronics and its applications for anthropological and medical purposes. Coll. Antropol. **41**, 169–172 (2017)
17. Ishakl, N.S., Awang, A.H., Bahri, N.N.S., Zaimi, A.M.M.: GSM activated watering system prototype. In: 2015 IEEE International RF and Microwave Conference (RFM), Kuching, Sarawak. IEEE (2015)

18. Pezol, N.S., Adnan, R., Tajjudin, M.: Design of an Internet of Things (IoT) based smart irrigation and fertilization system using fuzzy logic for chili plant. In: 2020 IEEE International Conference on Automatic Control and Intelligent Systems (I2CACIS), pp. 69–73 (2020)
19. Mayuree, M., Aishwarya, P., Bagubali, A.: Automatic plant watering system. In: 2019 International Conference on Vision Towards Emerging Trends in Communication and Networking (ViTECoN), pp. 1–3 (2019)

Security Assurance in the Software Development Process: A Systematic Literature Review

Kedir Lemma Arega[1]([✉]), Asrat Mulatu Beyene[2], and Sofonias Yitagesu[3]

[1] Department of Information Technology, Ambo University, Ambo, Ethiopia
kedirnaw1999@gmail.com
[2] Department of Electrical and Computer Engineering, Addis Ababa Science and Technology University, Addis Ababa, Ethiopia
[3] Debre Berhan University, Debre Berhan, Ethiopia

Abstract. A systematic review of the literature is a method for identifying, choosing, assessing, and critically evaluating recent research works to tackle ongoing research issues and concerns. This review attempts to investigate the current issues and faintness in system security assurance. A review protocol was created after a thorough analysis of the current methodology of the systematic review and consultation with subject matter specialists. A list of potential research topics, search strategy, potential sources, selection standards, selection process, and checklists for assessing the caliber of the research. Boolean ANDs and ORs were used to build the search strings, which were then put to the test against primary studies on system security assurance from well-known databases. Primary research studies that offered support for research questions were found and chosen using selection criteria. The inclusion criteria were as follows: research papers published between 2019 and 2023, software security assessment and evaluation of systems, and publications on software assurance and security that are only concerned with software.

Keywords: Software security · Software system · Systematic literature review · Software Assurance

1 Introduction

Software security is crucial for maintaining high-quality software integrity, confidentiality, and accessibility. The rise of internet apps, social networking platforms, cloud computing, and IoT has increased software vulnerabilities. Secure systems are hindered by flaws and design weaknesses, and after production, "penetrations and patches" are used to manage software security [1]. Software development techniques are intended to increase software quality by including quality-promoting practices. Software security is essential for quality, particularly in the age of Internet-distributed technologies. Individual developers are overlooked in research on producing high-quality and safe software [2]. Software systems have become a vital element of human society, necessitating security measures to satisfy user expectations and functional requirements. However,

S. Rajagopal et al (Eds.): ASCIS 2023, CCIS 2040, pp. 16–30, 2024.
https://doi.org/10.1007/978-3-031-59107-5_2

numerous software growth approaches don't specifically mention security concerns for software safeguards throughout program growth, potentially resulting in losses [3]. Security researchers are currently working to ensure the security and usability of healthcare software. Practitioners are developing approaches to improving security while maintaining usability. Quantitative usability and security testing are required to meet software security requirements [4]. The development of advanced defense schemes, such as cyberphysical structures, necessitates early, realistic security testing in software development. Despite various methods, restricted settings and access constraints hinder the creation of a robust defense system against cyberattacks. A recent study found that many software development methodologies do not incorporate package safety features into the development process [5]. Cyberattacks are increasing, necessitating new models for software development. Testing determines program quality and resolves security issues. Reactive measures prevent vulnerabilities but don't adequately safeguard systems. Software security breaches can negatively impact enterprises, and corporate brands, and allow access to client information [7]. Code clones pose challenges to software maintenance and debugging due to their vulnerability to malicious code. Scholars have been researching code clone detection for a long time. A comprehensive investigation is needed to evaluate published work and future research prospects, as threat modeling often involves expert opinions [8]. The study explores an automated risk-assessment method to enhance the quantitative nature of software system vulnerability identification, utilizing machine-learning algorithms to improve data operation during software development processes and leveraging industry knowledge on security vulnerabilities [9]. Businesses that specialize in creating software look into data sources to increase security and productivity using a clever knowledge management system that employs artificial intelligence approaches. Through modular design and integration, machine learning and deep learning model data can be used to create an intelligent system for controlling software security vulnerabilities [10]. Security assurance in software development minimizes risks and protects sensitive data by identifying challenges, assessing trends, analyzing vulnerabilities, implementing reliable measures, conducting regular testing, adhering to legislation, monitoring threats, and providing recommendations for improvement.

2   Related Works

Software security assurance has previously been the subject of assessments with narrow systematics, but there have been no dedicated works that take a thorough and methodical approach. The existing systematic reviews are compared with our work in this section and summarized. Most studies lack a systematic methodology and concentrate on a single application domain or a small portion of the security assurance process. The subject matter is discussed, and its contributions are summarized. Moyo et al. [2] proposed an agile secure software development paradigm that encourages quality and security in solitary developers' software outputs. To create secure agile software development practices, it combines quality and minimal security practices. Using Keramati and Mirian-Hosseinabadi's approach, a study combines quality and security principles from a single framework while maintaining agility. The methodology shows its efficiency in attaining the best results by producing high-quality, secure software solutions without losing agility. F. A., et al.: [4] The study aims to assess the serviceability and safety of healthcare packages and offer design guidelines for producing secure and useful software. It uses an innovative method that concurrently analyzes usability and security by integrating the Analytic Network Method (ANP), Fuzzy Sets (FS), and Techniques for Order of Preference by Similarity to the Ideal Solution (TOPSIS). The serviceability findings and security evaluations support the notion that this novel hybrid technique is the most precise and efficient way to analyze the usability and security of healthcare applications. These results will help with security management without affecting the usability of end users. C.-G. et al.: [5] cybersecurity risks to software can impact combat systems, which poses a significant risk to naval operations. To build a safe system that can withstand cyberattacks, comprehensive security testing must be conducted during combat system development. This study examines prior studies on software security testing, battle structure package characteristics, and recommendations aimed at package safety challenges of weapon system development in the Korean military. Grounded on the features then missions of the battle scheme, enhanced package security testing is suggested to boost cybersecurity. Althar, et al. [10] looked into the idea of combining data science and software development techniques to reduce software system vulnerabilities. An AI-founded scheme for handling information about software system vulnerabilities was created by combining various data sources in the proposed architecture. Deep learning models were employed for two-level processing in the customer dialogue module, and a data classifier was constructed to recognize security-related information. An integrated strategy that integrates risk calculation and threat modeling methodologies with mechanism knowledge models is suggested in the industry landscape module. Lastly, the structure was expanded to feed the data into the organization's main database. Using this approach, the knowledge processing platform will be able to develop over time, and software development procedures will become more effective. Ebad et al. [11] attempted to close this gap by applying the eight principles of Saltzer and Schroeder, as well as three additional concepts put forth by others, to an actual software project called the electronic promotion scheme (EPS). The majority of the 11 SDPs, including input validation, sound authentication, least privilege, secure fails to repay, and least-common-denominator techniques, were fully implemented; however, the separation of privileges and psychological acceptability were only partially used. Complete mediation and open design, the other two principles, did not play a significant role because ePS satisfied these two principles on its own. Leonardi et al. [12] proposed a method for improving actual package security through maintaining system schedulability. By incorporating response-time analysis for scheduling ability, the mixed-integer linear programming (MILP) design exploits security. The efficacy of this technique in a typical task collection was assessed experimentally. Bhuiyan et al. [13] conducted a comprehensive mapping investigation of investigate that employed security infection intelligence for a software susceptibility study via scanning five scholarly databases. They chose 46 articles that used security bug reports and highlighted three study topics: vulnerability categorization, vulnerability report summarizing, and vulnerability dataset development. 42 of the 46 publications reviewed focused on vulnerability classifications. Márquez et al. [14] presented a systematic mapping study (SMS) conducted to notice, establish, and describe security problems in telehealth systems. The findings emphasize three techniques (detecting, halting, mitigating, and reacting to attacks) and four security classes (attacks, vulnerabilities, weaknesses, and threats). Privacy and insecure data transfers are common research topics. Software design, specifications, and models are essential [15]. Khan et al. [16] studied the protection of software dangers and applied it to build secure software growth processes. Important studies were categorized for categorization purposes through a comprehensive literature review. The study highlights 424 recommendations for managing security throughout the SDLC, strengthening product security, and identifying 145 safety problems for firms that develop software. This determination also makes the designer more aware of safe development practices. Nina et al.: [17] attempting to distinguish between difficulties that have already been well explored and those that still need more investigation, this article aims to present an overview of Secure Software Development trends. A methodical charting assessment was undertaken employing Population Interest Context (PIC) search algorithms, and 867 papers were discovered, of which 528 were chosen for their review. The primary findings are related to software requirement security, anywhere evocation then misappropriation cases are more commonly reported, Software Design Security, Software Construction Security, and Software Testing Security. At each level of safe software development, there are various approaches, models, and tools with distinct goals. Medeiros et al.: [18] The efficiency of software metrics in locating weak code units is the subject of research. Using machine-learning techniques, the experiment pulls vulnerability-related knowledge from C/C++ software projects. Due to false positive rates, machine learning approaches are ineffective for low-criticality or non-critical systems, but they can reliably identify susceptible code units in security-critical systems. Al-Matouq et al.: [19], a framework is created to help software development companies design safe products more effectively. To create a Secure Software Design Maturity Model (SSDMM), 38 primary studies were found. The relevant data were then compiled into eight knowledge domains and 65 recommended practices. The framework was created using the Capability Maturity Model Integration (CMMI v2.0) structure and was assessed using case studies in actual work settings. The findings of the real-world investigation reinforce the Secure Software Design Maturity Model. (SSDMM) helps determine an organization's maturity level for the safe design phase of the SDLC. Kun Xu, et al.: [20] of a knowledge-based society is software, making the creation and use of software a key differentiator. The systematic software creation procedure and technology were compressed using software development methodology. Software systems are becoming larger in systematic terms, and as a result, their complexity is increasing quickly and is challenging to manage. In an aspect-oriented approach, similar traits are combined as overarching issues to comprehend and classify and are abstracted as "party". This essay primarily introduces the methodology and steps involved in software development based on software buses and then explores how they differ from traditional software development to determine their benefits. Azman, et al.: [21], explore the dependability and validity of an instrument developed to assess the risks of implementing software updates that affect software aging. The instrument is valuable for future investigations due to the excellent reliability of the questionnaire questions used in the pilot study that measured variables in the model. Although unavoidable, software aging can be slowed down or postponed. To attempt to establish risk mitigation effects on the relationship between software aging and anti-software aging from a software engineering perspective, this study evaluates the validity and logic of a tool used to assess the risks of adopting software changes that affect software aging. Capretz, et al.: [22] explores the motivators and demotivators that influence software professionals' decisions to pursue and maintain software testing professions in four different nations. To critically evaluate software testers' assessments of testing activities and view them as human-dependent tasks, research is essential. The majority of research indicates that working in the testing sector is unpleasant, with stress and being treated like a second-class citizen serving as common demotivators. To address issues with software professionals' motivation, managers and team leaders might benefit from analyzing motivation and demotivation causes. Manzano, et al.: [23] Software repositories are used to aid software development efforts. Forecasting is becoming increasingly important as a decision-making tool. They created a modular and adaptable forecasting solution that can link to various databases/data repositories. It is free and open-source software written in Java and R that exposes its functionality via a REST API. Architecture details are supplied, as well as a description of the features and an example of how they might be used to forecast software quality. Kanner et al.: [24], focus on the application of known automata and graph theory provisions to the challenge of testing software and hardware data security technologies (DST). DST consists of hardware components that implement critical security functions while restricting the use of various testing methodologies and instruments. The authors propose using a mathematical technique based on automata and graph theories to assure the completeness and optimality of testing. Özdemir et al.: [25]study aims to develop new technologies to improve web application vulnerability monitoring. Provides a dashboard tool for dynamic application security test result visualization and generates a generic data structure utilizing freely accessible sources. The publication also discusses a validation study in which individuals completed quizzes after using the tool prototype. To track evaluations and changes over several online projects, the research looks at 50 indicators for multi-project/phase settings. Stengele et al.: [26] looked into how existing software review and attestation tools and procedures might be used on the highest of distributed stages like Ethereum. A resistant of thought solution aimed at a distributed public software review was presented by combining prior works based on Ethereum with fresh enhancements both on-chain and off-chain. The technique given here could be used in cases other than software attestation. Systematic literature reviews are crucial in evidence-based methods, requiring rigorous and transparent processes to ensure reliability. They emphasize the need for a comprehensive approach to software security and assurance, encompassing all stages of the development lifecycle. A risk-based approach, continuous monitoring, and stakeholder involvement are essential for ensuring quality and security. Software security assurance has been the subject of limited systematic reviews, but few dedicated works take a thorough and methodical approach. Some studies propose an agile safe package growth paradigm that combines quality and security practices in solitary developers' software output. Cybersecurity risks to software can impact combat systems, and it is crucial to conduct systematic and useful security testing for combat systems during system development to understand their usefulness in varied circumstances, more study is required.

3   Methodology

A reliable strategy for locating, selecting, analyzing, and critically evaluating finished research works stays to conduct a methodical review of the literature. Its primary goal is to assess and understand current scheme security pledge research to tackle ongoing study issues and concerns. A review methodology has been devised to carry out the objective and systematic examination of the literature. The steps outlined in the guidelines for this systematic review: are review planning, review execution, and review report [27].

3.1   Review Plan

The present review of the literature attempts to investigate the current issues and weaknesses in system security assurance. For various systems and contexts, it will investigate needs, measurements, frameworks, and methodologies. The goal of this review is to provide a taxonomy of system security assurance and to look at important background information, technological advancements, research trends, and future directions.

3.2   Creating Protocols for Reviews

A review protocol is created after a thorough analysis of the systematic review's current methodology and consultation with subject-matter specialists. There are criteria for assessing the quality of the study as well as research topics, a search strategy, prospective sources, selection criteria, and a selection procedure. It also includes details on data extraction and synthesis, as well as key planning and management details such as the project timetable and dissemination plan.

3.3   Review and Evaluate the Protocol

a. Do the search terms match the research questions and are they appropriate?
b. Will the data extraction points adequately address the study questions?
c. Is the analysis process appropriate to achieve the review's objectives?

3.4   Developing Research Questions

Based on reflection, debate, and reformulation, the following research questions for these reviews were considered:

RQ. 1: What are the current methods, and frameworks for ensuring security during the software development process?"
RQ. 2: What are the primary difficulties encountered while trying to achieve security assurance during the software development process?
RQ. 3: How can we categorize the various software security assurance?

3.5   Conducting the Review

After the review methodology was properly created, the review process got underway.

3.5.1 Identification of Research

The work focuses on locating relevant primary studies that address research concerns and comparing search terms to current studies on system security assurance from well-known databases. Following consideration of three electronic sources, including IEEExplore, ELSEIVER, and Google Scholar, two search keywords, "Software Security Assurance" and "Software and Security and Assurance," are decided upon.

3.5.2 Study Choice

Selection criteria are used to identify and select key investigative studies that deliver indications for study issues. To reduce the possibility of bias, selection criteria were chosen depending on the study topics. The review used inclusion criteria.

  i. Research papers published between the years 2019 and 2023.
 ii. Software security assessment and evaluation of systems, such as requirements, frameworks, and models.
iii. Publications on software assurance and security that are only concerned with software.

Information and software security are excluded from the exclusion criteria, and the chosen papers will be continually updated through June 2023. We have selected the year 2019 to examine recent advancements in system security assurance during the previous 5 years.

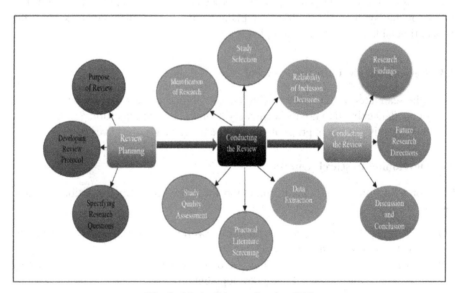

Fig. 1. Methodology of review [27]

3.5.3 Decisions on Inclusion are Reliable

Each electronic source is given to two researchers to increase the dependability of the inclusion selections. Two researchers evaluate each paper following the inclusion and exclusion criteria. To determine if academics agree on inclusion or exclusion, a list of publications with inclusion and exclusion criteria is kept. Any discrepancies or misunderstandings regarding any paper have been handled in the group's general meeting and have been resolved through discussion and professional counsel (Fig. 2 and Tables 1, 2, 3, 4).

Table 1. Research goals and inspirations

Id	Approach Questions	Inspirations
RQ1	What contemporary techniques and frameworks are there for guaranteeing security when developing software?	This research aims to explore the many strategies and approaches that have been looked into and discussed in the literature to guarantee software development security. Finding and assessing pertinent research papers, articles, and publications is what the systematic literature review entails to get an understanding of the techniques and knowledge that are currently known in the subject of security assurance Recognize the difficulties and roadblocks in establishing software security assurance
RQ2	What are the primary difficulties encountered while trying to achieve security assurance during the software development process?	Security problems can be caused by a lack of security awareness, a lack of time and resources, and a complex threat landscape. Although integrating security procedures into the SDLC is difficult, striking a balance between robust security and usability is crucial. To achieve this balance, stakeholders, testers, security specialists, and developers must work together effectively. For security assurance throughout the development process, a thorough strategy is essential. This includes continual training, applying secure coding principles, performing extensive testing, and encouraging tight cooperation between security teams and development teams
RQ3	How can we categorize the various software security assurance?	This study classifies software security assurance research projects according to their goals, methods, and application areas to efficiently arrange them. It is simpler to compare and evaluate these activities, find gaps or overlaps, and direct future research efforts in this field by developing a taxonomy or classification scheme for them

Table 2. Search string results per database. (2019–2023)

Software Assurance	Software Assurance	Software Assurance	Software Assurance	Software Assurance
(("software" OR "security" OR "software system" OR "constraint" OR"software security" "software development" OR "development" "software") AND ("software system model "OR "software security model")) Google Scholar (Search Engine)	IEEE Xplore IEEE Access Springer	2,390 213	14 41	3 23
Total		2,603	55	27

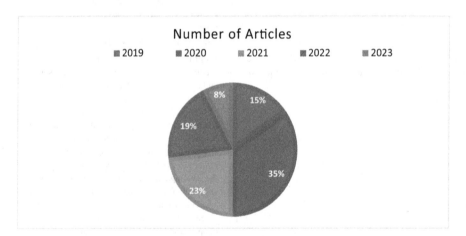

Fig. 2. Number of articles in the year

3.5.4 Study Quality Evaluation

The next phase in gathering possibly qualifying articles is the quality assessment. Stricter standards have been set to make sure that the targets are clearly defined, the research method is employed effectively, the outcome is evaluated appropriately, and the research work permits questions to be addressed. The use of acceptable research methodologies, the appraisal of the results, and the capacity to respond to queries are some of these characteristics.

Table 3. Inclusion and Exclusion

Category	Criteria for Inclusion and Exclusion
Inclusion	• In the paper, discuss at least a single matter relating to the necessities for software security, software systems, and safety in the background of the software development process • The articles are on the subjects of software manufacturing and computer science • Papers were peer-reviewed in journals and at conferences • Papers were published between 2019 and 2023
Exclusion	• The papers are not conducted in the context of a software security system • Papers on software security for experimentation and training • Journals are non-peer-reviewed then don't relate to an abstract of a whole volume or a journalistic • The papers concern the protection of software security

Table 4. Number of published articles by year

Publication years	Number of articles
2019	4
2020	9
2021	6
2022	5
2023	2

3.5.5 Real-World Literature Review

The literature screening has been done while taking into account the aforementioned processes and criteria. The outcomes of the various rounds are as follows:

The works were examined and composed from dissimilar electronic bases, resulting in 2,603 items. Duplicate entries were eliminated, leaving 55 items. Quality assessment was led using the aforementioned criteria, resulting in 26 items.

3.5.6 Extraction of Data

The purpose of the data extraction form is to gather details that will be useful in addressing research questions. Piloted a preliminary research sample to ensure completeness and avoid technological problems. Based on the research objectives, many form points have been chosen, and each point has been explicitly specified to prevent misunderstanding.

3.5.7 Report Review

The report is the ultimate step in generating a study literature review, and it entails describing and writing the results methodically and fluidly so that they may be replicated scientifically. The systematic literature review process is illustrated graphically in Fig. 1 (Table 5).

Table 5. List of selected titles

Author	Title	Reference
H. A.-M. e. al.: [2020]	Maturity Model for Secure Software Design: A Multivocal Study	[1]
S. Moyo, E. Mnkandla: [2020]	A Novel Lightweight Solo Software Development Methodology with Optimum Security Practices	[2]
R. A. K. e. al.: [2021]	Systematic Mapping Study on Security Approaches in Secure Software Engineering	[3]
F. A. Al-Zahrani: [2020]	Evaluating the Usable Security of Healthcare Software Through Unified Technique of Fuzzy Logic ANP and TOPSIS	[4]
C.-G. Yi, Y.-G. Kim: [2021]	Security Testing for Naval Ship Combat System Software,	[5]
R. Kumar et al., [2020]	A Hybrid Model of Hesitant Fuzzy Decision-Making Analysis for Estimating Usable Security of Software	[6]
J. C. S. Núñez et al.: [2020]	"A Preventive Secure Software Development Model for a Software Factory: A Case Study"	[7]
K. S. H. Zhang, [2021]	"A Survey of Software Clone Detection from a Security Perspective"	[8]
R. R. Althar et al.: [2022]	"Automated Risk Management Based Software Security Vulnerabilities Management"	[9]
R.R., Althar, et al. [2023]	"Design and Development of an Artificial Intelligence Knowledge Processing System for Optimizing the Security of Software System"	[10]
S. A. Ebad: [2022]	"Exploring How to Apply Secure Software Design Principles"	[11]

(continued)

Table 5. (*continued*)

Author	Title	Reference
S. D. L. e. al.: [2023]	"Maximizing the Security Level of Real-Time Software While Preserving Temporal Constraints"	[12]
F. A. Bhuiyan et al.: [2021]	"Security Bug Report Usage for Software Vulnerability Research: A Systematic Mapping Study"	[13]
G. Márquez et al.: [2019]	"Security in Telehealth Systems from a Software Engineering Viewpoint: A Systematic Mapping Study"	[14]
R. A. K. e. al.: [2022]	"Systematic Literature Review on Security Risks and Its Practices in Secure Software Development"	[15]
H. N. e. al.: [2021]	"Systematic Mapping of the Literature on Secure Software Development"	[16]
N. M. e. al.: [2020]	"Vulnerable Code Detection Using Software Metrics and Machine Learning"	[17]
H. Al-Matouq et al.: [2020]	"A Maturity Model for Secure Software Design: A Multivocal Study"	[18]
W. S. Kun Xu, [2020]	"Software Development Method Based on Software Bus"	[19]
T. I. Azman, N. C. Pa, R. N. H. Nor and Y. Y. Jusoh, [2019]	"Assessing the instrument reliability and validity of risk mitigation for the anti-software aging model during software maintenance"	[20]
L. F. Capretz, P. Waychal, J. Jia, D. Varona and Y. Lizama [2019]	"Studies on the Software Testing Profession"	[21]
M. Manzano, C. Ayala, C. Gomez and L. Lopez Cuesta [2019]	"A Software Service Supporting Software Quality Forecasting"	[22]
T. M. Kanner and A. M. Kanner [2020]	"Testing Software and Hardware Data Security Tools Using the Automata Theory and the Graph Theory"	[23]
F. Özdemir Sönmez, B. Günel Kiliç: [2021]	"Holistic Web Application Security Visualization for Multi-Project and Multi-Phase Dynamic Application Security Test Results"	[24]
O. S. e. al.: [2022]	Decentralized Review and Attestation of Software Attribute Claims	[25]
A. Shukla, B. Katt, L.O. Nweke et al., [2022]	System security assurance: A systematic literature review	[26]

4   Discussions

Systematic literature reviews are an important tool in evidence-based techniques for identifying knowledge gaps, scoping the literature, defining ideas, and examining research
practices. Software security is critical for high-quality software to protect its integrity,
confidentiality, and accessibility. This paper investigates Systematic literature evaluations on software security needs, limitations, and attack vectors that are significant to
software security improvement and offer a new security paradigm for the next generation.
Systematic evaluations necessitate rigorous and open approaches to ensure trustworthy
results. Clear guidance is essential to ensure that scoping reviews are not performed
for inappropriate reasons and vice versa. Because of their greater Systematic literature
and more expansive inclusion criteria, scoping reviews are viable review procedures for
specific indications. It is critical to precisely explain the key questions and objectives of
a scoping review.

5   Future Research Directions

A systematic literature review on software assurance and security systems should explore
emerging technologies, industry standards, cost-effectiveness, empirical studies, and
organizational culture. Limitations include potential bias towards specific industries and
not considering the latest trends. Existing methods are strong in detecting abnormalities
but struggle to identify their significance and potential hazards, presenting constraints and
future issues for security solutions. The review highlights the need for more research on
software security and software assurance constraints' effectiveness in real-world settings,
including technical and procedural constraints, organizational and cultural factors, software reliability and resilience, and the effectiveness of software assurance constraints in
various contexts and industries, including emerging technologies. Addressing these limitations and research gaps can advance understanding of software assurance constraints
and lead to more effective software security and reliability practices.

6   Conclusion

Systematic literature reviews are an important tool in evidence-based methods. They are
carried out for different reasons than systematic reviews, but they nevertheless require
rigorous and transparent processes to ensure the results are reliable. Systematic literature
reviews are a valid review approach for certain indications due to their broader Systematic
and more expansive inclusion criteria. They also differ from systematic reviews in their
overriding purpose, and it is important to clearly define the key questions and objectives
of a systematic review. A systematic literature review of software assurance and security
systems highlights the need for a comprehensive and systematic approach to software
security and assurance, encompassing all stages of the software development lifecycle.
Organizations should adopt a risk-based approach, focusing on identifying and mitigating critical threats. Product quality and security must incorporate security and assurance
into software development. It is a continuous process that includes continual monitoring
and enhancement of security measures. The involvement of all stakeholders, including

developers, testers, and end-users, is crucial for ensuring the security and assurance of software products. To meet the rising threat of software security breaches, a holistic and proactive strategy for software security and assurance is required. Collaboration and information exchange across businesses and sectors are critical for maintaining security and dependability. Constraints on software assurance are critical for doing this. Technical constraints like access control and encryption prevent unauthorized access and protect sensitive data. Procedural constraints like secure coding practices and peer code reviews identify vulnerabilities. Organizational constraints like compliance with security policies establish a security culture. The effectiveness of software assurance constraints depends on proper implementation and enforcement. Further research is needed to understand their effectiveness in various contexts and industries' products.

Acknowledgments. Not applicable.

Declarations.

Funding. Authors declare no funding for this research.

Competing Interests. The authors declare that they have no competing interests.

Conflicts of Interest. The authors declare that they have no conflict of interest.

Availability of Data. The datasets generated during and/or analyzed during the current study are not publicly available but are available from the corresponding author upon reasonable request.

Code availability. Not applicable.

References

1. Al-Matouq, H., Mahmood, S., Alshayeb, M., Niazi, M.: A maturity model for secure software design: a multivocal study. IEEE Access **8**, 1–19 (2020)
2. Mnkandla, S., Moyo, E.: A novel lightweight solo software development methodology with optimum security practices. IEEE Access **8**, 1–13 (2020)
3. Khan, R.A., Khan, S.U., Khan, H.U., Ilyas, M.: Systematic mapping study on security approaches in secure software engineering. IEEE Access **9**, 19139–19160 (2021)
4. Al-Zahrani, F.A.: Evaluating the usable-security of healthcare software through unified technique of fuzzy logic ANP and TOPSIS. IEEE Access **8**, 1–12 (2020)
5. Yi, C.-G., Kim, Y.-G.: Security testing for naval ship combat system software. IEEE Access **9**, 1–13 (2021)
6. Kumar, R., et al.: A hybrid model of hesitant fuzzy decision making analysis for estimating usable security of software. IEEE Access **8**, 1–19 (2020)
7. Núñez, J.C.S., et al.: A Preventive secure software development model for a software factory: a case study. IEEE Access **8**, 1–13 (2020)
8. Zhang, H., Sakurai, K.: A survey of software clone detection from security perspective. IEEE Access **8**, 1–17 (2021)
9. Althar, R.R., et al.: Automated risk management based software security vulnerabilities management. IEEE Access **10**, 1–12 (2022)

10. Althar, R.R., Samanta, D., Purushotham, S., et al.: Design and development of artificial intelligence knowledge processing system for optimizing security of software system. SN Comput. Sci. **4**, 1–12 (2023)

11. Ebad, S.A.: Exploring how to apply secure software design principles. IEEE Access **10**, 1–11 (2022)

12. Leonardi, S.D., et al.: Maximizing the security level of real-time software while preserving temporal constraints. IEEE Access **11**, 1–17 (2023)

13. Bhuiyan, F.A., et al.: Security bug report usage for software vulnerability research: a systematic mapping study. IEEE Access **9**, 1–25 (2021)

14. Márquez, G., et al.: Security in telehealth systems from a software engineering viewpoint: a systematic mapping study. IEEE Access **8**, 1–18 (2019)

15. Shanmugapriya, S., Devika, P.: A novel software engineering approach toward using machine learning for improving the efficiency of health systems. Int. J. Eng. Technol. Manage. Sci. **7**(2), 711–725 (2023)

16. Khan, R.A., et al.: Systematic literature review on security risks and its practices in secure software development. IEEE Access **10**, 1–26 (2022)

17. Nina, H., et al.: Systematic mapping of the literature on secure software development. IEEE Access **9**, 1–16 (2021)

18. Medeiros, N., Ivaki, N., Costa, P., Vieira, M.: Vulnerable code detection using software metrics and machine learning. IEEE Access **8**, 1–35 (2020)

19. Al-Matouq, H., et al.: A maturity model for secure software design: a multivocal study. IEEE Access **8**, 1–19 (2020)

20. Xu, K., Shen, W.: Software development method based on software bus. In: IEEE 2020 International Conference on Advance in Ambient Computing and Intelligence (ICAACI) (2020)

21. Azman, T.I., Pa, N.C., Nor, R.N.H., Jusoh, Y.Y.: Assessing the instrument reliability and validity of risk mitigation for the anti-software aging model during software maintenance. In: 2019 6th International Conference on Research and Innovation in Information Systems (ICRIIS), pp. 1–6. IEEE (2019)

22. Capretz, L.F., Waychal, P., Jia, J., Varona, D., Lizama, Y.: Studies on the software testing profession. In: IEEE 2019 IEEE/ACM 41st International Conference on Software Engineering: Companion Proceedings (ICSE-Companion), pp. 1–2 (2019)

23. Manzano, M., Ayala, C., Gomez, C., Lopez Cuesta, L.: A software service supporting software quality forecasting. In: IEEE 19th International Conference on Software Quality, Reliability and Security Companion (QRS-C), Sofia, Bulgaria, pp. 1–3 (2019)

24. Kanner, T.M., Kanner, A.M.: Testing software and hardware data security tools using the automata theory and the graph theory. In: IEEE 2020 Ural Symposium on Biomedical Engineering, Radioelectronics and Information Technology (USBEREIT), Yekaterinburg, Russia, pp. 1–4. IEEE (2020)

25. Sönmez, F.Ö., Kiliç, B.G.: Holistic web application security visualization for multi-project and multi-phase dynamic application security test results. IEEE Access **9**, 1–27 (2021)

26. Stengele, O., et al.: Decentralized review and attestation of software attribute claims. IEEE Access **10**, 1–17 (2022)

27. Shukla, A., Katt, B., Nweke, L.O., et al.: System security assurance: A systematic literature review. Comput. Sci. Rev. **45**, 1–29 (2022)

Edge Detection Using Watershed Algorithm for Polycystic Ovary Image Analysis: A Comprehensive Study

Kamini Solanki[1], Jaimin Undavia[1(✉)], Rahul Vaghela[2], Mittal Desai[1], and Chetan Dudhagra[3]

[1] CMPICA, Charotar University of Science and Technology (CHARUSAT), Changa, India
jaiminundavia.mca@charusat.ac.in
[2] Computer Engineering Department, Silver Oak University, Ahmedabad, India
[3] International Agribusiness Management Institute, AAU, Anand, India

Abstract. Polycystic ovary syndrome (PCOS) is a common endocrine disorder that affects reproductive-age women. Image analysis techniques, particularly edge detection, play a crucial role in PCOS diagnosis and treatment monitoring. This research paper presents a comprehensive study on edge detection using the Watershed algorithm for analyzing Polycystic Ovary (PCO) images. The paper explores the application of the Watershed algorithm in detecting and segmenting ovarian cysts, follicles, and other key structures in PCO images. Various approaches, modifications, and pre-processing techniques are investigated to enhance the performance of the Watershed algorithm in PCO image analysis. Additionally, the paper discusses the challenges, future directions, and potential applications of Watershed-based edge detection in PCOS research and clinical practice.

Keywords: PCOD · PCOS · Edge Detection · Watershed Algorithm

1 Introduction

PCO image analysis plays a crucial role in the diagnosis and treatment monitoring of Polycystic Ovary Syndrome (PCOS). PCOS is a common endocrine disorder affecting reproductive-age women, characterized by hormonal imbalances, ovarian dysfunction, and the presence of multiple small cysts on the ovaries. Accurate analysis of PCO images provides valuable insights into the morphology, size, and distribution of ovarian cysts and follicles, which are key diagnostic markers of PCOS. Accurate edge detection methods are essential in PCO image analysis to precisely identify and segment cysts, follicles, and other relevant structures. Edge detection allows the extraction of boundaries between different tissue regions and provides critical information for quantitative analysis. Accurate edge detection enables clinicians and researchers to measure cyst size, count follicles, and assess the spatial distribution of ovarian structures. It assists in tracking changes over time, evaluating treatment response, and identifying patterns associated with PCOS severity [9, 15].

S. Rajagopal et al (Eds.): ASCIS 2023, CCIS 2040, pp. 31–38, 2024.
https://doi.org/10.1007/978-3-031-59107-5_3

2 Objectives

- Diagnosis:
    Machine learning algorithms can undergo training using extensive sets of clinical and imaging data. The aim is to create accurate models capable of diagnosing Polycystic Ovary Syndrome (PCOD) with precision. For instance, a machine learning model can analyse elements like hormonal levels, ultrasound images of the ovaries, and patient demographics. This analysis helps identify patterns and enables predictions regarding PCOD diagnosis.
- PCOD Risk Prediction:
    Machine learning can scrutinize various risk determinants such as family history, lifestyle variables, and hormonal levels. The purpose is to construct predictive models that can evaluate the probability of a woman developing PCOD in the future. This process aids in pinpointing individuals at high risk and facilitates early interventions for prevention or management.
- Tailored Treatment Plans:
    Machine learning algorithms have the capacity to process substantial volumes of data, encompassing patient medical histories, symptoms, and responses to treatments. These algorithms then formulate treatment plans that are personalized for women with PCOD. The ultimate goal is to refine treatment strategies, curtail adverse effects, and enhance overall treatment outcomes.
- Real-time Monitoring and Management:
    Machine learning models can delve into data originating from wearable devices like activity trackers and hormonal monitors. The objective is to offer constant real-time monitoring and management of PCOD. This empowers women to trace their symptoms, keep an eye on hormonal levels, and proficiently handle their condition.
- Lifestyle Recommendations:
    Machine learning can engineer algorithms that dissect lifestyle factors including diet, physical activity, and sleep patterns. This analytical approach enables the provision of personalized recommendations for lifestyle adjustments. Such adjustments contribute to the management of PCOD symptoms and the advancement of overall well-being.
- Fertility Estimation:
    Machine learning models can evaluate an array of factors like regularity of menstrual cycles, hormone levels, and patient age. The purpose is to predict fertility outcomes among women with PCOD. This predictive capacity aids women with PCOD who are striving to conceive by furnishing them with informed choices concerning fertility treatments and family planning.

3 Importance of Edge Detection in PCO Image Analysis

Edge detection plays a crucial role in PCO image analysis for several reasons. Here are some key reasons highlighting the importance of edge detection in PCO image analysis [13]:

- Localization and Segmentation of Structures: Edge detection methods allow the precise localization and segmentation of important structures in PCO images, such as ovarian cysts and follicles. These structures are key diagnostic markers in PCOS, and accurate identification and delineation are essential for diagnosis, treatment monitoring, and research purposes.
- Quantitative Analysis: Edge detection provides the basis for quantitative analysis of PCO images. By extracting the boundaries of cysts and follicles, edge detection enables the measurement of their size, shape, and distribution. Quantitative analysis aids in objective assessment, comparison, and tracking of these structures over time, facilitating treatment monitoring and research investigations.
- Feature Extraction: Edge detection serves as a fundamental step in feature extraction for PCO image analysis. Extracting relevant features from edges allows the characterization and classification of different structures, such as distinguishing between cysts, follicles, and normal ovarian tissue. These extracted features can be used as inputs for machine learning algorithms, pattern recognition, or further analysis in PCOS research.
- Image Visualization and Interpretation: Edge detection enhances image visualization and interpretation by highlighting the boundaries and contours of structures of interest. By emphasizing the edges, important structures become more visually prominent, aiding clinicians and researchers in the visual analysis and interpretation of PCO images [16].
- Detection of Abnormalities: Edge detection methods can assist in detecting abnormalities or variations in the ovarian structures present in PCO images. Deviations from normal edge characteristics may indicate irregularities, such as atypical cysts or follicles, which can be further investigated and analysed for clinical decision-making.
- Automation and Efficiency: Edge detection techniques enable automation and efficiency in PCO image analysis. By automating the process of structure localization and segmentation, edge detection algorithms can save time and reduce subjectivity inherent in manual analysis. This is particularly valuable when analysing large datasets or when aiming for reproducible and consistent results across different clinicians or researchers [16].
- Integration with Other Analysis Techniques: Edge detection can be integrated with other image analysis techniques, such as morphological operations, texture analysis, or shape modelling, to provide a comprehensive analysis of PCO images. The combined use of edge detection with these techniques can yield more accurate and robust results, enabling a deeper understanding of the morphology and characteristics of PCO structures.

In summary, edge detection plays a vital role in PCO image analysis by enabling localization, segmentation, quantitative analysis, feature extraction, visualization, detection of abnormalities, automation, and integration with other analysis techniques. It contributes to the accurate assessment and interpretation of PCO images, facilitating diagnosis, treatment monitoring, and research advancements in PCOS.

4   Overview of Edge Detection Methods

Edge detection methods are fundamental techniques used in image processing and computer vision to identify and extract boundaries or edges between different regions in an image. These methods are crucial in various applications, including PCO image analysis in PCOS diagnosis and treatment monitoring. Here is an overview of commonly used edge detection methods:

4.1   Gradient-Based Methods

- Sobel Operator: The Sobel operator uses a pair of convolution kernels to approximate the gradient of the image intensity. It computes the first derivative in the horizontal and vertical directions, allowing the detection of edges based on intensity changes.
- Prewitt Operator: Similar to the Sobel operator, the Prewitt operator estimates the gradient by convolving the image with a pair of kernels. It is also used for edge detection based on intensity variations.

4.2   Laplacian-Based Methods

- Laplacian of Gaussian (LoG): The LoG operator combines the Laplacian operator and Gaussian smoothing. It convolves the image with a Gaussian kernel followed by the Laplacian operator to detect zero-crossings, which indicate the presence of edges.
- Difference of Gaussians (DoG): The DoG operator applies a difference filter between two Gaussian-smoothed versions of the image. It enhances edges by highlighting regions of rapid intensity changes.

4.3   Canny Edge Detection

- The Canny edge detection algorithm is a multi-stage approach that includes smoothing, gradient computation, non-maximum suppression, and hysteresis thresholding. It aims to find the optimal edges with good localization, minimal noise sensitivity, and thin contours.

4.4   Roberts Operator

- The Roberts operator utilizes a pair of simple gradient operators to estimate the gradients in the image. It calculates the gradient magnitude and direction to detect edges based on intensity variations.

4.5   Model-Based Approaches

- Active Contour Models (Snakes): Active contour models are energy-based algorithms that iteratively deform a contour to fit the image edges. They use edge information to guide the contour evolution and accurately capture the boundaries of objects in an image.
- Level Set Methods: Level set methods represent the boundaries as the zero level set of a higher-dimensional function. They evolve the level set function using partial differential equations, incorporating edge information to detect and track object boundaries.

4.6 Machine Learning-Based Approaches

- Deep Learning-based Methods: Deep learning approaches, particularly convolutional neural networks (CNNs), have shown remarkable success in edge detection tasks. CNN architectures can be trained to learn edge features directly from the data, enabling accurate and robust edge detection.

Each of these edge detection methods has its advantages, limitations, and specific use cases. The choice of the method depends on the characteristics of the images, the level of noise, the desired edge localization, and the specific requirements of the PCO image analysis task. Often, a combination of multiple methods or further modifications may be employed to improve the accuracy and robustness of edge detection in PCO image analysis.

5 Watershed Algorithm for PCO Image Analysis

- Pre-processing Techniques for PCO Images: Discuss specific pre-processing techniques suitable for PCO images, such as noise reduction, contrast enhancement, and normalization, to improve the accuracy of edge detection [17, 18].
- Marker Selection Strategies for PCO Edge Detection: Explore different strategies for selecting markers in PCO images, considering factors such as intensity thresholds, gradient magnitudes, or region-based approaches to initiate the Watershed algorithm [17, 18].
- Watershed-based Edge Detection for PCO Structures: Explain how the Watershed algorithm can be applied to detect and segment key structures in PCO images, including ovarian cysts, follicles, and boundaries between different tissue regions [17, 18].

6 Experimental Evaluation and Dataset

PCO Image Dataset: Our dataset which was utilized to train and validate of our models, was obtained from Kaggle [19] (Figs. 1, 3 and 4).

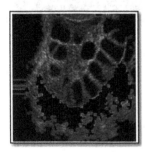  

Fig. 1. Infected images   **Fig. 2.** Threshold Processing   **Fig. 3.** Noise Removal

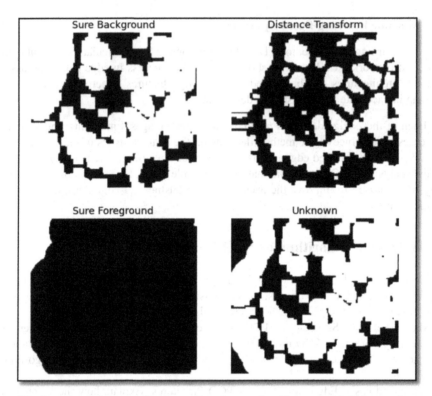

Fig. 4. a. Sure Background b. Distant Transform c. Sure Foreground d. Unknown Area

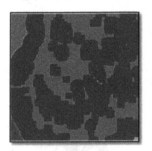
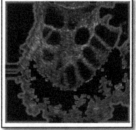

Fig. 5. Marker labelling   **Fig. 6.** Watershed Algorithm   **Fig. 7.** Elevation map using sobel

7   Discussion and Results

The experiments are performed to assess the performance of the proposed technique by utilizing the distance transform method for watershed segmentation, along with commonly employed differential edge detection operators like the Sobel edge detector or LoG edge detector, in combination with morphological watershed segmentation using distance transform. The proposed approach has been applied to an image of PCOD measuring {200 × 200} and containing 256 grey levels (Fig. 2). The segmentation outcomes are displayed in Figs. 5, 6, and 7. By observing the segmented images, it is evident that the final result obtained using the proposed approach (Fig. 7) exhibits superior performance compared to the traditional watershed segmentation using distance transform method (Fig. 6) and the typically utilized differential edge detection operators like the Sobel edge detector (Fig. 7).

8 Conclusion

In this paper, an effective morphological edge detection algorithm is proposed to detect image edge. The technique is very useful for Image segmentation and classification. The given experimental result shows that the algorithm produces more efficient results compared to traditional watershed segmentation using distance transform algorithm and the usually used differential edge detection operators such as Sobel edge detector or LoG edge detector with the combination of morphological watershed segmentation using distance transform. The detected edges are more sharp, pinpointed and clear with abundant edge information. Moreover, the proposed algorithm can filer the noise more effectively than traditional watershed segmentation using distance transform algorithm.

References

1. Chauhan, P., Patil, P., Rane, N., Raundale, P., Kanakia, H.: Comparative analysis of machine learning algorithms for prediction of PCOS. In: 2021 International Conference on Communication Information and Computing Technology (ICCICT), pp. 1–7. IEEE (2021)
2. Hassan, M.M., Mirza, T.: Comparative analysis of machine learning algorithms in diagnosis of polycystic ovarian syndrome. Int. J. Comput. Appl. **975**, 8887 (2020)
3. Kumari, S.: Classification of PCOS/PCOD using transfer learning and GAN architectures to generate pseudo ultrasound images. Ph.D. Dissertation, Dublin, National College of Ireland (2021)
4. Inan, M.S.K., Ulfath, R.E., Alam, F.I., Bappee, F.K., Hasan, R.: Improved sampling and feature selection to support extreme gradient boosting for PCOS diagnosis. In: 2021 IEEE 11th Annual Computing and Communication Workshop and Conference (CCWC), pp. 1046–1050. IEEE (2021)
5. Lv, W., et al.: Deep learning algorithm for automated detection of polycystic ovary syndrome using scleral images. Front. Endocrinol. **12**, 789878 (2021)
6. Soni, P., Vashisht, S.: Image segmentation for detecting polycystic ovarian disease using deep neural networks. Int. J. Comput. Sci. Eng. **7**(3), 534–537 (2019)
7. Srivastava, S., Kumar, P., Chaudhry, V., Singh, A.: Detection of ovarian cyst in ultrasound images using fine-tuned VGG-16 deep learning network. SN Comput. Sci. **1**(2), 1–8 (2020)
8. Zheng, E., et al.: Second-generation dual scan mammoscope with photoacoustic, ultrasound, and elastographic imaging capabilities. https://www.frontiersin.org/articles/10.3389/fonc.2021.779071/full
9. Dewi, R.M., Wisesty, U.N.: Classification of polycystic ovary based on ultrasound images using competitive neural network. J. Phys. Conf. Ser. **971**(1), 012005 (2018)
10. Manickam, S., Perumal, C., Prabha, R., Srilatha, K.: Study and detection of PCOS related diseases using CNN. IOP Conf. Ser. Mater. Sci. Eng. **1070**, 012062 (2021)

11. Nasim, S., Almutairi, M., Munir, K., Raza, A., Younas, F.: A novel approach for polycystic ovary syndrome prediction using machine learning in bioinformatics. IEEE Access **10**, 21038–21048 (2022)
12. Bećirović, L.S., Deumić, A., Pokvić, L.G., Badnjevic, A.: Artificial intelligence challenges in COPD management: a review. In: 2021 IEEE 21st International Conference on Bioinformatics and Bioengineering (BIBE), pp. 1–7 (2021)
13. Witchel, S.F., Oberfield, S.E., Peña, A.S.: Polycystic ovary syndrome: pathophysiology, presentation, and treatment with emphasis on adolescent girls. J. Endocr. Soc. **3**(8), 1545–1573 (2019)
14. Hasib, K.M., Sakib, S., Mahmud, J.A., Mithu, K., Rahman, M.S., Alam, M.S.: Covid-19 prediction based on infected cases and deaths of Bangladesh using deep transfer learning. In: 2022 IEEE World AI IoT Congress (AIIoT), pp. 296–302 (2022)
15. Aggarwal, S., Pandey, K.: Early identification of PCOS with commonly known diseases: obesity, diabetes, high blood pressure and heart disease using machine learning techniques. Exp. Syst. Appl. **217**, 119532 (2023)
16. Faris, N.N., Miften, F.S.: Proposed model for detection of PCOS using machine learning methods and feature selection. J. Educ. Pure Sci. **13**(11), 1–01 (2023)
17. Ma, W., Wang, L., Jiang, T., Yang, A., Zhang, Y.: Overlapping pellet size detection method based on marker watershed and GMM image segmentation. Metals **13**(2), 327 (2023)
18. Gharehchobogh, B.K., Kuzekanani, Z.D., Sobhi, J., Khiavi, A.M.: Flotation froth image segmentation using Mask R-CNN. Miner. Eng. **192**, 107959 (2023)
19. Choudhari, A.: PCOS detection using ultrasound images. https://www.kaggle.com/datasets/anaghachoudhari/pcos-detection-using-ultrasound-images

Sculpting the Perfect Workforce: A Study of Cognitive AI and Machine Learning Algorithms in Reshaping the Future of Talent Acquisition and Fostering Synergistic HR-Technology Ecosystems

Meeta Joshi[(✉)] [iD]

Faculty of Business Management, Marwadi University, Rajkot, India
meeta.joshi@marwadieducation.edu.in

Abstract. This study explores integrating Cognitive AI and ML algorithms into talent acquisition and assessing their impact on HR practices. The paper reviews the literature to contextualize this convergence, identifying gaps in real-world organizational usage. It outlines current trends, challenges, and opportunities. Discussions with HR professionals, AI experts, and executives employ a focus group approach. The qualitative framework spotlights applicant sourcing, screening, matching, and personalized experiences. Thematic analysis reveals fresh results and insights. Integrating Cognitive AI and ML induces a talent acquisition paradigm shift. Improved candidate sourcing accuracy and AI-based screening enhance the talent pipeline. Acknowledging challenges, like algorithmic bias, calls for ongoing vigilance and ethical considerations. The study underscores the transformative power of Cognitive AI and ML in talent acquisition while advocating ethical integration. Balancing innovation and deliberate adoption can steer enterprises toward an AI-empowered HR future.

Keywords: Cognitive AI · Machine Learning Algorithms · Talent Acquisition · HR-Technology Ecosystems

1 Introduction

The orchestration of talent acquisition arises in the turbulent expanse of the modern business ecosystem as a pivot that profoundly determines the course of corporate success, not just as a routine task. The ability to attract, assess, and secure elite personnel becomes increasingly crucial when industries experience seismic transformations brought on by the relentless march of technological advancement and escalating competitive currents (Jha et al. 2020). The traditional human resources (HR) structures, which were previously steadfast guardians of organizational development, are now feeling the strain from the intricate web of contemporary talent acquisition requirements. In light of this, the convergence of cognitive AI and machine learning algorithms is emerging as a disruptive phenomenon, signaling a paradigm shift that necessitates a recalibrating of how businesses think.

© The Author(s), under exclusive license to Springer Nature Switzerland AG 2024
S. Rajagopal et al (Eds.): ASCIS 2023, CCIS 2040, pp. 39–52, 2024.
https://doi.org/10.1007/978-3-031-59107-5_4

Talent acquisition appears as a cornerstone that underpins organizational dominance in the current digital era (George 2019). The trajectory of innovation and competitive strength is orchestrated by the gravitational pull of outstanding people. The empirical proof that a company's vitality is shaped by the quality of its staff emphasizes the imperative requirement for a skilled talent acquisition compass (Pan et al. 2022). The function of talent acquisition transforms from a purely transactional process into an intricate tapestry of strategic talent management and longevity as sectors delicately navigate the turbulent waters of technological disruption and workforce change. The evolution of talent acquisition parallels the larger transformative spirit permeating the modern organization. Regardless of their historical importance, enduring practices run the risk of vanishing in the aftermath of technological tides. This revolutionary change, which is heralded by the merger of Cognitive AI and ML algorithms, promises to seismically recalibrate HR paradigms. The iterative brilliance of ML and the agile linguistic capability of cognitive AI combine to provide a framework that improves candidate experiences and strengthens the foundation of HR decision-making.

1.1 Research Gap and Study Need

Although the combination of Cognitive AI and ML algorithms offers profound potential for HR practices, there is a crucial knowledge gap about its actual organizational applications and the ensuing effect on talent acquisition. Prior studies have frequently concentrated on theoretic aspects or particular elements of this integration. However, there hasn't been much research done on the complex relationships between cognitive AI, machine learning algorithms, and hiring practices. By exploring the complex interactions between these technologies and HR practices, this study seeks to close this gap by identifying trends, problems, and opportunities that have evaded thorough examination to until.

1.2 Research Objective

- To examine the effects of incorporating Cognitive AI and Machine Learning algorithms into candidate sourcing, screening, and matching procedures within talent acquisition, focusing on enhancements in candidate selection accuracy, effectiveness, and quality.
- To identify, evaluate, and recommend ways for mitigating the risks, moral issues, and potential biases related to the application of cognitive AI and machine learning algorithms in HR practices, particularly in the context of talent acquisition.
- To analyze how personalized applicant experiences including cognitive AI and machine learning algorithms can improve candidate engagement, satisfaction, and general perceptions of the organization's hiring process.

2   Literature Review

In the chaotic expanse of today's business ecosystem, the orchestration of talent acquisition appears as a fulcrum that intimately determines the trajectory of organizational victory. Industry changes are becoming more intense as a result of the relentless march of technology. Johansson and Herranen (2019) look into the use of artificial intelligence (AI) in human resource management, specifically the traditional recruitment process. To present a summary of the current state of AI's application in HRM with an emphasis on hiring procedures, their paper makes extensive use of an investigation of the existing literature.

The authors critically examine the numerous ways AI is incorporated into the recruiting process using a systematic review, detecting patterns and consequences. The integration of artificial intelligence (AI) and machine learning (ML) within the human resources (HR) domains is discussed by George and Thomas (2019). The potential transformational influence of these technologies on HR operations is highlighted by their investigation. The amalgamation of AI and ML has greatly increased interest in rethinking personnel management techniques and promoting more effective and efficient HR practices. The difficulties and potential remedies in integrating Artificial Intelligence (AI) into Human Resources (HR) management are covered in detail by Tambe et al. (2019). The authors draw attention to the challenges involved in effectively utilizing AI for hiring, performance evaluation, and staff training. Their work highlights the necessity for the implementation of morally sound and goal-aligned AI. The move from traditional human resource management (HRM) to intelligent HRM (IHRM), fueled by developments like artificial intelligence (AI), is the subject of Yabanci's essay from 2019.

The conceptual viewpoint imagines a purposeful blending of human knowledge with AI technologies in engagement, talent management, and decision-making processes. This paper offers insights into the potential of AI-driven IHRM in changing HR strategies for the future, adding to the ongoing discussion on HRM's development. The introduction of transparency into AI-ML models for forecasting and explaining employee turnover is examined by Chowdhury et al. (2023), with significant management implications. The paper emphasizes how transparent models offer useful support for HR decisions by shedding light on the intricate interactions between transparency, prediction accuracy, and turnover insights. This study contributes to the dialogue on AI-ML transparency by offering key insights for efficiently managing employee turnover.

In Chen's study from 2023, the synergistic potential of human recruiters and artificial intelligence (AI) to eliminate prejudice in work scenarios is carefully examined. The study dissects the complex dynamics of this collaboration, offering insight on how artificial intelligence's data-driven capabilities might combat subjective preconceptions. Makarius et al. (2020) provide a game-changing sociotechnical approach for integrating Artificial Intelligence (AI) into companies. The concept deftly investigates the interaction of AI and human dynamics inside organizational systems. The paper provides a strategic plan for efficient AI integration by unraveling the linkages between technology capabilities, organizational architecture, and human interactions. This study contributes to the discussion of AI integration methods by offering enterprises a holistic strategy to maximize AI's promise while navigating the obstacles of implementation. By addressing the essential worry of cognitive biases, Soleimani et al. (2022) provide a vital perspective on AI-assisted recruiting systems. Their research recommends a knowledge-sharing method to counteract the biases inherent in these systems. The authors acknowledge the possibility of bias impacting judgments and suggest a collaborative framework between human experts and AI to improve transparency and fairness.

An in-depth investigation on the use of artificial intelligence (AI) in employee recruiting, concentrating on the role of contextual factors, is presented by Pan et al. (2022). The study acknowledges the importance of organizational and environmental circumstances in driving AI adoption decisions. According to their findings, successful AI integration in recruiting is intricately entangled with company culture, strategy, and external variables. Focusing on its causes, integration, and multiple implications, Prikshat et al. (2023) thorough analysis of AI-augmented HRM. They identify key adoption factors, emphasize strategy alignment, and emphasize wide implications. This research greatly enhances HRM by providing insights into AI's nuanced effect across organizational levels. In order to address the issue of preparing employees for AI integration, research by Jaiswal et al. (2022) explores AI upskilling in global organizations. With artificial intelligence altering work roles, the report underlines the importance of strong upskilling initiatives. It examines the tactics and obstacles involved in retraining workforces to meet AI needs, emphasizing the significance of strategic planning and reskilling programs. This research gives insights on HR strategies for AI adoption, providing unique perspectives on how multinational businesses prepare their employees for an AI-driven future.

A substantial conceptual research on AI-driven re-cruitment is presented by Geetha and Bhanu (2018). Their study emphasizes artificial intelligence's revolutionary impact in improving the recruiting process, highlighting increased efficiency, objectivity, and strategic focus. Garg et al. (2022) provide a thorough examination of machine learning's implications in human resource management (HRM). Their research meticulously explores applications in the areas of recruiting, performance evaluation, talent management, and decision-making. They emphasize machine learning's potential to change HRM by improving operational efficiency and strategic effectiveness.

Human-centric multimodal machine learning and AI-based recruiting are examined by Peña et al. (2023) for their potential synergy. Their research demonstrates practical applications of this strategy, highlighting its revolutionary potential in improving recruiting procedures. This study provides important insights into the intersection of human-centric viewpoints and powerful machine-learning approaches, offering up new avenues for enhancing recruiting procedures. A study on machine learning-based predictive analytics in HR is conducted by Kakulapati et al. in 2020. Their study examines the use of machine learning approaches for outcome predicting in a variety of HR disciplines. The study emphasizes the potential of data-driven solutions to improve HR decision-making in a systematic manner.

Mahmoud et al. (2019) study the ability of machine learning to predict job performance in recruiting and appraisals. They emphasize the practical benefits of data-driven decision upgrades for hiring and assessments. Their research contributes to conversations about using machine learning into HR practices by demonstrating its strategic influence on performance forecasts and improvement. Indarapu et al. (2023) look into how machine learning models may be integrated into human resource management

(HRM) intelligence procedures. Their research looks at real-world examples, stressing machine learning's potential to improve HR procedures and decision-making. Analytically, the study emphasizes machine learning's transformational influence on human resource management, emphasizing its role in building data-driven HRM intelligence. Prikshat et al. (2023) perform a literature survey and analysis of AI-augmented Human Resource Management (HRM). In order to explore the interactions between HR practices and AI at various organizational levels, they suggest a multilayer paradigm for future study.

Albert (2019) provides a thorough examination of AI applications in talent acquisition, with an emphasis on recruiting and selection procedures. The paper investigates the use of AI in different disciplines critically, providing analytical insights into its numerous uses. The author emphasizes the role of AI in boosting efficiency and effectiveness by evaluating the strategic implications of AI in talent acquisition. Votto et al. (2021) conduct a thorough examination of the use of artificial intelligence (AI) in tactical human resource management (HRM). Their research thoroughly examines various AI applications inside tactical HRM practices, providing accurate insights into strategic implementation. The junction of innovative artificial intelligence (AI)-mediated knowledge sharing and talent experiences within an IT-multinational setting is explored by Malik et al. (2021). Their study focuses on the function of artificial intelligence in enabling information diffusion and cooperation. The report emphasizes the revolutionary impact of AI on talent engagement and expertise augmentation by rigorously assessing its impact. The practical integration of artificial intelligence (AI) for improving recruiting and selection processes is comprehensively examined by Jha, S. K., Jha, S., and Gupta, M. K. in their 2020 study. The authors show how, by employing AI-driven tools and algorithms, these technologies may greatly improve decision-making accuracy, candidate evaluation efficiency, and overall HR strategy optimization. The research highlights AI's power to transform established procedures, ushering in a new era of advanced and successful talent acquisition processes. Hunkenschroer and Luetge (2022) conduct a critical examination of the ethics of AI-enabled recruiting and selection. Their analysis dissects the complex ethical elements of AI integration, revealing biases, fairness concerns, and accountability challenges. The study emphasizes the importance of a strong ethical framework to drive responsible AI implementation in HR practices, underlining the need for more research in this area. Mahmoud's (2021) demonstrates the efficacy of AI-driven human resourcing. The paper emphasizes the potential benefits of introducing artificial intelligence into these procedures. While the emphasis is mostly on AI's efficacy, there is potential for further investigation of the ethical and data privacy implications. Furthermore, taking into account the current legislative framework and proposing modifications for responsible AI integration would add to the conversation.

3 Methodology

Focus groups and qualitative investigation are intertwined in the research approach chosen for this study. This integrated approach provides a sophisticated knowledge of the complex interplay between Cognitive Artificial Intelligence (AI) and Machine Learning (ML) algorithms in the context of talent acquisition methods. This study's rigorous curation of a cohort of 13 participants was designed to capture a broad range of skills and perspectives, guaranteeing a multi-faceted analysis of the issue. Thirty-one percent of the participants are HR experts, who offer their in-depth knowledge of the nuances of hiring and HR procedures. This group has intimate experience of present methods and issues. A technical dimension is added by the fact that 23% of the participants are specialists in artificial intelligence (AI). They use their knowledge of ML and cognitive AI algorithms to offer insightful analyses on their prospective strengths and weaknesses. Complementing these insights are organizational executives (46% of the cohort), who provide a strategic perspective by linking HR initiatives with larger company objectives. With a mean age of 38.5 years (SD = 6.8) and a gender distribution of 38% male and 62% female participants, the demographic characteristics show a varied age range. In terms of education, 31% have a bachelor's degree, 23% have a master's degree, and 15% have a doctorate. Their cumulative professional experience averages 9.2 years (SD = 3.5), and their geographical distribution throughout different areas of Gujarat adds region-specific views to the study's observations. This triangulated selection enhances the authenticity and richness of the acquired insights. Focus groups were chosen because they can reveal the underlying assumptions that are important in influencing the viewpoints of possible end users. Focus groups encourage lively dialogues among members, which improves our sophisticated understanding. Discussions were preceded by ethical approval. Participants were led by a researcher and began with informed consent and demographic questions. Deepening the discussions were open-ended questions like "How might AI revolutionize candidate sourcing?" and "What challenges could AI bring to data privacy?" Insights were also supplemented by queries such as "Can you elaborate on the concept of automated candidate screening?" and "How can HR strategies align with AI integration?" (Fig. 1).

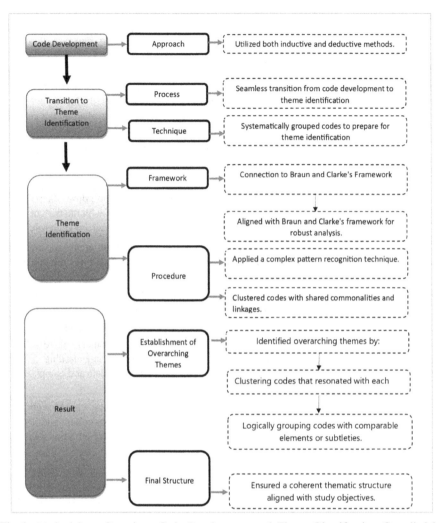

Fig. 1. Methodology Overview: Code Development and Theme Identification Complied by Author

These segments, known as codes, were developed using both inductive and deductive methods. Inductive coding enabled new patterns to arise from the data, whereas deductive coding used established categories associated with our study aims. The method then moved effortlessly into theme identification, which included the systematic grouping of codes that shared commonalities and linkages. This complex pattern recognition technique required clustering codes that resonated with one another, eventually establishing overarching themes. This theme identification procedure was well connected with Braun and Clarke's framework, allowing for the logical grouping of codes that essentially shared comparable elements or subtleties (Table 1).

Table 1. Thematic Analysis of Focus Group Discussions on the Transformative Potential of Cognitive AI and ML in Talent Acquisition and Synergistic HR-Technology Ecosystems.

Theme	Sub-Themes	Illustrative Quotations
Transformative Potential of Cognitive AI and ML in Talent Acquisition	– Advancing Candidate Sourcing Accuracy	"AI's precision in candidate sourcing is like having a magnifying glass on the perfect fit"
	– Streamlining Automated Candidate Screening	"Automation eases our load. It's like a helping hand during initial screening"
	– Elevating Candidate Matching Precision	"ML narrows down the pool, leaving us with the perfect puzzle pieces for each role"
	– Tailoring Personalized Candidate Experiences	"Candidates appreciate tailored messages. It's like the process is designed just for them"
Synergistic HR-Technology Ecosystems	– Ethical Implications and Bias Mitigation	"Bias checks are vital. We're ensuring fairness by keeping AI's decisions unbiased"
	– Navigating Data Privacy and Compliance	"Privacy matters. We're vigilant in safeguarding candidate data and complying with regulations"
	– Adapting to Organizational Change	"The journey with AI is about adapting our culture and practices. It's a harmonious change"
	– Aligning HR Strategy with Business Impact	"AI aligns our talent hunt with business needs. It's not just about hiring; it's about strategic growth"
	– Pioneering Future Workforce Dynamics	"AI shapes who we look for, preparing us for the talents of tomorrow"
	– Continuous Learning and Improvement	"AI is our teacher too. We're learning from its insights, making each hiring cycle smarter"
Challenges and Potential Pitfalls in AI-Driven Talent Acquisition	– Tackling Algorithmic Bias	"Guarding against bias is a must. AI's decisions must reflect our diverse society"

(continued)

Table 1. (*continued*)

Theme	Sub-Themes	Illustrative Quotations
	– Managing Technological Complexity	"AI brings complexity. It's about ensuring our teams can navigate the tech landscape"
	– Balancing Automation with Human Touch	"While automation helps, we can't lose sight of the human connection in recruitment"
	– Mitigating Privacy and Security Risks	"As AI handles data, we're cautious. Security measures must be robust to protect candidates' information"
	– Ensuring Ethical and Transparent AI Use	"Transparency is key. AI decisions should be clear, ensuring candidates understand the process"

4 Results and Findings

- **Transformative Potential of Cognitive AI and ML in Talent Acquisition**

The examination of the provided statements uncovers a narrative that delves into the profound transformative prospects presented by cognitive AI and machine learning (ML) in the realm of talent acquisition. The concept of "Advancing Candidate Sourcing Accuracy" emerges as a pivotal revelation, portraying AI's ability to hone candidate sourcing with a precision akin to a finely tuned lens focusing on the optimal fit. This imagery vividly captures AI's potential to significantly enhance proficiency of identifying the most suitable candidates. The theme of transformation further unfolds with the idea of "Streamlining Automated Candidate Screening," portraying automation as a valuable collaborator during initial screening. The metaphor of a guiding hand effectively captures how automation simplifies and accelerates the demanding task of evaluating a plethora of candidates, freeing up HR teams to concentrate on the more intricate dimensions of recruitment.

"Elevating Candidate Matching Precision" takes this transformation a step further, spotlighting ML's capacity to curate the candidate pool with the finesse of assembling a complex puzzle. This analogy succinctly illustrates how ML efficiently identifies candidates whose capabilities and traits seamlessly align with the prerequisites of each role. This aptly underscores ML's potential to considerably augment the accuracy and effectiveness of candidate selection. Lastly, the theme concludes with the concept of "Tailoring Personalized Candidate Experiences. "The comparison to a process custom-tailored for each candidate encapsulates the essence of personalized communication facilitated by AI. This approach emphasizes technology's potential to construct bespoke interactions that resonate with candidates, fostering a sense of individual attention and value.

- **Synergistic HR-Technology Ecosystems**

Moreover, the image of personalized experiences akin to tailored processes resonates deeply. It suggests that AI's competency in curating individualized interactions may usher in a paradigm where candidate engagement flourishes. This personal touch encapsulates AI's role in fostering engagement, painting a picture of a recruitment journey where candidates feel distinctly valued. The collective discourse thus weaves a tapestry that champions the transformative prowess of Cognitive AI and ML in redefining the very landscape of recruitment. This orchestration, characterized by heightened accuracy, streamlined efficiency, precision, and immersive engagement, heralds a new dawn for talent acquisition. In this scenario, the interplay between technology and human ingenuity is poised to sculpt a workforce acquisition narrative that is not only strategically aligned but also innately human-centric. The examined statements shed light on the multifaceted implications arising from the integration of AI and technology within HR ecosystems. The central theme of "bias checks" emerges prominently, highlighting the paramount significance of addressing algorithmic biases within decision-making processes. This underscores a recognition of the imperative nature of maintaining fairness and impartiality in AI-driven HR practices, with a concerted commitment towards eradicating biases that could potentially engender adverse effects for candidates.

Furthermore, the recurrent emphasis on "privacy" and "compliance" underscores a robust dedication to upholding the sanctity of candidate data and adhering rigorously to legal frameworks. This signifies a conscientious and principled approach to the adoption of technology, reflecting a concern for ethical considerations within the integration of AI. The focal point on "organizational change" underscores a strategic orientation toward harmonious assimilation of AI technology. This suggests a well-structured change management approach that facilitates a seamless transition, ensuring a comprehensive integration of AI while preserving cultural equilibrium. Moreover, the concept of "aligning HR strategy with business impact" accentuates the transformative potential of AI beyond conventional recruitment paradigms. This portrays an alignment strategy that transcends immediate hiring objectives, integrating AI into broader organizational strategies to foster holistic growth. The assertion of "pioneering future workforce dynamics" signifies AI's pivotal role in shaping the contours of talent acquisition, projecting a forward-looking perspective that anticipates forthcoming shifts in skills and expertise requirements. This resonance with the notion of "continuous learning and improvement" underscores the pedagogical role of AI as a catalyst for professional development. By assimilating insights from AI, each hiring cycle is poised to incrementally enhance its acumen, encapsulating a culture of perpetual advancement and responsiveness.

- **Challenges and Potential Pitfalls in AI-Driven Talent Acquisition**

The analysis of the provided statements reveals a series of crucial findings concerning challenges and potential pitfalls inherent in the utilization of AI-driven approaches within talent acquisition processes. Firstly, the imperative of "Tackling Algorithmic Bias" emerges prominently, emphasizing the vital importance of mitigating any biases present in AI algorithms to ensure that the decisions made reflect the diversity that exists within society. This underscores a commitment to equitable recruitment practices that avoid perpetuating biases embedded in the data. Secondly, the challenge of "Managing

Technological Complexity" surfaces as a significant consideration. The integration of AI introduces a layer of intricacy, necessitating a proactive approach to equip organizational teams with the necessary skills to adeptly navigate this complex technological landscape, ensuring optimal utilization of AI's potential. The third finding pertains to the critical task of "Balancing Automation with Human Touch." While AI-driven automation streamlines processes, the recognition of the irreplaceable value of human interaction in recruitment remains pivotal. Despite automation, maintaining a human touch and empathy in interactions with candidates is essential to foster meaningful connections. Fourthly, the "Mitigating Privacy and Security Risks" challenge comes to the forefront. The application of AI to handle candidate data underscores the need for a vigilant stance on privacy and security concerns. The commitment to robust security measures underscores a responsible approach to safeguarding sensitive candidate information, aligning with principles of data protection. Lastly, the importance of "Ensuring Ethical and Transparent AI Use" stands out. Transparency is highlighted as a cornerstone of ethical AI deployment, emphasizing the need for AI-driven decisions to be not only ethically sound but also comprehensible to candidates. This approach fosters trust and openness, ensuring candidates have a clear understanding of the role AI plays in decision-making processes. In essence, these findings collectively underscore a comprehensive approach to AI integration within talent acquisition, prioritizing fairness, human interaction, data security, and ethical considerations. Such an approach reflects a commitment to harnessing the benefits of AI while navigating potential pitfalls in a responsible and conscientious manner.

5 Implications

The extrapolated findings bear significant implications, encompassing both constructive and cautionary facets, for the evolving domain of talent acquisition. The transformative potential inherent in cognitive AI and machine learning presents a pioneering avenue with the capacity to revolutionize candidate sourcing accuracy, streamline intricate screening processes, refine candidate matching precision, and orchestrate bespoke candidate experiences. This holds the promise of elevating operational efficiency, augmenting precision, and fostering dynamic candidate engagement, thereby reshaping the contours of recruitment. However, amidst this promising landscape, the illuminated challenges and potential pitfalls underscore areas of imperative concern that warrant meticulous attention. These include the critical mandate to combat algorithmic bias, necessitating a comprehensive reevaluation of data and algorithms to uphold fairness and inclusivity. Additionally, proactive upskilling initiatives are mandated to empower professionals to navigate the intricate technological ecosystem, facilitating optimized integration of AI. Striking a balance between automation and the human touch requires nuanced recalibration, underscoring the continued significance of human empathy and interaction in fostering meaningful candidate connections.

Furthermore, the mounting importance of robust data privacy protocols and security measures is evident, where stringent safeguards are imperative to protect candidate information against potential breaches. Ensuring the ethical and transparent deployment of AI remains a pivotal pursuit, wherein the clarity of AI-driven decisions and processes is paramount for building stakeholder trust. By addressing these multifaceted implications judiciously, organizations can harness AI's transformative capabilities while preemptively averting pitfalls, thereby shaping a talent acquisition landscape that capitalizes on technology's potential while responsibly navigating its challenges. This synthesis of innovation and prudence stands as a cornerstone in fostering the evolution of talent acquisition practices within a digitally-driven era.

5.1 Strengths and Limitations

The article effectively highlights the transformative potential of cognitive AI and machine learning in talent acquisition, offering promising insights into their application. It underscores the benefits these technologies bring to the field, emphasizing their ability to enhance recruitment processes and decision-making. However, it is crucial to acknowledge certain challenges that temper this promising outlook. One notable limitation is the potential for algorithmic biases to persist despite ongoing efforts to address them. Additionally, navigating complex technological landscapes can present a challenge, requiring careful consideration and adaptability. Striking the right balance between automation and a human-centric approach also emerges as a key consideration, reflecting the need to maintain a harmonious integration of these technologies within the broader recruitment framework.

5.2 Conclusion

In conclusion, this comprehensive exploration underscores the profound implications of integrating cognitive AI and machine learning algorithms within the realm of talent acquisition and the broader HR ecosystem. The potential to enhance precision, streamline complex processes, and customize experiences represents a transformative advancement. As organizations prepare to harness these unprecedented advantages, they must also grapple with substantial challenges while recognizing the inherent potential for positive change. Foremost among these challenges is the imperative to address bias, a task that necessitates meticulous attention and unwavering dedication. This call for unbiased processes extends not only to talent acquisition but also resonates throughout the entire HR ecosystem, fostering an atmosphere of fairness and inclusivity that goes beyond recruitment, influencing all HR functions.

Furthermore, the need to cultivate and refine human skills remains paramount within the HR context. The interaction between technological capabilities and human expertise forms the core of this transformative synergy, influencing not just talent acquisition but also other critical aspects of HR, such as talent development, performance management, and employee engagement. Organizations could bolster their workforce's adaptability, creativity, and critical thinking by navigating this interface adeptly.

Equally crucial is the ethical responsibility associated with the implementation of these advanced tools across the HR spectrum. While ethical concerns undoubtedly loom, they also offer a chance for organizations to demonstrate their commitment to principled innovation across all HR functions. Upholding ethical standards can foster trust within the workforce and set a positive example for the industry, shaping a culture where technology adoption is synonymous with ethical integrity. As the landscape of talent acquisition and HR evolves, the orchestration of a harmonious symphony merging innovation and conscientiousness becomes the driving force. This symphony not only redefines how talent is acquired but also reshapes the fundamental tenets of workplaces and HR practices. The result is a new era of collaboration that seamlessly integrates human ingenuity, AI-driven technologies, and the evolving HR landscape. Thus, the narrative woven by cognitive AI and machine learning transcends mere technological advancement; it signifies a deep commitment to crafting a more dynamic, inclusive, and visionary HR ecosystem—one that embodies the harmonious fusion of technological progress and human aspirations in the realms of talent acquisition and beyond.

References

Albert, E.T.: AI in talent acquisition: a review of AI-applications used in recruitment and selection. Strateg. HR Rev. **18**(5), 215–221 (2019)

Braun, V., Clarke, V.: Using thematic analysis in psychology. Qual. Res. Psychol. **3**(2), 77–101 (2006)

Chen, Z.: Collaboration among recruiters and artificial intelligence: removing human prejudices in employment. Cogn. Technol. Work **25**(1), 135–149 (2023)

Chowdhury, S., Joel-Edgar, S., Dey, P.K., Bhattacharya, S., Kharlamov, A.: Embedding transparency in artificial intelligence machine learning models: managerial implications on predicting and explaining employee turnover. Int. J. Hum. Res. Manag. **34**(14), 2732–2764 (2023)

Garg, S., Sinha, S., Kar, A.K., Mani, M.: A review of machine learning applications in human resource management. Int. J. Product. Perform. Manag. **71**(5), 1590–1610 (2022)

Geetha, R., Bhanu, S.R.D.: Recruitment through artificial intelligence: a conceptual study. Int. J. Mech. Eng. Technol. **9**(7), 63–70 (2018)

George, G., Thomas, M.R.: Integration of artificial intelligence in human resource. Int. J. Innov. Technol. Explor. Eng **9**(2), 5069–5073 (2019)

Indarapu, S.R.K., Vodithala, S., Kumar, N., Kiran, S., Reddy, S.N., Dorthi, K.: Exploring human resource management intelligence practices using machine learning models. J. High Technol. Managem. Res. **34**(2), 100466 (2023)

Jaiswal, A., Arun, C.J., Varma, A.: Rebooting employees: upskilling for artificial intelligence in multinational corporations. Int. J. Hum. Res. Manag. **33**(6), 1179–1208 (2022)

Jha, S.K., Jha, S., Gupta, M.K.: Leveraging artificial intelligence for effective recruitment and selection processes. In: Bindhu, V., Chen, J., Tavares, J.M.R.S. (eds.) International Conference on Communication, Computing and Electronics Systems. LNEE, vol. 637, pp. 287–293. Springer, Singapore (2020). https://doi.org/10.1007/978-981-15-2612-1_27

Johansson, J., Herranen, S.: The application of artificial intelligence (AI) in human resource management: current state of AI and its impact on the traditional recruitment process (2019)

Kakulapati, V., Chaitanya, K.K., Chaitanya, K.V.G., Akshay, P.: Predictive analytics of HR-a machine learning approach. J. Stat. Manag. Syst. **23**(6), 959–969 (2020)

Malik, A., De Silva, M.T., Budhwar, P., Srikanth, N.R.: Elevating talents' experience through innovative artificial intelligence-mediated knowledge sharing: evidence from an IT-multinational enterprise. J. Int. Manag. **27**(4), 100871 (2021)

Pan, Y., Froese, F., Liu, N., Hu, Y., Ye, M.: The adoption of artificial intelligence in employee recruitment: the influence of contextual factors. Int. J. Hum. Res. Manag. **33**(6), 1125–1147 (2022)

Peña, A., et al.: Human-centric multimodal machine learning: recent advances and testbed on AI-based recruitment. SN Comput. Sci. **4**(5), 434 (2023)

Prikshat, V., Malik, A., Budhwar, P.: AI-augmented HRM: antecedents, assimilation and multilevel consequences. Hum. Res. Manag. Rev. **33**(1), 100860 (2023)

Soleimani, M., Intezari, A., Pauleen, D.J.: Mitigating cognitive biases in developing AI-assisted recruitment systems: a knowledge-sharing approach. Int. J. Knowl. Manag. (IJKM) **18**(1), 1–18 (2022)

Tambe, P., Cappelli, P., Yakubovich, V.: Artificial intelligence in human resources management: challenges and a path forward. Calif. Manag. Rev. **61**(4), 15–42 (2019)

Votto, A.M., Valecha, R., Najafirad, P., Rao, H.R.: Artificial intelligence in tactical human resource management: a systematic literature review. Int. J. Inf. Manag. Data Insights **1**(2), 100047 (2021)

Yabanci, O.: From human resource management to intelligent human resource management: a conceptual perspective. Hum.-Intell. Syst. Integrat. **1**(2–4), 101–109 (2019)

Analyzing the Performance: B-trees vs. Red-Black Trees with Caching Strategies

Medha Wayawahare, Chinmayee Awale[✉], Aditya Deshkahire, and Ashwinee Barabadekar

Vishwakarma Institute of Technology, Bibwewadi, Pune, India
{medha.wyawahare,chinmayee.awale20,aditya.deshkhaire20,
ashwini.barbadekar}@vit.edu

Abstract. The objective of this comparison study is to evaluate the effectiveness of B-trees and Red-black trees when used in conjunction with caching strategies. Red-black trees and B-trees are both frequently used data structures for effectively storing and retrieving huge datasets. Contrarily, caching is a widely used approach that keeps frequently accessed data in a quick memory, like RAM, to improve the performance of data access operations. In this study, we analyse the effect of caching using several measures, including search time, cache hit rate, and cache eviction rate, to assess how caching affects the performance of Red-black and B-trees. The findings of this study can assist developers select the best mix of data structures and caching methods for their particular use case by illuminating the advantages and disadvantages of each data structure and caching method.The dataset used for this study consists of integer keys that are inserted in the data structures. Integrating caching techniques in B-tree operations yields a notable performance boost, reducing the execution time from 1e-06s without caching to a mere 7e-07s with caching. The caching strategy implemented for the Red-Black Tree did not prove to be efficient, as evidenced by an increase in search time from 600 to 3500 ns. Reevaluation and optimization may be necessary to enhance performance.

Keywords: b tree · red-black tree · caching · memory · improved performance

1 Introduction

For arranging and storing enormous amounts of data, computer systems commonly use the self-balancing tree data structure known as the B-tree. It was created in 1972 by Bayer and McCreight to enhance file system performance by lowering disc access times. B-trees are frequently used in databases and file systems and are especially beneficial for handling big data collections. A balanced tree is referred to as a "B-tree" if each node can have any number of children, which are typically represented by the letter "B". B-trees are made to efficiently insert, remove, and update data while maintaining data organisation and searchability. The balancing property of B-trees ensures that the height of the tree is always logarithmic, reducing the temporal complexity of search, insertion,

S. Rajagopal et al (Eds.): ASCIS 2023, CCIS 2040, pp. 53–64, 2024.
https://doi.org/10.1007/978-3-031-59107-5_5

deletion, and update operations to O(log n), where n is the number of tree elements. As a result, B-trees are the best option for huge dataset storage and searching in computer systems.

Caching enables B-trees to run better by minimising the number of disc accesses necessary to obtain data from the tree. Accessing data from the disc can be time-consuming when a B-tree is used to store a lot of data, especially if the disc access time is slow. To recover frequently used data rapidly without having to touch the disk, a technique called caching is employed to store it in fast memory, such as RAM.

Caching can be used to store frequently requested tree nodes, like the root node and intermediate nodes, in the context of B-trees. These nodes can be cached in memory to speed up subsequent searches and operations by allowing data to be fetched from the cache rather than the disc. As the updated data can be cached in memory and sent to the disc in batches to minimise disc access, caching can also reduce the amount of disc writes necessary for insertions and updates.

A self-balancing binary search tree data structure called a red-black tree is used to store and retrieve data quickly. The red-black tree, like other self-balancing binary search trees, is intended to maintain tree height balance, making sure that all operations on the tree proceed in a predictable amount of time.

A binary tree known as a red-black tree has nodes that are either red or black in colour. By guaranteeing that no path from the root to a leaf node is longer than twice as long as any other path, the tree is kept in balance. Every time an addition or deletion throws the balance off, the tree is reorganized and recolored to restore it.

The red-black tree's balancing mechanism ensures that its search, insert, and delete times are O(log n), where n is the number of nodes. The red-black tree is a well-liked data structure for handling large datasets as a result, and it is utilised in a variety of applications, including databases, operating systems, and computer networking.

By lowering the number of memory accesses necessary to carry out operations on the tree, caching can enhance the speed of a red-black tree. Large datasets are frequently stored in red-black trees, and the time needed to access memory might be a performance barrier. By keeping frequently visited data in a quick memory, such a CPU cache, caching is a strategy for accelerating memory access.

2 Literature Review

In the database system domain, transaction management plays a crucial role in ensuring the consistency and reliability of data. A novel method for transaction management in B-tree indexed database systems is put forth in Paper [1]. The authors introduce a new data structure called the "transaction tree," which is a B-tree-like structure designed to efficiently handle commit and abort operations. They also present a lightweight locking protocol called "lightweight locking" that reduces overhead by allowing multiple transactions to share locks.

To understand the evolution and modern implementations of B-tree data structures, Paper [2] provides a comprehensive survey. The authors discuss various B-tree variants, including B + trees, T-trees, R-trees, and fractal trees, comparing their strengths and weaknesses. They also explore advanced topics such as concurrency control, compression, and multi-versioning. Additionally, the paper evaluates the performance of different B-tree implementations and addresses challenges in scaling B-tree databases to large datasets.

In the broader context of data structures for databases, Paper [3] offers an overview of various data structures and their suitability for modern database systems. The authors discuss B-trees, hash indexes, bitmap indexes, and column stores, examining their advantages, disadvantages, and suitability for different database workloads. They also delve into optimization techniques such as compression, parallelism, and query optimization, highlighting the importance of choosing efficient data structures for improved performance.

Cache optimization is a critical aspect of database systems, and Paper [4] proposes a novel approach called "persistently cached B-trees" for caching in B-tree-based database systems. By combining B-tree and log-structured merge (LSM) tree techniques, the authors introduce a hybrid data structure that optimizes both point and range queries as well as write and update operations. They also present an efficient logging mechanism called "update logging" for cache management and durability.

Improving cache utilization is also addressed in Paper [4], which focuses on optimizing the performance of dynamic binary trees, including B-trees and Red-Black trees. The authors propose a cache-sensitive memory layout (CSML) that groups together nodes likely to be accessed together in a single cache line. Their experimental results demonstrate significant reductions in cache misses and improvements in query performance, highlighting the effectiveness of CSML in dynamic binary tree structures.

For the specific case of Red-Black trees, Paper [5] presents an algorithm for performing operations optimally on these self-balancing binary search trees. Traditional algorithms for Red-Black trees often exhibit suboptimal time complexity, especially for insertion and deletion operations. The authors propose a new algorithm that leverages the properties of Red-Black trees to achieve optimal time complexity for all operations, surpassing existing algorithms in terms of speed and performance.

Real-time memory databases utilizing Red-Black trees are examined in Paper [6]. The authors analyze various data organization schemes within Red-Black trees, considering depth-first, breadth-first, and hybrid schemes. Their findings indicate that the hybrid scheme, combining elements of depth-first and breadth-first, achieves the best tradeoff between query response time and memory usage. They emphasize the significance of data organization in real-time memory databases and propose the hybrid scheme as an effective optimization technique.

Memory organization in real-time databases based on Red-Black trees is further explored in Paper [6]. The authors propose a memory allocation scheme that minimizes fragmentation and improves cache utilization by grouping nodes likely to be accessed together. Their scheme outperforms traditional allocation schemes, reducing memory fragmentation and enhancing query performance.

Concurrency in Red-Black trees is addressed in Paper [7], which presents a concurrent implementation of a Red-Black tree. The authors describe the challenges associated with implementing a concurrent version of the tree and propose an algorithm that combines fine-grained locking and optimistic concurrency control. Their algorithm outperforms other concurrent.

3 Methodology

3.1 BTree

To create a B-tree with caching, you can follow a step-by-step approach. First, determine the order of the B-tree, denoted as 't', which determines the maximum number of keys and child pointers a node can have. Additionally, specify the cache size and choose a caching strategy, such as LRU (Least Recently Used) or LFU (Least Frequently Used).

Next, design the node structure for the B-tree. Each node should have fields to store keys, child pointers, and any additional metadata required for the implementation. Additionally, include fields specific to caching, such as a cache data structure and an eviction policy.

Start by creating an empty root node for the B-tree. This node initially has no keys or children. Alongside that, create an empty cache structure with the specified cache size and caching strategy.

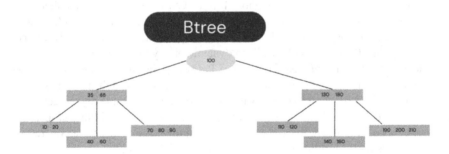

Fig. 1. BTree Structure

When inserting data into the B-tree with caching, you can utilize the caching mechanism to optimize access. Before performing an insert, check if the key already exists in the cache. If it does, update the B-tree node accordingly based on the cache hit, such as by updating the frequency count of the key.

If the key cannot be located in the cache, navigate the B-tree from the root to the proper leaf node and insert the key there. After finding it, place the key within the leaf node to update the cache by including the key.

To handle cache capacity, if the cache is full, apply the eviction policy to remove the least frequently used or least recently used key from the cache. The specific eviction policy depends on the chosen caching strategy.

In the depicted B-tree structure, Fig. 1, all leaf nodes are uniformly positioned at the same level, ensuring a balanced arrangement. Furthermore, each non-leaf node exhibits a notable pattern: there are no empty subtrees, and the number of keys within these nodes consistently remains one less than the count of their associated children. This balanced and well-defined structure is a characteristic property of B-trees, contributing to their efficiency in storage and retrieval operations.

When searching for the value 120 in the B-tree, the process involves a strategic comparison starting at the root. Initially comparing with 100, the algorithm navigates to the right node due to the value being greater. Subsequently, within the range of 130 to 180, the algorithm opts to explore the left node as 120 falls below 130. This approach significantly streamlines the search by narrowing down potential locations for the key-containing value. By selectively traversing nodes based on value comparisons, the search algorithm efficiently eliminates unnecessary branches, reducing the search space and enhancing overall retrieval speed.

3.2 Red-Black Tree

To create an RBTree with caching, you can follow a step-by-step approach. First, design the node structure for the RBTree. Each node should have fields to store the key, color (red or black), parent pointer, left and right child pointers, and any additional metadata required for the implementation. Additionally, include fields specific to caching, such as a cache data structure and an eviction policy.

Next, create an empty root node for the RBTree. This node initially has no key or children. Alongside that, create an empty cache structure with the specified cache size and caching strategy, such as LRU (Least Recently Used) or LFU (Least Frequently Used).

When inserting or searching for data in the RBTree with caching, utilize the caching mechanism to optimize access. Before performing an operation, check if the key already exists in the cache. If it does, update the RBTree node accordingly based on the cache hit, such as by performing any required rotations or color adjustments for insertion, or returning the cached value for search.

If the key is not found in the cache, traverse the RBTree from the root to find the appropriate position for insertion or search. Once the desired location is determined, perform the insertion or search operation in the RBTree and update the cache by adding the key-value pair to it.

To handle cache capacity, if the cache is full, apply the eviction policy to remove the least frequently used or least recently used key from the cache. The specific eviction policy depends on the chosen caching strategy.

3.3 Time Complexities

Search: It is necessary to move up the tree from the root to the correct leaf node while looking for a key in a B-Tree. A B-Tree's search time complexity is O(log N), where N is the tree's element count. The balanced nature of the B-Tree, in which each level of the tree has a fixed amount of keys, results in its logarithmic complexity [2].

Insertion: Inserting a new key into a B-Tree involves two steps: searching for the appropriate position to insert the key and performing the actual insertion. The time complexity of insertion in a B-Tree is also O(log N). Similar to search, insertion takes advantage of the balanced nature of the B-Tree, resulting in logarithmic time complexity [2].

Table 1. BTree Time Complexities

Sr. No.	Function	T(n)
1	Insertion	O(logn)
2	Deletion	O(logn)
3	Searching	O(logn)

Deletion: Deleting a key from a B-Tree requires locating the key in the tree and then performing the deletion operation. The time complexity of deletion in a B-Tree is also O(log N). Like search and insertion, deletion benefits from the balanced structure of the B-Tree, ensuring efficient removal of keys [2].

Table 2. RedBlack Tree Time Complexities

Sr. No.	Function	T(n)
1	Insertion	O(logn)
2	Deletion	O(logn)
3	Searching	O(logn)

A Red-Black Tree's search, insertion, and deletion operations have an O(log n) time complexity, where "n" stands for the number of nodes in the tree [16].

Self-balancing binary search trees called Red-Black Trees use colour attributes and tree rotation operations to keep their structure balanced. These characteristics make guarantee that the tree's height is always logarithmic in relation to the number of nodes.

During the search operation, starting from the root, comparisons are made to determine the direction in which to traverse the tree. At each step, the search progresses towards the desired node or determines that it does not exist in the tree. Since Red-Black Trees are balanced, the height of the tree is constrained to be logarithmic, which means that the number of comparisons required to search for a specific node is proportional to the logarithm of the number of nodes in the tree, resulting in an O(log n) time complexity.

For insertion and deletion operations, the tree may need to be modified to maintain the Red-Black Tree properties. These modifications include rotations and color changes. The maximum number of rotations or color changes that need to be performed during these operations is also proportional to the height of the tree, which is O(log n). Therefore, the time complexity for insertion and deletion operations in a Red-Black Tree is also O(log n) [16].

From Table 1 and 2 we can infer that the time complexities for both the data structures is same, ie O(log n).

The proof for the time complexity of B-trees and Red-Black trees involves analyzing their structural properties and ensuring that certain invariants are maintained.

B-Tree Time Complexity Proof

Balanced Structure: B-trees are designed to be balanced. During insertion or deletion, if a node becomes overfull or underfull, keys are redistributed between neighboring nodes to maintain balance.

Bounding the Number of Keys: In a B-tree of order m, each internal node can have at most m-1 keys, and at least $\lceil m/2 \rceil$ - 1 keys, where $\lceil m/2 \rceil$ is the ceiling of m/2.

Height Analysis: By ensuring that each node has a minimum number of keys, B-trees achieve a logarithmic height. The height is O(log n), where n is the number of keys.

Red-Black Tree Time Complexity Proof

Properties Maintenance: Red-Black trees maintain properties like color balance and black height during insertions and deletions.

Bounding Black Height: The black height (number of black nodes on any path) is maintained. This ensures that the longest path is no more than twice the shortest path.

Height Analysis: The properties maintained in Red-Black trees guarantee a logarithmic height. The height is O(log n), where n is the number of nodes.

3.4 Effect of Caching on the Data Structures

When there are n elements stored in the tree, the temporal complexity of B-tree operations like search, insertion, and deletion is typically O(log n). Effective caching techniques can considerably reduce the actual execution time of these activities. A high cache hit rate can decrease the amount of disc accesses, which shortens execution time. It is crucial to remember that the precise reduction in time complexity will rely on a number of variables, including cache size, cache hit rate, disc access speed, and the specific caching approach used.

Similarly, the time complexity of Red-Black tree operations is also O(log n), where n is the number of elements in the tree. The use of a caching technique can help reduce the constant factors associated with memory lookups or disk accesses, leading to improved performance in practice. Again, the actual improvement in time complexity will depend on the effectiveness of the caching technique and the specific implementation details.

In both cases, the caching technique does not fundamentally change the asymptotic time complexity of B-trees or Red-Black trees, which remains logarithmic. However, it can significantly improve the actual running time by reducing the number of costly disk accesses or memory lookups, resulting in faster execution and improved performance in practice.

Following is the function used for caching in Btree

```
BTreeNode* result = (root == NULL) ? NULL : root->search(k);
if (cache.count(k) > 0) return cache[k];
cache[k] = result; // Store the result in cache
return result;
```

Before performing the actual search operation, the code checks whether the result for the given key k is already present in the cache.

If the result is found in the cache (i.e., cache.count(k) > 0), the cached result is immediately returned. This avoids re-executing the search operation.

If the result is not found in the cache, the actual search operation is performed (root-> search(k)), and the result is stored in the cache for future use (cache[k] = result). The final result of the search operation is returned.

Following is the function for caching technique used in Red Black tree:

```
NodePtr searchTreeHelper(NodePtr node, int key)
{ if (cache.find(key) != cache.end())
{ return cache[key]; }
// Perform the search operation NodePtr result = nullptr;
// ... (search logic)
cache[key] = result;
return result; }
```

Before performing the search operation, the code checks whether the key is already present in the cache (cache.find(key) ! = cache.end()).

If the key is found in the cache, the corresponding value (cached result) is returned directly without executing the search operation again.

If the key is not found, the regular search operation is performed.

After obtaining the search result (NodePtr result), it is stored in the cache for future use (cache[key] = result).

```
void deleteNodeHelper(NodePtr node, int key) {
// ... (delete logic)

// Update the cache after deletion
cache.erase(key);
}
```

After performing a deletion operation, the cache is updated by removing the entry corresponding to the deleted key (cache.erase(key)).

4   Results and Discussions

The performance of Btree is different than Red Black tree is calculated based on the time both structures needed to execute. The following was done using < chrono > library.

Table 3. Performance of Btree

Function	Without Caching	With Caching
Search	1e-06s	7e-07s

From Table 3 we understand that the B-tree demonstrated improved performance with caching compared to without caching.

Without caching: The search operation took approximately 1 ms on average. This indicates that without caching, the B-tree had to access disk or main memory for every search operation. Disk or memory access can be relatively slow compared to accessing data from cache.

With caching: The search operation took approximately 0.7 ms on average. With caching, the B-tree likely benefited from storing frequently accessed keys or nodes in a cache, such as CPU cache or a memory cache. Caching reduces the time required to access frequently used data, as it is readily available in a faster cache memory. By caching frequently accessed keys or nodes, the B-tree reduces the number of disk or memory accesses, resulting in faster search operations.

The inference is that caching improves B-tree performance by reducing the time required to access frequently accessed keys or nodes, leading to faster search operations. Caching exploits the principle of locality, where recently accessed data is more likely to be accessed again in the near future.

The hyperparameter that was changed for optimizing the algorithm is adding a "unordered_map" named "cache".

An unordered_map is a standard C++ container that implements an associative array (a map) using a hash table. It allows efficient insertion, deletion, and search operations with an average time complexity of $O(1)$ for each operation (assuming a good hash function and uniform distribution of keys). The unordered_map is part of the C++ Standard Template Library (STL).

Table 4. Performance of Red Black tree

Function	Without Caching	With Caching
Search	600 ns	3500 ns

From Table 4 we understand that the Red-Black tree demonstrated degraded performance with caching compared to without caching.

Without caching: The search operation took approximately 600 ns on average. Without caching, the Red-Black tree had to access disk or main memory for every search operation, similar to the B-tree without caching. The search time of 600 ns indicates the time required to access data from disk or memory.

With caching: The search operation took approximately 3500 ns on average. Surprisingly, the search time increased significantly with caching. This suggests that caching might not be effective for Red-Black trees due to their structural properties.

The changes made to implement the caching technique are as follows:

1. The caching implementation uses an unordered_map < int, NodePtr > cache to store previously searched nodes and improve the search operation's efficiency where as the normal implementation doesn't use caching. It performs a direct search without maintaining a cache.
2. In the caching implementation, the searchTreeHelper function first checks if the key is present in the cache before performing the search operation. If the key is found

in the cache, it returns the cached result; otherwise, it proceeds with the search and updates the cache.

In the normal implementation, the searchTreeHelper function directly performs the search without using a cache.

5 Conclusion

The inference is that caching has a negative impact on the Red-Black tree's search performance. This could be due to the following reasons:

Red-Black trees have a more balanced structure compared to B-trees. The structure of a Red-Black tree inherently provides better locality of reference, reducing the need for caching.

The overhead of maintaining and updating the cache for a Red-Black tree might outweigh the benefits of caching, leading to increased search times.

It's important to note that the specific implementation details and the characteristics of the dataset can influence the performance results. The performance of different data structures can vary depending on factors such as the size of the dataset, the distribution of data, the specific hardware and caching mechanisms used, and the implementation details of the data structure. Therefore, it is crucial to consider these factors and conduct thorough performance evaluations in real-world scenarios.

The comparative study of B-trees and Red-Black trees with caching techniques highlights the impact of caching on their performance and efficiency. B-trees, when combined with caching techniques, exhibit improved performance in scenarios where disk-based storage and retrieval are critical. By caching frequently accessed nodes in memory, B-trees can reduce disk I/O operations, resulting in faster data access and manipulation. This makes B-trees with caching well-suited for applications with large datasets and slow disk access times, such as databases. On the other hand, Red-Black trees with caching techniques offer enhanced performance for in-memory operations. By caching frequently accessed nodes or subtrees in memory, Red-Black trees can reduce memory lookups and improve overall time complexity. This makes Red-Black trees with caching suitable for applications that require fast in-memory access and modification, such as dynamic data structures and algorithms.

The choice between B-trees and Red-Black trees with caching depends on the specific requirements of the application. If the emphasis is on efficient disk-based storage and retrieval, B-trees with caching provide an advantage. On the other hand, if the focus is on efficient in-memory operations, Red-Black trees with caching techniques offer better performance.

Overall, the comparative study demonstrates that the choice between B-trees and Red-Black trees with caching techniques relies on understanding the specific needs of the application and considering factors such as storage medium, data size, access patterns, and performance requirements. By carefully evaluating these factors, developers can select the most suitable data structure to optimize their application's performance and efficiency.

6 Future Scope

In the future development of the database structure, several enhancements can be considered to improve the overall efficiency and robustness. First and foremost, the addition of comprehensive error handling mechanisms is crucial to ensure the reliability of the system. This involves anticipating and managing various types of invalid inputs, which can be especially important for maintaining data integrity and preventing potential vulnerabilities. Additionally, exploring advanced caching techniques, such as B + tree caching, can significantly enhance the database's performance by reducing the retrieval time for frequently accessed data. The implementation of B + tree caching, with its ability to efficiently handle range queries, can further optimize the database for scenarios where ordered retrieval of data is essential. Moreover, to leverage the strengths of different data structures, a hybrid approach can be pursued by incorporating both Red-Black Tree and B-tree implementations. This optimized data structure can provide a well-balanced solution, taking advantage of the efficient search and insertion capabilities of Red-Black Trees along with the balanced and disk-friendly properties of B-trees. Such a hybrid structure has the potential to deliver improved performance and scalability, making it well-suited for a variety of database applications.

References

1. Jaluta, I.: Transaction management in b-tree-indexed database systems. In: In 2014 International Conference on Information Science, Electronics and Electrical Engineering, vol. 3, pp. 1968–1975. IEEE (2014)
2. Graefe, G.: Modern B-tree techniques. Found. Trends® Databases 3(4), 203–402 (2011)
3. Hammer, J., Schneider, M.: Data structures for databases. In: Handbook of Data Structures and Applications, pp. 967–981. Chapman and Hall/CRC, Boca Raton (2018)
4. Saikkonen, R., Soisalon-Soininen, E.: Cache-sensitive memory layout for dynamic binary trees. Comput. J. **59**(5), 630–649 (2016)
5. Chen, L., Schott, R.: Optimal operations on red-black trees. Int. J. Found. Comput. Sci. **7**(03), 227–239 (1996)
6. Li, J., Xu, Y., Guo, H.: Memory organization in a real-time database based on red-black tree structure. In: Fifth World Congress on Intelligent Control and Automation (IEEE Cat. No. 04EX788), vol. 5, pp. 3971–3974. IEEE (2004)
7. Besa, J., Eterovic, Y.: A concurrent red–black tree. J. Parallel Distrib. Comput. **73**(4), 434–449 (2013)
8. Holenderski, M., Bril, R.J., Lukkien, J.J.: Red-black trees with relative node keys. Inf. Process. Lett. **114**(11), 591–596 (2014)
9. Blelloch, G., Ferizovic, D., Sun, Y.: Parallel ordered sets using join. arXiv preprint arXiv: 1602.02120 (2016)
10. Awad, M.A., Ashkiani, S., Johnson, R., Farach-Colton, M., Owens, J.D.: Engineering a high-performance GPU B-Tree. In: Proceedings of the 24th Symposium on Principles and Practice of Parallel Programming, pp. 145–157 (2019)
11. Brodal, G.S., Fagerberg, R., Jacob, R.: Cache oblivious search trees via binary trees of small height. BRICS Rep. Ser. **36** (2001)
12. Bender, M.A., Demaine, E.D., Farach-Colton, M.: Cache-oblivious B-trees. In: Proceedings 41st Annual Symposium on Foundations of Computer Science, pp. 399–409. IEEE (2000)

13. Aglin, G., Nijssen, S., Schaus, P.: Learning optimal decision trees using caching branch-and-bound search. In: Proceedings of the AAAI Conference on Artificial Intelligence, vol. 34, no. 04, pp. 3146–3153 (2020)
14. Rao, J., Ross, K.A.: Making B+-trees cache conscious in main memory. In: In: Proceedings of the 2000 ACM SIGMOD International Conference on Management of Data, pp. 475–486 (2000)
15. Havasi, F.: An improved B+ tree for flash file systems. In: Černá, I., et al. (eds.) SOFSEM 2011. LNCS, vol. 6543, pp. 297–307. Springer, Heidelberg (2011). https://doi.org/10.1007/978-3-642-18381-2_25
16. Cormen, T.H., Leiserson, C.E., Rivest, R.L., Stein, C.: Introduction to Algorithms. MIT press, Cambridge (2022)

A Bird's Eye View of Microservice Architecture from the Lens of Cloud Computing

Nidhi Vaniyawala[1]([✉]) and Kamlendu Kumar Pandey[2]

[1] Department of Computer Science, Sarvajanik University, Surat 395001, India
nidhi.vaniyawala@srki.ac.in
[2] Department of Information and Communication Technology, Gujarat University,
Veer Narmad South, Surat 395007, India
kspandey@vnsgu.ac.in

Abstract. In past couple of years, cloud computing has emerged as one of the fastest growing technologies across the globe. In order to keep pace with the advancements taking place in the cloud computing paradigm and to cater the needs of current businesses, there is a continuous evolution in the architectural patterns for building the distributed systems as well. Microservices is one of those architectural patterns which has emerged as an advanced variant of Service Oriented architectural style. Microservices architecture is entirely an amalgamation of notions like domain-driven design, continuous integration continuous delivery, DevOps, containerization, highly scalable and agile systems. As a part of the study, an exhaustive survey is carried out around the ecosystem of microservices architecture. This paper aims at exploring the recent development in microservice architectural pattern, emerging trends and the potential research gaps. The paper outlines the survey of the efforts done by various researchers in discrete aspects of microservice like design and implementation of applications in different domains based on microservices, strategies to empower maintainability and scalability of microservices, security aspects of microservices, strategies for data management and fault tolerance in microservices, orchestration of microservice and frameworks to achieve event sourcing in microservice architecture. The findings of this survey will set a path ahead for addressing the current challenges in various aspects of microservices architecture discussed in the study and further innovations to the same.

Keywords: Microservices · Cloud Computing · Kubernetes · Orchestration · Event Sourcing · Containerization

1 Introduction

The past decade has witnessed a massive development of applications based on the technology of distributed and layered client-server architecture. Even though applications are developed based on logically modular architecture, but ironically, most of the applications are packaged and deployed as a monolith. Hence, the essence of "distributed" gets lost as in most of the scenarios all the layers of the application were deployed on

S. Rajagopal et al (Eds.): ASCIS 2023, CCIS 2040, pp. 65–97, 2024.
https://doi.org/10.1007/978-3-031-59107-5_6

a single or clustered servers. Further, the distributed layered architecture did not meet the performance expectation of industry. The servers may scale up and down as per the requirement, but it scales all the modules rather than scaling only the modules which are in demand. Secondly, it is extremely problematic to adopt a new development stack in a monolithic application because then the entire application has to be rewritten. Large monolithic applications are actually an obstacle to frequent changes and deployments. In order to update a single component, the entire application has to go through the redeployment process. Hence, organizations whose primary focus is to boost productivity, adopt agility and enhance customer experience should leave behind monolithic web applications and embrace micro services, whose loosely-coupled architectures expedite the entire process of development, testing, deployment, and monitoring while accommodating present and future digital requirements. The micro service architectural style is an approach that enables to develop applications as a collection of relatively small independent services, each running in its own process. In order to communicate with each other relentlessly, the microservices utilize lightweight mechanisms like HTTP REST API. These services are mapped with each of the business capabilities and are loosely coupled. The gap between development and production environment is solved by containerization technology like Docker. Nesting of containers and scaling is taken care by orchestration tools like Docker Swarm and Kubernetes (open-source platform developed by Google). The approaches like CI/CD creates a complete eco system to develop applications under micro services architecture. Since, microservices function independently, it helps DevOps teams accomplish milestones in less time. Unlike monolithic software where errors in a single module adversely affects the working of the entire application, the effect of a micro service defect is restricted to only that micro service where fault has occurred.

According to a report published by "Predictive Market Research", the global market size for Microservice Architecture is expected to hit multi million by year 2028, as compared to the year 2021, at an exceptional compound annual growth rate during 2022–2028. The reason behind such immense popularity is its promising efficacy and its favorable utility which spans across varied areas like healthcare, Government, IT and Telecommunication, Entertainment, Retail, Manufacturing, etc. A number of giant market players including Cognizant, Nginx Inc., Salesforce.com, Microsoft Corporation, Infosys Limited, etc. is making the market for microservice architecture far more competitive [16].

2 Motivation for Research

Microservice Architecture is one of the most preferred design patterns nowadays for building distributed systems. The applications that are built based on microservice leverage benefits like 1. Enhanced scalability due its ability to scale independently. 2. Improved maintainability owing to its loosely coupled nature. 3. Lightweight and cost effective compared to monolith applications due to containerization. 4. Automatic workload balancing on distributed cloud environment achieved through Kubernetes. 5. High level of reliability is achieved through Event Sourcing in microservices 6. It very well complements the DevOps ideology which in turns makes it a perfect architectural candidate for software systems which requires Continuous Integration and Continuous Delivery (CI/CD).

So far, these aspects are studied in a very scattered and isolated manner. However, still there is a need of the hour to get a bird's eye view of the entire ecosystem of microservices as a whole, in order to detect the loopholes in the current state of architecture and address the same. Moreover, there seems to be very unbalanced research in reference to different aspects of microservice ecosystem. Hence, one of the intentions to conduct this study is also to find out the unexplored corners of microservices which demands more research engagements.

3   Scope of Research

This study is not restricted to a specific aspect of micro services. Rather, we have laid efforts to conduct a comprehensive and methodical survey, casing all the significant aspects revolving around the entire micro services tool chain and tried to find out the areas where there is more room for research and development. Consequently, the study will give a wider purview over the subject.

4   Research Methodology

This paper intends to identify, analyze and interpret the state of the art of microservices architecture (MSA). Hence, we conducted an SLR (Systematic Literature Review) taking reference of the guidelines given by Kitchenham and Charters [108]. The reason behind going for SLR is that SLR allow researchers to carry out a meticulous study and analysis of the literature available on the targeted research area. We started the entire process of SLR with defining the research questions. It is then followed by strategizing the search process, deciding selection criteria, devising methods for data extraction and developing methods for data synthesis. The entire flow of activities performed is shown in Fig. 1.

4.1   Define Research Questions

We concentrated our research around a number of research questions (RQ1-RQ4) answering to which, led us to proceed on our way of exploring varied significant studies related to microservices carried out by various researchers.

RQ1: What is the publication trend and primary focus behind microservices related research?
The answer to this question will create a strong base for analysis of existing studies on MSA and classify them into relevant themes.

RQ2: What are the trade-offs of migrating from monolithic architecture to microservices based architecture? What are the available approaches for such migration?
Answering this question will enable us to get idea about the pains and gains of switching

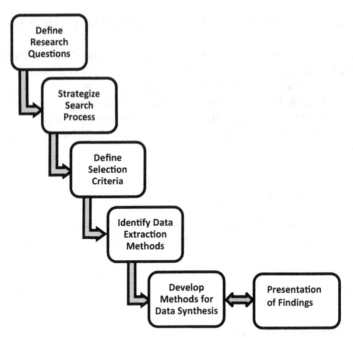

Fig. 1. Steps for Systematic Literature Review

to microservice based architecture. Further, it also brings in to focus various approaches of identifying microservices from a monolithic application.

RQ3: Which quality attributes have been addressed with reference to distributed systems? What are the issues and solutions associated with these attributes?
The main aim behind this question is to identify and figure out the quality attributes focused by various researchers, the issues identified by them and the solutions discussed. This will open door for future research opportunities to work on reported problem and evaluate the efficacy of proposed solutions.

RQ4: What is the state of research with reference to coordination and deployment of microservices?
The primary objective is to study various approaches of coordination and deployment of microservices proposed by various researchers.

4.2 Strategize Search Process

We conducted the search operation in two stages. Stage1 involves performing search operation using the predefined search strings on selected research databases. Stage2 is concerned with the snowballing technique (Fig. 2).

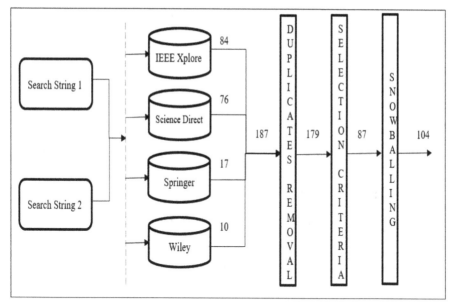

Fig. 2. The search and selection process

4.2.1 Stage1: Primary Search

The primary search is carried out by querying the digital databases based on a combination of search strings as shown below in Table 1.

Table 1. Search string used for querying database.

Search Strings	
String1:	("Micro service" OR "Microservice" OR "Micro-service") AND ("Architecture" OR "Design" OR "System")
String2:	("Cloud" OR "Cloud Computing") AND ("Architecture" OR "Design")

The digital libraries that we used for searching the research studies includes IEEE Xplore, Science Direct, Springer and Wiley.

4.2.2 Stage2: Snowballing Technique

At this stage, in order to get more studies relevant to search criteria, we performed forward and backward snowballing. The forward snowballing activity involved gathering studies which has cited the selected studies. The backward snowballing is done by gathering the relevant studies from the references of selected studies (Table 2).

Table 2. Research databases searched.

Online Database	Link	Studies initially retrieved
IEEE Xplore	http://ieeexplore.ieee.org/	84
Science Direct	https://www.sciencedirect.com/	76
Springer	http://link.springer.com/	17
Wiley	https://onlinelibrary.wiley.com/	10
	Total	**187**

4.3 Define Selection Criteria

We started with the selection process by evaluating the titles and abstracts of individual papers to filter out relevant studies. Further, the full-text of filtered studies were examined to make sure that the studies meet our inclusion criteria. The filtration criteria used to perform selection on studies is given in Table 3.

Table 3. Selection criteria

ID	Description	Yes	No
IEC1	Does the study primarily revolve around microservices?	**Include**	**Exclude**
IEC2	Is the study written in English language?	**Include**	**Exclude**
IEC4	Is full text of paper available?	**Include**	**Exclude**
IEC5	Is the paper/article published between year 2016–2023	**Include**	**Exclude**

4.4 Identify Data Extraction Methods

The data extraction process is undertaken by studying the entire content of all studies selected in previous phase. The attributes from each study are examined, extracted and recorded as against a number of pre-defined parameters. Data items A1–A6 are used to extract the basic information about the studies. Attribute A7 is used to record the domain on which a study is primarily based. Data items A8–A9 basically address each of the research questions specified in the Sect. 4.1. MS Excel spreadsheets are used to classify and record the extracted data from selected studies (Table 4).

Table 4. Study attributes extracted with relevant research question addressed

ID	Study Attributes	Description	Research Question
A1	ID	The unique ID of Study	Metadata
A2	Title	The title of research	Metadata
A3	Authors	The name of all authors	Metadata
A4	Publication Source	The source of publication	Metadata
A5	Publication Year	The year when study was published	Metadata
A6	Publication Type	Conference, journal paper, technical report	Metadata
A7	Domain	The internal classification of aspects related to microservices	Demography
A8	Outline	The gist of the research work	RQ1, RQ2
A9	Quality Attributes Addressed	The challenges unveiled in the research work	RQ3
A10	Proposed Solutions	The solutions suggested or implemented to address the challenges uncovered in the study	RQ3
A11	Coordination and Deployment approach	The techniques used for microservices deployment and coordination	RQ4

4.5 Develop Methods for Data Synthesis

With the primary objective of comprehending, analyzing, and categorizing existing research on architecting microservices, the data synthesis activity entails gathering and summarising the data taken from the original studies. Particularly, we used content analysis to classify and encode the studies under general thematic categories. Moreover, we also used narrative synthesis to analyse and explain in more detail the findings from the content analysis.

5 Findings

5.1 Demography of Selected Studies (RQ1)

This section discusses the overall demography of selected studies in terms of year-wise publication, publication type, publication venues and themes. The corresponding findings will also help in answering the research question RQ1.

5.1.1 Year-Wise Publication

One of the significant aspects of analysing the selected studies is from the perspective of year wise publication. This perspective brings out the information regarding the interest of researchers over the period of time in various research areas with microservices at the focal point. With this intention, we also presented the research trends in terms of publication year in Fig. 3. With reference to the studies selected for further analysis.

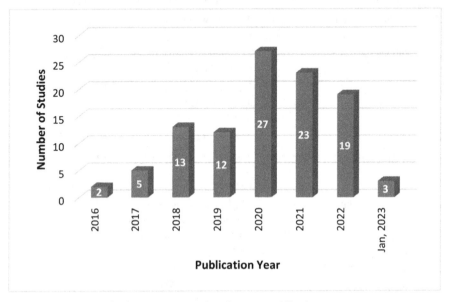

Fig. 3. Distribution of studies over publication years

5.1.2 Distribution of Studies over Themes and Subthemes

Figure 4 shows the classification of varied research themes and subthemes identified from the selected studies. The study is classified into primarily three themes namely i) Paradigm shift from monolith to microservices. ii) Operational and quality aspects of microservices. Iii) Coordination and deployment techniques. The listed themes are further classified into more precise subthemes.

In all, there are thirteen subthemes divided amongst three themes listed earlier. There are in all four subthemes under theme1, seven subthemes under theme2 and two sub-themes under theme 3. The subthemes are then mapped to the studies (citation number in reference) addressing that particular subtheme. The further analysis of this classifica-tion suggests that Database Management, Transaction Management, Security, Deploy-ment and Containerization with reference to micro services architecture is the hot cake amongst researchers.

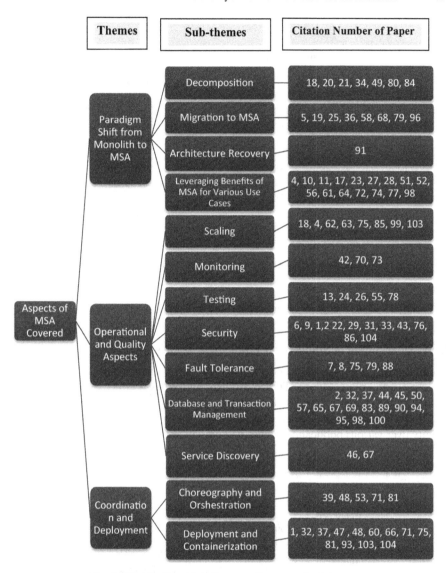

Fig. 4. Distribution of studies over themes and subthemes

5.1.3 Publication Type

The distribution of studies in context of publication type is shown in Fig. 5. The figure depicts, out of selected studies, majority of them i.e., 59% and 40% are sourced from journals and conference proceedings respectively. Rest of the studies are from sources like technical reports and workshops.

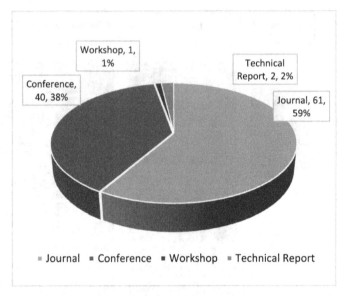

Fig. 5. Distribution of studies over publication type

5.1.4 Distribution of Studies over Publication Venues

As discussed in Sect. 4.2, the primary search was carried out across four online libraries namely, IEEE Xplore, Science Direct, Springer and Wiley. Further, as a part of snow-balling process, studies from other journals and conference proceedings were also included. The distribution of selected studies from primary as well as snowballing search activity over various publication venues is represented in Fig. 6.

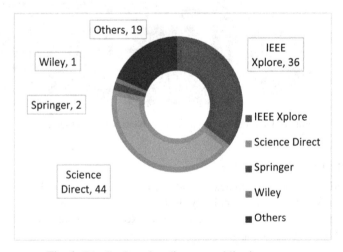

Fig. 6. Distribution of studies over publication venues

5.2 Studies Investigated

This section presents the studies related to the paradigm shift from monolith to micro service architecture, various operational and quality aspects in terms of its challenges and solutions as identified and suggested by various researchers and a number of deployment and containerization techniques proposed in selected studies with their strengths and weaknesses.

5.2.1 Paradigm shift from Monolith to Microservice Architecture (RQ2)

Decomposition Techniques

Sellami et al. introduced a technique named MS Extractor that performs cost-effective extraction of microservices from legacy enterprise systems ensuring sufficient granularity and cohesion. Extractor basically use the Indicator-Based Evolutionary Algorithm (IBEA) to guide a search process towards an optimal decomposition of a particular legacy software system while taking structural and semantic relationships in the source code into account. Further, a practical evaluation is carried out on seven system software and the result proves the outstanding performance of the proposed approach in extracting cohesive and loosely couple services [20].

Hassan et al. outlined the issue of deciding the granularity level of microservices i.e., when and how to integrate or decompose the microservices. To address the issue, a catalogue is designed that helps in identifying the metrics which plays significant role in taking decisions regarding the scalability-aware granularity adaptions [18].

Li et al. Suggested a novel approach based on knowledge graph to extract microservices during the re-architecting phase of existing monolithic software systems. The right candidates for microservices are identified using a constrained Louvain community detection algorithm. The algorithm passed the evaluation test on two open-source projects in terms of team size reduction, cohesion, coupling and code reduction. The major strength of study lies in less dependency on human experience for constructing the knowledge graph [21].

Daoud et al. recommended an approach that automatically finds the microservices which best suits the requirements of an organization. The model basically captures the dependencies between business processes. A clustering algorithm is also designed which further combines all the extracted dependencies for the identification of microservices. The proposed model takes into consideration the aspects like cohesion and decoupling while identifying the microservices [34].

D. Kuryazov et al. has also touched on the aspect of decomposition of microservices. The authors have defined a 6-step process to simplify the decomposition of monolithic system into microservices. This technique is claimed to be more efficient than the conventional decomposition method as it takes into consideration the runtime behaviour of the system like context, method call, etc. Further they also affirmed that following this decomposition technique will help determine accurately whether to introduce a new service or not which can increase resilience of the application by up to 10 times compared to the monolith system. It will also make scaling and testing easier [49].

Li et al. addressed the challenge of decomposing the microservices through a simple approach. As a result, a dataflow driven method is proposed for decomposing microservices in four steps. Step1: To analyse the requirements. Step2: Construct the detailed

DFDs (Data Flow Diagrams) including the process-datastore version of DFD. Step3: Condense the process-datastore version of DFD into decomposable DFDs. Step4: Identify feasible microservice candidates from the decomposable DFDs. The efficacy of the proposed approach is then tested taking a use case of a cargo tracking system. The results suggests that the proposed methodology for decomposition recommends the candidates for microservices taking into account the aspect of cohesion and coupling [80].

De Alwis et al. presented a novel approach for re-structuring the enterprise system into microservices. The approach is purely based on queuing theory and business object relationships. The main objective of this technique is to optimize the process of discovering the microservices resulting into highly scalable, available and cohesive system. The experiments conducted based on proposed technique is able to achieve desired characteristics of the system [84].

Migration to Microservice Architecture
Debauche et al. conducted an exhaustive review around the cloud architectures for data management in agriculture 4.0. In the due course of study an attempt is made to figure out the storage and processing architectures which goes well with the agriculture 4.0 applications and the feasibility of using generic architectures for agriculture 4.0 applications. Reviewing the previous studies revealed that micro services architecture highly complements applications based on IoT platform [5].

Makris et al. touched the issues faced by the developers who are looking for an architectural switch over from monolithic to microservice based architecture. The study covers varied aspects involved around microservices like performance, granularity, scalability, security, load balancing, orchestration, service discovery and hosting environments. Hence, the study covers the current state of trends and development going on in microservice which will guide developers in adopting the architecture [19].

Yang et al. in their paper have discussed the drawbacks of conventional layered architecture against the benefits leveraged by using the microservice architecture for application development. They introduced micro services into the traditional layered Architecture by decomposing the traditional application and deploying the three layers - data management, model management and the presentation independently [25].

Auer et al. presented an assessment framework with an aim to assist the organizations which are planning to shift from distributed and layered architecture to microservices based architecture regarding the feasibility of the same. The framework comprises of a set of metrics which can aide organizations in taking the decision of whether migrating to microservices is recommended or not. This will help organizations in avoiding the cost and efforts of migration if they are not going to leverage any substantial benefit out of it [36].

Lenarduzzi et al. compared and analysed the technical debt of a system pre and post migration to microservices. SonarQube is used to quantify the technical debt at code level. The results suggest that initially during the development of independent microservices, the technically debt seems to grow swiftly. However, once the microservices are stabilised, developers confirmed the decrease in maintenance complexity and increase in operational velocity. Moreover, the increased velocity and the autonomous working of teams led to the reduction in overall efforts [58].

Dr. Kamlendu Kumar Pandey proposed an evaluation matrix for guiding the software architects and developers in selecting the combination of toolchain that best fits the requirements of a microservice based application. The evaluation matrix is divided into six categories namely Architectural evaluation, Executional evaluation, Inter-Operational evaluation, Deployment evaluation, Performance and Cost evaluation and Support evaluation [68].

Abidi et al. dealt with the security related issues encountered in the service-oriented architecture when web service or data is deployed on cloud. For instance, Denial-Of-Service (DoS) attack and data deletion by unauthorized access. To overcome these vulnerabilities, a Web Service Security Governance approach based on micro service architecture is proposed which incorporates a part of General Data Protection Regulation (GDPR) rules and predefined security policies [76].

Djogic et al. presented study on architectural redesign from Service Oriented Architecture to Microservice based Architecture in order to cater the benefits of scalability, maintainability, and easy deployment. The study discusses a number of steps to be followed for such transition as follows - 1: Identify microservices. 2: Implement REST based microservice for database operations. 3: Decompose components into small microservices. 4: Remove dependencies between service contracts. 5: Configure database for each service 6: Set up messaging queues for each microservices [96].

Architecture Recovery
N. Alshuqayran, N. Ali and R. Evans outlined the challenges faced in performing downstream engineering tasks like migration, audit, integration etc. in micro service-based system due to lack of clear architectural model. Since, no architecture recovery technique has been explored for micro service-based system, they carried out an empirical study on performing architecture recovery in context of microservice architecture and developed an approach called Micro Service Architecture Recovery (MiSAR) [91].

Leveraging Benefits of MSA for Various Use Cases
J. Zaki et al. carried out an exhaustive study on the healthcare systems developed across various conventional architectural frameworks. This helped them to bring the challenges in the conventional frameworks used for developing healthcare systems like scalability, availability, integration with other healthcare systems, etc. As a part of their study, the authors have proposed and used a microservice based framework for the implementation of healthcare services on cloud infrastructure to address all these problems. The result of microservice framework implementation is expressed in form of qualitative assessment carried out based on the opinions of a number of industry experts like developers, architects, project manager and requirement engineer which further proves the efficacy of micro service architecture over the conventional service-oriented architecture in terms of response time and resource utilization [4].

Owing to the challenges of monolithic architecture in handling scaling and concurrency, Gu et al. recommended and implemented online teaching platform using microservice architecture. The resulting system solves the issues of traditional architecture and improves the concurrent performance of the system, scalability and operational efficiency [17].

L. Pei et al. designed and implemented a course selection system based on Spring Cloud Micro-Service Architecture. The system is divided into teacher side system, student side system and the administrator system. In their course of implementation, the authors concluded that Spring Cloud's microservices architecture works well with the relationships between projects as against the distributed projects combined with Dubbo and Zookeeper. Spring Cloud's framework also offers high availability and small service granularity. [23].

Qian et al. has put in the effort to explore the design and application of Manufacturing Execution System (MES) through an architectural shift from traditional to microservice architecture. The use case of MES for tobacco enterprise is considered for the execution of the architecture and the resulting application is observed to have high scalability, improved performance and overcomes security threats encountered in conventional architecture-based MES [27].

Campbell et al. set forth the need for an integrated micro service framework to manage business and student services of University of Technology, Jamaica. As a part of study, the University enterprise system ISAS - Integrated Student Assessment System is taken as a reference which is then fit into micro service architectural framework. The aim is to serve as a reference for the universities planning to go for serverless and containerized design architecture [28].

A. Luntovskyy et al. defined the term HDS (Highly Distributed System) and precisely differentiated it from the traditional distributed systems. In their study, they also discussed various architectures currently known for HDS. In addition to it, the micro service architecture is stated favourable for building modern highly distributed application due to the benefits it yields like Quality of Experience (QoE), high performance, better flexibility, enhanced scalability and loose coupling [51].

A. Haque et al. et al. stated that a scalable, multi-functional and resilient energy management system is required to fully utilize the advancements made in the fields of IoT. Such features are ensured by micro service architecture. Hence, the building energy management system (BEMS) is constructed utilising the proposed architecture based on microservices. The results of implementation are presented as a case study illustrating the advantages of using the microservice approach for the development of a BEMS. The framework consists of three layers - "Core layer" consisting of microservices, "API layer" which serves as a gateway for all requests and "Service layer" depicting the SAAS functionalities used by the end users. The researchers further aim at focusing on improvisation of architecture to accommodate better data access for machine learning algorithms, new IoT devices and software based transactive energy platforms [52].

Y. Gong et al. identified the performance issues arising in conventional java web applications due to the fact that frontend and backend are highly blended together. Hence, they came up with the solution of decoupling the front-end and back-end and adopted Spring cloud microservice framework for application development to improvise the performance of the system with reference to the Campus Information System. The outcome of the study suggests that using microservices for separating the front-end and the back-end enhances the user experience to a large extent as compared to the conventional web application [56].

Sha et al. introduced the design of microservice architecture crafted specifically for edge computing. The toolchain of proposed design consists of PostgreSQL for data storage, Flask framework for back-end services, VueJs which takes care of front-end part and docker containers for deployment [61].

Tao et al. implemented civil affairs informatization using microservice architecture. The architecture is specifically selected due to its capability of fostering the changes quickly. The application also leveraged the benefits of high scalability and maintainability by adopting MSA [64].

Ştefan et al. addressed the open learning platform from software architecture perspective. The paper discusses leveraging the benefits of microservices architecture and blockchain technology to fulfil the needs of open learning communities. The combination of both of these architectures very well addresses the issues related to de-centralization, security, reliability, auditability and user-identity. The driving force of this research is based on the similarities between microservices and smart contracts [72].

N. Cui et al. designed an intelligent workshop cloud platform composed of micro services. In order to ensure the security aspects of the system, role-based access is given to each user for all resources. The framework consists of three layers: physical data sensing layer, data service layer and business processing layer. The data gathered across the production process is transformed and presented to the user in order to support decision making [74].

Zhou Yi et al. implemented a manufacturing cloud platform for SME. As the business processes varies for small and medium scale business, relatively small modules are built around business processes. For this, Microservice architecture is used to decouple the entire system in order to swiftly deploy services that too packaged in docker containers. Each of these microservices run independently and communicate with each other through REST API [77].

S. S. Kumar et al. implemented an eLearning platform using microservice architecture. In their requirement gathering phase they stated that the system must be highly scalable, available and robust. Taking these features into consideration, they found MSA more preferable over the monolithic architecture. They divided each operation into small micro services and connected them through APIs. They achieved very loosely coupled architecture by implementing separate database per service [98].

5.2.2 Operational and Quality Aspects (RQ3)

Scaling

Nguyen et al. conducted extensive research of existing studies focusing on the use of Graph Neural Networks for addressing the issues of autoscaling in Microservice based cloud applications. Further research directions are suggested for leveraging Spatiotemporal Graph Neural Network (STGNN) and dynamic graph neural networks (DGNN) for microservice based applications [14].

Henning et al. introduced Theodolite - A technique used for benchmarking scalability of distributed stream processing engines in microservices. Different benchmarks are designed based on varying use cases. Consequently, benchmarks for 4 different use cases and 7 different workload dimensions are designed. The experiments suggested that Kafka Streams and Apache Flink appears to be highly scalable for all use cases considered.

Moreover, the decision regarding which deployment option is selected, highly influences the scalability of stream processing engines [41].

Srirama et al. proposed a container-based strategy focusing on auto-scaling, resource provisioning and scheduling of microservices deployed in cloud environment. The issue of resource provisioning is addressed by proposing the technique which enables to find the container that best fits the resource requirements of each microservice hence optimizes the cost and processing time. Another major issue of cold start in container-based scheduling is solved by reusing warm containers which significantly reduces the deployment time of containers. The efficiency of the proposed strategy is evaluated and compared with the strategies used by Docker Swarm [60].

Avritzer et al. introduced an approach for the quantitative analysis of various configuration options available for microservice deployment in order to efficiently scale automatically without performance degradation. The approach comprises of analysis of operation profile data, building experiments, automatically calculating the baseline requirements and executing the experiment [62].

Taherizadeh et al. presented a set of key factors which should be considered while building auto-scaling methods so as to cope up with application performance requirements. The key factors focused in study are - conservative constant, Control loop time period and stopping at most one container instance in each adaption interval. The proposed approach is applied on Kubernetes auto-scaler that too for three different workload patterns - predictable bursting workload pattern, unpredictable bursting workload pattern and on-and-off workload pattern [63].

M. Song et al. presented an API Gateway system as an entry point to backend microservices. The researchers have also implemented an autoscaling system using Kubernetes and Prometheus which can dynamically increase the number of instances based on the load of API Gateway. The proposed system seems to optimize resource utilization while ensuring the high availability and quality of API Gateway's service [85].

P. Nguyen et al. presented the architecture and implementation of MONAD, a self-adaptive micro-service-based infrastructure for heterogeneous scientific workflows. By isolating task dependencies from its implementation, the proposed micro-service-based method increases the flexibility and scalability of workflow design and execution. Moreover, the feedback control-based resource adaption technique aids in taking decisions regarding resource allocation without pre-knowledge of workflow structures [99].

Monitoring
Apolinário et al. introduced SYMBIOTE technique to monitor the coupling evolution of microservice architecture-based systems. The technique uses service coupling metrics and gives warning to the developers when modifications in the system adversely affects the maintainability. The technique is tested with a real-world open-source project and have proven its potential in identifying the architectural degradation via coupling metrics [42].

M. Song et al. implemented a distributed tracing solution which implements call tracing between micro services. The system is compatible across programming languages and helps developers in troubleshooting and sorting the call chain. The tracing system can be easily embedded in the existing system and can trace the fault location without much affecting the performance of existing system [73].

Testing

Camilli et al. proposed a technique in which load testing on microservices is carried out based on pre-fixed specifications and that too for varied deployment configurations. The approach is an amalgamation of specification driven load testing sessions and Bayesian inference to develop a performance model of the target microservices system in terms of a CTMC (continuous-time Markov chain). Hence, the entire testing process can be eliminated once we get the inferred model with stable parameters. This further, can bring down the overall cost as well [13].

T. Duan et al. expressed that due to the loose coupling nature of microservices, the services usually have multiple interfaces which further complicates the testing of micro services. As a part of research, the author introduced a decision tree algorithm in order to automatically categorise and screen various test cases. The proposed technique aims at reducing the labour cost and enhance the efficacy through automated testing. The experiment results states that the model achieved 94.1% accuracy. However, the author also claimed that the accuracy will tend to increase with the increase in the volume of test cases in the training set [24].

T. Vassiliou-Gioles identified the aspects which poses challenges in the way of trusting the results of integration testing in the context of microservices. The proposed technique simply embeds instance identification within the service to increase the expressiveness and trust on the results of integration testing. This provides information on regular basis to the developers. Further it also helped in avoiding the interaction with the wrong instance of the service due to version updates of that service [26].

Raychev et al. in their study expressed the need of test automation in micro services architecture due to the fact that with increase in the number of micro services, the number of connections and dependencies increases which leads to the complexity in testing them. As a part of study, they proposed test automation techniques namely Karma for End-to-End testing, Agile testing, PaaS with API Gateway, service network for open tracing and degradation testing. All these techniques were experimented and worked well with the micro service architecture [55].

Shang-Pin Ma et al. proposed an innovative approach for the development of microservice based applications – GSMART (Graph-based and Scenario-driven Microservice Analysis, Retrieval and Testing) which mainly supports Java-based Spring Boot Framework. The significant features of the proposed technique are - It generates Service Dependency Graphs automatically which enables to view the dependency relationship among microservices and identify the faults arising out of cyclic dependencies. It also generates the test cases automatically owing to changes in system for regression testing. Further, the experiments prove the efficacy of all the significant features of GSMART [78].

Security

Nasab et al. conducted an empirical study by analysing microservices security points sourced from GitHub, Stack overflow posts, wiki pages etc. Consequently, the research led to the identification of 28 security practices to overcome security issues pertaining to microservices which are further divided into categories: Authorization and Authentication, Token and Credentials, Internal and External Microservices, Microservices Communications, Private Microservices, and Database and Environments [6].

Jacob et al. worked in the direction of securing microservice from cyber-attacks. A Diffusion Convolutional Recurrent Neural Network is used to model the set of distributed traces based on application traffic. Further, this model is used to make predictions and detect the asymmetrical microservice activity indicating the potential cyber-attack. This technique is capable of detecting brute force attack, batch registration of bot accounts and Distributed Denial of Service attack [9].

Nuno Mateus-Coelho et al. focused on security aspect of micro service architecture. The study unveils potential risks and security threats in microservices architecture like password complexity, weak authentication mechanisms, injection attacks, cross-site scripting, broken authentication and session management, cross-site request forgery, broken access control, etc. In addition to this, counter measures like service-to-service authentication and authorization, securing data at REST and tracking through activity logs are also discussed precisely to overcome such potential threats [29].

Hannousse et al. focused their study on securing microservices and examined 46 research papers since 2011. The findings showed that the threats that are currently being investigated and addressed by studies include unauthorised access, sensitive data leakage, and compromising individual microservices. The study also revealed that more research efforts have been given on external attacks and mitigation techniques. Hence, it is suggested to focus on internal attacks and prevention techniques as well [31].

Nasab et al. outlined the significance of the security discussions that can assist practitioners in taking informed security decisions in the future or detect security threats (e.g., security bugs, security mistakes, etc.) in microservices systems more swiftly. To achieve this, fifteen Deep learning models are developed which detects the security related discussions in context of microservices over GitHub and Stack Overflow posts. The findings suggest that DeepM1 model gives most accurate results [33].

Miller et al. recommended and implemented an architecture for preventing leakage of data on cloud platform. Taking the principle of zero-trust into the account, a system enables to exchange data between non-trusted parties with an assurance of secured communication at rest, in transport or by either of the party. The experiments further confirms that the method is capable of scaling well with the increasing workflow complexity [43].

G. Fu et al. in their paper have analysed and outlined the challenges of using the conventional access control mechanisms in micro-service environment and have proposed an optimized model for access control based on RBAC. The mechanism enables the existing RBAC users to directly access the ABE (Attribute Based Encryption) encrypted data in micro-services. This technique enhances the expression ability of access rules, decreases the computational cost to a certain amount, and enhances the security and operational efficiency of microservices when compared to the previous schemes of trivial equality and bit matching [86].

J. Chelladhurai et al. discussed various security aspects with regards to the Docker containers as well as the recent advancements in this area. Different solutions to overcome the security issues have also been outlined in the study. In addition to that, a pragmatic approach has also been proposed and experimented to combat DoS attacks on Docker containers and the results are found promising. [104].

Fault Tolerance

Chen et al. focused on locating fault in large microservices application. Hence, a framework is proposed to locate fault based on fault correlation of microservices by examining the dependency calling relationship in context of microservices [7].

Cinque et al. focused the research on log mining for detection of anomalies in micro services architecture. To deal with the heterogeneous logs generated in microservices based applications, a novel approach to log mining - Micro2vec is proposed which does not require any knowledge regarding application in advance. [8].

Chen et al. proposed a machine learning framework to keep track of the traffic of RPC and detect the points of anomalies. The framework is applied to a dataset of more than 7 billion lines of RPC logs extracted from a huge Kubernetes system. Consequently, the proposed framework successfully found RPC chain patterns and detected anomalous points in a complex microservice system. [12].

Leila et al. identified different architectures for deploying microservices with Kubernetes and evaluated Kubernetes in terms of availability of applications. However, during study it was discovered that service availability is an issue while using Kubernetes as an orchestration platform for microservice based applications. The reason observed is that in some cases service recovery is not guaranteed and the repair actions of Kubernetes does not satisfy the high availability requirements. Consequently, a High Availability State Controller is integrated with Kubernetes which replicates the application state and automatically redirects the request to the healthy microservice instances. This allows service recovery and repair actions to take place without affecting the availability of microservices. The results of experiment shows that the proposed solution can improve the recovery time of microservices by 50% when compared with the other existing architectures [39].

Baboi et al. proposed an architecture which enables creation and integration of new microservices smoothly. The architecture addresses the challenges of scaling and fault tolerance with reference to microservices. Basically, the monolithic architecture is modified to leverage the flexibility feature of microservices. The proposed architecture provides auto scaling based on parameters like number of calls to task and the time to execute it [79].

W. Lin et al. introduced FacGraph - a framework to detect anomalies and root cause in a micro service architecture. Due to its loosely coupled nature, it is often difficult to find out the root cause service which is creating an anomaly. The proposed framework is evaluated in real production environment IBM Bluemix. The findings shows that the use of Breadth First Order Search has proven its ability to detect anomalies faster through frequent graph mining compared to the other known approaches. The strength of this approach lies within the fact that it treats micro-service architecture as a "Black Box". Hence, no predefined knowledge is needed and it can be applied to a numerous use case. [88].

Database and Transaction Management

González-Aparicio et al. proposed a novel transaction platform that works on asynchronous protocols for microservice based architecture. The platform intends to handle processing of big data stored in NoSQL database cluster. The platform is tested and evaluated through a system that simulates "Transport for London" which provides bus service in London. The results suggests that the proposed platform performs well in terms of reliability, data consistency and application correctness. However, it lacks to perform well in context of response time and throughput [2].

Sadek et al. explored two architectural paradigms - serverless and microservices, for the design and implementation of a Medical Searching System. However, it was found that using microservices together with serverless function overcomes the restrictions posed by serverless providers. Hence design and implementation of Medical Searching System's framework is done using AWS lambda functions and microservices. Microservices architectural design made the system flexible and easy to scale [11].

Laigner et al. furnished a comprehensive study on various state of the art approaches of data management present in microservice based architecture. To start with, the analysis of numerous open-source microservice application is done. The researchers ran an online poll with 120 software architects and researchers to cross-validate their analysis of a number of well-known open-source applications. With this step they were able to classify the current status of data management techniques in microservices and identify a number of fundamental issues like lack of asynchronous and event driven approach, inconsistencies between heterogeneous database system and eventual consistency [44].

Overeem et al. presented a thorough understanding of event sourcing pattern. The discussion and benefits of the pattern like reduced complexity, improved maintainability, improved reliability and enhanced scalability is affirmed by the experience of 25 engineers who were interviewed during the study. The study also outlines challenges of working with the event sourced system like event system evolution, the steep learning curve, unavailability of required technology, rebuilding projections, and data confidentiality. The tactics like versioning events, weak schema, upcasting and in-place transformation are discussed in the later part of the study to address the issue of event store evolution [45].

S. Chandrasena compared the performance of monolithic service and micro service architectures for web-based database management systems by measuring the response time for READ operations with various record sizes. For this, two versions of same software are built. So, the first version is a generalized web service that can return the result for a SQL query submitted to the service via http request. The second version consists of a component comprising a set of services. The component splits the submitted query into smaller queries and send them to the small microservices. The experiment was carried out on various environments like local computer, Docker, Google cloud instances Google Kubernetes Engine. Further, the response time on all environment was analysed using JMeter which revealed that using microservices for database access systems gives best results on local computer environment and Google's Kubernetes Engine. Further, the results also confirmed that using micro service architecture over monolithic architecture for data intensive applications substantially improves performance and results in less response time [50].

H. Lv. et al. proposed a real time big data processing platform to cater the decision-making requirements of modern businesses. For this, they have built an event driven system based on Spring Cloud Stream microservice where they have used Apache Kafka as a message broker and stream API of Spark. The data collected from various sensors in the ecosystem is sent by Spring cloud stream to Kafka topic. The big data framework spark then fetches the data from Kafka topic using stream API for further data analysis [57].

Abhijeet et al. discussed the issues of synchronization of data and state of all microservices in an application. The said issue is however addressed through the use of event sourcing mechanism which comes with the capabilities of stream processing and message queue system. It is recommended not to use event sourcing pattern where consistency is at the focal point. Event sourcing is recommended for scenarios where availability and resilience is desired [65].

Dr. Kamlendu Kumar Pandey et al. analysed the microservice architecture very precisely. The main focus of the study is drawn towards challenges related to synchronous communication, transaction fallback, inconsistencies in highly decoupled system application and strenuous service discovery. With reference to the challenges discussed, a method is proposed to calculate a challenge handling index i.e., the intensity to which challenges are handled during design and implementation of microservice based applications [67].

Dr. Kamlendu Kumar Pandey et al. considered a hypothetical application for their study, identified the problems with respect to microservice architecture and laid down potential solutions to address those problems. The major problems identified and addressed in the study are related to the coupling of microservices, data inconsistency, synchronous communication and transaction fallback. The techniques discussed as a part of solution are event driven architecture, event-based streaming, command query responsibility segregation and choreography and orchestration technique [69].

Zhelev et al. presented a detailed study of the complementing nature of microservices for processing big data. The study covers various aspects like implementation of microservices and event driven architecture in context of big data stream processing. The proposed platform is then analysed taking a use case of autonomous vehicle application [83].

X. J. Hong et al. presented a comparison between RabbitMQ and REST API implemented as the message-oriented middleware for microservice web applications. The result of their experiment depicts that when the number of concurrent user request is less, REST API outperforms the RabbitMQ method. However, as the number of user requests grows in volume, a drastic drop in performance of REST API can be observed and more often the request is not served. On the contrary, with substantially high number of requests RabbitMQ remains stable [89].

Y. Xie et.al. proposed an architecture for the development of integrated platform application. The architecture is based on micro services and focuses on solving issues of Distributed transaction, service invocation and session sharing. The experiments conducted, establishes the evidence that numerous application services deployed over distributed cluster accommodates and supports session sharing, load balancing and distributed transactions. Additionally, the architecture smoothens the development and maintenance of the application [90].

Wauer et al. presented research regarding the need of scalable platform to manage geospatial and sensor data which is highly heterogeneous in nature. For this, a message driven approach is adopted for scalable integration of microservices. The proposed platform consists of services which extract, transform, link and transmit such complex data with utmost efficacy [95].

Service Discovery
P. Y. Tilak et al., in their paper have proposed a platform consisting of three applications-consumer app, creator app and administrator app in order to assist software development teams to collaboratively work on functionality in various software systems. The applications together work as a repository which helps developers of an organization to expose their microservices to the world and consumers to discover and use the microservices as per their requirements [46].

5.2.3 Coordination and Deployment Techniques (RQ4)

Choreography and Orchestration
Xue et al. addressed the issue of coordination amongst participants in the decentralized microservices composition. The study proposes different approaches built on SAGA technique for coordination amongst microservices based on the data dependencies they share. The corresponding approaches are experimented and proved to be effective for making different microservices reach consensus at runtime [37].

Stutz et al. in their study, discussed that choreography only makes up a small portion of association techniques. Because choreographies lack hierarchical architecture and complexity-hiding techniques, using them in bigger associations is not recommended. Choreographies excel in more manageable, less intricate associations than numerous decentralized entities. Based on this observation, the authors have presented the discussion and practical implementation of choreography within industrial automation with a specific focus on the interaction mechanisms of choreographies. The overall findings suggest that the potential for combining sub-elementary services spanning across several process equipment assemblies to provide new service functions makes a choreographic approach look viable [48].

S. Lee et al. proposed cloud-native workload profiling system with Kubernetes orchestrated multi-cluster configuration for micro services. The part of research includes designing an operating software which chooses optimal resources across a number of cloud-native cluster through continuous monitoring. Additionally, general service workloads are defined in order to operate across multiple clusters. Finally, variation in resource utilization is calculated based on initial resource usage and average resource usage [53].

D. Bhamare et al. addresses the challenges of scheduling micro-services spanning across multiple clouds. As a part of their work, they have proposed "Fair Weighted Affinity-Based Scheduling" (FWS) strategy to overcome the stated challenge. In addition to the proposed FWS approach, different variants of greedy algorithms (Least-full first with First Finish (LFFF), Most-full first with First time (MFFF), Least-full first with Decreasing time (LFDT), Most-full first with Decreasing Finish (MFDT) were also implemented. The efficacy of FWS is proven by comparing the performance metrices like turnaround time and number of user requests fulfilled as recorded for all the strategies implemented. It was observed that with FWS approach, the percentage of user requests fulfilled was around 96% which was way higher than the other approaches [100].

Deployment and Containerization

It has been a popular research area to figure out how to cost-effectively and robustly deploy edge AI microservices in Multi-access Edge Computing (MEC) situations that are highly prone to failure. Wu et al. took into consideration an edge AI microservice that can be implemented by combining multiple Deep Neural Networks (DNN) models. In doing so, features from various DNN models are combined together, and the deployment cost can be further brought down while still meeting the Quality-of-Service (QoS) requirement. Additionally, a Three-Dimensional Dynamic Programming (TDDP)-based technique is proposed to produce multi-DNN load allocation and orchestration plans that are both affordable and efficient. Real-world edge environment experiments have proven that the introduced orchestration and placement technique have the potential to achieve cheaper deployment costs and less Quality-of-Service loss in case of edge node failures compared to the conventional methods [1].

Karabey et al. discussed deployment mechanisms and communication patterns pertaining to microservices based systems. Across seven different communication patterns considered during the study, publish/subscribe pattern is found to be more often used communication pattern. Amongst deployment approaches, Service Instance per container pattern appeared to be more preferred amongst all the approaches covered [32].

Dharmaji et al. conducted a detailed study on containerization of microservices. The study concludes that containers are the best runtime contenders for microservices. The rationale for being the superior choice for microservices has a direct association with the benefits that containers bring with them like agility, continuous integration and continuous delivery and modularity [66].

Dr. Kamlendu Kumar Pandey conducted an empirical study through the practical implementation and evaluation of a microservice based containerized application. The aim of research is to monitor, analyze and evaluate the performance of application under varying load on services. The toolchain used for the experimentation purpose comprise of Kubernetes, docker, Ingress gateway, Prometheus, Apache JMeter and payara micro server. The results of experiment suggests that microservices remains stable under varying load on services and containers helps in keeping the application light weight and easy to scale [70].

Kayal et al. carried out research on IoT applications composed of microservices in fog. The study further demonstrates the practical feasibility of using tools like docker for deploying containerized IoT based applications on devices like raspberry pi. Kubernetes is used as an orchestrator to instantiate and manage the containers hosted on different cloud servers. The experiment further depicts a significant delay in terms of time while working with the mobile nodes placed at varying distance [71].

S. Eismann et al. evaluated various self-management approaches of microservices to automate scaling, fault tolerance and parameter tuning taking the reference of a Tea Store application built on micro service architecture. The study also consists of the discussion of various deployment models for the reference microservice application namely - Application server, Container and Kubernetes. It also explains how to run different load profiles and gather performance matrices [75].

Yu et al. expressed the problem related to service request routing and instance deployment in microservice ecosystem. The problem is then addressed through the inception of a three-stage technique - LEGO. Stage 1 is meant for optimizing the decision related to allocation of resources considering the incoming requests. At stage 2, a set of instances of microservice is created and the incoming traffic is routed to the instances in a balanced manner. At the later stage i.e., stage 3, a minimum number of servers are consumed for the deployment of service instances [81].

Wan et al. carried out study related to the optimization of containerized application deployment on cloud platform with an aim to minimize the deployment as well as the operation cost. As a part of study, a cost efficient and scalable resource allocation algorithm is proposed. The proposed algorithm is then evaluated and compared with the existing strategies being used in docker swarm based on real data traces. The result of evaluation suggest that the proposed algorithm considerably reduces the deployment cost by balancing the wake-up cost of physical machine, installation cost of supporting library and communication cost [93].

D. Guo et al. introduced a new Cloud ware PaaS platform based on lightweight container technology and microservice design. Without making any modifications, users may directly deploy conventional software on this platform that offers services to customers through browsers. Leveraging the benefits of microservices, this platform features scalability, auto-deployment, disaster recovery, and elastic configuration [103].

6   Discussions

During the study, we found that there is a progressive surge in the volume of studies related to microservices architecture over a period of last 5 years. From the studies investigated so far, it is quite evident that the primary reason for this paradigm shift is due to the benefits like agility, scalability, continuous integration and deployment, maintainability, security and fault tolerance furnished by microservices. However, "With power comes great responsibility." Though, a lot of research has been done by various researchers across different arena of microservice architecture, there are many areas of microservices which are still vulnerable and needs to be addressed through research. Few of them are challenges related to complex service discovery, monitoring the complicated mesh of microservices, coordination and orchestration of service request between microservices. Since, services are deployed on multi-cloud environment, handling all these challenges becomes quite tricky job. we studied and presented varied aspects of microservices pertaining to migration from monolith to microservice architecture, operational and quality aspects of microservices and state of the art coordination and deployment techniques proposed in selected studies. Further, we have put forward out point of view in each of the listed categories and comprehended the same in the study. This can serve as a primary literature and a reference for those who are looking for best approach and tool chain for microservice implementation as per their application need.

As far as database and transaction management is concerned, the database per service concept is suggested as one of the ideal conditions for experiencing the desired level of loose coupling in microservice applications by Chris Richardson [106]. Further, the database systems must be aware of events spanning across multiple cloud environment. As observed during the study, seamless communication across services deployed on multiple clouds is achieved through asynchronous event driven message queues. However, enforcing consistency seems to be the biggest challenge in real-time systems where one cannot afford to accommodate eventual consistency in the system. Hence, there is still a considerably huge research gap when it comes to addressing challenges of eventual consistency and performance degradation in event driven transaction management approach.

Ample amount of research work has been carried out in context of securing microservices covering various security aspects from end-to end secure communication to securing the containers. It has been observed that highest number of attacks in microservices based architecture occur in form of user-based attacks through various techniques like Brute Force Attack, Spoofing, Cross-Site Request Forgery etc. However, software attacks like Denial of Service and Injection also hold a considerable share in compromising microservice security. Out of various techniques studied for securing microservices, the technique of using JSON Web Token (JWT) and OAuth2 seems promising and flawless for authentication and authorization. In addition to this, continuous auditing through logs also has proven its efficacy when tested on sample applications by researchers.

The organizations looking for a paradigm shift from a monolith to a microservice based application often face a bigger challenge of identifying the boundaries of microservices while maintaining the standard level of coupling and cohesion. In recent years, a lot of research work has been carried out regarding the decomposition and granularity of microservices. Consequently, a lot of techniques have been proposed by various researchers for the identification of ideal microservice candidate via decomposition. Amongst them, microservice identification using knowledge graph seems to be most effective. The efficacy of this technique is also proven, as the algorithm passed the evaluation test on two open-source projects in terms of parameters like team size reduction, cohesion, coupling and code reduction. The major strength of study lies in less dependency on human experience for constructing the knowledge graph.

One of the features responsible for making microservice architecture a cost-effective solution is its ability to scale services independently rather than scaling the entire application. Significant work has been done in developing auto-scaling techniques for optimum utilization of resources and automatic load balancing. Amongst all the studies covered, Kafka Streams and Apache Flink appears to be highly scalable. Moreover, the decision regarding which deployment option is selected highly influences the scalability of the system. During the study, it is also observed that Kubernetes Auto scalar is highly used by researchers and industry experts to gain the benefit of auto scaling. From the studies covered, it is evident that containers are the best runtime contenders for microservices and they are cost efficient to scale. The publication trend also clearly shows that Docker is the popular choice for packaging and deploying microservices on cloud platform.

API gateways serves as an entry point for all incoming request which are eventually routed to concerned microservices. However, it is also worth noting that API gateway congestion is equally is bigger challenge as far as scaling is concerned. So, there is still a considerable room for research regarding the scaling techniques for API gateways.

In context of large-scale applications, the challenge of identifying the root cause of faults in an ecosystem of enormous number of interconnected microservices is a problem which deserves due attention of researchers. Moreover, the fault propagation relationship in microservices is quite complex compared to the conventional architecture. Various fault diagnosis methods have been proposed to address the issue. It is observed that using Kubernetes as an orchestrator affects the availability of the application due to the lack of assurance of service repair. Hence, relying solely on Kubernetes for managing the faults in service mesh is not recommended. Rather, some mechanism must be used in combination, for continuously logging the health of the application and mining the logs regularly to detect the fault and identify its root.

To sum it up, though a lot of work still needs to be done in the area of microservice architecture, the applicability, acceptance and popularity of microservice based architecture in software community can be affirmed by its usage for architecting applications in diversified domains like IoT and edge computing, ERP software solutions, big data analytics, Blockchain and countless other commercial application domains.

7   Limitations of Research

Since, the research is intended to carry out a broader and comprehensive outlook over various aspect of microservices, an in-depth study on each and every aspect of micro service ecosystem is not incorporated. Moreover, aspects like the compatibility of no code environment with microservices, utility of microservices in Agent Based Computing and AIOps i.e., Artificial Intelligence for IT Operations are not covered.

8   Conclusion

In this article, a systematic literature review methodology is adopted in order to concisely discuss the state of the art of microservice architecture. We took into account 104 primary studies from year 2016 to 2023. It is quite evident that microservice architecture is by far the most trending service-oriented architecture which very well complements the cloud applications. The finding of this study will also set a path ahead for researchers and software architects in evaluating the trade-offs of each aspect of microservices they are looking to adopt and implement. Moreover, in our upcoming work, we plan to dig deep and work on the challenges discussed and which are still less explored in researcher's community.

References

1. Wu, C., Peng, Q., Xia, Y., Jin, Y., Zhentao, H.: Towards cost-effective and robust AI microservice deployment in edge computing environments. Futur. Gener. Comput. Syst. **141**, 129–142 (2023)

2. González-Aparicio, M.T., Younas, M., Tuya, J., Casado, R.: A transaction platform for microservices-based big data systems. Simul. Model. Pract. Theory **123**, 102709 (2023)
3. Zhou, X., et al.: Revisiting the practices and pains of microservice architecture in reality: An industrial inquiry. J. Syst. Softw. **195**, 111521 (2023)
4. Zaki, J., Islam, S.M.R., Alghamdi, N.S., Abdullah-Al-Wadud, M., Kwak, K.-S.: Introducing cloud-assisted micro-service-based software development framework for healthcare systems. IEEE Access **10**, 33332–33348 (2022). https://doi.org/10.1109/ACCESS.2022.316 1455
5. Debauche, O., Mahmoudi, S., Manneback, P., Lebeau, F.: Cloud and distributed architectures for data management in agriculture 4.0: review and future trends. J. King Saud Univ. – Comput. Inf. Sci. **34**(9), 7494–7514 (2022). ISSN 1319–1578. https://doi.org/10.1016/j.jks uci.2021.09.015
6. Nasab, A.R., Shahin, M., Raviz, S.A.H., Liang, P., Mashmool, A., Lenarduzzi, V.: An empirical study of security practices for microservices systems. J. Syst. Softw. **198**, 111563 (2023). ISSN 0164–1212, https://doi.org/10.1016/j.jss.2022.111563
7. Chen, Y., Xu, D., Chen, N., Wu, X.: FRL-MFPG: propagation-aware fault root cause location for microservice intelligent operation and maintenance. Inf. Softw. Technol. **153**, 107083 (2023). ISSN 0950–5849. https://doi.org/10.1016/j.infsof.2022.107083
8. Cinque, M., Della Corte, R., Pecchia, A.: Micro2vec: anomaly detection in microservices systems by mining numeric representations of computer logs. J. Netw. Comput. Appl. **208**, 103515 (2022). ISSN 1084–8045. https://doi.org/10.1016/j.jnca.2022.103515
9. Jacob, S., Qiao, Y., Ye, Y., Lee, B.: Anomalous distributed traffic: Detecting cyber security attacks amongst microservices using graph convolutional networks. Comput. Secur. **118**, 102728 (2022). ISSN 0167–4048. https://doi.org/10.1016/j.cose.2022.102728
10. Atitallah, S.B., Driss, M., Ghzela, H.B.: Microservices for data analytics in IoT applications: current solutions, open challenges, and future research directions. Procedia Comput. Sci. **207**, 3938–3947 (2022). https://doi.org/10.1016/j.procs.2022.09.456
11. Sadek, J., Craig, D., Trenell, M.: Design and implementation of medical searching system based on microservices and serverless architectures. Procedia Comput. Sci. **196**, 615–622 (2022). ISSN 1877–0509. https://doi.org/10.1016/j.procs.2021.12.056
12. Chen, J., Huang, H., Chen, H.: Informer: irregular traffic detection for containerized microservices RPC in the real world. High-Confidence Comput. **2**(2), 100050 (2022). ISSN 2667–2952
13. Camilli, M., Janes, A., Russo, B.: Automated test-based learning and verification of performance models for microservices systems. J. Syst. Softw. **187**, 111225 (2022). ISSN 0164–1212. https://doi.org/10.1016/j.jss.2022.111225
14. Nguyen, H.X., Zhu, S., Liu, M.: A survey on graph neural networks for microservice-based cloud applications. Sensors **22**(23), 9492 (2022)
15. Söylemez, M., Tekinerdogan, B., Tarhan, A.K.: Challenges and solution directions of microservice architectures: a systematic literature review. Appl. Sci. **12**(11), 5507 (2022)
16. https://www.marketwatch.com/press-release/microservice-architecture-market-research-report-by-type-installation-application-region---global-forecast-to-2028---cumulative-impact-of-covid-19-2022-12-23
17. Gu, H., Yang, S., Gu, M., Yuan, M.: Research on online teaching platform system based on microservice architecture. In: MATEC Web of Conferences, vol. 355, p. 03058. EDP Sciences (2022)
18. Hassan, S., Bahsoon, R., Buyya, R.: Systematic scalability analysis for microservices granularity adaptation design decisions. Softw. Pract. Exp. **52**(6), 1378–1401 (2022)
19. Makris, A., Tserpes, K., Varvarigou, T.: Transition from monolithic to microservice-based applications: challenges from the developer perspective. Open Res. Europe **2**, 24 (2022)

20. Sellami, K., Ouni, A., Saied, M.A., Bouktif, S., Mkaouer, M.W.: Improving microservices extraction using evolutionary search. Inf. Softw. Technol. **151**, 106996 (2022)
21. Li, Z., Shang, C., Jianjie, W., Li, Y.: Microservice extraction based on knowledge graph from monolithic applications. Inf. Softw. Technol. **150**, 106992 (2022)
22. Ponce, F., Soldani, J., Astudillo, H., Brogi, A.: Smells and refactorings for microservices security: a multivocal literature review. J. Syst. Softw. **192**, 111393 (2022)
23. Pei, L., Peng, L.: Design and implementation of course selection system based on spring-cloud micro-service architecture. In: 2021 3rd International Conference on Applied Machine Learning (ICAML), Changsha, China, pp. 132–135 (2021). https://doi.org/10.1109/ICAML54311.2021.00035
24. Duan, T., et al.: Design and implementation of intelligent automated testing of microservice application. In: 2021 IEEE 5th Information Technology, Networking, Electronic and Automation Control Conference (ITNEC), Xi'an, China, pp. 1306–1309 (2021). https://doi.org/10.1109/ITNEC52019.2021.9587260
25. Yang, K.-K., Li, Y., Lang, Q.-M., Zhang, Y.-S., Guo, S.-Z.: Design of information sy stem model management system based on micro-service. In: 2021 4th International Conference on Advanced Electronic Materials, Computers and Software Engineering (AEMCSE), Changsha, China, pp. 632–636 (2021). https://doi.org/10.1109/AEMCSE51986.2021.00131
26. Vassiliou-Gioles, T.: Quality assurance of micro-services - when to trust your micro-service test results? In: 2021 IEEE 21st International Conference on Software Quality, Reliability and Security Companion (QRS-C), Hainan, China, pp. 01–06 (2021). https://doi.org/10.1109/QRS-C55045.2021.00024
27. Jin, W., Qian, J., Zhang, Q., Gao, X., Xu, Y.: Research and application of MES technology architecture in tobacco industry based on micro service. In: 2021 IEEE International Conference on Power, Intelligent Computing and Systems (ICPICS), Shenyang, China, pp. 222–225 (2021). https://doi.org/10.1109/ICPICS52425.2021.9524169
28. Campbell, A., Thorpe, S., Edwards, T., Panther, C., Ramsey, S., White, D.: Towards an integrated micro-services architecture for campus environments. In: 2021 IEEE 7th International Conference on Collaboration and Internet Computing (CIC), Atlanta, GA, USA, pp. 125–128 (2021). https://doi.org/10.1109/CIC52973.2021.00023
29. Mateus-Coelho, N., Cruz-Cunha, M., Ferreira, L.G.: Security in microservices architectures. Procedia Comput. Sci. **181**, 1225–1236 (2021). ISSN 1877–0509. https://doi.org/10.1016/j.procs.2021.01.320
30. Waseem, M., Liang, P., Shahin, M., Di Salle, A., Márquez, G.: Design, monitoring, and testing of microservices systems: the practitioners' perspective. J. Syst. Softw. **182**, 111061 (2021). ISSN 0164–1212. https://doi.org/10.1016/j.jss.2021.111061
31. Hannousse, A., Yahiouche, S.: Securing microservices and microservice architectures: a systematic mapping study. Comput. Sci. Rev. **41**, 100415 (2021). ISSN 1574–0137. https://doi.org/10.1016/j.cosrev.2021.100415
32. Aksakalli, I.K., Çelik, T., Can, A.B., Tekinerdoğan, B.: Deployment and communication patterns in microservice architectures: a systematic literature review. J. Syst. Softw. **180**, 111014 (2021). ISSN 0164–1212. https://doi.org/10.1016/j.jss.2021.111014
33. Nasab, A.R., et al.: Automated identification of security discussions in microservices systems: industrial surveys and experiments. J. Syst. Softw. **181**, 111046 (2021). ISSN 0164–1212. https://doi.org/10.1016/j.jss.2021.111046
34. Daoud, M., El Mezouari, A., Faci, N., Benslimane, D., Maamar, Z., El Fazziki, A.: A multi-model based microservices identification approach. J. Syst. Arch. **118**, 102200 (2021). ISSN 1383–7621. https://doi.org/10.1016/j.sysarc.2021.102200
35. de Nardin, I.F., et al.: On revisiting energy and performance in microservices applications: a cloud elasticity-driven approach. Parallel Comput. **108**, 102858 (2021). ISSN 0167–8191. https://doi.org/10.1016/j.parco.2021.102858

36. Laigner, R., Zhou, Y., Vaz Salles, M.A., Liu, Y., Kalinowski, M.: Data management in microservices: State of the practice, challenges, and research directions. arXiv preprint arXiv: 2103.00170 (2021)
37. Auer, F., Lenarduzzi, V., Felderer, M., Taibi, D.: From monolithic systems to Microservices: an assessment framework. Inf. Softw. Technol. **137**, 106600 (2021). ISSN 0950–5849. https://doi.org/10.1016/j.infsof.2021.106600
38. Xue, G., Deng, S., Liu, D., Yan, Z.: Reaching consensus in decentralized coordination of distributed microservices. Comput. Netw. **187**, 107786 (2021) ISSN 1389–1286. https://doi.org/10.1016/j.comnet.2020.107786
39. de Toledo, S.S., Martini, A., Sjøberg, D.I.K.: Identifying architectural technical debt, principal, and interest in microservices: a multiple-case study. J. Syst. Softw. **177**, 110968 (2021). ISSN 0164–1212. https://doi.org/10.1016/j.jss.2021.110968
40. Vayghan, L.A., Saied, M.A., Toeroe, M., Khendek, F.: A Kubernetes controller for managing the availability of elastic microservice based stateful applications. J. Syst. Softw. **175**, 110924 (2021). ISSN 0164–1212. https://doi.org/10.1016/j.jss.2021.110924
41. Li, S., et al.: Understanding and addressing quality attributes of microservices architecture: a systematic literature review. Inf. Softw. Technol. **131**, 106449 (2021). ISSN 0950–5849. https://doi.org/10.1016/j.infsof.2020.106449
42. Henning, S., Hasselbring, W.: Theodolite: scalability benchmarking of distributed stream processing engines in microservice architectures. Big Data Res. **25**, 100209 (2021). ISSN 2214–5796. https://doi.org/10.1016/j.bdr.2021.100209
43. Apolinário, D.R., de França, B.B.: A method for monitoring the coupling evolution of microservice-based architectures. J. Brazil. Comput. Soc. **27**(1), 17 (2021)
44. Miller, L., Mérindol, P., Gallais, A., Pelsser, C.: Securing workflows using microservices and metagraphs. Electronics **10**(24), 3087 (2021)
45. Overeem, M., Spoor, M., Jansen, S., Brinkkemper, S.: An empirical characterization of event sourced systems and their schema evolution—Lessons from industry. J. Syst. Softw. **178**, 110970 (2021)
46. Tilak, P.Y., Yadav, V., Dharmendra, S.D., Bolloju, N.: A platform for enhancing application developer productivity using microservices and micro-frontends. In: 2020 IEEE-HYDCON, Hyderabad, India, pp. 1–4 (2020). https://doi.org/10.1109/HYDCON48903.2020.9242913
47. Avritzer, A.: Challenges and approaches for the assessment of micro-service architecture deployment alternatives in DevOps: a tutorial presented at ICSA 2020. In: 2020 IEEE International Conference on Software Architecture Companion (ICSA-C), Salvador, Brazil, pp. 1–2 (2020). https://doi.org/10.1109/ICSA-C50368.2020.00007
48. Stutz, A., Fay, A., Barth, M., Maurmaier, M.: Choreographies in microservice-based automation architectures: next level of flexibility for industrial cyber-physical systems. In: 2020 IEEE Conference on Industrial Cyberphysical Systems (ICPS), Tampere, Finland, pp. 411–416 (2020). https://doi.org/10.1109/ICPS48405.2020.9274719
49. Kuryazov, D., Jabborov, D., Khujamuratov, B.: Towards decomposing monolithic applications into microservices. In: 2020 IEEE 14th International Conference on Application of Information and Communication Technologies (AICT), Tashkent, Uzbekistan, pp. 1–4 (2020). https://doi.org/10.1109/AICT50176.2020.9368571
50. Chandrasena, S.: Generalized micro-service architecture for web based database management systems. In: 2020 20th International Conference on Advances in ICT for Emerging Regions (ICTer), Colombo, Sri Lanka, pp. 274–275 (2020). https://doi.org/10.1109/ICTer51097.2020.9325482
51. Luntovskyy, A., Shubyn, B.: Highly-distributed systems based on micro-services and their construction paradigms. In: 2020 IEEE 15th International Conference on Advanced Trends in Radioelectronics, Telecommunications and Computer Engineering (TCSET), Lviv-Slavske, Ukraine, pp. 7–14 (2020). https://doi.org/10.1109/TCSET49122.2020.235378

52. Haque, A., Rahman, R., Rahman, S.: Microservice-based architecture of a software as a service (SaaS) building energy management platform. In: 2020 6th IEEE International Energy Conference (ENERGYCon), Gammarth, Tunisia, pp. 967–972 (2020). https://doi.org/10.1109/ENERGYCon48941.2020.9236617

53. Lee, S., Son, S., Han, J., Kim, J.: Refining micro services placement over multiple kubernetes-orchestrated clusters employing resource monitoring. In: 2020 IEEE 40th International Conference on Distributed Computing Systems (ICDCS), Singapore, Singapore, pp. 1328–1332 (2020). https://doi.org/10.1109/ICDCS47774.2020.00173

54. Rasheedh, J.A., Saradha, S.: Review of micro-services architectures and runtime dynamic binding. In: 2020 Fourth International Conference on I-SMAC (IoT in Social, Mobile, Analytics and Cloud) (I-SMAC), Palladam, India, pp. 1130–1137 (2020). https://doi.org/10.1109/I-SMAC49090.2020.9243335

55. Raychev, N.: Test automation in microservice architecture. IEEE Spectrum (2020)

56. Gong, Y., Gu, F., Chen, K., Wang, F.: The architecture of micro-services and the separation of frond-end and back-end applied in a campus information system. In: 2020 IEEE International Conference on Advances in Electrical Engineering and Computer Applications (AEECA), Dalian, China, pp. 321–324 (2020). https://doi.org/10.1109/AEECA49918.2020.9213662

57. Lv, H., Zhang, T., Zhao, Z., Xu, J., He, T.: The development of real-time large data processing platform based on reactive micro-service architecture. In: 2020 IEEE 4th Information Technology, Networking, Electronic and Automation Control Conference (ITNEC), Chongqing, China, pp. 2003–2006 (2020). https://doi.org/10.1109/ITNEC48623.2020.9084717

58. Lenarduzzi, V., Lomio, F., Saarimäki, N., Taibi, D.: Does migrating a monolithic system to microservices decrease the technical debt?. J. Syst. Softw. **169**, 110710 (2020). ISSN 0164–1212. https://doi.org/10.1016/j.jss.2020.110710

59. Waseem, M., Liang, P., Shahin, M.: A systematic mapping study on microservices architecture in DevOps. J. Syst. Softw. **170**, 110798 (2020). ISSN 0164–1212. https://doi.org/10.1016/j.jss.2020.110798.

60. Srirama, S.N., Adhikari, M., Paul, S.: Application deployment using containers with auto-scaling for microservices in cloud environment. J. Netw. Comput. Appl. **160**, 102629 (2020). ISSN 1084–8045. https://doi.org/10.1016/j.jnca.2020.102629

61. Sha, P., Chen, S., Zheng, L., Liu, X., Tang, H., Li, Y.: Design and implement of microservice system for edge computing. IFAC-PapersOnLine **53**(5), 507–511 (2020). https://doi.org/10.1016/j.ifacol.2021.04.137

62. Avritzer, A., et al.: Scalability assessment of microservice architecture deployment configurations: a domain-based approach leveraging operational profiles and load tests. J. Syst. Softw. **165**, 110564 (2020). ISSN 0164–1212. https://doi.org/10.1016/j.jss.2020.110564

63. Taherizadeh, S., Grobelnik, M.:Key influencing factors of the Kubernetes auto-scaler for computing-intensive microservice-native cloud-based applications. Adv. Eng. Softw. **140**, 102734 (2020). ISSN 0965–9978. https://doi.org/10.1016/j.advengsoft.2019.102734

64. Tao, L., Fan, Y., Zhang, T., Zhao, C., Yang, T.: Research and application on microservices architecture in civil affairs informatization. In: Journal of Physics: Conference Series, vol. 1575, no. 1, p. 012076. IOP Publishing (2020)

65. Abhijeet, K., Smitha, G.R.: Building microservices with event sourcing: a comprehensive review (2020)

66. Dharmaji, N.: A study of containerization as a micro service deployment model. Int. J. Res. Appl. Sci. Eng. Technol. **8**, 1365–1367 (2020). https://doi.org/10.22214/ijraset.2020.5216

67. Kayal, P.: Kubernetes: towards deployment of distributed iot applications in fog computing. In: Companion of the ACM/SPEC International Conference on Performance Engineering, pp. 32–33 2020

68. Pandey, K.K., Joshi, D.: Challenges in realizing the software applications based on micro services architecture. Int. J. Adv. Sci. Technol. **29**(11s), 2301–2313 (2020)

69. Pandey, K.K.: development of an evaluation model for micro services development platforms. Compliance Eng. J. **11**(6), 51–63 (2020). ISSN NO: 0898–3577

70. Pandey, K.K., Joshi, D.: Solutions to challenges in realizing the software applications based on micro services architecture. Int. J. Adv. Sci. Technol. **29**(7), 12687–12698 (2020)

71. Pandey, K.K.: Empirical and practical evaluation of micro services with containerized deployment. Compl. Eng. J. **11**(6), 134–143 (2020). ISSN NO: 0898–3577

72. Ştefan, L.: Blockchain technologies and microservices for open learning communities. a software architecture perspective. In: Conference proceedings of» eLearning and Software for Education (eLSE), vol. 16, no. 03, pp. 126–133. Carol I National Defence University Publishing House (2020)

73. Song, M., Liu, Q., Haihong, E.: A mirco-service tracing system based on istio and kubernetes. In: 2019 IEEE 10th International Conference on Software Engineering and Service Science (ICSESS), Beijing, China, pp. 613–616 (2019). https://doi.org/10.1109/ICSESS47205.2019.9040783

74. Cui, N., Hu, Y., Yu, D., Han, F.: Research and implementation of intelligent workshop IoT cloud platform based on micro-services. In: 2019 IEEE International Conference on Signal Processing, Communications and Computing (ICSPCC), Dalian, China, pp. 1–5 (2019). https://doi.org/10.1109/ICSPCC46631.2019.8960804

75. Eismann, S., Kistowski, J., Grohmann, J., Bauer, A., Schmitt, N., Kounev, S.: TeaStore - a micro-service reference application. In: 2019 IEEE 4th International Workshops on Foundations and Applications of Self* Systems (FAS*W), Umea, Sweden, pp. 263–264 (2019). https://doi.org/10.1109/FAS-W.2019.00073

76. Abidi, S., Essafi, M., Guegan, C.G., Fakhri, M., Witti, H., Ghezala, H.H.B.: A web service security governance approach based on dedicated micro-services. Procedia Comput. Sci. **159**, 372–386 (2019). ISSN 1877–0509. https://doi.org/10.1016/j.procs.2019.09.192

77. Yi, Z., Wang, M., Chen, R.Y., Wang, Y.S., Wang, J.: Research on application of SME manufacturing cloud platform based on micro service architecture. Procedia CIRP **83**, 596–600 (2019). ISSN 2212–8271. https://doi.org/10.1016/j.procir.2019.04.091

78. Ma, S.P., Fan, C.Y., Chuang, Y., Liu, I.H., Lan, C.W.: Graph-based and scenario-driven microservice analysis, retrieval, and testing. Future Gener. Comput. Syst. **100**, 724–735 (2019). ISSN 0167–739X. https://doi.org/10.1016/j.future.2019.05.048

79. Baboi, M., Iftene, A., Gîfu, D.: Dynamic microservices to create scalable and fault tolerance architecture. Procedia Comput. Sci. **159**, 1035–1044. ISSN 1877–0509. https://doi.org/10.1016/j.procs.2019.09.271

80. Li, S., et al.: A dataflow-driven approach to identifying microservices from monolithic applications. J. Syst. Softw. **157**, 110380 (2019). ISSN 0164–1212. https://doi.org/10.1016/j.jss.2019.07.008

81. Yu, Y., Yang, J., Guo, C., Zheng, H., He, J.: Joint optimization of service request routing and instance placement in the microservice system. J. Netw. Comput. Appl. **147**, 102441 (2019). ISSN 1084–8045, https://doi.org/10.1016/j.jnca.2019.102441

82. Di Francesco, P., Lago, P., Malavolta, I.: Architecting with microservices: a systematic mapping study. J. Syst. Softw. **150**, 77–97 (2019). ISSN 0164–1212. https://doi.org/10.1016/j.jss.2019.01.001

83. Zhelev, S., Rozeva, A.: Using microservices and event driven architecture for big data stream processing. In: AIP Conference Proceedings, vol. 2172, no. 1, p. 090010. AIP Publishing LLC (2019)

84. De Alwis, A.A.C., Barros, A., Fidge, C., Polyvyanyy, A.: Availability and scalability optimized microservice discovery from enterprise systems. In: Panetto, H., Debruyne, C., Hepp, M., Lewis, D., Ardagna, C.A., Meersman, R. (eds.) OTM 2019. LNCS, vol. 11877, pp. 496–514. Springer, Cham (2019). https://doi.org/10.1007/978-3-030-33246-4_31

85. Song, M., Zhang, C., Haihong, E.: An auto scaling system for API gateway based on kubernetes. In: 2018 IEEE 9th International Conference on Software Engineering and Service Science (ICSESS), Beijing, China, pp. 109–112 (2018). https://doi.org/10.1109/ICSESS.2018.8663784

86. Fu, G., Sun, J., Zhao, J.: An optimized control access mechanism based on micro-service architecture. In: 2018 2nd IEEE Conference on Energy Internet and Energy System Integration (EI2), Beijing, China, pp. 1–5 (2018). https://doi.org/10.1109/EI2.2018.8582628

87. Premchand, A., Choudhry, A.: Architecture simplification at large institutions using micro services. In: 2018 International Conference on Communication, Computing and Internet of Things (IC3IoT), Chennai, India, pp. 30–35 (2018). https://doi.org/10.1109/IC3IoT.2018.8668173

88. Lin, W., Ma, M., Pan, D., Wang, P.: FacGraph: frequent anomaly correlation graph mining for root cause diagnose in micro-service architecture. In: 2018 IEEE 37th International Performance Computing and Communications Conference (IPCCC), Orlando, FL, USA, pp. 1–8 (2018). https://doi.org/10.1109/PCCC.2018.8711092

89. Hong, X.J., Yang, H.S., Kim, Y.H.: Performance analysis of RESTful API and RabbitMQ for microservice web application. In: 2018 International Conference on Information and Communication Technology Convergence (ICTC), Jeju, Korea (South), pp. 257–259 (2018). https://doi.org/10.1109/ICTC.2018.8539409

90. Xie, Y., Zhou, X., Xie, H., Li, G., Tao, Y.: Research on the architecture and key technologies of integrated platform based on micro service. In: 2018 IEEE 3rd Advanced Information Technology, Electronic and Automation Control Conference (IAEAC), Chongqing, China, pp. 887–893 (2018). https://doi.org/10.1109/IAEAC.2018.8577921

91. Alshuqayran, N., Ali, N., Evans, R.: Towards micro service architecture recovery: an empirical study. In: 2018 IEEE International Conference on Software Architecture (ICSA), Seattle, WA, USA, pp. 47–4709 (2018). https://doi.org/10.1109/ICSA.2018.00014

92. Soldani, J., Tamburri, D.A., Van Den Heuvel, W.J.: The pains and gains of microservices: a systematic grey literature review. J. Syst. Softw. **146**, 215–232 (2018). ISSN 0164–1212. https://doi.org/10.1016/j.jss.2018.09.082

93. Wan, X., Guan, X., Wang, T., Bai, G., Choi, B.Y.: Application deployment using microservice and docker containers: framework and optimization. J. Netw. Comput. Appl. **119**, 97–109 (2018). ISSN 1084–8045. https://doi.org/10.1016/j.jnca.2018.07.003

94. Hiraman, B.R.: A study of apache kafka in big data stream processing. In: 2018 International Conference on Information, Communication, Engineering and Technology (ICICET), pp. 1–3. IEEE (2018)

95. Wauer, M., Sherif, M.A., Ngomo, A.C.N.: Towards a semantic message-driven microservice platform for geospatial and sensor data. In: GeoLD-QuWeDa@ ESWC, pp. 47–58 (2018)

96. Djogic, E., Ribic, S., Donko, D.: Monolithic to microservices redesign of event driven integration platform. In: 2018 41st International Convention on Information and Communication Technology, Electronics and Microelectronics (MIPRO), pp. 1411–1414. IEEE (2018)

97. Containerized Microservices Architecture. https://www.academia.edu/49354877/Containerized_Microservice_architecture

98. Kumar, S.S., Shastry, P.M.M.: Database-per-service for e-learning system with micro-service architecture. In: 2017 International Conference on Smart Technologies for Smart Nation (SmartTechCon), Bengaluru, India, pp. 705–708 (2017). https://doi.org/10.1109/SmartTechCon.2017.8358462

99. Nguyen, P., Nahrstedt, K.: MONAD: self-adaptive micro-service infrastructure for heterogeneous scientific workflows. In: 2017 IEEE International Conference on Autonomic Computing (ICAC), Columbus, OH, USA, pp. 187–196 (2017). https://doi.org/10.1109/ICAC.2017.38

100. Bhamare, D., Samaka, M., Erbad, A., Jain, R., Gupta, L., Chan, H.A.: Multi-objective scheduling of micro-services for optimal service function chains. In: 2017 IEEE International Conference on Communications (ICC), Paris, France, pp. 1–6 (2017). https://doi.org/10.1109/ICC.2017.7996729

101. Vural, H., Koyuncu, M., Guney, S.: A systematic literature review on microservices. In: Gervasi, O., et al. (eds.) ICCSA 2017. LNCS, vol. 10409, pp. 203–217. Springer, Cham (2017). https://doi.org/10.1007/978-3-319-62407-5_14

102. Di Francesco, P., Malavolta, I., Lago, P.: Research on architecting microservices: trends, focus, and potential for industrial adoption. In: 2017 IEEE International Conference on Software Architecture (ICSA), pp. 21–30. IEEE (2017)

103. Guo, D., Wang, W., Zeng, G., Wei, Z.: Microservices architecture based cloudware deployment platform for service computing. In: 2016 IEEE Symposium on Service-Oriented System Engineering (SOSE), Oxford, UK, pp. 358–363 (2016). https://doi.org/10.1109/SOSE.2016.22

104. Chelladhurai, J., Chelliah, P.R., Kumar, S.A.: Securing docker containers from denial of service (DoS) attacks. In: 2016 IEEE International Conference on Services Computing (SCC), San Francisco, CA, USA, pp. 856–859 (2016). https://doi.org/10.1109/SCC.2016.123

105. Napoleão, B., Felizardo, K.R., de Souza, E.F., Vijaykumar, N.L.: Practical similarities and differences between systematic literature reviews and systematic mappings: a tertiary study. In: SEKE, vol. 2017, pp. 85–90 (2017)

106. Richardson, C., Smith, F.: Microservices: From Design to development

107. Newman, S.: Building Micro services. O'Reilly Media, Inc., Boston (2015)

108. Kitchenham, B., Charters, S.: Guidelines for performing systematic literature reviews in software engineering. Engineering **2**, 1051–1052 (2007)

State of the Art in Zero-Knowledge Machine Learning: A Comprehensive Survey

Aneesh Sathe[(✉)], Varun Saxena, P. Akshay Bharadwaj, and S. Sandosh

Vellore Institute of Technology, Chennai, India
aneeshashwinikumar.sathe2021@vitstudent.ac.in

Abstract. In recent years, the field of Machine Learning (ML) has witnessed significant expansion, with its applications spanning various domains such as finance, healthcare, and cybersecurity. However, this expansion has brought about significant challenges concerning privacy and security, particularly as ML models deal with sensitive data. Both organizations and individuals have reservations about sharing proprietary or personal information, primarily due to concerns about potential data breaches and misuse. Furthermore, doubts surrounding model integrity and transparency have raised questions about the reliability of ML predictions. To address these issues, Zero Knowledge Proofs (ZKPs) have emerged as a promising cryptographic technique. ZKPs allow secure computations on encrypted data without revealing any sensitive information. They enable a prover to convince a verifier of a statement's truthfulness without disclosing any underlying data, thereby ensuring data privacy and confidentiality. The paper under consideration conducts an extensive analysis of the burgeoning field of Zero Knowledge Proofs within the context of machine learning applications. It emphasizes the advantages and limitations of ZKPs in preserving data privacy, ensuring computation integrity, and enhancing the security of machine learning systems. The ultimate goal is to foster a deeper understanding of the potentials and challenges associated with integrating ZKPs into modern ML workflows and systems.

Keywords: Zero Knowledge Proofs · Machine Learning · Data Privacy · Data Integrity

1 Introduction

The field of machine learning has undergone significant advancements, revolutionizing data processing and analysis across various domains. However, the rise of these advancements has also brought forth concerns regarding privacy and security. With machine learning models relying on sensitive data, ensuring privacy and maintaining the integrity of the learning process have emerged as critical challenges. In response to these concerns, the concept of zero-knowledge machine learning has gained substantial attention.

Zero-knowledge machine learning aims to strike a delicate balance between preserving privacy and leveraging the utility of machine learning models. By incorporating

S. Rajagopal et al (Eds.): ASCIS 2023, CCIS 2040, pp. 98–110, 2024.
https://doi.org/10.1007/978-3-031-59107-5_7

cryptographic techniques such as zero-knowledge proofs, secure multi-party computation, and homomorphic encryption, researchers have developed innovative approaches that enable privacy-preserving machine learning without compromising model accuracy and effectiveness. This survey paper provides a comprehensive overview of the advancements, challenges, and opportunities within the field of zero-knowledge machine learning.

By examining a diverse range of reference papers, it explores the various techniques and methodologies proposed for preserving privacy in the context of machine learning. The goal is to provide a comprehensive perspective on the current advancements in this emerging field, shedding light on potential applications and limitations of zero-knowledge techniques. Throughout the paper, different approaches used to achieve privacy-preserving machine learning are explored. The Survey includes secure computation protocols, cryptographic primitives, and differential privacy. By discussing the benefits and trade-offs associated with each approach, The survey paper strives to offer perspectives on the applicability and efficiency of these methods.

Furthermore, existing research and implementations are analyzed to offer a clear perspective on the current landscape of zero-knowledge machine learning. The aim of this survey paper is to contribute significantly to the growing body of knowledge within the domain of zero-knowledge machine learning, aiming to offer guidance to researchers, practitioners, and policy-makers who seek insights into and wish to implement privacy-preserving machine learning techniques. By surveying the literature and presenting a comprehensive analysis, it seeks to inspire further innovation and facilitate the development of secure and privacy-enhancing machine learning systems that can address the increasing privacy concerns and regulatory requirements of our time.

2 Related Works

Lee et al. [1] propose an efficient method for verifying the correctness of AI inference services in Convolutional Neural Networks (CNNs) without revealing the weight values. The need for verification arises as clients require assurance that the calculations performed by AI services are accurate, even without access to the weight values. To enable verification without input and weight values, the authors employ Zero-Knowledge Succinct Non-Interactive Arguments of Knowledge (zk-SNARKs) [10]. This work presents several notable contributions.

Firstly, an optimized QAP relation for convolutions is proposed, resulting in an efficient zk-SNARK scheme for CNN verification. Secondly, an efficient construction of the verifiable CNN (vCNN) framework is developed, incorporating QAP-based zk-SNARKs optimized for convolutions, as well as QAP-based zk-SNARKs for Pooling and ReLU operations. These components are interconnected using CP-SNARKs. To address the limitation of slow proving time in zk-SNARKs for practical AI applications, an optimized Quadratic Arithmetic Program (QAP) formula is utilized for convolution operations, significantly reducing the number of multiplications. By leveraging this optimized QAP formula, an efficient zk-SNARK scheme for verifying CNNs is constructed, with the size and proving time linearly dependent on the input and kernel size. The research work [1] also showcases the computational knowledge soundness and the flawless zero-knowledge characteristics of the vCNN construction they put forth. Additionally, the implementation and performance of vCNN are compared to existing zk-SNARK schemes, highlighting significant improvements in key generation, proving time, and CRS size across various CNN models. Experimental results demonstrate the superior performance of vCNN compared to existing schemes.

For instance, the proposed scheme reduces the proving time from 10 years to 8 hours for the VGG16 model, and the CRS size from 1400 TB to 80 GB. These improvements make the proposed vCNN the first efficient verifiable convolutional neural network solution, revolutionizing the feasibility of verification in CNNs. The Authors provided the efficient solution for verifying the correctness of CNN models using zk-SNARKs is provided, enabling clients and third parties to validate AI inference services without access to sensitive weight values. The proposed vCNN framework demonstrates significant performance gains in terms of proving time and CRS size, making it a practical and scalable solution for real-world CNN applications (Table 1).

Table 1. vCNN and Gro16 (Comparative Study Metrics)

	vCNN				
	setup	prove	verify	|CRS|	|proof|
LeNet-5	19.47 s	9.34 s	75ms	40.07MB	
AlexNet	20 min	18 min	130ms	2.1 GB	2803 bits
VGG16	10 hours	8 hours	19.4s	83 GB	
VGG16wFC	2 days	2 days	19.4s	420 GB	

Gro16				
setup	prove	verify	|CRS|	|proof|
1.5 hours	0.75 hours	75ms	11 GB	
16 days	14 days	130 ms	2.5 TB	1019 bits
13 years	10 years	19.4s	1400 TB	
13 years	10 years	19.4s	1400 TB	

Feng et al. [2] introduce ZEN, which is an optimizing compiler designed to generate efficient zero-knowledge neural network inference schemes that can be verified. The Paper addresses the computational cost challenge by incorporating two key optimizations: R1CS friendly quantization and stranded encoding of R1CS Constraints. These optimizations significantly reduce the number of constraints in the generated schemes compared to a vanilla implementation in zk-SNARK, with an average reduction of $15.35\times$ in R1CS Constraints.

ZEN's primary advancements encompass pioneering the field as the initial optimizing compiler capable of generating efficient verifiable zero-knowledge neural network inference schemes. It offers potential applications in privacy-preserving tasks like medical AI, identity verification, and blockchain oracles.ZEN's implementation comprises three main components: a quantization engine, circuit generators, and a scheme aggregator. The quantization engine is responsible for converting a pre-trained floating-point PyTorch model into a quantized model using quantizations suitable for zk-SNARK protocols. Circuit generators create circuit components for different kernel types, such as fully connected, convolutional, average pooling, ReLU, and commitment. Stranded encoding optimization is applied to fully connected and convolutional circuit generators. The ultimate zero-knowledge proof systems in the ZENinfer scheme are generated by the scheme aggregator, which integrates all components together.

Upon analyzing the constraint size distribution in the LeNet-Face-Large model, it is observed that convolution and fully connected kernels emerge as the primary contributors to the constraints. The commitment scheme contributes a smaller portion of the constraints. In ZEN, notable optimizations lead to a substantial reduction in the number of constraints associated with the neural network inference part. Meanwhile, enhancements in commitment efficiency are identified as potential areas for future exploration and development. The runtime examination of ZEN's proving phase demonstrates that as the number of constraints rises, the inlining of linear combinations becomes a predominant factor. ZEN's optimization techniques successfully curtail the count of these linear combinations, leading to heightened efficiency. The findings indicate that models with an increased count of constraints result in extended prover and setup durations and necessitate a larger Common Reference String (CRS) size. As the number of constraints grows, the overall computational cost of ZENinfer also escalates. In the case of larger models, such as LeNet-Face-large applied to the ORL dataset, which involves over 318,505 thousand constraints, ZENinfer demands roughly 20,000 seconds for setup and proving, with the CRS size expanding to approximately 100 gigabytes.

To address the resource-intensive characteristics of ZENacc, the paper introduces an alternative approach that focuses on parallelizing the inference step for the testing dataset across multiple machines. This method incorporates a prediction accuracy commitment sum check circuit, offering a means to alleviate the memory and time requirements typically associated with ZENacc (Tables 2 and 3).

Table 2. Overall performance of ZENinfer. * indicates an estimated value

Model-Dataset	Constraints (K)	Linear Combinations (K)	Setup (s)	Comm. (s)	Prove (s)	Verify (s)	CRS Size (GB)
ShallowNet-MNIST	4,380	18,008	154.87	0.310	147.07	0.097	1.395
LeNet-small-CIFAR	4,061	19,863	137.67	0.255	125.53	0.023	1.144
LeNet-medium-CIFAR	23,681	130,054	1033.59	1.069	1000.79	0.106	7.059
LeNet-Face-small-ORL	20,607	95,406	787.79	1.226	766.76	0.103	6.359
LeNet-Face-medium-ORL	83,416	474,277	4915.39	3.779	4710.13	0.372	25.531
LeNet-Face-large-ORL	318,353	1,818,988	20,000*	15.058	20,000*	1.5*	100*

Table 3. Overall Performance of ZENacc Scheme

Model-Dataset	Constraints (K)	Linear Combinations (K)	Setup (s)	Comm. (s)	Prove (s)	Verify (s)	CRS Size (GB)
ShallowNet-MNIST	13,181	75,210	291.67	0.366	256.02	0.17	1.75
LeNet-small-CIFAR	88,294	675,365	466.21	0.265	413.24	0.13	2.21
LeNet-medium-CIFAR	563,545	5,762,645	1511.20	1.069	1323.67	0.21	8.13
LeNet-Face-small-ORL	284,341	2,395,061	1316.51	1.081	1158.21	0.21	7.43
LeNet-Face-medium-ORL	1,809,239	21,266,440	5350.75	3.737	4863.41	0.47	26.61
LeNet-Face-large-ORL	5,792,208	77,689,757	20,000*	14.587	20,000*	1.5*	100*

3 Convolutional Neural Networks with Zero-Knowledge Techniques

In the work by Liu et al. [3], they introduce zkCNN, an innovative zero-knowledge proof framework designed specifically for Convolutional Neural Networks (CNNs). The primary objective of zkCNN is to enable the owner of a CNN model to furnish evidence of the model's predictions while safeguarding the confidentiality of any sensitive information pertaining to the model. Additionally, this framework extends its capabilities to demonstrate the accuracy of a confidential CNN model when applied to a publicly available dataset.

To achieve this, the paper introduces a new sum-check protocol that is designed to accelerate the computation of Fast Fourier Transforms (FFT) and convolutions. This protocol enables the efficient calculation of proofs with linear prover time, surpassing the asymptotic computation result. Specifically, the protocol is applied to two-dimensional (2-D) convolutions and achieves optimal prover time and proof size, resulting in highly efficient proof generation. The paper proposes various improvements and extensions to interactive proof techniques for validating Convolutional Neural Network (CNN) predictions. These enhancements encompass the validation of multiple components within CNNs, such as verifying the accuracy of the convolutional layer, assessing the correctness of the ReLU activation function, and confirming the integrity of the max pooling operation.

Notably, Liu et al. [3] designed an efficient circuit gadget that computes ReLU activation function as well as performs max-pooling, requiring only a single bit-decomposition per number. The zkCNN scheme is implemented and evaluated using various CNN models, such as LeNet, VGG11, and VGG16, along with popular datasets like MNIST and CIFAR-10. The practical performance of zkCNN is demonstrated, showcasing fast prover and verifier times as well as compact proof sizes. As an example, the process of generating a proof for a prediction made by LeNet on an MNIST dataset sample requires just 0.44 seconds, while the prover time for VGG16 is a mere 88 seconds. Remarkably, the verifier time is exceptionally fast, even outperforming local computation of CNN predictions. The memory consumption of zkCNN when running on VGG16 is well-suited for typical personal computer configurations.

Comparative analysis against existing schemes highlights the superior prover time efficiency of zkCNN. It significantly outperforms vCNN and ZEN on various CNN models, enabling the provability of large CNN predictions within minutes. Although zkCNN exhibits a larger proof size compared to some existing schemes, it does not necessitate a trusted setup or a large common reference string. Furthermore, the research paper introduces zkCNN, which tackles the issue of verifying the precision of CNN models across numerous input samples, a task that has not been previously tackled in other studies due to scalability constraints. The efficiency of zkCNN in verifying accuracy on a dataset comprising 20 images is demonstrated by the authors. The results showcase faster prover time, a compact proof size, and rapid verifier time, indicating its effectiveness (Tables 4 and 5).

Table 4. Performance of zkCNN

	LeNet	VGG11	VGG16
sumcheck	0.280s	28.9s	57.7s
poly commit	0.161s	19.0s	30.6s
Total prover	**0.441s**	**47.8s**	**88.3s**
sumcheck	0.900ms	2.70ms	3.80ms
poly commit	4.90ms	36.5ms	55.5ms
Total verifier	**5.80ms**	**39.3ms**	**59.3ms**
sumcheck	45.9KB	110KB	147KB
poly commit	25.4KB	194KB	194KB
Total proof	**71.3KB**	**304KB**	**341KB**

Table 5. Comparison of zkCNN to existing schemes. * indicates an expected value

LeNet (average pooling)			
	prover	proof	verifier
Ours	0.49s	63.6KB	5.5ms
vCNN [34]	5.49s	0.34KB	84ms
LeNet (CIFAR-10 & average pooling)			
	prover	proof	verifier
Ours	0.56s	68.4KB	5.6ms
ZEN [23]	119.5s	0.28KB	18.6ms
VGG16			
Ours	88.3s	341KB	59.3ms
vCNN [34]	31 hours*	0.34KB	20s*

4   Zero-Knowledge Machine Learning (Zk-Ml) Inference Pipeline

Zhang et al. [4] introduce an innovative approach to efficient and secure machine learning (ML) inference. The authors propose ezDPS, a zero-knowledge ML inference pipeline that enables the processing of data in multiple stages while ensuring verifiability without revealing private model parameters. The paper addresses the limitations of previous zero-knowledge ML schemes, which often suffer from accuracy issues or rely on large-scale training data.

The core idea behind ezDPS is to leverage well-established ML algorithms, such as Discrete Wavelet Transformation (DWT), Principal Components Analysis (PCA), and Support Vector Machine (SVM), in multiple stages to achieve high accuracy. To facilitate essential ML operations, the authors introduce new gadgets and present a formal security analysis of the proposed scheme.

The methodology utilized in the research paper involves employing an argument of knowledge for NP relations and a commit-and-prove zero-knowledge proof protocol. To support NP statements expressed as Rank-1 Constraint System (R1CS), the authors adopt the Spartan zero-knowledge proof system. The ezDPS framework encompasses three distinct phases: data preprocessing, feature extraction (using DWT and PCA), and ML classification (employing SVM).

To ensure the accuracy of the model, the server commits to the model parameters and provides a zero-knowledge Proof-of-Accuracy (zkPoA).Extensive experimental results exemplify that ezDPS surpasses generic circuit-based approaches in terms of both efficiency and accuracy. The proposed scheme exhibits superior performance while addressing the privacy concerns associated with ML models. Furthermore, ezDPS holds immense potential for various applications, including proof-of-genuine ML services, fair ML model trading platforms, and mitigating the reproducibility problem in ML research. The investigation conducted in this paper showcases compelling findings regarding the efficiency metrics of ezDPS compared to the baseline approach. The Authors' analysis consistently demonstrates the superior performance of ezDPS, outperforming the baseline by one to three orders of magnitude across all metrics.

Notably, as the number of classes increases, the advantages of ezDPS become even more pronounced. The ezDPS technique demonstrates striking efficiency when compared to the baseline approach, exhibiting improvements of up to three orders of magnitudes across all measured metrics. Comparative analysis across various datasets reveals substantial gains in proving, verification, and proof size reduction with ezDPS. For instance, on the UCR-ECG dataset, ezDPS achieves proving times 321 to 518 seconds faster for 4 to 42 classes, outperforming the baseline. Similarly, on the LFW dataset, ezDPS achieves a proving time that is approximately 1842 times faster for 2048 classes. The verification time and proof size also exhibit significant improvements with ezDPS, which offers highly efficient verification and optimal bandwidth utilization, making it a compelling alternative to the baseline approach (Fig. 1).

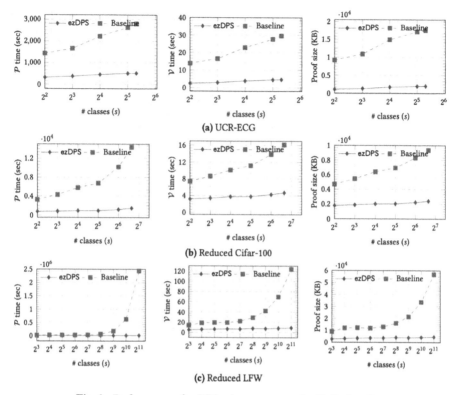

Fig. 1. Performance of ezDPS scheme compared with the baseline

5 Federated Learning with Zero-Knowledge Proofs

Xing et al. [5] present a novel approach called Zero-Knowledge Proof-based Federated Learning (ZKP-FL) scheme, which utilizes blockchain technology to mitigate privacy concerns associated with data sharing. The primary objective is to enable collaborative learning while ensuring the confidentiality of user data. The ZKP-FL scheme encompasses three distinct phases: model distribution, model training, and model aggregation. During the model distribution phase, the training algorithm is partitioned into identical pieces, and a shared reference string is generated for zero-knowledge proof generation and verification. These algorithm pieces, along with the reference string and constraints, are then transmitted to the trainers.

In the subsequent model training phase, trainers utilize their respective datasets to train local models while generating zero-knowledge proofs to validate the training process. To preserve data privacy, trainers apply modifications to the proofs and data before transmitting them to the publisher. Finally, in the model aggregation phase, the publisher verifies the proofs, engages in a secure sum protocol with select trainers, and computes the global model without revealing individual local models. The research paper also addresses practical challenges encountered in the ZKP-FL scheme, such as handling fractional and integer values and accommodating non-linear operations. To overcome these obstacles, the authors propose the Practical ZKP-FL scheme, which effectively resolves these issues. The Authors emphasize the significance of partitioning the training algorithm within the secure sum protocol to optimize time and computation. This approach enables practical setup operations and parallel execution of proof generation and verification, leading to a substantial reduction in time requirements. Furthermore, the study investigates the impact of algorithmic piece size on running costs. Smaller pieces result in shorter running times for trainers, enhancing system efficiency. These findings underscore the advantages of these techniques in enhancing the performance of privacy-preserving federated learning systems (Tables 6 and 7).

Table 6. The experimental results of a classification task and a prediction task

Task	Setup Time (s)	Proof Generation Time (per proof) (s)	Proof Verification Time (per proof) (s)	Number of Proof	Accuracy
Iris classification	950.34	89.99	25.75	90,000	96%
Price prediction	514.19	50.09	1.55	500	88%

Table 7. The experimental results of the impact of the piece size

Piece Size (number of epoch)	1	2	3	5	10	15
Setup Time (s)	508.25	966.43	1518.59	2622.10	5247.52	7268.61
Proof generation (per proof) (s)	50.74	95.95	140.70	225.10	439.16	533.24
Proof verification (per proof) (s)	1.56	1.54	1.19	1.15	1.13	1.12
Circuit Constraints	973,617	1,923,246	2,873,142	4,773,477	9,525,930	14,279,460
Points in CRS	968,155	1,912,324	2,856,760	4,746,175	9,471,328	14,197,558
Arithmetic Circuit Size (KB)	162,612	323,291	484,035	805,678	1,610,476	2,416,076
Proving Key Size (KB)	347,279	687,122	1,092,583	1,903,677	3,800,842	5,674,057
Verification Key Size (per proof) (KB)	2	2	2	2	2	2
Proof Size (per proof) (KB)	5	5	5	5	5	5

6 Mystique

Weng et al. [6] present design, development, and evaluation of a zero-knowledge (ZK) system called Mystique. This system addresses the limitations of existing ZK protocols in proving results about complex computations efficiently. The authors suggest effective methodologies for three types of conversions: arithmetic to boolean values, committed to authenticated values, and fixed-point to floating-point values.

Furthermore, the system is integrated into Rosetta, a privacy-preserving framework based on TensorFlow, demonstrating that Mystique can prove the correctness of private image inference using committed ResNet-101 models with minimal loss of accuracy. Notably, this is the first system to support ZK proofs for neural-network models with over 100 layers. This integration enables ZK proofs for neural-network inference on large models with millions of parameters.

Mystique incorporates fundamental components for producing efficient ZK proofs in large-scale neural network inference. Additionally, the researchers introduce optimized protocols to facilitate seamless transitions between numeric and Boolean values, committed and authenticated values, and fixed-point and floating-point numbers (Fig. 2).

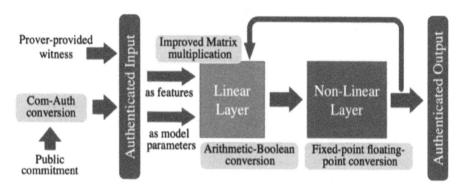

Fig. 2. Summary of the ZK neural-network Inference System

The paper provides detailed information on the methodology employed for arithmetic-Boolean conversion in ZK proofs. The authors utilise, Πzk-edaBits, that efficiently constructs ZK-friendly extended doubly authenticated bits (zk-edaBits).

These zk-edaBits are then utilized for secure conversions between arithmetic and Boolean circuits. Additionally, the authors present protocols, ΠA2B and ΠB2A, for converting authenticated wire values from arithmetic to Boolean circuits and vice versa. The security of the protocols is proven in the presence of static, malicious adversaries, and the statistical error is analyzed. The authors benchmarked the performance of the ZK protocols using three neural network models: LeNet-52, ResNet-50, and ResNet-101. The experiments demonstrated the scalability and efficiency of the protocols, with significant improvements compared to existing approaches. The paper also discusses the accuracy of the ZK protocols and their applicability to large-scale machine learning inference. The ZK proof for matrix multiplication achieves a sevenfold improvement when compared to the state-of-the-art protocol. The integration of the building blocks into a ZK system enables ZK proofs for large neural networks, with performance summarized for LeNet-5, ResNet-50, and ResNet-101 models.

The paper [6] explores three distinct scenarios that involve the privacy of model parameters and feature input. Within these scenarios, the parameters and the input can be either privately held by the prover or shared between both parties. The research concentrates on three distinct neural networks: LeNet-5, ResNet-50, and ResNet-101. While

LeNet-5 is relatively straightforward, ResNet-50 and ResNet-101 represent cutting-edge models in terms of accuracy and complexity.

Additional examination indicates that when the model is kept private, the overall execution time is longer compared to when the model parameters are made public. This discrepancy arises due to the increased computational requirements of zero-knowledge proofs for private models. Irrespective of the specific setting, the inference process for LeNet-5 alone takes several seconds to complete. In terms of timing, the study reports that ResNet-50 requires approximately 2.6-5.6 minutes, while ResNet-101, on a 200 Mbps network, typically requires between 4.4 to 9 minutes to complete their specific tasks. These findings provide insights into the timeframes necessary for the considered neural networks to perform their operations in the given scenarios. The paper also discusses the performance and execution times for specific applications, such as ZK proofs for evasion attacks and private benchmarking (Tables 8 and 9).

Table 8. Performance of zero-knowledge neural-network inference (CIFAR-10 dataset has been used to train all models)

Model	Image	LeNet-5	ResNet-50	ResNet-101
Communication				
Private	Private	16.5 MB	1.27 GB	1.98 GB
Private	Public	16.5 MB	1.27 GB	1.98 GB
Public	Private	16.4 MB	0.53 GB	0.99 GB
Execution time (seconds) in a 50 Mbps network				
Private	Private	7.3	465	736
Private	Public	7.5	463	735
Public	Private	6.5	210	369
Execution time (seconds) in a 200 Mbps network				
Private	Private	5.9	333	535
Private	Public	5.5	336	541
Public	Private	4.9	158	262

Table 9. Efficiency of the Zero-Knowledge system, tested on different applications (200 Mbps Network utilized for reporting Execution Time)

ML applications	LeNet-5	ResNet-50	ResNet-101
ZK for evasion attacks	9.8 *s*	316 *s*	524 *s*
ZK for genuine inference	7.2 *s*	16.4 *m*	28 *m*
ZK for private benchmark	8.2 *m*	4.4 *h*	7.3 *h*

7 Conclusion

In conclusion, the use of Zero Knowledge Proofs (ZKPs) in machine learning holds great promise for addressing privacy and security concerns while still enabling valuable insights and data-driven decision-making. ZKPs provide a powerful mechanism to validate the correctness of computations without revealing sensitive input data, allowing for trust and transparency in collaborative settings. Furthermore, the emergence of ZK-STARKs and ZK-Rollups further enhances the potential of ZKPs in machine learning. ZK-STARKs offer efficient proof generation and verification processes, reducing computational overhead and enabling scalability. On the other hand, ZK-Rollups provide an avenue for aggregating and compressing large amounts of data, improving the efficiency of computations and reducing storage requirements. By leveraging these advancements, ZKPs can significantly enhance the existing results in machine learning, fostering a future where privacy and accuracy can coexist harmoniously. Future research should strive to refine protocols, address scalability, and explore new applications of existing technology, creating a seamless integration of Zero Knowledge Proofs into modern Machine Learning workflows. Through innovation, the convergence of privacy, security, and data driven decision-making will define the next frontier in Privacy-Preserving Machine Learning.

References

1. Lee, S., Ko, H., Kim, J., Oh, H.: vCNN: verifiable convolutional neural network. IACR Cryptology ePrint Archive, 2020/584 (2020)
2. Feng, B., Qin, L., Zhang, Z., Ding, Y., Chu, S.: ZEN: an optimizing compiler for verifiable, zero-knowledge neural network inferences (2021)
3. Liu, T., Xie, X., Zhang, Y.: zkCNN: zero knowledge proofs for convolutional neural network predictions and accuracy. In: CCS 2021 - Proceedings of the 2021 ACM SIGSAC Conference on Computer and Communications Security. Proceedings of the ACM Conference on Computer and Communications Security, 27th ACM Annual Conference on Computer and Communication Security, CCS 2021, Virtual, Republic of Korea, pp. 2968–2985. Association for Computing Machinery (2021). https://doi.org/10.1145/3460120.3485379
4. Wang, H., Hoang, T.: ezDPS: an efficient and zero-knowledge machine learning inference pipeline. In: Proceedings on Privacy Enhancing Technologies 2023, pp. 430–448 (2023). https://doi.org/10.56553/popets-2023-0061

5. Xing, Z., et al.: Zero-knowledge proof-based practical federated learning on blockchain (2023)
6. Weng, C., Yang, K., Xie, X., Katz, J., Wang, X.S.: Mystique: efficient conversions for zero-knowledge proofs with applications to machine learning. IACR Cryptology ePrint Archive, 2021/730 (2021)
7. Zhang, J., Fang, Z., Zhang, Y., Song, D.: Zero knowledge proofs for decision tree predictions and accuracy, pp. 2039–2053 (2020). https://doi.org/10.1145/3372297.3417278
8. Thaler, J.: Time-optimal interactive proofs for circuit evaluation. In: Canetti, R., Garay, J.A. (eds.) CRYPTO 2013. LNCS, vol. 8043, pp. 71–89. Springer, Heidelberg (2013). https://doi.org/10.1007/978-3-642-40084-1_5
9. Ben-Sasson, E., Chiesa, A., Genkin, D., Tromer, E., Virza, M.: SNARKs for C: verifying program executions succinctly and in zero knowledge. In: Canetti, R., Garay, J.A. (eds.) CRYPTO 2013. LNCS, vol. 8043, pp. 90–108. Springer, Heidelberg (2013). https://doi.org/10.1007/978-3-642-40084-1_6
10. Chen, T., Lu, H., Kunpittaya, T., Luo, A.: A review of zk-SNARKs. arXiv preprint arXiv:2202.06877 (2022)
11. Campanelli, M., Fiore, D., Querol, A.: LegoSNARK: modular design and composition of succinct zero-knowledge proofs. In: Proceedings of the 2019 ACM SIGSAC Conference on Computer and Communications Security (CCS 2019), pp. 2075–2092. Association for Computing Machinery, New York (2019). https://doi.org/10.1145/3319535.3339820
12. Xie, T., Zhang, J., Zhang, Y., Papamanthou, C., Song, D.: Libra: succinct zero-knowledge proofs with optimal prover computation. In: Boldyreva, A., Micciancio, D. (eds.) CRYPTO 2019. LNCS, vol. 11694, pp. 733–764. Springer, Cham (2019). https://doi.org/10.1007/978-3-030-26954-8_24
13. Zhang, Y., Genkin, D., Katz, J., Papadopoulos, D., Papamanthou, C.: A zero-knowledge version of vSQL. IACR Cryptology ePrint Archive, 2017/1146 (2017)
14. Lavaur, T., Detchart, J., Lacan, J., Chanel, C.P.C.: Modular zk-rollup on-demand. J. Netw. Comput. Appl. **217**, 103678 (2023). https://doi.org/10.1016/j.jnca.2023.103678
15. Santoso, I., Christyono, Y.: Zk-SNARKs as a cryptographic solution for data privacy and security in the digital era. Int. J. Mech. Comput. Manuf. Res. **12**, 53–58 (2023). https://doi.org/10.35335/computational.v12i2.122
16. Baghery, K.: Reducing trust and improving security in zk-SNARKs and commitments (2020). https://doi.org/10.13140/RG.2.2.16777.47205
17. Panait, A.-E., Olimid, R.F.: On using zk-SNARKs and zk-STARKs in blockchain-based identity management. In: Maimut, D., Oprina, A.-G., Sauveron, D. (eds.) SecITC 2020. LNCS, vol. 12596, pp. 130–145. Springer, Cham (2021). https://doi.org/10.1007/978-3-030-69255-1_9
18. Hou, D., Zhang, J., Huang, S., Peng, Z., Ma, J., Zhu, X.: Privacy-preserving energy trading using blockchain and zero knowledge proof. In: 2022 IEEE International Conference on Blockchain (Blockchain), Espoo, Finland, pp. 412–418 (2022). https://doi.org/10.1109/Blockchain55522.2022.00064
19. Dang, H.-V., Phuong, T.V.X., Nguyen, T.D., Hoang, T.: ZAC: efficient zero-knowledge dynamic universal accumulator and application to zero-knowledge elementary database. In: 2022 IEEE 4th International Conference on Trust, Privacy and Security in Intelligent Systems, and Applications (TPS-ISA), Atlanta, GA, USA, pp. 248–257 (2022). https://doi.org/10.1109/TPS-ISA56441.2022.00038
20. Chen, P., et al.: ZeroKBC: a comprehensive benchmark for zero-shot knowledge base completion. In: 2022 IEEE International Conference on Data Mining Workshops (ICDMW), Orlando, FL, USA, pp. 1–6 (2022). https://doi.org/10.1109/ICDMW58026.2022.00117
21. Ryu, H., Kang, D., Won, D.: On a partially verifiable multi-party multi-argument zero-knowledge proof. In: 2021 15th International Conference on Ubiquitous Information Management and Communication (IMCOM), Seoul, Korea (South), pp. 1–8 (2021). https://doi.org/10.1109/IMCOM51814.2021.9377407

IoT Based ECG to Grayscale Representation for the Prediction of Artery Deposition

G. Pandiselvi[1,2(✉)], C. P. Chandran[2], and S. Rajathi[3]

[1] Department of Computer Science, Madurai Kamaraj University, Madurai 625 021,
Tamil Nadu, India
pandiselvi89.g@gmail.com

[2] Department of Computer Science, Ayya Nadar Janaki Ammal College, Sivakasi 626 124,
Tamil Nadu, India
chandran_ts115@anjaconline.org

[3] Department of Computer Science, M.V. Muthiah Government College for Women,
Dindigul 624 001, Tamil Nadu, India

Abstract. The study and design entitled "IoT based ECG Grayscale representation for the prediction of Artery Deposition" was designed in response to the recent sharp rise in the number of different heart abnormalities affecting both older and younger people. The Internet of Things (IoT) age is far more beneficial for a variety of applications. The purpose of this study is to make it easier to get the ECGs of the patients, to continually monitor them, and to identify any patient problems. The Internet of Things (IoT) components needed to get a person's ECG include an Arduino UNO microcontroller, an AD8232 ECG Sensor, and ECG Electrodes. There are three phases to this work. Using IoT devices, we physically collect an ECG signal from a person in the first phase. We are removing the noisy data from the ECG we acquired in the second step. Additionally, we divided the ECG's 12 leads into segments, which were then represented as a grayscale image. To determine if the ECG is normal or abnormal, we analyze the data from the previous phase in the final phase.

Keywords: IoT · Heart Monitoring system · Segmentation · Classification · machine learning

1 Introduction

ECG monitoring technologies are flattering supplementary and more ubiquitous within the literature. It is outstandingly complicated for researchers and healthcare professionals to select, measure up to, and appraise systems that meet their goals and the requirements for monitoring [2, 3]. During this study, we use reasonably priced, clear-cut IoT devices to easily and quickly get the ECG using sensor technologies.

S. Rajagopal et al (Eds.): ASCIS 2023, CCIS 2040, pp. 111–124, 2024.
https://doi.org/10.1007/978-3-031-59107-5_8

2   System Specifications

2.1   Hardware Description

2.1.1   Arduino Uno Microcontroller

It is an open-source microcontroller board designed, based on the Microchip ATmega328P microprocessor [1]. It can be programmed using the Arduino IDE with a type B USB cable [4]. It resembles the Arduino Nano and Leonardo in certain ways [5, 6] (Fig. 1).

Fig. 1. Arduino Uno Microcontroller

2.1.2   AD8232 ECG Sensor

An integrated signal conditioning block for ECG and other biopotential measurement applications is the AD8232 ECG Sensor (Fig. 2).

Fig. 2. AD8232 ECG Sensor

2.1.3 ECG Electrodes

A circular self-adhesive pad and a flat, paper-thin sticker are typical electrodes. The first is usually used in a single ECG recording. The second is used for uninterrupted recordings because it sticks improved. ECG Electrodes' functions include strong adhesion, simple fixation and removal, high conductivity solid gel, hypoallergenic properties, and foam base (Fig. 3).

Fig. 3. Electrodes

2.1.4 Arudino IDE

Apart from a text editor for writing code, a message area, a text console, a toolbar with buttons for frequently used operations, are available. An Arduino sketch must contain the functions setup() and loop().The programming language used by Arduino is comparable to C++ and Python.

2.1.5 C++ Code for IoT Devices

One of the most popular languages for creating Internet of Things (IoT) applications and hardware is C++. C++, an extension of the C language, offers low-level projects and embedded programming, both of which are necessary for creating IoT devices.

3 System Analysis

3.1 Previous Works

The embedded technology has practically permeated every aspect of daily life, and the healthcare industry is no exception. As people's awareness of their health issues increases, there is an increasing need for diagnostic centers and health clinics that are fully equipped. Different physiological and abnormal heart conditions can be identified by an ECG signal. The heart examining system also aids in influential whether or not a person has any heart conditions. It is consummate by measuring the heart rate. In that system, an Atmega controller is used to scan the ECG signal and hunt for patterns contained by a regular choice. If the patterns fall within that range, the system declares the patient to be in the normal range; if not, a heart condition of some sort is present. On the Internet of Things, the result is sent as an alert message. They use IoTGecko in this instance to create the internet-based IoT signaling component.

3.2 Proposed System

With the AD8232 ECG Sensor and Arduino, we present this work on Internet of Things-based ECG and heart monitoring. To view a pattern from a one-dimensional ECG signal, researchers have studied the algorithm for converting ECGs to grayscale mapping. The study's goals are to improve ECG using time series and grayscale mapping. We used the contour technique to convert the images to grayscale, find the trace, and then extract only the necessary signal from the images. A one-dimensional signal is created from the original image. The image is then scaled using MinMaxScaler. Save the 1D signal values in a.csv file for each lead (1–12) signal present in each ECG image. Combine all 12 lead values with the target label added into a single csv file. We determine whether the ECG is normal or abnormal after dimensionality reduction.

4   Methodology

Phase 1, Phase 2, and Phase 3 are the three phases that make up the methodology (Fig. 4).

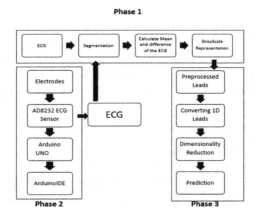

Fig. 4. Methodology used

4.1   Module Description

4.1.1   Phase 1: ECG to Grayscale Representation

- ECG Signal
- Segmentation
- Calculate mean and difference of ECG
- Grayscale Representation

4.1.2   Phase 2: IoT to ECG Signal

- Electrodes
- AD8232 ECG SENSOR
- ARDUINO UNO
- ARDUINO IDE

4.1.3   Phase 3: Grayscale Representation to Prediction

- Preprocessed Leads
- Converting 1D Signals
- Dimensionality Reduction

Phase 1: ECG to Grayscale Representation ECG Signal
Electrical signal from the heart is recorded by an electrocardiogram (ECG or EKG) to glance for diverse heart conditions. Electrodes are placed on the chest to capture the electrical impulses that drive heartbeat.

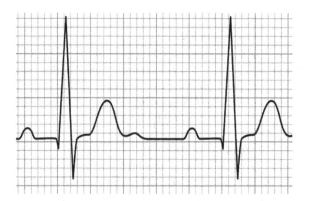

Fig. 5. ECG or EKG Signal

An ECG is used to stumble on Arrhythmias, Coronary Artery Disease, Heart Attacks, and Cardiomyopathy. A series of ECGs can also be used to observe a patient over time if they have already been diagnosed with a heart condition or are taking medication that is known to have potentially negative effects on the heart [7].

Segmentation
Segmentation is the process of dividing an image into areas with comparable characteristics, such as contrast, brightness, color, and texture. To divide the objects in an image, segmentation is used. By isolating only necessary areas, medical image segmentation enables a more accurate analysis of anatomical data, which is one of its main advantages. It is necessary to segment out specific structures for some procedures, like implant design, for instance in heart disease like cardiovascular disease. The best imaging for segmentation includes computed tomography (CT), digital mammography, and magnetic resonance imaging (MRI).

In this work, we converted the ECG signal to leads using watershed segmentation. In a grayscale image, watersheds are changing. Through the detection of lines that form ridges and basins, this method identifies the areas between the watershed lines. Based on pixel height, it divides images into various regions, grouping pixels with the same gray value. The processing of medical images is one of the key use cases for the watershed technique.

Calculate Mean and Difference of ECG

Image input is required for two-dimensional data. Therefore, by plotting each ECG beat as a separate 128 × 128 grayscale image, we converted ECG signals into ECG images. The Q-wave peak time is used to slice each ECG beat. Thus, by centering the Q-wave peak signal and excluding the first and last ECG signals from the prior and subsequent Q-wave peak signals, we were able to define a single ECG beat image. A single ECG beat range can be defined as follows using the time information:

$$T(n) = T(Qpeak(n + 1) + T(Qpeak(n + 1) - 20)$$

Three steps are involved in converting an ECG signal to grayscale, and they are as follows: [1].

Step 1: Calculate the Difference ECGs

In this step, the signal amplitude variation for each time instant (epoch) of the signal as shown in (Fig. 5) will be examined. We can examine a signal's hidden attribute by looking at how its amplitude changes. Following the difference ECG calculations, the positive value of the difference is determined by applying the absolute sign to the difference ECG results. For step two, the fundamental information is provided by difference ECGs and absolute difference ECGs.

Step 2: Calculate the Mean of the signal

The signal's mean gives information about the fluctuation in the signal. The Mean of ECGs (MECG), Mean Difference of ECGs (MD), and Mean Absolute Difference of ECGs (MAD) signals are the three difference signals for which the mean can be calculated in this implementation. These three means value signals offer a wealth of data for the interpretation of ECGs. There are nine (9) different window sizes in this case, and the means have been calculated for each of them in order to obtain more precise information for the interpretation of ECGs. For performing grayscale conversion, this next step yields a very helpful result.

Step3: Performing the Grayscale conversion

Once the signals' means have been determined, converting to grayscale is simple to do. For this task, a 9 × 9 grouped pixel matrix is set up as a display to convert ECG into patterns. A 9 × 9 covariance matrix can be produced by converting the nine window sizes from step two into vectors, and this matrix can then be used to produce a 9 × 9 matrix for 2D grayscale mapping.

Grayscale Representation

A grayscale image is one in which the value of each pixel is a single sample in lieu of only an amount of light; Grayscale images are distinct from one-bit bitonal black-and-white images, which, in the context of computer imaging, are images with only two colors: black and white (also called bilevel or binary images). Grayscale is a collection of tones with no discernible color. The amount of light that each grayscale display pixel on a monitor carries varies from the lightest amount, or black, to the brightest amount, or white [8] (Fig. 6).

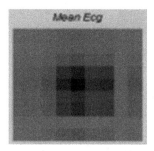

Fig. 6. Grayscale

Phase 2: IoT to ECG Signal

The literature is preparatory to mention ECG monitoring technologies more and more frequently. As a result, it is very challenging for researchers and medical professionals to choose, evaluate, and compare systems that satisfy their objectives and monitoring needs. With developments in sensor technologies, communication infrastructure, data processing and modeling, and analytics algorithms, the risk of impairments could be better controlled than in the past. These systems have significantly evolved over the past few decades due to the development and widespread use of ECG monitoring systems in the healthcare industry, as well as the emergence of smart supporting technologies. In this study, we obtain the ECG quickly and easily using inexpensive, simple IoT devices.

Serial Plotter

In our work, the Arduino IDE window's plotter displays the ECG signal. One useful tool for tracking various types of data sent from our Arduino board is the Serial Plotter tool. It prints data "terminal style" in a manner similar to our regular Serial Monitor tool, but it's a more powerful visual aid that will improve our comprehension and ability to compare our data. Available in Arduino versions 1.6.6 and higher is the Serial Plotter. It's a useful tool for quickly visualizing data that comes in, like from a sensor. If the data is changing too quickly, we might not be able to detect the changes with Serial Monitor. The changes will be visually displayed by the serial plotter. The Serial Plotter can also plot multiple values at a time (Fig. 7).

When working on Arduino projects, the Serial Monitor is a vital tool. It can be used to test ideas, debug problems, or establish direct communication with the Arduino board. Since the Serial Monitor tool is integrated with the editor in the Arduino IDE 2.0, using it doesn't require opening an external window. This implies that we are able to run multiple windows, each utilizing a separate Serial Monitor.

Phase 3: Grayscale Representation to Prediction

Preprocessed Leads

Images are processed using morphology based on their shapes. The operation is defined as a dilation or erosion by the rule that processes the pixels (Fig. 8).

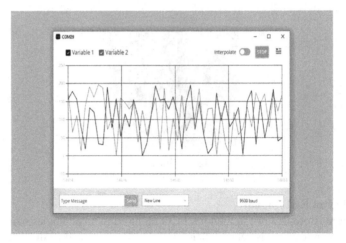

Fig. 7. Serial Plotter

Structuring Element

A small shape or template that morphological techniques use to analyze an image is called a structuring element. These methods compare each potential placement of the structuring element to the corresponding pixel neighborhood in the image.

1. Fit: When every pixel in the structuring element fully encircles every pixel in the target object
2. Hit: When the pixels of an object and at least one structural element overlap
3. Miss: When there are no pixels in the structuring element that cover any of the object's pixels.

While some tests look for instances where an object "hits" or intersects the environment, others determine whether it "fits" into its surroundings.

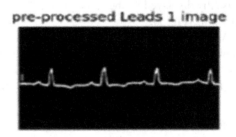

Fig. 8. Preprocessed Leads

Converting 1D Signals

Contour Images

The line connecting all of the equally intense points along an image's border is known as its contour. Shape analysis, object detection, and determining the size of the object of interest can all benefit from contours. As can be seen above, contours are a shape's equally intense boundaries. It saves a shape's boundary's (x, y) coordinates. Does it, however, save every coordinate? A pass on cv2.CHAIN_APPROX_NONE stores every boundary point. Do we really need all the points, though? For example, all we need are the two endpoints of a straight line if we are trying to find its contour. This is the function of cv2.CHAIN_APPROX_SIMPLE. Memory is saved by eliminating all unnecessary points and compressing the contour. This is the entire procedure that we will use to successfully identify contours in an image for increased accuracy.

- Image to a binary image. Typically, the input image is a binary image (which is typically the outcome of edge detection or a thresholded image).
- Using the OpenCV function findContours() to locate the contours.
- Sketch these outlines and present the picture.

After locating the contour images, we proceed as directed to transform the preprocessed leads into values that represent one-dimensional signals.

- We used the contour technique to trace and extract only the necessary signal from images.
- The image is transformed into a signal that is only one dimension.
- The image is then scaled using MinMaxScaler.
- Save the 1D signal values in a.csv file for each lead (1–12) signal in the entire ecg image.
- Combine all 12 lead values with the target label added into a single CSV file.

Dimensionality Reduction

The process of obtaining a set of principal variables and then reducing the number of random variables under consideration is known as dimensionality reduction. It is separated into two categories: feature extraction and feature selection.

In our work we use PCA (Principal Component Analysis) for dimensionality reduction. In order to enhance performance, dimensionality reduction is carried out in the pre-processing phase prior to model construction.

To identify and predict cardiac anomalies, numerous researchers have used a variety of data mining techniques, including neural networks, KNN, decision trees, and classification based on clustering. In this work, we apply a number of supervised classification algorithms, such as Support Vector Machine (SVM), Logistic Regression, KNN, and Voting Based Ensemble Classifier, using CSV data. ECG images typical of four patient categories (myocardial infarction, abnormal heartbeat, history of myocardial infarction, and good health) are aggregated at the lead level (from 1 to 12) prior to data modeling. After that, the target column is transformed into numeric using an array (['No', 'HB', 'MI', 'PM']) and groups encoder. The data are interpreted using principal component analysis, a post-dimension reduction technique, which also verifies that the variance explained is within allowable bounds.

5 Circuit Diagram

From the following circuit diagram we all need to connect the wires for the appropriate places like in our code (Fig. 9).

$$GVD \to GND$$
$$3.3\ V \to 3.3\ V$$
$$Output \to A0$$
$$LO- \to 10$$
$$LO+ \to 11$$

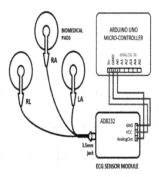

Fig. 9. Circuit diagram for IoT

6 Results and Discussion

(See Figs. 10, 11, 12, 13, 14 and 15).

There are three phases to this work. Using IoT devices, we physically collected an ECG signal from a person in the first phase. We have removed the noisy data from the ECG we acquired in the second step. Additionally, we divided the ECG's 12 leads into segments, which were then represented as a grayscale image. To determine if the ECG is normal or abnormal, we analyze the data from the previous phase in the final phase.

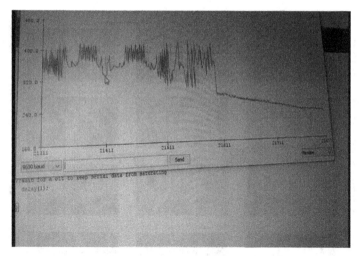

Fig. 10. Serial Plotter for ECG

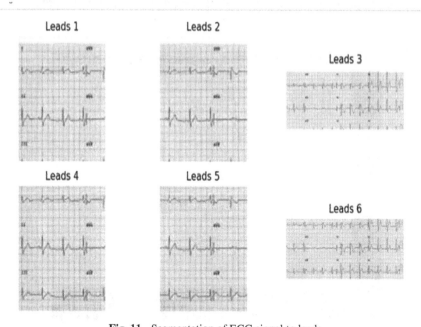

Fig. 11. Segmentation of ECG signal to leads

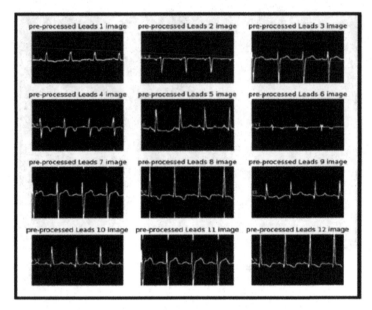

Fig. 12. Preprocessed Leads

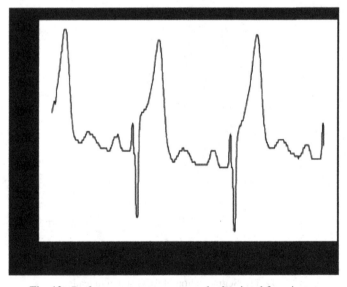

Fig. 13. Perform contours separate only the signal from image

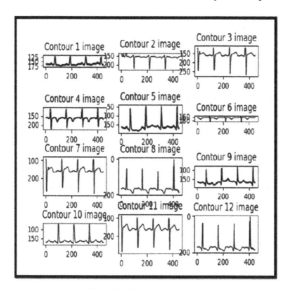

Fig. 14. Contour images

0	1	2	...	1728	1729	1730
0.859944	0.871148	0.87395	...	0.826331	0.826331	0.826331

Fig. 15. Dimensionality Reduction

7 Conclusion

An individual's ECG is obtained using IoT and Python, and the ECG is then examined for further analysis to produce a result. This work makes it simple and affordable for people to check their heart rates. Because it can affect both young and old people so quickly, heart disease has recently emerged as a serious issue in healthcare. In order to help in measuring the heart rate in both older and younger people, we are therefore developing the study. It can be enhanced to more accurately and precisely analyze the ECG, producing results that are more precise. The algorithm of translating ECGs to grayscale mapping has been studied in order to view pattern from one dimensional ECG signal. The website is finished, but we may still develop a mobile application to facilitate using the website.

References

1. Leis, J.W.: Digital Signal Processing Using MATLAB for Students and Researchers, 1st edn. Wiley, Hoboken (2011)
2. Kisku, D.R.: Design and Implementation of Healthcare Bio Metrics Systems. IGI Global (2019)
3. Izadhah, H.: Deep Learning in Bioinformatics: Techniques and Applications in Practice, 2nd edn. Elsevier Science, Amsterdam (2022)

4. Rojo-Alvarez, J.L., Martinez-Ramon, M., Munoz-Mari, J.: Digital Signal Processing with Kernel Methods. Wiley, Hoboken (2018)
5. Rajathi, S., Radhamani, G.: A Survey on Cloud Computing with Classification and Swarm Intelligence for Cardiac Healthcare and Prediction of Rheumatic Heart Disease. EDU World, vol. XII, no. 20, pp. 198–214, Special issue. APH Publishing Corporation (2018)
6. Chandran, C.P., Rajathi, S., Pandiselvi, G.: Deep learning based Artery Deposition Analysis using Segmentation and CNN Classification. Patent Application No. 20224100837 A, Published on 4.2.2022 Ministry of Commerce and Industry Government of India, Field of Invention: Bio Medical Engineering. https://ipindia.nic.in/index.html
7. https://www.anaconda.com
8. Shiva Varshini, K., Yuvasri, S., Chandran, C.P.: Automatic transformation of ECG signal into grayscale representation using segmentation. In: 3rd International Conference on Mathematical Modeling & Computational Science, ICMMCS 2023. Mother Teresa University (2023)

AHP-MOORA Approach for Industrial Robot Selection in Car Paint: An Industrial Case Study

Ashish Yadav[✉] ⓘ, Anand Jaiswal ⓘ, and Teena Singh ⓘ

New Delhi Institute of Management, New Delhi, India
ashish.yadav@ndimdelhi.org

Abstract. Industrial robots are crucial elements of advanced manufacturing technologies because they allow manufacturing companies to generate high-quality products affordably. Industrial robots may carry out a wide range of operations, including welding, painting, assembling, disassembly, placing printed circuit boards precisely, palletizing, packaging, labeling, and product testing. All features are completed with extreme endurance, quickness, and accuracy. Several competing parameters that must be taken into account simultaneously in a thorough selection process affect how well industrial robots function. The practical method for choosing an industrial robot for vehicle painting activities is presented in this study article. It streamlines the decision-making process by combining the Analytical Hierarchy Process (AHP) and Multi-Objective Optimization by Ratio Analysis (MOORA) methods. It is a strategy that is used to rank and evaluate alternatives while taking into account their relative importance and effectiveness. The ranking derived using the MOORA method is displayed. The outcomes demonstrated the value of MCDM techniques for robot selection. The study's originality is in using MOORA MCDM approaches to select industrial car painting robots.

Keywords: Industrial Robots · Car painting · Multi-Criteria Decision-Making · AHP Process MOORA Method · Robot Selection

1 Introduction

The word "robot" is derived from the Czech word "robota," which denotes a slave or forced laborer. Robots are essentially robots made to aid people automatically or semi-automatically in a variety of multidisciplinary sectors. Robotics is the study of these machines, including how they work, how they are made, and how they are used. Robots are autonomously controlled, reprogrammable manipulators that can perform several tasks and are programmable in three or more axes, according to the International Organization for Standardization (ISO). These robots, which can be mobile or stationary, are frequently employed in industrial automation applications. The necessity for accuracy and precision in operations that demand repetition and continuity is what motivates industries to employ robotics [1].

The development of robotics has made it possible for researchers and businesses to operate in risky and challenging conditions where performing human operations would

S. Rajagopal et al (Eds.): ASCIS 2023, CCIS 2040, pp. 125–143, 2024.
https://doi.org/10.1007/978-3-031-59107-5_9

be dangerous. Robots are proficiently carrying out repetitive, challenging, and dangerous activities. Additionally, robots are essential in a variety of industry sectors, including machining, hospitality, space science, the automobile industry, the medical field and the sports sector. According to human intervention, different robots have varied levels of autonomy, ranging from entirely human-controlled robots to an aiding robot that helps to lessen human work to a fully autonomous one that doesn't need any outside assistance. Rising market competitiveness and rising consumer demands may make this a viable sector for robots to play a significant role to enhance quality and productivity [2, 3].

1.1 Steps Involved in Industrial Robots Painting Cars

Industrial robots paint cars using a carefully planned procedure that includes several crucial steps. The process starts with meticulous surface preparation, when the exterior of the car is painstakingly washed and buffed to provide a flawless surface for painting. Following the preparation stage, the car goes through a priming process in which a coat of primer is applied to improve adhesion and durability. The application must be precise at this point, and industrial robots equipped with paint guns make sure that it is. The genuine color of the car's basecoat is subsequently applied with robotic precision. The robots execute this operation with extraordinary accuracy, ensuring uniformity across the whole vehicle. A clear coat is then applied to the paint to protect it and make it appear lustrous [4].

The painted car then goes through a controlled drying and curing phase to set the paint. Automated inspection systems are used to examine the paint's quality and identify any flaws that should be fixed. The car may go through polishing and buffing procedures to obtain a flawless, glossy appearance after the paint passes inspection. Industrial robots are essential to this complex process because they provide accuracy, consistency, and efficiency, which helps the auto industry produce vehicles with flawless paint finishes [5].

Furthermore, the automotive painting procedure highlights the blending of advanced technology and expertise. It starts with meticulous surface preparation, cleaning the exterior of the car and assuring a perfect base. Industrial robots equipped with paint guns apply the primer, basecoat, and clearcoat with imperceptible error as precision takes center stage. Their relentless accuracy ensures brilliance and homogeneity in the final paint finish. The car is placed in regulated drying and curing circumstances once the paint has been applied to ensure the paint's endurance. Automated inspection systems employ cameras and sensors to closely examine the quality of the paint, spotting any imperfections for prompt rectification. The ability of industrial robots to provide a consistently high-quality finish is seen here [6].

After this, polishing and buffing are required to give the paint finish a glossy sheen. Each phase takes the environment into account, and there are thorough controls in place to limit paint fumes and follow strict environmental rules. The integration of technology and craftsmanship in car painting is a prime example of the automotive industry's dedication to providing vehicles with flawless paint quality, and this is made possible in large part by the invaluable contribution of industrial robots. Figure 1 depicts the crucial steps involved in industrial robots painting cars.

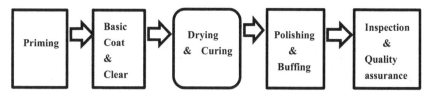

Fig. 1. Steps involved in industrial robots painting cars

Our review centers around a complete examination and arrangement approach for the difficulties experienced in modern robot determination utilizing the Multi-Models Navigation (MCDM) approach. We especially underline situations including the assessment of different modern robot options in view of numerous rules. Our essential point is to disentangle the unmistakable qualities related with every robot elective inside the setting of MCDM for determination. To accomplish an ideal decision of modern robot, we attempt to devise proficient dynamic approaches custom-made to different mixes of choice models. In quest for accuracy and viability, we have fostered a multi-objective MCDM arrangement approach that influences laid out MCDM strategies like Analytical Hierarchy process (AHP) and Multi-Objective Optimization by Ratio Analysis (MOORA) method is described in this work. This approach is planned not exclusively to give doable robot determinations yet in addition to recognize ideal decisions, taking into account the complicated idea of robot choice models. To guarantee the commonsense relevance of our examination, we have led a top to bottom examination concerning genuine modern settings, inspecting contextual investigations across different assembling spaces [7].

In our investigation, we have painstakingly illustrated the basic suspicions that support these contextual investigations, in this way offering a complete and context oriented comprehension of their complexities. Perceiving the multi-layered nature of modern robot choice prerequisites and administrative contemplations, we have zeroed in on one-layered targets as well as rather embraced a more extensive range of standards that describe viable robot determination. By enveloping different administrative perspectives and considering the exhibition of modern robots in contrast to numerous standards, our review tries to give an all-encompassing and noteworthy system for the determination of modern robots utilizing the MCDM approach.

The manuscript is organized into distinct sections to present a comprehensive study. In Sect. 2, we delve into the literature on industrial robot selection process. Section 3 introduces the methodology of our research, detailing the MOORA method and its steps. In Sect. 4, we discuss the results of MOORA method. Finally, Sect. 5 concludes the manuscript by summarizing our findings and outlining future research directions for industrial robot selection.

2 Literature Review

TOPSIS and OCRA were compared by Rao [8] in the context of robot selection. The foundation of TOPSIS is the idea of finding "ideal" and "anti-ideal" solutions and rating options according to how closely they adhere to these standards. OCRA, on the other hand, is a technique for measuring performance. In the context of robot selection, Chatterjee [9] contrasted ELECTRE, an outranking method, and VIKOR, a compromise ranking method. Kumar and Garg [10] provided a quantitative strategy for assessing, choosing, and rating different robots based on the DBA. In this method, the distances in a multidimensional space between options and ideal solutions are measured. Bairagi [11] addressed the robot selection conundrum using the MMMCA method. To provide a final ranking, this model multiplies performance scores with criteria weights. The ROBSEL decision support system, a two-phase method created to help decision-makers choose robots, was introduced by Baležentis [12].

Wu [13] introduced a fuzzy set-based decision support system to help managers choose the best robot for particular applications. Khouja and Booth [14] put out a decision-making framework that makes use of fuzzy cluster analysis to deal with instances in which a robot's performance falls short of what the manufacturer had predicted. Chu and Lin's [15] introduction of a fuzzy TOPSIS method for robot selection expanded the original TOPSIS strategy to accommodate linguistic and fuzzy information. Kapoor and Tak [16] proposed a methodology that makes the Analytic Hierarchy Process (AHP) for robot selection more permeable to subjective assessments by using fuzzy linguistic variables. A fuzzy hierarchical TOPSIS model was put forth by Kahraman [17] offering a structured method for dealing with fuzziness and uncertainty in robot selection. Sharma [18] addressed AHP and Fuzzy SWARA based process for lean management concept.

Bairagi [19] suggests the Technique of Accurate Ranking Order (TARO), a unique MCDM methodology. In this approach first measure the weights of the final selection values using an enhanced version of the entropy weighting method. Sharma [20] represent hybrid AHP with ISM –MICMAC based approach of lean in robots. Sharma [21] represents SWARA-WASPAS concept which help to solve real world problem. Dağsuyu & Kokangül [22] develop the effective criteria for surface protection procedures have been determined, and the level of significance of these criteria for surface quality has been determined using a method based on the Analytic Hierarchy Process (AHP) and the process capability (Cp) values.

The choice of industrial robots using MCDM techniques is receiving more and more attention in the manufacturing and automation sectors. A substantial body of literature has emerged to address the challenging decision-making process involved in choosing the optimal robot for specific industrial applications. Researchers have looked into a number of MCDM methodologies, such as the Analytic Hierarchy Process (AHP), Technique for Order Preference by Similarity to Ideal Solution (TOPSIS), and entropy-based methods, to evaluate and rank industrial robots based on various criteria. These specifications often consider things like load capacity, accuracy, speed, energy efficiency, and cost-effectiveness. In order to account for fresh developments like collaborative robotics (cobots) and sustainability norms for the industry, studies have also expanded their focus to encompass non-traditional industrial settings.

The study found a growing demand for trustworthy software programs and decision-making aids that may aid professionals in navigating the intricate realm of robot selection. As industrial automation develops, this body of research provides a foundation for enhancing the efficacy and adaptability of production processes by selecting the best robots for the job.

Our analysis reveals a critical flaw in the current landscape of industrial robot selection: the absence of a precise solution strategy capable of successfully reducing workload while taking into account selection process limits. This gap in the literature emphasizes the demand for novel strategies to tackle these complex problems. As a result, our research aims to close this gap by presenting a fresh solution framework based on the ideas of MCDM. In particular, our goal is to create a thorough decision-making model that not only takes into account a variety of factors but also complies with the changing demands of contemporary production environments. Our study intends to add to the conversation about industrial robot selection by filling in these important research gaps, ultimately giving practitioners useful information and advancing of both theory and practice in this vital domain.

3 Problem Statement

A complex difficulty exists when choosing the best industrial robot for a certain application in the context of sophisticated production processes. The issue at hand entails determining and ranking the essential elements that affect the decision to use an industrial robot, taking into account characteristics like repeatability, accuracy, and speed as well as payload capacity and speed to different jobs. Depending on the particular needs of the industrial application, these aspects vary in importance, and making an informed choice requires a methodical strategy that successfully balances these criteria. The selection procedure is further complicated by the growing complexity of robotic systems and the quick improvements in robotics technology. Consequently, solving the industrial robot selection issue calls for the creation of a strong decision-making framework that maximizes performance, reduces costs, and aligns interests.

3.1 Robot Selection Factors in an Industrial Technical Context

The selection procedure in the field of industrial robots is comparable to a meticulously staged play. It starts with a thorough analysis of performance parameters, taking into account elements like repeatability, accuracy, and speed as well as payload capacity and speed. Versatility is increased by the capacity to adapt and switch between tasks with ease.

Consistent operations are ensured through dependability and low maintenance needs, while cost considerations and safety precautions are crucial in both the financial and human elements. The ensemble is completed by the robot's integration into the manufacturing ecosystem, sustainability, and strong supplier support. This selection process influences industrial efficiency, quality, and cost-effectiveness in ways that go beyond simple decision-making. It is the ultimate example of contemporary manufactured art.

Quality, service level, product variety, cost, lead time, and robustness are undoubtedly important factors or criteria to take into account when choosing industrial robots for vehicle painting and manufacturing procedures. Each criterion helps to achieve the overall goal of minimizing cost and lead time while maximizing the quality and product variety, service level and robustness as shown in the following ways:

1. **Quality:** Painting is especially important when it comes to vehicle manufacture. To achieve quality standards, industrial robots must make sure that paint finishes are flawless and consistent. Superior quality is made possible by robots with precise control mechanisms and cutting-edge coating techniques.
2. **Cost:** The initial outlay for robotics equipment as well as continuous operational costs is both taken into account. It's crucial to choose robots that strike a balance between price and performance. Lower running expenses can also be achieved with energy-efficient robots and cost-effective maintenance.
3. **Lead Time:** Lead time has a direct impact on delivery schedules and manufacturing efficiency. Lead times are shortened by quicker robots and effective production techniques. In order to meet client needs and stay competitive, lead times must be kept to a minimum.
4. **Service Level:** For the selected robots, service level refers to the accessibility of technical assistance, replacement components, and maintenance services. Robots from companies with robust support networks will execute consistently with little downtime.
5. **Product Variety:** A large range of vehicle types and variants are frequently produced in contemporary automobile manufacturing. To handle different product kinds without requiring considerable reconfiguration, robots with adjustable end-effectors and programming flexibility are essential.
6. **Robustness:** Robots need to be able to withstand the harsh industrial environment. They ought to be able to survive constant use, the elements, and potential wear and tear. Costs for maintenance and replacement are reduced with robust robots.

3.2 Robot Selection Characteristics in an Industrial Technical Context

Robot selection attributes or characteristics, in an industrial technical context, refer to the characteristics that are essential when selecting the best industrial robot for a given application or task. These characteristics aid in ensuring that the chosen robot can fulfill the operational needs and performance standards of the industrial or manufacturing process. Here are some crucial factors for choosing a robot in an industrial setting:

1. **Degree of freedom:** The number of independent movements the robot's arm or end-effector may perform is referred to as degrees of freedom. More independence allows us greater flexibility while managing challenging tasks.
2. **Working envelope:** The working envelope defines the range of motion and workspace that the robot can cover. Understanding the working envelope is essential to ensure that the robot can access all the necessary work areas within its operational space.
3. **Speed:** How quickly the robot can move is shown by its qualities for speed and acceleration. For applications requiring quick cycle times or rapid response, these qualities are crucial.

4. **Payload:** The greatest weight that the robot can safely handle is referred to as payload capacity. When choosing a robot for activities that include lifting or transferring large components, it is essential to understand the payload capacity.

5. **Positional Accuracy:** A crucial specification that describes how precisely the robot can position its tooling or end-effector is called positional accuracy. This enables the robot to put its tool precisely, making it possible to complete activities like painting or assembly that call for precise placement with little to no error.

6. **Repeatability:** Repeatability measures the robot's ability to consistently return to a specified position. This level of repeatability is critical for tasks where precision and consistency are paramount, such as in applications where the robot must repeatedly perform the same operation with minimal deviation.

7. **Adaptability to the environment:** When determining a robot's environmental compatibility, experts look at things like severe temperatures, humidity levels, and cleanroom specifications.

8. **Efficiency in Energy:** Aspects of energy efficiency take into account the robot's operational power usage.

4 Methodology

A team starts the process of making positive decisions by gathering pertinent information about the potential solutions. The team then carefully weighs each factor based on its importance before identifying the factor necessary for making the choice. The options are then meticulously evaluated utilizing the gathered information against these standards. The team then uses the suggested evaluation process to rank and evaluate the alternatives in accordance, which finally results in a well-informed decision. Figure 2 shows the research methodology steps those are mentioned below:

In this process more focus on gathering information that is unique to each option, enabling a detailed examination of each one's characteristics. After the data is gathered, the process of identifying critical components begins, allowing for the distinction of elements that are important within the context of decision-making. After that, each criterion is given a weight using the Analytical Hierarchy Process (AHP), which offers an organized way to rank the elements according to importance. The team uses the previously acquired data to rate each alternative on a separate criterion after putting weighted criteria in place. Lastly, the alternatives are thoroughly assessed using the Multi-Objective Optimization by Ratio Analysis (MOORA) method, which takes into account both their relative importance and efficacy.

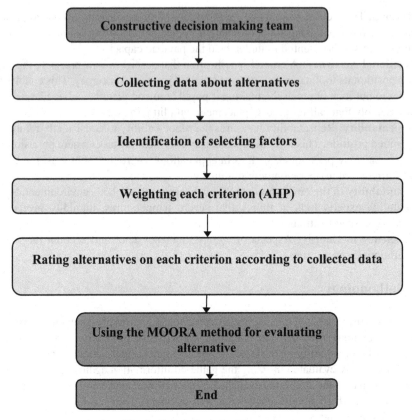

Fig. 2. Research methodology steps

5   Solution Approaches

The author discussed the AHP and MOORA methodologies' solution processes in three of the subsections in this part, along with the computational outcomes. Using an Excel solver with an Intel Core i5, 3.20 GHz processor, and 4 GB of RAM, the computed results were produced.

5.1   Analytic Hierarchy Process (AHP)

The Analytic Hierarchy Process (AHP) for industrial robot selection entails a methodical set of stages to rank and select the best robot for a certain application. First, the choice problem is stated, and then the selection-relevant criteria and sub-criteria are found. These requirements might cover things like payload capacity, reach, precision, and price. Second, pairwise comparisons are performed, often using a Saaty scale, to determine the relative relevance of these criteria and sub-criteria. A similar pairwise comparison procedure is then used to assess how well each robot alternative performed in relation to each criterion. These comparisons produce numerical values that reflect decision-makers' preferences. After that, consistency tests are carried out to guarantee the accuracy of the comparisons.

A clear and logical framework for choosing the best industrial robot is eventually provided by the AHP software or method, which determines the weights for each criterion and sub-criterion before ranking the robot alternatives based on their weighted sums.

5.2 MOORA (Multi-objective Optimization by Ratio Analysis)

The MOORA (Multi-Objective Optimization by Ratio Analysis) method stands out for its usability and efficacy, when it comes to decision-making. Regardless of their mathematical expertise, decision-makers from various sectors can use it because of its simplicity. In order to streamline the decision-making process, MOORA has the unique capacity to combine many performance criteria into a single, all-encompassing score. Interestingly, MOORA allows for both qualitative and quantitative criteria, which is a useful feature for addressing factors that are difficult to quantify and assuring a full evaluation. The risk of information loss is reduced by MOORA's use of different mathematical models for benefit and non-benefit criteria, which maintains vital data during the evaluation. Because of its adaptability, it may be tailored to the particular requirements of each decision-making scenario, taking into account both subjective and objective variables.

In order to ensure a methodical evaluation of each criterion's importance, MOORA also makes the frequently difficult work of defining criteria weights simpler. Additionally, MOORA's adaptability extends to its capacity for seamless integration with other multiple attribute decision-making methodologies, offering a thorough and durable framework for informed decision-making. In this process following steps are followed:

Step 1: The first step entails defining the objective and identifying the pertinent evaluation standards.

Step 2: The matrix X is m x n in size, where m is the number of robot choices. A Decision matrix frequently abbreviated as X, illustrates the performance of various options across various qualities.

The number n denotes the number of evaluation criteria or qualities. Each xij member of the matrix represents the performance measure of the ith choice (robot). To make sure that all of the attributes are on the same scale, these performance measurements are standardized.

To enable understandable comparisons, normalization may entail changing the numbers to a common range, frequently between 0 and 1.

$$X = \left[x_{ij}\right]_{m \times n} = \begin{matrix} x_{11} & x_{12} & \cdots \\ x_{21} & x_{22} & \cdots \\ \vdots & \vdots & \vdots \end{matrix} \tag{1}$$

Determine the selection criteria for the manufacturing selection issue under consideration, and shortlist the manufacturing system based on the criteria that the identified selection criteria satisfy. There are two categories of attributes: those that are beneficial and those that are not beneficial.

Step 3: The results of Brauers et al. (2008) suggest that the square root of the sum of squares computed for each alternative per attribute is the best option for the denominator in this situation. They offer a number of different phrases or formulas to represent this ratio as a result;

$$X_{ij}^* = x_{ij} \bigg/ \sqrt{\left[\sum_{i=1}^m x_{ij}^2\right]} \tag{2}$$

where x_{ij} represents the normalized performance of the ith alternative and j_{th} attribute, and x_i is a dimensionless value in the range [0, 1].

Step 4: In multi-objective optimization, the aim is to strike a balance between maximizing positive attributes by adding normalized performances and minimizing negative attributes by deleting them. This challenging work requires simultaneous optimization of many objectives using various criteria, necessitating an effective method to maximize positive characteristics while minimizing negative ones. The optimization challenge then is:

$$Y_i = \sum_{j=1}^g x_{ij}^* - \sum_{j=g+1}^n x_{ij}^* \tag{3}$$

"Yi" denotes the normalized assessment value for the ith alternative across all attributes in this context. While (n-g) denotes the number of attributes to decrease, "g" represents the count of attributes to maximize. This format makes it easier to determine an attribute's weight in a choice. Taking into account these attribute weights, Eq. 4 is transformed as follows:

$$Y_i = \sum_{j=1}^g w_j x_{ij}^* - \sum_{j=g+1}^n w_j x_{ij}^* \tag{4}$$

Step 5: In our research, we underline the critical importance of the "yi" values, which are produced by adding the maxima (useful characteristics) and minima (non-benefit attributes) in the decision matrix. The alternatives are ranked using these values, whether they are positive or negative. The option with the highest "yi" value is the best one, while the option with the lowest value is the least preferable. This method improves decision-making precision and clarity, making a significant addition to the field of decision science.

This work proposes a ranking value assessment on a fuzzy conversion scale utilizing fuzzy set theory. With the help of the provided numerical approximation system, fuzzy numbers can be generated from linguistic concepts in a consistent manner. In this research, an 11-point scale is suggested for a better comprehension and illustration of the qualitative quality.

The given set of abbreviations represents a range of qualitative rankings used to assess various attributes or characteristics. "H" signifies a rating of "High," indicating a superior level or performance, while "VH" represents "Very High," indicating an even greater level of excellence. "EH" stands for "Extremely High," and "OH" stands for "Outstanding high" indicating the highest level of achievement. Conversely, "L" denotes "Low," implying a subpar or unsatisfactory rating, while "VL" stands for "Very Low," indicating an even poorer level of performance. "EL" stands for "Extremely Low," and "OL" stands for "Outstanding low" indicating the lower level of process. "BA" stands for "Below Average," suggesting performance falling short of expectations, while "AA" represents "Above Average," signifying performance exceeding the norm. Lastly, "A" is an abbreviation for "Average," representing a performance level considered typical or in line with expectations. It is advised that users assign values based on Table 1.

Table 1. Values of the selection attribute of industrial robot

Qualitative analysis of selection characteristic	Fuzzy Numbers	Crisp Scores
OL	R1	0.04556
EL	R2	0.13647
VL	R3	0.22738
L	R4	0.31825
BA	R5	0.40916
A	R6	0.50000
AA	R7	0.59095
H	R8	0.68186
VH	R9	0.77278
EH	R10	0.86365
OH	R11	0.95456

5.3 Case Study: MOORA-Based Decision-Making for Industrial Robot Selection

XYZ Company is a leading automotive manufacturer specializing in the production of high-quality vehicles. To enhance their manufacturing processes and maintain a competitive edge, the company is embarking on the task of selecting the most suitable industrial robot for vehicle painting and manufacturing. The decision-makers at XYZ Company are considering various factors to optimize their selection, including quality, service level, cost, lead time, product variety, and robustness. Table 2 shows the characteristics for selecting industrial robots.

Table 2. Characteristics for selecting industrial robots

Characteristic Representation	Characteristics
C-1	Degree of freedom
C-2	Working envelope
C-3	Speed
C-4	Payload
C-5	Positional Accuracy
C-6	Repeatability
C-7	Adaptability to the environment
C-8	Efficiency in Energy

Several important elements that are each identified by an acronym come into play when choosing an industrial robot. Quality, or "Q," is essential to ensuring that the selected robot performs precisely and flawlessly. Budgetary restrictions and the pursuit of quality must coexist while keeping an eye on "C" for cost. Lead time, sometimes known as "LT," is a significant component that affects productivity and timeliness. For dependable technical assistance and maintenance, the letter "SL," which stands for service level, is required. "PV," or product variation, refers to the robot's adaptability to various manufacturing requirements. The letter "R" stands for robustness, which is essential for meeting the demanding requirements of continuous operation. These elements work together to create a thorough framework for selecting industrial robots that is in line with the particular needs of the manufacturing environment. Table 3 presents a comprehensive overview of the essential factors that influence the selection of industrial robots for various applications.

Table 3. Industrial robot selection factors

Factor Presentation	Factor	Benefit Factors	Non-benefit Factors
F-1	Q	• (+)	–
F-2	C	–	• (−)
F-3	LT	–	• (−)
F-4	SL	• (+)	–
F-5	PV	• (+)	–
F-6	R	• (+)	–

Table 4 shows the primary decision matrix using the Analytic Hierarchy Process (AHP) methodology, a framework pioneered by T.L. Saaty and his corresponding scale.

Table 4. AHP matrix with Saaty scale

	F-1(+)	F-2(−)	F-3(−)	F-4(+)	F-5(+)	F-6(+)
F-1	1	9	5	3	5	7
F-2	1/9	1	2	3	4	3
F-3	1/5	1/2	1	2	3	2
F-4	1/3	1/5	1/3	1	1/5	1/7
F-5	1/5	1/3	1/2	5	1	1/3
F-6	1/7	1/2	1/2	1/3	5	1

Table 5 shows the Fuzzy Scale (Word) interrelationship between characteristics and factors for industrial robot selection.

Table 5. Fuzzy Scale (Word) interrelationship between characteristics and factors

	F-1(+)	F-2(−)	F-3(−)	F-4(+)	F-5(+)	F-6(+)
C-1	H	VH	H	H	L	L
C-2	H	H	H	VH	VH	VH
C-3	H	VH	H	VH	H	H
C-4	VH	VL	EH	EH	BA	BA
C-5	H	BA	AA	OH	AA	AA
C-6	VH	H	BA	VH	H	VH
C-7	EH	EL	AA	AA	VH	H
C-8	OH	A	EH	L	EH	EH

Table 6 serves as a comprehensive reference, delineating the intricate relationship between key characteristics and influential factors within the context of the decision-making process.

Table 7 illustrates the connection between the summation of characteristics-factors and the square root of this summation, providing insights into the interplay of these crucial elements in the decision-making process.

Table 8 examines how the normalized decision matrix and characteristics-aspects interact, offering information on how these two factors relates to decision-making.

Table 6. Fuzzy Scale (Number) interrelationship between characteristics and factors

	F-1(+)	F-2(−)	F-3(−)	F-4(+)	F-5(+)	F-6(+)
C-1	0.68186	0.77278	0.68186	0.68186	0.31825	0.31825
C-2	0.68186	0.68186	0.68186	0.77178	0.77178	0.77178
C-3	0.68186	0.77278	0.68186	0.77178	0.68186	0.68186
C-4	0.77278	0.22735	0.86365	0.86365	0.40916	0.40916
C-5	0.68186	0.40916	0.59095	0.95456	0.59095	0.59095
C-6	0.77128	0.68186	0.40916	0.77128	0.68186	0.77128
C-7	0.86365	0.13646	0.59095	0.59095	0.77128	0.68186
C-8	0.95456	0.50000	0.86365	0.31827	0.86365	0.86365

Table 7. Interrelationship between characteristics-factor's summation and square root of summation

	F-1(+)	F-2(−)	F-3(−)	F-4(+)	F-5(+)	F-6(+)
m $\Sigma(X_{ij})\,2\,i = 1$	4.7112	2.6125	3.9934	4.3641	3.4883	3.4883
m SQRT$\Sigma(X_{ij})2\,i = 1$	2.17053	1.6162	1.99825	2.08925	1.86762	1.86762
Weight Factor	**0.5071**	**0.1751**	**0.1275**	**0.0364**	**0.0765**	**0.0774**

Table 8. Interrelationship between characteristics-factor's and normalized decision matrix

	F-1(+)	F-2(−)	F-3(−)	F-4(+)		F-5(+)	F-6(+)
WF	**0.5071**	**0.1751**		**0.1275**	**0.0364**	**0.0765**	**0.0774**
C-1	0.31925	0.47978		0.35422	0.32756	0.17777	0.17081
C-2	0.31002	0.42232		0.33841	0.37119	0.41257	0.42005
C-3	0.31510	0.47855		0.33841	0.36543	0.36387	0.35975
C-4	0.35705	0.14122		0.46061	0.40950	0.22051	0.22077
C-5	0.31510	0.25923		0.30102	0.46750	0.30921	0.31034
C-6	0.35129	0.41551		0.21519	0.37478	0.36387	0.41385
C-7	0.39857	0.08377		0.30629	0.26429	0.41879	0.36519
C-8	0.44001	0.30922		0.45007	0.15747	0.46232	0.46400

Table 9 explores the relationship between the weighted normalized choice matrix and the characteristics-factors, revealing their crucial interplay in the decision-making process.

Table 9. Interrelationship between characteristics-factor's and weighted normalized decision matrix

WF	0.5071	0.1751	0.1275	0.0364	0.0765	0.0774
C-1	0.14420	0.08372	0.04351	0.01188	0.01304	0.01389
C-2	0.14420	0.07387	0.04351	0.01346	0.03165	0.03203
C-3	0.14420	0.08372	0.04351	0.01346	0.02793	0.02826
C-4	0.18054	0.024631	0.05510	0.01504	0.01677	0.01696
C-5	0.14420	0.04433	0.03370	0.01663	0.02421	0.02449
C-6	0.18054	0.07387	0.02611	0.01346	0.02793	0.03203
C-7	0.20177	0.01478	0.03770	0.01030	0.03165	0.02826
C-8	0.22301	0.05417	0.05510	0.00554	0.03538	0.03579

Choosing an industrial robot by utilize a specialized equation to calculate relative and maximum significance values. Table 10 show the deriving relative and maximum significance values through a specific equation for the industrial robot selection.

Table 10. Show the deriving relative and maximum significance values through a specific equation for the industrial robot selection

Factor	Value	Rank
C-1	0.071317	8
C-2	0.117555	6
C-3	0.101692	7
C-4	0.146186	4
C-5	0.14055	5
C-6	0.151371	3
C-7	0.218113	1
C-8	0.188365	2

A team starts the process of making positive decisions by gathering pertinent information about the potential solutions. The team then carefully weighs each factor based on its importance before identifying the factor necessary for making the choice. The options are then meticulously evaluated utilizing the gathered information against these standards. The team then uses the suggested evaluation process to rank and evaluate the alternatives in accordance, which finally results in a well-informed decision.

Figure 3 show the Pie chart representation of factors and rank where Pie chart helps to clearly illustrate the factors and their rankings while also providing a concise representation of the importance distribution. In the chart, factors that are carefully considered during the decision-making process are represented by segments that correspond to their respective rank percentages. Additional customization options that improve the chart's comprehensibility include color modifications and appropriate labeling. Because it gives researcher a quick overview of the complex hierarchy of factors, the resulting visualization becomes a valuable tool for better informed decision-making.

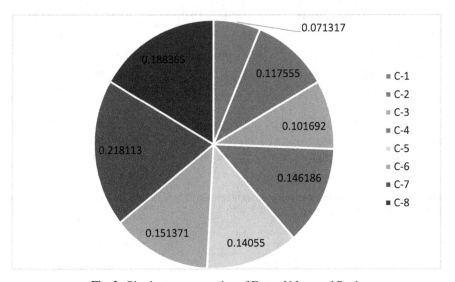

Fig. 3. Pie chart representation of Factor Values and Rank

6   Results and Discussion

A variety of elements are taken into consideration when choosing an industrial robot to make sure that it completely matches the demands and performance requirements of an industrial or manufacturing process. Every consideration has a different weight when making a decision. The given information gives a prioritized list of these crucial elements, illuminating their relative importance. It is noteworthy that the components are ranked according to their relative values, with a lower numerical value denoting a larger relevance.

For instance, in this context, "Degree of Freedom" is acknowledged as the top-ranking factor, emphasizing its vital importance. It means that while choosing an industrial robot, a robot's capacity for independent mobility is a crucial feature. The relevance of "Working Envelope," "Speed," "Payload," and "Positional Accuracy" is similarly close behind. These rankings highlight how important these characteristics are when selecting a robot for activities that need intricate movements, wide-ranging workspace coverage, quick movements, and exact positioning.

Additionally, "Repeatability," "Adaptability to the Environment," and "Efficiency in Energy" are also crucial elements, albeit having numerical values that are a little bit higher and showing their importance but with a little bit less weight than the top-ranked variables. Decision-makers can clearly grasp the important factors to take into account when choosing an industrial robot thanks to this data-driven evaluation of features, which enables them to make decisions that satisfy their operational needs and performance standards.

Effectiveness and efficiency are essential components of a strong paradigm for decision-making. Efficient use of time and resources guarantees a smooth process, reducing waiting times and maximizing resource distribution. This also applies to the fundamentals of data gathering and processing, where effectiveness is critical to gaining timely, insightful information that is required for making well-informed decisions.

The Analytical Hierarchy Process (AHP) increases productivity even more by quickly weighing criteria and quickly recognizing and classifying important factors. Effectiveness simultaneously becomes the cornerstone of decision impact and quality, guaranteeing that decisions are in line with overarching objectives. Ratio analysis-based Multi-Objective Optimization (MOORA) improves efficacy by providing a detailed assessment that appropriately contrasts alternatives based on predetermined standards.

7 Conclusion and Future Research Scope

In conclusion, our research has shown that the Multi-Criteria Decision-Making (MCDM) technique is useful and applicable for choosing industrial robots in a variety of production settings. We have demonstrated how MCDM methods like MOORA and AHP may help decision-makers choose the best industrial robot for certain applications by a systematic study of many parameters, including Degree of freedom, Working envelope, Speed, Payload, Positional Accuracy, Repeatability, Adaptability to the environment, Efficiency in Energy. Our research has shed light on the difficulties of selecting robots, emphasizing the necessity of weighing several competing variables at once.

The MOORA (Multi-Objective Optimization by Ratio Analysis) technique shines in the field of decision-making processes as a very accessible and powerful instrument, even for decision makers lacking a profound understanding of its underlying physical complexity. Through the creation of a consolidated performance criterion that explicitly reflects its impact on the values of the compared criteria, this strategy not only empowers decision makers but also streamlines the complex decision-making process. By using different mathematical models for benefit and non-benefit criteria, including those of a qualitative and graphical type, MOORA stands out from other Multi-Criteria Decision-Making (MCDM) systems. This strategic division makes sure that vital data is preserved, greatly lowering the possibility of data loss during the MOORA-based decision-making process. MOORA is a valuable tool because of its adaptability and simplicity. It can demystify the subjective aspect of using a comprehensive multiple attribute decision-making approach, improving the evaluation process and laying the groundwork for future study in this area.

There are numerous directions that the field of industrial robot selection utilizing the MCDM approach can go in the future. The precision and automation of the process could be improved by incorporating cutting-edge machine learning and artificial intelligence approaches for data-driven decision-making in robot selection. The incorporation of collaborative robots (cobots) and their unique requirements into the MCDM framework would also be a key area of investigation given the changing landscape of industrial automation. Additionally, the development of software tools and decision support systems that assist industry practitioners in choosing MCDM-based robots could accelerate the decision-making process. Finally, the modification of our strategy to take sustainability and environmental effect considerations into account when choosing robots is in line with the rising importance of environmentally friendly production methods. Overall, there is a lot of room for improvement in the efficiency and effectiveness of industrial robot selection in the future scope of research in this area, which would further progress the manufacturing and automation industries.

Subsequent investigations into the application of industrial robotics for vehicle painting tasks may delve into developments in robotic technologies that augment versatility, agility, and cooperation. Robots that can easily integrate into intelligent, networked production systems are becoming more and more necessary as manufacturing processes change. Subsequent research endeavors may concentrate on enhancing the sensory capacities of robots and developing artificial intelligence algorithms that would empower them to adjust to fluctuations in the painting milieu and manage intricate assignments with heightened self-sufficiency. Furthermore, investigating energy-efficient and sustainable robotic systems can be a major focus, in line with the increased emphasis on ecologically friendly production techniques. Additionally, studies could focus on human-robot cooperation techniques, examining how humans and robots can cooperate harmoniously to maximize efficiency.

References

1. Athawale, V.M., Chakraborty, S.: A comparative study on the ranking performance of some multi-criteria decision-making methods for industrial robot selection. Int. J. Ind. Eng. Comput. **2**(4), 831–850 (2011)
2. Brauers, W.K., Zavadskas, E.K.: The MOORA method and its application to privatization in a transition economy. Control. Cybern. **35**(2), 445–469 (2006)
3. Parkan, C., Wu, M.L.: Decision-making and performance measurement models with applications to robot selection. Comput. Ind. Eng. **36**(3), 503–523 (1999)
4. Goh, C.H.: Analytic hierarchy process for robot selection. J. Manuf. Syst. **16**(5), 381–386 (1997)
5. Bhangale, P.P., Agrawal, V.P., Saha, S.K.: Attribute based specification, comparison and selection of a robot. Mech. Mach. Theory **39**(12), 1345–1366 (2004)
6. Chakraborty, S.: Applications of the MOORA method for decision making in manufacturing environment. Int. J. Adv. Manuf. Technol. **54**, 1155–1166 (2011)
7. Karsak, E.E.: Robot selection using an integrated approach based on quality function deployment and fuzzy regression. Int. J. Prod. Res. **46**(3), 723–738 (2008)
8. Rao, R.V., Patel, B.K., Parnichkun, M.: Industrial robot selection using a novel decision making method considering objective and subjective preferences. Robot. Auton. Syst. **59**(6), 367–375 (2011)
9. Chatterjee, P., Athawale, V.M., Chakraborty, S.: Selection of industrial robots using compromise ranking and outranking methods. Robot. Comput.-Integr. Manuf. **26**(5), 483–489 (2010)

10. Kumar, R., Garg, R.K.: Optimal selection of robots by using distance based approach method. Robot. Comput.-Integr. Manuf. **26**(5), 500–506 (2010)
11. Bairagi, B., Dey, B., Sarkar, B., Sanyal, S.: A novel multiplicative model of multi criteria analysis for robot selection. Int. J. Soft Comput. Artif. Intell. Appl. **1**(3), 1–9 (2012)
12. Baležentis, A., Baležentis, T., Brauers, W.K.: MULTIMOORA-FG: a multi-objective decision making method for linguistic reasoning with an application to personnel selection. Informatica **23**(2), 173–190 (2012)
13. Wu, C.Y.: Robot selection decision support system: a fuzzy set approach. Math. Comput. Model. **14**, 440–443 (1990)
14. Khouja, M., Booth, D.E.: Fuzzy clustering procedure for evaluation and selection of industrial robots. J. Manuf. Syst. **14**(4), 244–251 (1995)
15. Chu, T.C., Lin, Y.C.: A fuzzy TOPSIS method for robot selection. Int. J. Adv. Manuf. Technol. **21**, 284–290 (2003)
16. Kapoor, V., Tak, S.S.: Fuzzy application to the analytic hierarchy process for robot selection. Fuzzy Optim. Decis. Making **4**(3), 209–234 (2005)
17. Kahraman, C., Çevik, S., Ates, N.Y., Gülbay, M.: Fuzzy multi-criteria evaluation of industrial robotic systems. Comput. Ind. Eng. **52**(4), 414–433 (2007)
18. Sharma, H., Sohani, N., Yadav, A.: Comparative analysis of ranking the lean supply chain enablers: an AHP, BWM and fuzzy SWARA based approach. Int. J. Qual. Reliab. Manag. **39**(9), 2252–2271 (2022)
19. Bairagi, B.: Technique of Accurate Ranking Order (TARO): a novel multi criteria analysis approach in performance evaluation of industrial robots for material handling. Decis. Sci. Lett. **11**(4), 563–589 (2022)
20. Sharma, H., Sohani, N., Yadav, A.: Structural modeling of lean supply chain enablers: a hybrid AHP and ISM-MICMAC based approach. J. Eng. Des. Technol. **21**(6), 1658–1689 (2021)
21. Sharma, H., Sohani, N., Yadav, A.: A fuzzy SWARA-WASPAS based approach for determining the role of lean practices in enabling the supply chain agility. Int. J. Syst. Assur. Eng. Manag. **14**(Suppl 1), 492–511 (2023)
22. Dağsuyu, C., Polat, U., Kokangül, A.: Integrated process capability and multi-criteria decision-making approach. Soft. Comput. **25**(10), 7169–7180 (2021)

Review on Gene Expression Meta-analysis: Techniques and Implementations

P. Marimuktu[1,2(✉)]

[1] Department of Computer Applications, Ayya Nadar Janaki Ammal College (Autonomous),
Sivakasi, India
pmanjac@gmail.com

[2] Madurai Kamaraj University Madurai, Tamil Nadu, India

Abstract. The massive use of high-efficiency gene expression evaluation progress over the last twenty years and certainty the majority of the produced research are stored in shared repositories. All further information's offers an essential resource for remodel to result in new understanding and scientific discovery. In this situation, considerable interest has been concentrated on meta-analysis techniques to blend and mutually inspect mismatched gene expression datasets. Here, this review outlines the major evolution in the gene expression meta-analysis, from data composition to the modern statistical techniques. This review addresses the major sets of applications and issues that could be addressed in protein expression meta-analysis studies and allows a relative outline of the useful software and bioinformatics tools. This review paper gives the researchers an overview of the approaches used to conduct meta-analysis on genome-wide data and new approaches can be invented with the help of previous one. This review has the aim of helping researchers to understand methodologies to perform meta-analyses based on gene expression data.

Keywords: protein expression · meta-syntheses · data integration · biomarker discovery · public tools

1 Introduction

The progress of high-performance gene expression quantification technologies has been major in the evolution of biomedical investigation, permitting investigator to estimate genome-vast gene expression samples in an assessment set-up. From the National Center for Biotechnology Information (NCBI) [1] Gene Expression Omnibus (GEO) general databases is available, which stores expression data from more than 100,000 different works with a total of more than 3 million samples, or Array Express [2], which keeps expression data carries over and above 2.3 million preferred samples. These resources gather information from different platforms and organisms, but there are also specialized databases that concentrate on specific illness, living thing, or tissues, like GTEx [3] where the data is gathered from 54 tissue sites in non-diseased humans, specifically from around 1,000 individuals. The wealth of information available is incredibly beneficial

S. Rajagopal et al (Eds.): ASCIS 2023, CCIS 2040, pp. 144–162, 2024.
https://doi.org/10.1007/978-3-031-59107-5_10

for reusing and analyzing together to produce fresh findings and understanding. Meta-analysis techniques refer to a set of statistical methods that merge several distinct studies together in order to generate a singular and significant outcome. In the field of gene expression, a meta-analysis can investigate data collections from various cohorts or studies to identify shared molecular patterns, enhance the consistency of results, and acquire more dependable biomarkers [4, 5]. In the past few years, there has been a significant growth in the amount of research articles focused on gene expression meta-analysis. Huan T. [6] a cluster of 7017 blood-sugar and hypertension samples from dissimilar learning's were brought together and analyzed. Through this analysis, distinct sets of genes were identified that are linked to specific clinical presentations within the disorder. The research conducted by de Magalhães JP [7]. The researchers utilized 27 sets of data from the Gene Aging Nexus [8] and GEO databases to identify patterns of gene expression that are related to aging. They found 56 genes that showed an increase in expression as age increased. Meta-analyses are commonly employed in different cancer contexts to discover biomarkers that can indicate the presence and advancement of the disease [9, 10].

Meta-analyses are especially beneficial when it comes to uncommon or infrequently studied illnesses that have a restricted number of research studies and a small patient population. Meta-analysis has the potential to increase sample size by combining samples from different groups, which strengthens the statistical significance and reliability of results. The work conducted by Piras IS Manchia M [5], they provided successful instances of meta-analyses. The researchers conducted a systematic-review using set of three GEO databases, as described by Su-et al. [11] discovered a set of modified biological processes by analyzing multiple separate research studies on Alzheimer's disease. In this assessment, the summary outlines the main statistical methods used in meta-analysis of gene expression and describes the primary purposes for which these methods are utilized. Different patient cohorts [12]. The following Fig. 1 shows Workflow of microarray meta-analysis.

2   Advances in Systematic Review of Gene Expression Data

Figure 2 displays the advancement of the meta-analysis. This part, provide an explanation of significant factors to consider and essential actions to take when conducting a gene expression meta-analysis [13–15].

- *Selection of hypotheses and data.* The selection criteria for the search and selection of data sets to be included are determined based on the objective of the study. Public repositories enable rapid searches using keywords or ontologies automatically. When choosing the data, various factors need to be considered since they have the potential to impact the outcomes. Study heterogeneity refers to how diverse, technical or biological the studies are. Selecting high or low heterogeneity between studies can serve different purposes: a high degree of heterogeneity between studies reduces statistical significance, but actually increases the generalizability of results [15, 16].
- In different circumstances, it's pivotal to work with balanced data regarding the number of instance from each class and the instance size of each study in order to homogenize the weight that each study exerts on the results. As a general rule, the isolated

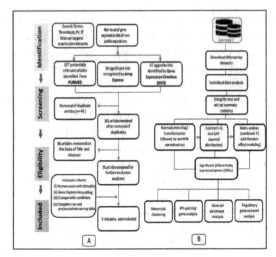

Fig. 1. Workflow of microarray meta-analysis. (A) Selection process of eligible microarray datasets for meta-analysis of the shared signatures between thrombosis, essential thrombocythemia (ET) and polycythemia vera (PV), according to Prisma 2009 flow diagram. (B) Depiction of the flow chart of the process involved in integrated meta-analysis of the selected microarray datasets.

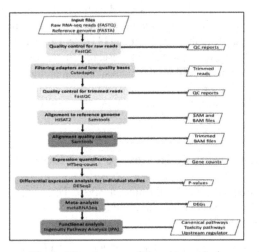

Fig. 2. The advances of the meta-analysis

effect of a study is minimized with a lesser number of studies, so the general meaning of the results is in the focus (17).

- *Data preprocessing and normalization.* As you have raw data, the first thing you need to do is generate an expression matrix for every set of data. The process varies depending on the type of technology utilized to produce the data. For example, RNA-Seq-Reads must be compared to a reference genome to obtain gene counts, while microarray data must be processed with different techniques depending on the platform. A common and important preprocessing step is normalization to minimize non-biological variation [18]. There are excellent reviews on this topic for RNASeq [19] and Formicroar [20]. Public data stores often have pre-processed data. Data preprocessing should be standardized as much as possible between studies to minimize technical heterogeneity.

- *Single quality control.* It is important to conduct quality checks to detect any exceptions, discrepancies in measurements, technical issues with samples, and so on. Outliers in the data lead to biases in subsequent analysis, leading to underestimated or overestimated results. Dealing with missing sample data is an example of a common problem that can induce mutable outcome when such samples are used to infer a population. Therefore, the results are highly influenced on the techniques used to process absent values and exceptions [21]. The detection of anomalies in expression studies typically involves identifying values that significantly deviate from normal patterns or using methods like correlations, clusters, Mahalanobis distances, or principal component analysis to determine similarity between samples [18, 22]. The issue of incomplete gene values in a dataset can be evaluated through imputation. There are several commonly used imputation methods that can be employed. One approach is to substitute the missing value with the average expression of that gene. A different approach includes utilizing models created by comparing genes, like the K nearest neighbor algorithm [23, 24].

- *Genetic malfunction and data summary.* To merge data sets from different platforms, it is necessary to assign common and standardized identifiers (like the Entrez gene identifier, set ID, or gene symbol) to the probe sets. After doing so, you should aggregate the expression values for all probes associated in it. The primary methods involve combining individual genes into a research that represents the greatest or smallest mean, absolute mean, or variance. Another approach is to aggregate a gene by calculating the mean of all its probes [26]. There are new solutions being developed to tackle this issue, such as using regression models to estimate gene expression by utilizing the genes found in all the available data sets [27].

- *Batch effect.* However, if the objective is to reduce variations in technical aspects, a technique called batch effect rectification can be used to lessen or eliminate the influence of external factors and technical biases that can strongly affect the examination of gene expression in various gene states. That means the adjustment of the batch effect. It is utilized for the purpose of eliminating undesired sources of variation. Some of the most commonly employed perspectives include empirical Bayesian methods using gathered data [28], which can be corrected by taking into account covariates or removing the influence of to obtain variation produced by substitute variables, the limma and sva-R packages are considered two of the most significant aid to utilize [28, 29].

- *Choice of the meta-analysis approach.* Objectives of the investigation. The efficiency of a particular approach will depend on the unique characteristics of the data being studied and the intended goals of the analysis. Analytical design is the methodical examination and assessment of different elements within a design in order to make knowledgeable choices and enhancements. The action that was asked for has been finished. The Meta-analysis techniques section provides a thorough explanation of the various methods used for selecting meta-analysis techniques. To consider, besides the quantity of research and the thoroughness of the examination, one must also take into consideration the diversity in technology (varying platforms) and diversity in biology (varying study conditions or phenotypes). Several methods exist for evaluating heterogeneity, including Cochran's Q test, which is commonly used in many studies. Another method is the utilization of the I2 statistic, which is calculated, based on Cochran's Q and indicates the proportion of dissimilarity among studies that can be attributed to heterogeneity, rather than random variation. Crucially, the I2 statistic is unaffected by the quantity of studies examined in the analysis [30, 31].

- *The understanding of the outcome.* In general, a gene expression meta-analysis will produce a list of genes that show varying levels of expression in several studies. Visualization aids such as heat maps or diagrams have been utilized in various studies to display the interaction network of these genes. Help is needed to perform an initial analysis, and other types of analyses are usually used to comprehend and explain the important biological functions related to the demise of the genetic signature [32].

3 Meta-synthesis Techniques

There are three main meta-analysis techniques: meta-analysis using rank combination, meta-analysis using effect size combination, and meta-analysis using P-value combination.

Approaches that Involve Utilizing the Combined Effect Sizes

This approach is designed to clarify the variation in the intensity of a phenomenon (referred to as the effect) across various studies. The determined effect size depends on the particular data type and the nature of the studies conducted [33]. For instance, in genomic studies that encompass the entire genome (GWAS), which extensively utilizes this particular approach [34], The calculated impact is associated with the probability ratio [35, 36]. In the provided demonstration of gene expression data, the term "effect size" denotes the variation in levels of expression that can be observed between two groups, such as cases and controls. This difference is expected to adhere to a normal distribution [37]. The Hedges G estimator is often recommended as a popular approach to determine the effect size when calculating [38–40]:

$$\mathbf{Ti} = c(m)\frac{\bar{\mathbf{y}}\mathbf{E} - \bar{\mathbf{y}}\mathbf{C}}{S} \tag{1}$$

where,

- Ti represents the impact magnitude of a specific gene on the ith dataset.
- The correct degrees of freedom can be represented by the equation $m = nE + nC - 2$.

The Fig. 3. The main recommendations for selecting the best meta-analysis approach while taking the peculiarities of the data into account are outlined in this book. The gene will also be significant in all other investigations if it turns out to be significant in the meta-analysis. HSB: If the gene significantly influences the meta-analysis, it significantly influences at least one individual research as well. These recommendations are tailored

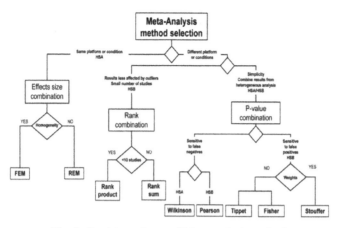

Fig. 3. Decision scheme of Meta-analysis method.

to the features of the data. It is crucial to keep the meta analysis's goal in mind when selecting a method.

$$c(m) = 1 - \frac{3}{4m - 1!} = 1 - \frac{3}{4(nE + nC) - 9}$$

is a factor that enhances the positive bias

- $\bar{y}_E$ and $\bar{y}_C$ the gene expression means of the case (experimental) and control groups

$$S = \sqrt{\frac{(n_E - 1)S_E^2 + (n_C - 1)S_C^2}{n_E + n_C - 2}} \tag{2}$$

Studies' standard deviation, where nE and nC are the sample sizes for the experimental and control groups, respectively.

The variances of the experimental and control groups are S2E and S2C, respectively. Additionally, an impact size's variance is calculated:

$$V(T_i) = \frac{n_E + n_C}{n_E \times n_C} + \frac{(T_i)^2}{2(n_E + n_C)} \tag{3}$$

The objective is to determine a cumulative effect of all the effect sizes and their variations for each gene. You can determine whether a gene is expressed differently across all experiments thanks to its combined effect. The fixed effects model (FEM) and the random effects model (REM) are two practical approaches for obtaining the combined effect.

The FEM fixed effects model is a linear model that considers the fact that different studies have a similar impact magnitude, or real effect. The total impact is computed as [41]

$$\bar{T} = \frac{\sum \omega_i T_i}{\sum \omega_i} \tag{4}$$

here ω_i are the different weights assigned to each study, that is, the inverse within-study variance, $V(T_i)$

$$\omega_i = \frac{1}{V(T_i)} \tag{5}$$

The variance of the combined effect is defined as

$$V(\overline{T}.) = \frac{1}{\Sigma \omega_i} \tag{6}$$

The combined effect value for a standard normal

$$Z = \frac{\overline{T}.}{\sqrt{V(\overline{T}.)}} \tag{7}$$

Therefore, we can calculate the two-trailed P value

$$P = 2[1 - (\Phi(|Z|))] \tag{8}$$

where Φ is the standard normal cumulative distribution function.

If there is homogeneity among the many studies or if it is assumed that all samples come from the same population, this model is advised [42]. As a result, this approach is extremely constrained and needs to be used with care.

The REM Random Effects Model
According to the REM Random Effects Model, a distribution of real effect sizes exists, reflecting the overall influence of the population mean. The FEM, in contrast, anticipates that all studies will have the same, single effect size as in the FEM [39, 41]. The total effect $\overline{T}$ in this REM effect model is It is calculated in a manner similar to how the PEF is calculated [39, 42].

$$\overline{T}^* = \frac{\sum_{i=1}^{k} \omega_i^* T_i}{\sum_{i=1}^{k} \omega_i^*} \tag{9}$$

The primary distinction lies in how the weights w^*_i are acquired. There are two sources of error in the weighting of this model: Variation within a study and variation between studies. The variance within a study (vi) is determined by calculating the observed effect, but it is important to also obtain the variance across different studies ($\tau2$). In order to determine the variation between studies, one must first calculate the overall variance and subsequently separate the variance within each study. The variance in total is a statistical metric. The total sum of all deviations is known as Q.

$$Q = \sum_{i=1}^{k} \omega_i (T_i - \overline{T}) \tag{10}$$

where,

- $\overline{T}.$ is the total impact computed using the finite element method,

- T_i is the effect that was observed,
- w_i is the determined weights for the FEM, and

After obtaining the Q statistic, it is decomposed to yield the between-study variance (τ^2).

$$\tau^2 = \begin{cases} \frac{Q-df}{C} & \text{if } Q > df \\ 0 & \text{if } Q \leq df \end{cases} \tag{11}$$

where,

$$C = \sum_{i=1}^{k} \omega_i - \frac{\sum_{i=1}^{k} \omega_i^2}{\sum_{i=1}^{k} \omega_i}$$

When the error within each study is the only factor affecting variance, the degrees of freedom (df) are equal to the number of studies minus one. The weights for each study can be calculated once the between-study variation has been determined.

$$\omega_i^* = \frac{1}{v_i^*} \tag{12}$$

where $\mathbf{v}^*_i$ is

$$v_i^* = V(T_i) + \tau^2 \tag{13}$$

The following is the definition of the combined effect's variance:

$$V\left(\overline{T}^*\right) = \frac{1}{\sum_{i=1}^{k} \omega_i^*} \tag{14}$$

The aggregate impact measure for a standard normal variable

$$Z = \frac{\overline{T}^*}{\sqrt{V\left(\overline{T}^*\right)}} \tag{15}$$

As a result, we can calculate the P value for each end of the distribution.

$$P = 2[1 - (\Phi(|Z|))] \tag{16}$$

Ø is a representation of the typical normal cumulative distribution function. Many meta-analysis techniques typically use this specific paradigm [43]. It is recommended that studies vary a little, but there shouldn't be any big differences between them. The text provided is incomplete, therefore it cannot be summarized. One advantage is that it generally aligns better with biological accuracy and is less restrictive than FEM [15, 42].

P-values from different analyses are combined into a single P-value for each gene using techniques that rely on merging P-values. One feature of these methodologies is that every study consistently influences the results, no matter its size. This is because the individual P values are directly combined, unless modifications such as including weights or using effect size approximations are made. Another benefit of these methods is that they enable the direct integration of diverse analyses [44].

Nevertheless, methodologies that rely on the P value suffer from a significant disadvantage - they fail to capture the directional aspect of the expression model [43]. For instance, in the search for similar trends and a Geneis notably/significantly In certain studies, the gene is found to be highly expressed while in others it is found to be expressed at a lower level. Even though the expression patterns varied between investigations, a significant total P value could still be determined. Selecting genes that show the same fold change (FC) direction is one potential solution. "Remove the genes that are in contradiction with each other" [45]. It is crucial to check for any variations in expression between the case and control groups, just like when combining effect sizes. Multiple techniques or approaches enable the pairing once the P values for each individual study have been computed.

The Fisher Method

An individual named Fisher developed a system or procedure known as the Fisher method. The statistical metric used in this method is the sum of the logarithms of the P values [43, 46], which means:

$$-2 \times \sum\nolimits_{i=1}^{k} \ln(p_i) \tag{17}$$

where pi stands for any P value discovered through various studies. The hypothesis being tested in this instance is that there is no variation in gene expression across the numerous studies, and if there is, it follows a distribution that is similar to ax2 with 2 times the number of studies (k) of degrees of freedom. When a gene is labeled as significant, it means that it has been found to be important in one or more research. A single study that produces surprisingly significant results can lead to a substantial combined P value because Fisher's approach can identify even the tiniest P values [47, 48].

Pearson's Approach

The method's statistic is

$$-2 \times \sum\nolimits_{i=1}^{k} \ln(1 - p_i) \tag{18}$$

This approach shares similar characteristics In relation to Fisher's approach and strategy can be applied in identical circumstances. The method's only distinction lies in its heightened sensitivity towards high values of P, resulting in an increased number of incorrect negative outcomes. [47].

Stouffer's Approach

This method is predicated on:

$$Z_i = \Phi^{-1}(1 - p_i) \tag{19}$$

A mathematical formula Φ is used to represent the standard normal cumulative distribution function. The statistical data are the ones used in this technique.

$$\frac{\sum_{i=1}^{k} Z_i}{\sqrt{k}} \tag{20}$$

When the null hypothesis is correct, the distribution has the shape of a normal distribution and is designated as N (0.1). This method has the advantage of allowing for the insertion of exam weights. The statistic in this instance is

$$\frac{\sum_{i=1}^{k} \omega_i Z_i}{\sqrt{\sum_{i=1}^{k} \omega_i^2}} \tag{21}$$

Weights (wi) should be assigned depending on the inverse variance of the data used to calculate various P values. The square roots of the sample sizes n, on the other hand, They can also be used since they generate good outcomes even when these differences cannot be computed [49, 50]. When calculating weights, the Stouffer's method is preferred over Fisher's or the unweight Stouffer's method because it produces more accurate results [50].

Tippet's Approach
Tippet's method involves selecting the P-values with the lowest values. The statistic for this strategy is the lowest P-value across all investigations.

$$\min (p1, p2, \ldots \ldots, pi, \ldots \ldots .pk) \tag{22}$$

It is distributed as Beta(1, k) under the null hypothesis [47]. When a gene is considered important, meaning it is significant in one or more studies, it can result in a number of falsely positive results. Therefore, this method is suggested when the goal is to eradicate a certain gene [47].

Wilkinson Approach
The Wilkinson approach is being used. This method is also known as maximizing the P value. The maximum statistic is the highest value for this technique. P-values derived from all studies:

$$\max (p1, p2, \ldots \ldots, pi, \ldots \ldots .pk) \tag{23}$$

The distribution is assumed to follow a Beta distribution with parameters (k, 1) based on the null hypothesis [46]. This approach of combining P-values differs from others in that it ensures that if a gene is important, it will be deemed significant in all investigations. However, it is possible that it will produce a large number of false negative findings. As a result, this method is recommended for selecting the most powerful genes [47].

Non-Parametric Techniques: Rank Combination
Rank Combination approaches allow the combination of many studies using any measurable criteria that can be put in a certain order, with HR being the most widely used statistic.

Once the CFs have been estimated, they are transformed into ranks. The gene with the least HR value The gene ranking would follow a sequence where the first place would be occupied by the highest value gene. To find the genes that are not expressed enough, perform calculations and then reverse the process. In order to determine the genes that are over expressed, an analysis needs to be performed.

The capacity to integrate diverse types of data, regardless of format or content, is one of the advantages of adopting these technologies. The technique handles heterogeneous data or data obtained from diverse platforms, guaranteeing that very significant P-values from individual studies do not effect the overall conclusions [43, 51].

Furthermore, these methods typically yield more precise and resilient outcomes compared to the P-value combination approaches [52]. However, a downside of these techniques is their high sensitivity to variations in diversity. For example, changes in diversity can significantly reduce the accuracy of approaches used to categorize genes based on differential expression. As previously demonstrated by Breitling and Herzyk [53], these results in incorrectly relevant P values. Furthermore, if these methods employ a two-tailed P value, they might fail to identify the opposite direction in the hazard ratio. [18, 48, 57]; hence, it is advisable to employ a single-sided Referring to the significance level in statistical analysis; the p-value is being mentioned to use these methods effectively.

Rank Product
In this approach, the overall rank for each gene is determined by multiplying their ranks from different studies [43]:

$$RP_g = \prod_i^k r_{ig} \tag{24}$$

Following that, an empirical P-value is calculated by randomizing the values in the rank matrix. And recalculates the position multiplication for the modified integers. If the sequence is randomized If a gene's value is greater than its original value, one is added to the gene's mistake count. The method is performed n times, and the empirical P value for a gene is computed by dividing the total error collected by n [43, 53, 54]. However, when a product is used, the computing cost is extremely significant [53].

Rank Total
The total values derived by ranking a set of data, often containing the sum of ranks for two groups or categories, are referred to as rank sums. The only difference between this strategy and the previous one is that the sum of the rank combination is

$$RS_g = \sum_i^K r_{ig} \tag{24}$$

A computation was performed instead of the product. [43]: While the sorted product method may produce more reliable results, this alternate strategy is more efficient when working with a large number of trials. Less computational resources are required [53].

4 Implementation

Methods for gene expression meta-analysis have been used in a variety of applications, and they can be categorized into three types of implementation. The most common strategy is to analyze multiple groups with comparable features.

There is a need to improve statistical power in order to discover genes that display consistent differences across groups with cases and control groups. So, this particular method of meta-analysis is appropriate for identifying reliable biomarkers and is commonly practiced in cancer research. [9, 55], autoimmune diseases [56, 57] or mental disorders [58].

The second approach is to look for similar patterns of gene expression across situations; for example, genes with differential levels of expression in several diseases compared to healthy samples, distinct disease stages, or diverse drug-influenced gene profiles. This technique is useful for discovering shared molecular processes and biological pathways among different phenotypes. This method, for example, has been used to investigate shared patterns of gene activation in autoimmune illnesses [59–61] or neurological disorders [62].

The third application is The third approach is to use gene expression data to find patterns of inverted gene expression. Amid many ailments or illnesses. The basic goal is to discover sets of genes that are over-expressed in one phenotype while being under-expressed in another. (In this situation,) Ibaez et al. [63]. Provide an example of how this can be done. We used several gene expression data sets to find opposing gene patterns in Alzheimer's disease and cancer, showing a reverse comorbidity. This procedure can also be used to undertake drug reuse analyses. Simply defined, drug reuse analysis finds additional medicinal uses for existing pharmaceuticals and identifies links between an illness and the genetic alterations generated by a drug. This remark implies that if a medicine can induce genetic patterns that are diametrically opposed to those seen in an illness, it may be able to reverse the disease's destructive qualities [64, 65].

5 Tools

In this section, I explain in detail the tools and software packages that can be shared openly for assessing gene expression. The emphasis is primarily on web tools and R packages. In this section, I will provide a brief analysis of each of their traits, benefits, and drawbacks. It should be noted that before making a decision, I consider all tools. Techniques that have been implemented are considered strengths, whilst techniques that have not been implemented are considered weaknesses.

Web-based programs

• Network Analyst [66] is a popular web-based meta-analysis application built with Java Server Faces 2.0 technology. It includes quality control procedures (such as batch effect correction and various normalization approaches for microarray and RNASeq data) as well as meta-analysis methodologies. It also includes viewing and investigation options, such as functional analysis with the KEGG [67] and Gene Ontology [68] databases. The biggest downside of this software is that it does not support data from public repositories. The biggest downside of this software is that it does not support data from public repositories. Before being posted to the app, gene expression records must be downloaded and prepared. Non-biotechnology users may find this format requirement problematic.

ImaGEO [69] (Institute for Meta-Analysis of Public Gene Expression) is a Shiny and R-based web application. Its primary use is meta-analysis of public gene expression. Tools are classified based on whether they employ combination approaches (e.g., effect size, p-value, ranges, or a mix of these). The font color shows the type of implementation (for example, blue for web tool and black for R package).

Data is saved in the GEO database. Select the GEO identifier of the study to be analyzed directly. Upload your own data. Identify outliers and filter data based on missing values. The most popular meta-analytical techniques, such as effects-based meta-analytical and P value integration, are included. ImaGEO uses the gene ontology database to perform quality control (QC) and functional analysis (FAA).

- *Gemma* [70] is Gemma is a A web-based tool for evaluating and exploring data about public expression. Meta-analysis is a sort of analysis in which P-values are combined. Gemma includes over 3,000 pre-loaded and carefully selected public-exchange-oriented (GEO) datasets, including human, rat, and mouse studies. You may also use Gemma to upload your own data (registration is required). While Gemma is an excellent tool for studying public expression data, meta-analysis techniques are limited to combining P-values.
- *ExAtlas* [71] It is yet another web-based meta-analysis tool that can perform meta-analysis on both public (GEO-supplied) and user-defined (user-defined) data. ExAtlas provides a diverse set of analysis approaches and outputs, including co-expression analysis, functional analysis, and meta-analysis, all of which are based on databases such as ENCODE, Gene Ontology, and KEGG. [79].
- *ShinyMDE* [72] shinyMDE is a R and Shiny-based online utility. It enables the integration of several gene expression data sets from Affymetrix or Illumina microarrays. You can begin with raw data and apply the P-value combination method. One restriction of the program is that no log generated by separate platforms can be integrated. The utility takes as input a table of computed p-values. As a result, before using the program, you must first do differential gene expression analysis.

R Packages

- **MetaOmics** [73, 74] is an interactive meta-analysis application based on shiny, but I included it here because you need some knowledge of r to install shiny dependencies and run it locally. MetaOmics offers various modules that allow you to do all meta-analytic stages interactively, including most meta-analytic procedures based on effect size, p-value, range combination, and so on. Additionally, metaOmics provides modules to analyze meta-analytic results (network analyzers, path analyzers, principal component analyzers, etc.).
- **MetaIntegrator** [75] is a R package that implements meta-analysis and visualization techniques. It is compatible with the REM and Fisher procedures.
- **MetaP** [76] performs various techniques for integrating p-values, such as those described in Techniques, as well as other non-proprietary techniques like sum or mean p-values.
- **GeneMeta** [77] is a R package that compiles expression matrices from individual studies and performs Meta analyses based on effect size combinations.
- **metaMA and metaRNASeq** [44, 45] MetaMA is an R package that contains functions to carry out meta-analyze based on P-value and effect size (MetaMA only).

MetaMA is a package for microarrays. MetaRNASeq is a package for RNASeq and metaMA data. MetaMA allows you to start from expression matrix as well as gene lists with t statistics. MetaRNASQ combines lists of p values with fisher or stouffer methods. MetaMA & metaRNASQ are implemented as interactive tool by galaxy [79].

- **RankProd** [78] is RankProd in R is a package that deals with the product and the sum of ranks. It can be used for differential expressions between two conditions as well as for meta-analyses.
- **RankAggreg** [79]. Using the rank sum algorithm, this R package can be used to perform meta-analyses of ranked lists (e.g. FC sorted genes) obtained from various studies.
- **Order list** [80]. This R package works with gene sorting lists. This R package can be used to sort lists of genes. The algorithm calculates the list's similarity score based on the number of genes detected in the list.
- **metahdep** [80]. Metahdep Metahdep is an R package that compiles meta-analyses based on effect
- **metaSeq** [81]. R package to apply Fisher and Stouf techniques to RNASeq differential expression analysis. MetaVolcanoR [82]. This R package applies
- *Random Effects Model* (REM) and Fisher's method to expression matrices. Its main advantage is the graphical output: volcano and forest diagrams may be built from the meta-analysis data.
- **Cross goal** [83]. R package for raw microarray data download and E-processing GEO. Combine effect sizes and meta-analyze routes.

Figure 4 categorizes the various tools based on the methods they have implemented.

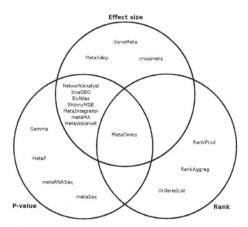

Fig. 4. Overview of the existing tools for conducting meta-analysis on gene expression. The tools are categorized based on whether they use the methods of combining impact. Dimensions, statistical significance, order or multiple of them. The color of the font indicates the category of tool used for implementation (blue represents web tools, while black represents R packages). (Color figure online)

6 Conclusions and Future Scope

For the past few years, reproducibility of results has been a serious problem in biomedical research, particularly in high throughput experiments such as gene expression microarrays or genome wide association analyses involving thousands of hypotheses. These irreproducibility issues are mainly due to technical and biological differences. These differences are integrated with the analytical basis using significant P values instead of effect sizes or independent validation [14].

High-performance technologies, combined with the need to publish experimental data in open repositories, have generated unprecedented amounts of data. This has opened up new ways to enhance reproducibility by combining multiple data sets through genome-wide meta-analysis, as well as new methods for testing and generating new hypotheses. This has led to a dramatic increase in the number of systematic review and meta-analyze publications over the past decade. Different techniques and variations on them have also emerged, providing the researcher with a broad array of options.

While meta-analysis software such as METAL [84] and PLINK [85] have been consolidated by GWAS and a full series of meta-analysis review articles have been published, the meta-analysis of gene expression data is still relatively underused. This is partly due to the fact that there are many different gene expression platforms and experimental designs, as well as the fact that the data itself is much more diverse. In this meta-analysis review article covers the most often used meta-analysis techniques for gene expression data and discuss the benefits and drawbacks of each based on the application. In addition, This review cover the main applications of meta-analysis for gene expression, the workflow for a common meta-analysis trial and also highlighted key points that users should think about when performing the analysis. Lastly, This review present a comparison of the different public tools for conducting genome-wide meta-analysis using gene expression data and specialize in meta-analysis methodologies, data entry and quality control, and analysis functionalities.

The future scope of this review paper gives the researchers an overview of the approaches used to conduct meta-analysis on genome-wide data and new approaches can be invented with the help of previous one. This review has the aim of helping researchers to understand methodologies to perform meta-analyses based on gene expression data.

References

1. Barrett, T., Wilhite, S.E., Ledoux, P., et al.: NCBI GEO: archive for functional genomics data sets—update. Nucleic Acids Res. 41, D991–D995 (2013)
2. Athar, A., Füllgrabe, A., George, N., et al.: ArrayExpress update - from bulk to single-cell expression data. Nucleic Acids Res. 47, D711–D715 (2019)
3. Consortium GTE. The genotype-tissue expression (GTEx) project. Nat Genet 45, 580 (2013)
4. Cho, H., Kim, H., Na, D., et al.: Meta-analysis method for discovering reliable biomarkers by integrating statistical and biological approaches: an application to liver toxicity. Biochem. Biophys. Res. Commun. 471, 274–81 (2016)
5. Piras, I.S., Manchia, M., Huentelman, M.J., et al.: Peripheral biomarkers in schizophrenia: a meta- analysis of microarray gene expression datasets. Int. J. Neuro. Psychopharmacol. 22, 186–193 (2018)

6. Huan, T., Esko, T., Peters, M.J., et al.: A meta-analysis of gene expression signatures of blood pressure and hypertension. PLoS Genet. **11**(3) (2015)

7. de Magalhães, J.P., Curado, J., Church, G.M.: Meta-analysis of age-related gene expression pro files identifies common signatures of aging. Bioinformatics **25**, 875–881 (2009)

8. Pan, F., Chiu, C.-H., Pulapura, S., et al.: Gene Aging Nexus: a web database and data mining platform for microarray data on aging. Nucleic Acids Res. **35**, D756–D759 (2007)

9. Bell, R., Barraclough, R., Vasieva, O.: Gene expression meta- analysis of potential metastatic breast cancer markers. Curr. Mol. Med.. Mol. Med. **17**, 200–210 (2017)

10. Chen, R., Khatri, P., Mazur, P.K., et al.: A meta-analysis of lung cancer gene expression identifies PTK7 as a survival gene in lung adenocarcinoma. Cancer Res. **74**, 2892–2902 (2014)

11. Su, L., Chen, S., Zheng, C., et al.: Meta-analysis of gene expression and identification of biological regulatory mechanisms in Alzheimer's disease. Front. Neurosci.Neurosci. **13**, 633 (2019)

12. Ch'ng, C., Kwok, W., Rogic, S., et al.: Meta-analysis of gene expression in autism spectrum disorder. Autism Res. **8**, 593–608 (2015)

13. Ramasamy, A., Mondry, A., Holmes, C.C., et al.: Key issues in conducting a meta-analysis of gene expression microarray datasets. PLoS Med. Med. **5**, e184 (2008)

14. Sweeney, T.E., Haynes, W.A., Vallania, F., et al.: Methods to increase reproducibility in differential gene expression via meta-analysis. Nucleic Acids Res. **45**, e1 (2017)

15. Waldron, L., Riester, M.: Meta-analysis in gene expression studies. Stat. Genom. **1418**, 161–176 (2016)

16. Jaksik, R., Iwanaszko, M., Rzeszowska-Wolny, J., et al.: Microar- ray experiments and factors which affect their reliability. Biol. Direct **10**, 46 (2015)

17. Ioannidis, J.P.A.: Why most published research findings are false. PLoS Med. **2**, e124 (2005)

18. Filzmoser, P., Maronna, R., Werner, M.: Outlier identification in high dimensions. Comput. Stat. Data Anal. **52**, 1694–1711 (2008)

19. Conesa, A., Madrigal, P., Tarazona, S., et al.: A survey ofbest practices for RNA-seq data analysis. Genome Biol. **17**(13) (2016)

20. Tarca, A.L., Romero, R., Draghici, S.: Analysis of microarray experiments of gene expression profiling. Am. J. Obstet. Gynecol. **195**, 373–388 (2006)

21. Kwak, S.K., Kim, J.H.: Statistical data preparation: management of missing values and outliers. Korean J. Anesthesiol.Anesthesiol. **70**, 407–411 (2017)

22. Shieh, A.D., Hung, Y.S.: Detecting outlier samples in microarray data. Stat. Appl. Genet. Mol. Biol. **8**, 13 (2009)

23. Aittokallio, T.: Dealing with missing values in large-scale studies: microarray data imputation and beyond. Brief Bioinf. **11**, 253–264 (2010)

24. Liew, A.W.-C., Law, N.-F., Yan, H.: Missing value imputation for gene expression data: computational techniques to recover missing data from available information. Brief Bioinf. **12**, 498–513 (2011)

25. Miller, J.A., Cai, C., Langfelder, P., et al.: Strategies for aggregating gene expression data: the collapse Rows R function. BMC Bioinf. **12**, 322 (2011)

26. Wang, K.Y., Vankov, E.R., Lin, D.D.M.: Predictors of clinical out- come in pediatric oligoden droglioma: meta-analysis of individual patient data and multiple imputation. J. Neurosurg. Pediatr.Pediatr. **21**, 153–163 (2018)

27. Johnson, W.E., Li, C., Rabinovic, A.: Adjusting batch effects in microarray expression data using empirical Bayes meth-ods. Biostatistics **8**, 118–127 (2007)

28. Ritchie, M.E., Phipson, B., Wu, D., et al.: Limma powers differential expression analyses for RNA-sequencing and microarray studies. Nucleic Acids Res. **43**, e47 (2015)

29. Leek, J.T., Johnson, W.E., Parker, H.S., et al.: The sva package for removing batch effects and other unwanted variation in high-throughput experiments. Bioinformatics **28**, 882–883 (2012)
30. Higgins, J.P.T., Thompson, S.G., Deeks, J.J., et al.: Measuring inconsistency in meta-analyses. BMJ **327**, 557–560 (2003)
31. Higgins, J.P.T., Thompson, S.G.: Quantifying heterogeneity in a meta-analysis. Stat. Med. **21**, 1539–1558 (2002)
32. Nakagawa, S., Cuthill, I.C.: Effect size, confidence interval and statistical significance: a practical guide for biologists. Biol. Rev. Camb. Philos. Soc.**82**, 591–605 (2007)
33. Tang, L.L., Caudy, M., Taxman, F.: A statistical method for synthesizing meta-analyses. Comput. Math. Methods Med.. Math. Methods Med. **2013**, 732989 (2013)
34. Kavvoura, F.K., Ioannidis, J.P.A.: Methods for meta-analysis in genetic association studies: a review of their potential and pitfalls. Hum. Genet. **123**, 1–14 (2008)
35. Jakobsdottir, J., Gorin, M.B., Conley, Y.P., et al.: Interpretation of genetic association studies: markers with replicated highly significant odds ratios may be poor classifiers. PLoS Genet. Genet. **5**, e1000337 (2009)
36. Stringer, S., Wray, N.R., Kahn, R.S., et al.: Underestimated effect sizes in GWAS: fundamental limitations of single SNP analysis for dichotomous phenotypes. PLoS ONE **6**, e27964 (2011)
37. Hedges, L.V.: Fitting categorical models to effect sizes from a series of experiments. J. Educ. Stat. **7**, 119–137 (1982)
38. Cohn, L.D., Becker, B.J.: Howmeta-analysis increases statistical power. Psychol. Methods **8**, 243–253 (2003)
39. Ellis, P.D.: The Essential Guide to Effect Sizes: Statistical Power, Meta-Analysis, and the Interpretation of Research Results. Cambridge University Press, Cam- bridge (2010)
40. Borenstein, M., Hedges, L.V., Higgins, J.P.T., et al.: Introduction to Meta-Analysis. John Wiley & Sons Inc, New York (2009)
41. Nakagawa, S., Santos, E.S.A.: Methodological issues and advances in biological meta-analysis. Evol. Ecol.. Ecol. **26**, 1253–1274 (2012)
42. Siangphoe, U., Archer, K.J.: Estimation of random effects and identifying heterogeneous genes in meta-analysis of gene expression studies. Brief. Bioinform.Bioinform. **18**, 602–618 (2017)
43. Marot, G., Foulley, J.-L., Mayer, C.-D., et al.: Moderated effect size and P-value combinations for microarray meta-analyses. Bioinformatics **25**, 2692–2699 (2009)
44. Rau, A., Marot, G., Jaffrézic, F.: Differential meta-analysis of RNA-seq data from multiple studies. BMC Bioinform. **15**, 91 (2014)
45. Li, J., Tseng, G.C.: An adaptively weighted statistic for detect- ing differential gene expression when combining multiple transcriptomic studies. Ann. Appl. Stat. **5**, 994–1019 (2011)
46. Heard, N., Rubin-Delanchy, P.: Choosing between methods of combining p-values. Biometrika **105**, 239–246 (2018)
47. Song, C., Tseng, G.C.: Hypothesis setting and order statis- tic for robust genomic META-analysis. Ann. Appl. Stat. **8**, 777–800 (2014)
48. Zaykin, D.V.: Optimally weighted Z-test is a powerfulmethod for combining probabilities in meta-analysis. J. Evol. Biol.Evol. Biol. **24**, 1836–1841 (2011)
49. Whitlock, M.C.: Combining probability from independent tests: the weighted Z-method is superior to Fisher's approach. J. Evol. Biol.Evol. Biol. **18**, 1368–1373 (2005)
50. Tseng, G.C., Ghosh, D., Feingold, E.: Comprehensive literature review and statistical considerations for microarray meta- analysis. Nucleic Acids Res. **40**, 3785–3799 (2012)
51. Hong, F., Breitling, R.: A comparison of meta-analysis methods for detecting differentially expressed genes in microar- ray experiments. Bioinformatics **24**, 374–382 (2008)

52. Breitling, R., Herzyk, P.: Rank-based methods as a non-parametric alternative of the T-statistic for the analysis of biological microarray data. J. Bioinform. Comput. Biol.Bioinform. Comput. Biol. **3**, 1171–1189 (2005)
53. Breitling, R., Armengaud, P., Amtmann, A., et al.: Rank products:a simple, yet powerful, new method to detect differentially regulated genes in replicated microarray experiments. FEBS Lett. **573**, 83–92 (2004)
54. O'Mara, T.A., Zhao, M., Spurdle, A.B.: Meta-analysis of gene expression studies in endometrial cancer identifies gene expression profiles associated with aggressive disease and patient outcome. Sci. Rep. **6**, 36677 (2016)
55. Song, G.G., Kim, J.-H., Seo, Y.H., et al.: Meta-analysis of differen- tially expressed genes in primary Sjogren's syndrome by using microarray. Hum. Immunol. **75**, 98–104 (2014)
56. Patel H, Dobson RJB, Newhouse SJ. A meta-analysis of Alzheimer's disease brain transcriptomic data. J. Alzheimers Dis. **68**, 1635–56
57. Badr, M.T., Häcker, G.: Gene expression profiling meta- analysis reveals novel gene signatures and pathways shared between tuberculosis and rheumatoid arthritis. PLoS ONE **14**, e0213470 (2019)
58. Toro-Domínguez, D., Carmona-Sáez, P., Alarcón-Riquelme, M.E.: Shared signatures between rheumatoid arthritis, systemic lupus rythematosus and Sjögren's syndrome uncovered through gene expression meta-analysis. Arthritis Res. Ther.Ther. **16**, 489 (2014)
59. Tuller, T., Atar, S., Ruppin, E., et al.: Common and specific signatures of gene expression and protein-protein interactions in autoimmune diseases. GenesImmun **14**, 67–82 (2013)
60. Kelly, J., Moyeed, R., Carroll, C., et al.: Gene expression meta- analysis of Parkinson's disease and its relationship with Alzheimer's disease. Mol. Brain **12**, 16 (2019)
61. Lamb, J., Crawford, E.D., Peck, D., et al.: The connectivity map: using gene-expression signa tures to connect small molecules, genes, and disease. Science **313**, 1929–1935 (2006)
62. Kanehisa, M., Goto SKEGG.: Kyoto encyclopedia of genes and genomes. Nucleic Acids Res. 28, 27–30 (2000)
63. The gene ontology (GO) database and informatics resource. Nucleic Acids Res. **32**, D258–61 (2004)
64. Toro-Domínguez, D., Martorell-Marugán, J., López- Domínguez, R., et al.: ImaGEO: integra tive gene expression meta-analysis from GEO database. Bioinformatics **35**, 880–2 (2019)
65. Zoubarev, A., Hamer, K.M., Keshav, K.D., et al.: Gemma: a resource for the reuse, sharing and meta-analysis of expression profiling data. Bioinformatics **28**, 2272–2273 (2012)
66. Sharov, A.A., Schlessinger, D., Ko, M.S.H.: ExAtlas: an interactive online tool for meta-analysis of gene expression data. J. Bioinform. Comput. **13**, 1550019 (2015)
67. ENCODE Project Consortium: An integrated encyclope- dia of DNA elements in the hu man genome. Nature **489**, 57–74 (2012)
68. Shashirekha, H.L., Wani, A.H.: ShinyMDE: shiny tool for microarraymeta-analysis for differ entially expressed gene detection. International Conference on Bioinformatics and Systems Biology (BSB) **2016**, 1–5 (2016)
69. Ma, T., Huo, Z., Kuo, A., et al.: MetaOmics: analysis pipeline and browser-based software suite for transcriptomicmeta- analysis. Ioinformatics, **35**, 1597–9 (2019)
70. Forero, D.A.: Available software for meta-analyses of genome-wide expression studies. PeerJ Preprints **7**, e27708v1 (2019)
71. Haynes, W.A., Vallania, F., Liu, C., et al.: Empowering multi- cohort gene expression analysis to increase reproducibility. Pac. Symp. Biocomput.Biocomput. **22**, 144–153 (2016)
72. Dewey, M.: metap: meta-analysis of significance values (2019)
73. Lusa, L., Gentleman, R., Ruschhaupt, M.: GeneMeta: Meta Analysis for high throughput ex periments. In: (2019)
74. Blanck, S., Marot, G.: SMAGEXP: a galaxy tool suite for transcriptomics data meta analysis. *arXiv* 2018;1802:08251 q-bio, stat

75. Hong, F., Breitling, R., McEntee, C.W., et al.: RankProd: a bioconductor package for detecting differentially expressed genes in meta-analysis. Bioinformatics **22**, 2825–2827 (2006)
76. Pihur, V., Datta, S., Datta, S.: RankAggreg, an R package for weighted rank aggregation. BMC Bioinformatics **10**, 62 (2009)
77. Lottaz, C., Yang, X., Scheid, S., et al.: OrderedList–a bioconductor package for detecting similarity in ordered gene lists. Bioinformatics **22**, 2315–2316 (2006)
78. Stevens, J.R., Nicholas, G.: metahdep: meta-analysis of hierarchically dependent gene expression studies. Bioinformatics **25**, 2619–2620 (2009)
79. Tsuyuzaki, K., Nikaido, I.: metaSeq: Meta-Analysis of RNA-Seq Count Data in Multiple Studies (2019)
80. Prada, C., Lima, D., Nakaya, H.: MetaVolcanoR: Gene Expression Meta-analysis Visualization Tool (2020)
81. Pickering, A.: Crossmeta: Cross Platform Meta-Analysis of Microarray Data (2020)
82. Goodman, S.N., Fanelli, D., Ioannidis, J.P.A.: What does research reproducibility mean? Sci. Transl. Med. **8,** 341ps12 (2016)
83. Shi, L., Jones, W.D., Jensen, R.V., et al.: The balance of reproducibility, sensitivity, and specificity of lists of differentially expressed genes in microarray studies. BMC Bioinformatics **9**, S10 (2008)
84. Willer, C.J., Li, Y., Abecasis, G.R.: METAL: fast and efficient meta-analysis of genome wide association scans. Bioinformatics **26**, 2190–1 (2010)
85. Willer, C.J., Li, Y., Abecasis, G.R.: METAL: fast and efficientmeta- analysis of genomewide association scans. Bioinformatics **26**, 2190–2191 (2010)
86. Purcell, S., Neale, B., Todd-Brown, K., et al.: PLINK: a tool set for whole-genome association and population-based linkage analyses. Am. J. Hum. Genet. **81**, 559–575 (2007)

Exploring the Effectiveness of On-Page SEO for Webpage Ranking: A Critical Study

Ravi S. Patel[✉], Jignesh A. Chauhan, Kirit C. Patel, and Krupa Bhavsar

Department of Computer Science, Ganpat University, Mehsana, India
rsp01@ganpatuniversity.ac.in

Abstract. A research paper titled "Exploring the Effectiveness of On-Page SEO for Webpage Ranking" investigates the importance of on-page SEO strategies on the ranking of webpages in search engine results. With the increasing importance of online visibility and website traffic for businesses and organizations, understanding the factors that influence search engine rankings has become crucial.

The study employs a comprehensive approach, incorporating data from various sources, to assess the importance of on page SEO factors in influencing webpage rankings. To achieve this, a diverse set of webpages from different domains and industries were analyzed, focusing on key on-page SEO elements such as keyword optimization, meta tags, content quality, URL structure, and internal linking. Through a rigorous analysis of these on-page SEO factors and their correlation with webpage rankings, the research reveals valuable insights into the practices that can positively impact search engine visibility. Additionally, the study considers the evolving algorithms of major search engines and their effects on ranking mechanisms, offering a forward-looking perspective on SEO strategies.

The findings of this research underscore the significance of on-page SEO as an important factor of a successful ranking strategy. By identifying best practices and areas for improvement, website owners, marketers, and SEO professionals can make informed decisions to enhance their webpage rankings and overall online presence.

In conclusion, this research paper contributes valuable knowledge to the field of SEO by investigating the effectiveness of on-page optimization techniques on webpage rankings. It provides actionable recommendations for website owners and digital marketers seeking to improve their search engine visibility and achieve higher rankings for their webpages, ultimately leading to increased organic traffic and potential business growth.

Keywords: Digital Marketing · On-Page Seo · Off-Page Seo · Seo · Technical Seo · Web Page Ranking · Google Ranking

1 Introduction

The Internet is fully crowded with lots of different information. Billions of webpages vying for online visibility and user attention. Amidst this vast ocean of data, search engines play a pivotal role in helping users discover relevant content by presenting search

S. Rajagopal et al (Eds.): ASCIS 2023, CCIS 2040, pp. 163–171, 2024.
https://doi.org/10.1007/978-3-031-59107-5_11

results based on sophisticated algorithms. For businesses and organizations, the ability to rank prominently in search engine results is a critical factor in driving website traffic, attracting potential customers, and achieving overall success in the digital landscape.

Search Engine Optimization (SEO) has emerged as a strategic discipline aimed at enhancing a website's visibility in search engine rankings. While various aspects of SEO have been extensively studied, the significance of on-page SEO factors in determining webpage rankings cannot be underestimated. On-page SEO involves optimizing individual webpages to improve their relevancy and alignment with search engine algorithms. Techniques such as keyword optimization, meta tags, content quality, URL structure, and internal linking all fall under the umbrella of on-page SEO.

Understanding the impact of on-page SEO on webpage rankings is vital for website owners, digital marketers, and SEO professionals. Despite the growing importance of this topic, there remains a need for empirical research that delves into the effectiveness of on-page SEO practices and their influence on search engine visibility (Fig. 1).

2   Working Mechanism of Search Engines

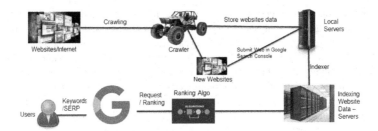

Fig. 1. Search Engine I How Search engines works I Crawling I Indexing I Ranking:

The Google search engine works based on a complex and constantly evolving algorithm. Here is a simplified overview of its working mechanism:

2.1   Crawling

Google uses automated software called "web crawlers" or "spiders" to browse the World Wide Web. These crawlers start searching for relevant content as per user query. They continuously crawl the web, collecting information about web pages, such as the content, links, and metadata.

2.2   Indexing

After crawling web pages, Google's algorithms process the collected data and create an index. It helps Google quickly find relevant pages when a user submits a search query.

2.3 Ranking

When a user find a specific content on web, Google's search algorithms come into play. They analyze the query to understand the user's intent and then search the index for web pages that are most relevant to that query.

3 Literature Review

SEO stands for Search Engine Optimization. It's a simple game for achieving top ranking on different search engines like Google. SEO is the bunch of technical activities of increasing quality and quantity of visitors on website, which is also known as Web traffic. The general meaning of the optimization is the action of making the best or most effective, here we are talking about the search engine it means prepare the best or most effective website according to search engines criteria. Search engine optimization (SEO) is the systematic step by step bulk of organic and inorganic activities using some technical tricks and tools for getting the higher rank in search engine such as Google.

Search engine you all of know very well, It's a one type of software system, which search systematically different types of information on internet according to your queries and give the result in the format of WebPages, textual, images, video, articles, info graphics etc., Which is known as search engine result pages. (SERPs). Example of Search engines: Google, Bing, Yahoo, Baidu, DuckDuckGo, Ask, AOL.

3.1 Importance of Search Engine Optimization

The first page results on Google get 75% of all clicks, and you get an idea of why search engine optimization is so important. SEO is the best business growing technique because it makes your website more visible on web, and It means more visitors on your website and more opportunities to convert visitors into customers. If you have a web site or blog, SEO can help you to get targeted free traffic from search engines and build your brand in specific domain. SEO friendly websites also improve the user experience and usability.

SEO experts mainly use two types of techniques for higher page ranking in Google or any search engines. On page Search engine optimization and Off page search engine optimization (Tables 1 and 2).

3.2 Search Engine Algorithms

Table 1. Study & Analysis of Search Engine Algorithms.

No	Google Algorithms Updates	Important Parameters
1	Caffeine (2010)	More Content, find new Contents
2	Panda (2011)	Keyword Stuffing. Spammy content will removing it from top ranking
3	Penguin (2012)	Link Building tactics

(*continued*)

Table 1. (*continued*)

No	Google Algorithms Updates	Important Parameters
4	Venice (2012)	geographical proximity to the searcher. Local Search
5	Pirate (2012)	copyright infringement. Content copyright
6	Hummingbird (2013)	Most relevant contents based on query or keywords
7	Pigeon (2013)	local search community. Local Search
8	HTTPS/SSL (2014)	HTTPS/SSL Certification, Technical SEO
9	Mobilegeddon (2015)	Mobile friendliness became a new ranking. Mobile Friendly
10	Rank Brain (2015)	Using AI, Search engine gives most relevant and Quality search results for a given query
11	Possum (2016)	Google improved filters based on address and location
12	Mobile Page Speed Update (2018)	mobile-first initiative
13	BERT (2019)	Quality Contents

3.3 Study and Analysis or Research Paper

Table 2. Study & Analysis of Research Papers.

Sr. No.	Paper Title	Author/Publication/Journal/Conference	Parameters
1	Optimizing Website effectiveness using various SEO Techniques	Dr. Seema Verma©2020 IEEE/Conference	Title Optimization: Body text optimization: Hyperlinks, Meta Tags Optimization: Sitemaps, Image optimization, Off page optimization
2	New Technique to Rank Without Off Page Search Engine Optimization	Asad Nadeem IEEE Xplore./Conference	Suggest a keyword planning tools for selecting proper high-volume keywords for content writing in a blog
3	Implementation of search engine Optimization	Mayank Kumar Mittal ICACCCN Conference/IEEE	Content: Alttags: Meta Tags:Robots.txt,Internal Links:Sitemaps:Keyword Research:

(*continued*)

Table 2. (*continued*)

Sr. No.	Paper Title	Author/Publication/Journal/Conference	Parameters
4	An Empirical Study on the Search Engine Optimization Technique and Its Outcomes	Fuxue Wang, Yi Li, Yiwen ZhangIEEE Xplore./ Conference	Internal linking means a page navigation and external linking to quality websites are important factors for web page ranking
5	Optimized Technique for Ranking Webpage on Search Engine Optimization	Ankita Tiwari IEEE Conference	Arrange the clusters of clicked URLs/Web pages according to the content's relevancy
6	Comparative Study Of Google Search Engine Optimization Algorithms: Panda, Penguin and Hummingbird	Akshita Patil IEEE 2021/Conference	Thin Content, Duplicate content, Poor User Experience, Plagiarism, Keyword Stuffing are the important parameters
7	Enhancing the Page Ranking for Search Engine Optimization Based on Weightage of In-Linked Web Pages	Rekha Singhal ICRAIE-2016/Conference	It also gives the priority on Quality backlinks
8	Search Engine Optimization: Success Factors	Swati Gupta IEEE Conference	DA/PA Domain Authority, Page Authority

3.4 Here Are the Most Effective on Page SEO Factors Are Listed

- URL Structure, Title of Article, Headings (H1–H6), Meta Description
- ALT Tag, Keywords, Key Phrases/Long tail keywords, Keyword Difficulty
- Fresh Updated Contents, Image Optimization, Internal Linking/Friendly Navigation
- Page Loading Seed, Domain Authority, Page Authority
- Site Map, Robot.txt, Privacy Policy, SSL Certificat, Small Video Insertion
- Favicon, Broken Links, Bounce Rate

4 On-Page SEO Parameters

4.1 URL Structure

URL stands for Uniform Resource Locator. It is a unique address of specific webpage, where resources (Text, Image, Video, data, etc) of that webpage are located. URL Example: http://digitalvidhyam.com/why-digital-marketing/

- URL should be short and sweet.
- URL should contain a keyword, which you want to rank.
  http://digitalvidhyam.com (Keyword = digital)
- URL should be related with your contents of blog.
- Use Hyphens (-)In-Between Words of URL
- Do not use underscore (_) in URL.

4.2 Title of Article

Actually Title tag is the important element of HTML, Which plays the crucial role in the ranking of any search engine.

- Title should contain the main keyword of article.
- Title should be written in 65 characters.
- Example: What Is Search Engine Optimization?

4.3 Heading Tags (H1–H6)

Generally, we read newspapers headings first other than small contents because headings are in big, bold and colored format. Exactly this things are applies in SEO. H1 to H6 are HTML tags for heading of article. HTML use for the development of static web application. H1 to H6 are priority based heading tags, used for writing the main and sub headings of articles.

- Use H1 tag only once in your page or article for main heading.
- H2 or H3 used in sub headings of article and so on.
- WordPress provides user-friendly platform for writing contents or heading in specific SEO friendly criteria.

  Example: Cyber Laws in India: < H1 > Importance of Cyber Laws: < H2 > India IT Act 2000: < H2 > Challenges of Cyber Laws: < H2 >

4.4 Meta Description

Meta description is also a part of HTML code. Meta description is a small content about the article or page.

- Meta description should be up to 155 characters.
- It should contain the main keywords of your article or page.
- Content should be unique and related with your page.

  < h1 > what is SEO < h1 > Importance of SEO I Future of SEO I On Page & Off Page SEO I M – 99241 97787 I Certificate Program 6 Month I Fees 15000 I

4.5 Alt Attribute

ALT tag is used for writing the alternative text for specific image on website, which is also known as the ALT attribute or ALT description of an image. Sometimes search engines robots cannot interpret the image due to some server errors, so alternative text is useful to understand the image for crawlers.

4.6   Keywords/Key Phrases/Long Tail Keywords

The most important part of SEO friendly web applications are Keywords. Keywords are still important element for search engine ranking.

4.7   Keyword Difficulty

Keyword difficulty is a truly associated with keyword research process. It is the process of evaluating how difficult it is to rank in Google's organic search results for a specific term. Keyword difficulty helps you choose the best keywords for SEO. Use only those keywords whose difficulty is below 30 as per Ahreafs tool.

4.8   Fresh Updated Contents

Fresh content means updated content in an article or blog. It is required to change your content frequently on blog. Search engines give higher priority to updated content compared to old ones.

4.9   Image Optimization

Page load time of website is an important factor of every websites. So we need to decrease the content size on websites. Heavy content may increase the loading time of websites. So you need to optimize your images for blog articles.

5   Implementation of Listed SEO On-Page Parameters

We implement the above-listed parameters on the following websites (Fig. 2).

1. https://digitalravi.site/
2. https://cyberlaws.online/
3. https://automonkey.co/

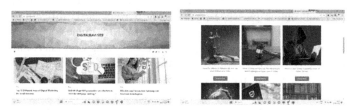

Fig. 2. On-Page SEO Implementation

6 SEO Tools (Used)

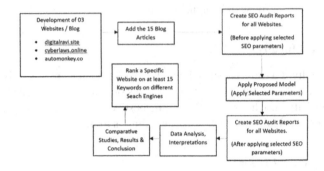

Sr. No	SEO Tools	Use/Importance
1	Google Search Console	Its also known as Google Web Master, used to submit newly launched websites for Search engine ranking
2	SEMrush	SEMrush is a versatile and comprehensive digital marketing tool that offers a wide range of features and functionalities. It is useful for various purposes in the field of online marketing, SEO (Search Engine Optimization), and competitive analysis
3	Google Analytics	Find out the different statistics of websites
4	Woorank	Used for SEO audit reports

7 SEO Audit Report/Conclusion

An SEO (Search Engine Optimization) audit report is a comprehensive analysis of a website's performance in terms of search engine visibility, user experience, and overall, SEO health. The primary purpose of an SEO audit report is to identify areas where a website can be improved to achieve a better rank in search engine results pages and enhance its overall online presence on web. We developed 03 different websites in different domains on WordPress platform and uploaded 15 articles on it. After that, we examine those all three websites with SEO audit reports using woo-rank online platform for checking their visibility on search engine ranking and its weakness. In the initial stage all three websites have the same search engine ranking position. After that we did lots of study and analysis on search engine algorithms and research articles and found those important parameters which have a highest priority on ranking. We applied those parameters on specific websites and finally we got excellent results with listed parameters. Now our www.automonkey.co website ranked in different search engines on more than 15+ keywords.

References

1. Sharma, D., Shukla, R., Giri, A.K., Kumar, S.: A brief review on search engine optimization. In: 2019 9th International Conference on Cloud Computing, Data Science & Engineering (Confluence), pp. 687–692 (2019). https://doi.org/10.1109/CONFLUENCE.2019.8776976
2. Alhaidari, F., Alwarthan, S., Alamoudi, A.: User preference based weighted page ranking algorithm. In: 2020 3rd International Conference on Computer Applications & Information Security (ICCAIS), pp. 1–6 (2020). https://doi.org/10.1109/ICCAIS48893.2020.9096823
3. Sharma, S., Verma, S.: Optimizing website effectiveness using various SEO techniques. In: 2020 7th International Conference on Signal Processing and Integrated Networks (SPIN), pp. 918–922 (2020). https://doi.org/10.1109/SPIN48934.2020.9070893
4. Nadeem, A., Hussain, M., Iftikhar, A.: New technique to rank without off page search engine optimization. In: 2020 IEEE 23rd International Multitopic Conference (INMIC), pp. 1–6 (2020). https://doi.org/10.1109/INMIC50486.2020.9318166
5. Andonov, A.D.: The application of search engine optimization in internet marketing. In: 2020 55th International Scientific Conference on Information, Communication and Energy Systems and Technologies (ICEST), pp. 37–41 (2020). https://doi.org/10.1109/ICEST49890.2020.9232740
6. Dramilio, A., Faustine, C., Sanjaya, S., Soewito, B.: The effect and technique in search engine optimization. In: 2020 International Conference on Information Management and Technology (ICIMTech), pp. 348–353 (2020). https://doi.org/10.1109/ICIMTech50083.2020.9211171
7. Joglekar, B., Bhatia, R., Jayaprakash, S., Raina, K., Mulchandani, S.: Search engine optimization using unsupervised learning. In: 2019 5th International Conference on Computing, Communication, Control And Automation (ICCUBEA), pp. 1–5. (2019). https://doi.org/10.1109/ICCUBEA47591.2019.9129011
8. Killoran, J.B.: How to use search engine optimization techniques to increase website visibility. IEEE Trans. Prof. Commun. **56**(1), 50–66 (2013). https://doi.org/10.1109/TPC.2012.2237255
9. Madiudia, I., Porplytsya, N., Nagara, M.: Mathematical model for prediction the dynamics of organic traffic at E-commerce web-site in the process of its search engine optimization. In: 2020 10th International Conference on Advanced Computer Information Technologies (ACIT), pp. 577–580 (2020). https://doi.org/10.1109/ACIT49673.2020.9208886
10. Matta, H., Gupta, R., Agarwal, S.: Search engine optimization in digital marketing: present scenario and future scope. In: 2020 International Conference on Intelligent Engineering and Management (ICIEM), pp. 530–534 (2020). https://doi.org/10.1109/ICIEM48762.2020.9160016
11. Patel, S.K., Prajapati, J.B., Patel, R.S.: SEO and content management system. Int. J. Electron. Comput. Sci. Eng. **1**(3), 953–959 (2012)
12. Parikh, S., Patel, R.S., Chauhan, J.A.: A survey on effective on-page and off-page search engine optimization factors to improve the website visibility on google search engine platform. AEGAEUM J. **09**(04), 296–303

Precision Tuning of PID Controller Parameters for Dynamic Stability Enhancement in GPSS-SMIB Systems: The HB-PSO Optimization Approach

Yogesh Kalidas Kirange$^{(\boxtimes)}$ ⓘ and Pragya Nema ⓘ

Department of Electrical and Electronics Engineering, Oriental University, Indore,
Madhya Pradesh 453555, India
yogesh.kirange@gmail.com

Abstract. This research work proposes to boost the transient stability of general purpose simulation system (GPSS) connected one machine unlimited bus system through proportional-integral-derivative (PID) controller parameters optimized using hybrid optimization approach. The major intention is to render flexible environment for modelling, simulating, and analyzing the functioning of an electrical power system to enhance the system's dynamic stability. It paves the way for sophisticated control system design by enabling comprehensive system modelling, dynamic simulations, parameter tuning, stability analysis, and development. Hybrid optimization approaches significantly improve stability of systems by fine-tuning PID controllers. This work focuses on hybrid butterfly-particle swarm optimization (HBPSO) uses to calibrate PID controller parameters for SMIB system is to enhance dynamic stability and control performance. HBPSO aims to effectively identify optimal or near-optimal PID controller settings by combining BOA and PSO. Its unique combination of PSO and BO improves control quality with decreased overshoot, settling time, steady-state error, robustness, responsiveness to changing system dynamics, enhancing SMIB system stability and reliability at various operating conditions. This research demonstrates the complex and nonlinear nature of power system dynamics through extensive GPSS simulation experiments and exhaustive simulations that an HB-PSO-optimized PID controller effectively provides the required stability and disturbance attenuation. Simulation results demonstrate that the proposed HBPSO-based PID-MPSS configuration enhances damping performance compared to conventional MPSS approaches, validated through eigenvalue analysis confirming a favorable shift of unstable eigenvalues towards the stable region. Stability analysis for the hybrid controller at reducing 5%, 10%, and 15% load, the output of eigenvalue and damping ratio are $-1.59 \pm j4.34$ and 0.298. Also, implementing this technique not only settling time improve to 9, 4, and 3 s but also overshoot time to 7, 4, and 2 s by reducing 5%,10%, and 15% load.

Keywords: BOA · GPSS · HBPSO · PID Controller · PSO · SMIB system

S. Rajagopal et al (Eds.): ASCIS 2023, CCIS 2040, pp. 172–193, 2024.
https://doi.org/10.1007/978-3-031-59107-5_12

1 Introduction

The PID controller, an important tool in machine and power system control systems that evaluates errors using proportional, integral, and derivative parameters are introduced. The goal of tweaking the PID controller is to satisfy expectations of performance, which might be difficult owing to compromises amongst various parameters.

Dynamic stability, which is fundamental to the secure and reliable passage of energy, is one of the most crucial characteristics of power systems. It is connected to a SMIB system; the GPSS offers a simplified model for evaluating power system stability. Establishing dynamic stability in these systems requires meticulous calibration of the PID controllers that comprise the framework of the regulating architecture. The unpredictability and constant evolution of power network dynamics hinder this endeavor. Therefore, optimization techniques have become more valuable in fine-tuning PID controller settings, enhancing the dynamic stability of GPSS-SMIB systems. This optimization-driven technique is significant because it can simplify and accelerate the painstaking process of calibrating PID controllers.

In today's complex grid, manual adjustments may be laborious and may not result in the optimal parameters for power system stability. Consequently, numerous optimization techniques have evolved into valuable resources. This category includes sophisticated algorithms such as differential evolution (DE), PSO, and genetic algorithms (GA). The primary objective is determining the optimal parameters for the newly designed PID controller, enabling the power system to recover rapidly from disturbances without sacrificing stability. The complex, multimodal nature of optimization problems in power systems has led to the rise in popularity of hybrid optimization techniques, such as HBPSO. Their contributions to the search for enhanced and robust dynamic stability within GPSS-SMIB systems demonstrate the significance of these optimization methodologies within the larger field of power system engineering.

Providing consistent energy demands a strong power system. A SMIB system tests dynamic stability to recover from brief perturbations. Generator regulation in SMIB systems is generally controlled via PID controllers. PID controller settings must be fine-tuned to optimize power system. This problem has been overcome by many PID controller parameter tuning optimization methods. These methods range from heuristics to complex computer algorithms. System complexity and performance criteria are key strategic considerations. Enhancing SMIB system dynamic stability is vital and ever-changing as power systems include renewable energy and smart grid technologies. This research examines BOA, PSO and HB-PSO optimization methodologies to determine their principles, efficacy, and usefulness in improving power network reliability.

Many considerations must be addressed while adjusting PID controller settings to improve dynamic stability in SMIB systems. SMIB systems show power grid dynamics clearly and informatively because dynamic stability is crucial. PID controllers are often utilized in SMIB generator management systems. The complexity of power system dynamics makes PID controller settings difficult to fine-tune. Changes in demand, grid topology, and renewable energy sources make this task more difficult and need flexible management. One needs grasp system dynamics and PID control theory to alter PID controller settings. Traditional, heuristic, and cutting-edge computational optimization procedures have pros and cons, so choosing the best one is crucial. Renewable energy sources and smart grid technologies have created a dynamic energy environment, making SMIB system reliability more important than ever. Researchers must constantly find new control techniques to overcome these challenges and maintain the reliability of modern power networks.

Motivating the investigation of the difficulties of enhancing dynamic stability in SMIB systems through PID controller parameter optimization is the need to ensure a reliable supply of electrical energy. Dynamic stability, which is required for power system resilience during transient disruptions, is portrayed in the SMIB model, making it the focus of investigation. Despite their adaptability, PID controllers require precise parameter adjustment, a challenging task given the dynamic character of modern power systems. This research work seeks to provide an overview of the multifarious PID controller optimization strategies for those navigating the arduous path to power grid stability.

The research requirement on optimization methods for PID parameters in SMIB systems subject to varying conditions and disturbances, comparative research needs to be more complete. Additionally, new optimization techniques that are resource-friendly and efficient should be investigated. To address this area of limited understanding, our study employed a Hybrid Butterfly-Particle Swarm Optimisation (HBPSO) method to optimize the PID controller configurations of an SMIB linked to GPSS. To enhance the efficiency of both local exploitation and global exploration, the HBPSO algorithm integrates the methodologies of Particle Swarm Optimisation and Butterfly Optimisation. Based on our comprehensive simulations, the outcomes demonstrate that the HBPSO-based approach we propose surpasses traditional PID controllers and alternative optimization methods. This is achieved by effectively ascertaining the optimal PID parameters and enhancing the steady-state and transient stability of the SMIB system, which is of utmost importance for the reliability and security of power systems.

The main primary goal is to gain as much knowledge as possible regarding SMIB system PID controller parameter adjustment. Conducting a comprehensive comparison of traditional heuristic and cutting-edge optimization techniques to identify the most effective methods and their practical value.

This research work contributes to the energy sector by synthesizing existing information, analyzing optimization efforts critically, providing practical insights. Adapting to the ever-changing dynamics of the energy, this work seeks to provide a valuable resource that not only consolidates the comprehension of PID controller parameter tuning but also guides researchers in making informed decisions to better the power system's stability.

2   Methodological Surveys

2.1   Tuning of Parameters of PID Controller

The efficacy of PID controllers, which includes the minimization of non-linear stability issues [5] and the mitigation of low-frequency oscillations (LFO) [6], is suitable for a variety of applications, including the stability of power systems, and is therefore favoured by a large number of researchers. However, PID parameter adjustment is notoriously problematic. The proportionality (Kp), integral (Ki), and derivative (Kd) parameters are the fundamental elements of a proportional-integral derivative controller [7]. The dynamic reactivity of a system may be enhanced by adequately adjusting these parameters. Overshoot is reduced, steady-state error is eliminated, and system stability is boosted. Equation (1) characterizes the transfer function of a Proportional-Integral-Derivative (PID) controller, as expressed by the following definition [4]:

$$u(t) = K_p * e(t) + K_i * \int e(t) + K_d * \frac{d(e(t))}{dt} \tag{1}$$

(See Fig. 1) depicts the fundamental architecture of a PID mechanism system. The variance amongst the modified reference point and tangible outcome can then be calculated. The instruction signal u (t) that is sent to the plant model is derived from the error signal e (t) via a proportional, integral, and derivative arrangement [8], with the scaled and averaged signals resulting from this arrangement. It will be possible to get a diversity of signals at the output. The controller will be supplied with a new, variable actual signal, and the error signal will be recalculated as shown in Eq. (1). A control signal, u(t), will be transmitted to the facility. An error will be reduced in the stable state if this process is repeated indefinitely.

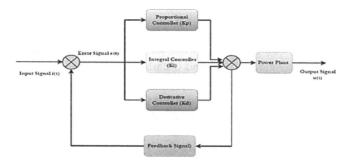

Fig. 1. PID Controller architecture

While the system's order remains constant, the proportional term increases its responsiveness when the closed-loop time constant decreases in tandem with the proportional constant, because the system's output is purely proportional to the input [9]. The inaccuracy cannot be corrected by any quantity of proportional perpetual. The integral word abolishes the deviation and escalations the system's performance and reducing the system's reaction time. The derivative term introduces persistent oscillations. The major goal of this term is to attenuate the system's oscillatory response. No changes are made to the system's type of order, or offset. Changing the constants of these proportionality components influences the sensitivity of the system. To achieve PID tuning, which entails adjusting the proportionality constants of the PID controller, is essential a variety of PID tuning techniques have been endeavored. Generally, these approaches can be categorized into two main groups: traditional methods and computational techniques.

2.1.1 Conventional Procedures

Attempt to derive optimal controller settings by constructing a logical or graphical representation of the process based on predetermined assumptions about the plant and the desired output. These techniques require few computer resources and can produce results rapidly. However, owing to the established norms, the default controller settings seldom provide the anticipated outcomes without further fine-tuning.

2.1.2 Optimization Methods

Have been utilized for PID tuning and are frequently employed for data modelling and cost function optimization. A few examples of computational models that can simulate complex systems are neural networks, genetic algorithms, and differential evolution. Utilizing optimization techniques, cost functions are minimized. These are examples of cost functions as integral absolute error, integral square error, integral time absolute error, integral time square error. When it comes to self- or auto-tuning PID controllers, mathematical representations are essential for defining the PID parameters and simulating the fundamental procedure. The resulting model enables constant output monitoring and comparison by permitting instantaneous PID parameter adjustments whenever process deviations are detected to maintain the intended system behaviour.

2.2 Soft Computing Techniques

Several techniques have evolved for improving PID parameters to increase SMIB power system stability, however there is a knowledge vacuum in comparing optimization strategies under diverse operating settings and disturbance instances. Better, more reliable optimization algorithms with faster convergence, less computing overhead, and fewer false positives are desperately needed.

Despite the abundance of literature on optimizing PID parameters for power system stability in SMIB systems, comparative studies of various methods under varying operating circumstances and disturbances still need to be improved. Further investigation into the creation of trustworthy optimization methods with enhanced efficiency and reduced computing resource requirements is necessary.

Numerous PID controller adjustment methods apply to a given set of objectives. Numerous authors and researchers have established PID tuning method hierarchies as shown in (See Fig. 2) [1] classified PID adjustment techniques based on the possibility of a control system and the model type. These divisions are divided into four distinct groups:

i) **Empirical Approaches** are no models or defined points with these techniques. Therefore, clear determination of essential classical nodes or a structured model should not be relied upon.

ii) **Non-parametric prediction approach methods** utilize normal, steady-state representation and frequency location data that is less comprehensive than that used by parametric models. The methods function most effectively in an online environment. In most instances, they can be utilized without prior knowledge of the organisms in question.

iii) **Comprehensive data collection techniques** provide a comfortable medium between parametric and non-parametric approaches. Like subspace strategy and self-tuned fuzzy logic systems [3, 10, 11, 12, 15] use grey knowledge for tuning, process data is also employed.

iv) **Parametric model techniques** can be used to acquire the essential model data for parametric model techniques. A matrices/space model of the system's transfer function and a linear model are required. These approaches are better suited for isolated PID fine-tuning. The three major classifications of parametric strategies are non-optimal parametric, optimal restricted structure control and optimal control signal matching [8, 13, 14].

Tuning PID parameters using computational methods requires data modelling and cost function optimization techniques. In this manner, parameters for the controller can be optimized by minimizing a cost function. Typically, six (6) standard cost functions are employed when configuring PID controller parameters. Here are some common examples of cost functions [8]:

a) Integral Time Absolute Error (ITAE) can be expressed in Eq. (2)

$$ITAE = \int_0^t t * |e(t)| * dt \tag{2}$$

b) Integral Absolute Error (IAE) can be given in Eq. (3)

$$IAE = \int_0^t |e(t)| * dt \tag{3}$$

c) Mean Square Error (MSE) [1] can be defined in Eq. (4)

$$MSE = \frac{\int_0^t e(t)^2 * dt}{t} \tag{4}$$

d) Integral Error (IE) can be represented in Eq. (5)

$$IE = \int_0^t e(t) * dt \tag{5}$$

e) Integral Square Error (ISE) can be represented in Eq. (6)

$$ISE = \int_0^t |e(t)|^2 * dt \tag{6}$$

f) Integral Time Square Error (ITSE) can be represented in Eq. (7) as

$$ITSE = \int_0^t t * |e(t)|^2 * dt \tag{7}$$

Self-regulating PID controller parameters must be fine-tuned using computational techniques. According to [8], there are five primary ways to classify these controllers according to their characteristics and applications: analytical methods, heuristic approaches, frequency response techniques, optimization algorithms, and adaptive tuning methodologies.

2.2.1 Genetic Algorithm (GA)

Foundation of natural selection and genetics forms. GA, a type of optimization technique. (See Fig. 3) indicates the process flowchart of GA. Also, (See Fig. 3) describes how GA works well and gives the best solution [8]. Create a candidate pool for use in problem-solving. They are comparing the fitness of the population to the problem's objective. Select progenitors for the next generation from the general population. The selection process tends to favor fitter individuals. Combine the DNA of a mother and father to produce a child. Encourage variation in the population by manipulating the DNA of random offspring. Replace the previous generation with your children and perhaps your parents if they survived. Consider termination points (such as an acceptable response or a limited number of generations). The algorithm terminates if the condition holds; otherwise, it returns to the evaluation phase. By progressively refining solutions over time, GAs imitate the process of natural selection. Their vast array of optimization applications necessitates fine-tuning several parameters, including population size and mutation rate.

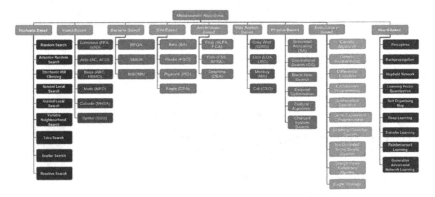

Fig. 2. Operational procedure-based metaheuristic categorization summary [2]

2.2.2 Butterfly Optimization Algorithm (BOA)

(See Fig. 4) depicts the process flow chart of the BOA algorithm. (See Fig. 4) describes how the BOA algorithm works well and gives the best solution. Consider, as a beginning point, a population of insects. Each butterfly compares its current fitness level to its previous best, and if the latter is more remarkable, it enhances its personal best. Select the butterfly with the highest fitness value as the new global best solution (g_{best}). Adjust the

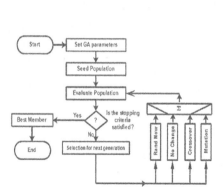

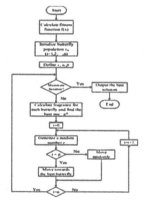

Fig. 3. GA algorithm process flowchart [8]

Fig. 4. BOA algorithm process flowchart [8]

pace and location of each butterfly so that they average out to the global and individual bests, correspondingly. Assess Fitness Determine each butterfly's fitness level using the problem's objective function. Examine the termination points (such as the allowed number of iterations or the presence of a viable solution). Continuing if conditions are met; otherwise, returning to update personal best. BOA effectively examines and leverages the search space by balancing individual and community knowledge. Depending on the character of the optimization problem at hand, parameters may need to be adjusted for optimal results.

2.2.3 Particle Swarm Optimization Algorithm (PSO)

(See Fig. 5) indicates the process flowchart of PSO. It entails a particle population exploring a search space. They adjust their positions and rates following their best responses and the most incredible solutions identified globally. By repeating this procedure until a termination requirement is met, we can more rapidly arrive at the optimal solution as shown in Fig. 5. The parameters must be tuned for optimal performance.

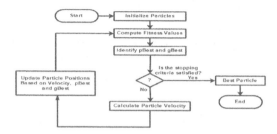

Fig. 5. PSO algorithm process flowchart [2]

2.2.4 Hybrid Butterfly Particle Swarm Optimization (HBPSO)

Combines the strength of the PSO and BO algorithms. It employs the particle swarm mechanism for wide-area search and butterfly optimization for precision work in a limited area. HBPSO may find the best answer by splitting the search space and assigning each particle a location. Butterfly optimization improves convergence speed and accuracy by optimizing particle positions. Simulation testing has supported the Heffron-Phillip SMIB PID controller setting optimization approach to replicate the HBPSO algorithm. The proposed method outperforms existing PID controllers and other optimization methods. SMIB system transient and steady-state stability may be enhanced by adopting the optimal PID parameter settings. HBPSO gives better dynamic response as compared to fuzzy [3, 10–12], BAT [16], PSO [17], Grey Wolf Optimization (GWO) [18], harmony search (HSA) [19] and BOA algorithm [20].

2.2.5 Stability Assessment Methods

Use to fine-tune the dynamic stability of the SMIB system, it is necessary to evaluate the angular stability to significant disturbances (transient stability). Research into temporary stability is essential. There are numerous methods for ensuring research consistency. The fundamental assumptions and modeling approaches differentiate them;

2.2.5.1 Progressive Approaches Correlated to Statistical Integration has the objective to discover a mathematical model representing the network and machine dynamics before, during, and after a disturbance. Using digital integration techniques, differential equations in the time domain are solved. The most prevalent approaches are the Runge-Kutta fourth-order and modified Euler methods.

2.2.5.2 Vigorous Approaches of Lyapunov [21] is the foundation for the strategies used in these approaches. The equal-areas criterion is widespread due to its effectiveness and simplicity of application. The essential machines and stability margin used to characterize the system's stability are determined using a combination of direct and hybrid techniques.

2.2.5.3 Randomized Techniques maintain the transient stability of electrical networks, stochastic research employing a variety of methodologies makes significantly more use of statistical data. A probabilistic technique based on form recognition and the Monte Carlo method has been developed specifically.

2.2.5.4 Examines stability under dynamic perturbations are numerous methods for evaluating stability, but eigenvalue analysis and linearized power system model analysis are two of the most effective. These methods can be used to determine whether or not a system is stable.

2.2.6 Methods for Enhancing Stability

Focuses on the network's response to both minor and significant perturbations. As long as it remains within its limits and serves its customers, the network will remain stable until the disruption is resolved. There are numerous possible causes and symptoms of network instability. In electrical network analysis, it is crucial to identify causes of network instability and knowledge-based methods that can improve network stability. The proposed strategy will concentrate on the PSS and the various techniques PSSs and FACTS devices use to enhance stability. The materials and methods sections employ and discuss intelligent control methods such as GA (Genetic Algorithm) and, PSO (Particles swarms Optimisation) and other soft computing methods.

2.2.6.1 Enhanced Stability by Innovative Technology may be enhanced by employing closed-loop systems furnished with suitable control mechanisms. Over the years, there has been considerable effort to enhance these controllers' design. Stability can be improved in two significant ways: An additional controlling signal is produced by attaching a controller to the generator side's excitation system another control signal for FACTS systems involving the use of a transmission line-side controller.

2.2.6.2 Power System Stabilizer (PSS) can be outfitted with power quality sensors (PSS) controllers [22] to reduce electromechanical vibrations [23]. This controller initiates an input signal to the automatic voltage regulator based on the generator's output and rotor speed data. The generator's additional torque attenuation compensates for the unfavorable influence of the excitation mechanism on the oscillations. PSS controllers are the most commonly used systems to increase stability at moderate disturbances because they are simple, straightforward to implement, practically practical, inexpensive, and effective. Consequently, we will utilize them in this investigation.

3 Materials and Methods

3.1 Proposed Methodology

A common power system model for transient stability research is the GPSS connected SMIB system. Incorporating a PID controller to regulate the generator's excitation voltage can improve the system's transient response. Optimization methods are typically used to fine-tune the controller parameters for maximum efficiency. The HBPSO algorithm is a cross between the butterfly algorithm for optimization and the PSO technique for optimization. The purpose of this technology is to stabilize the electrical grid and keep the frequency constant regardless of the load. Figure 6 illustrates the steps involved in optimizing PID parameters for the GPSS-SMIB model using the HBPSO algorithm. The HBPSO algorithm follows the steps outlined in (See Fig. 6) to evaluate the best optimal solution.

The HBPSO algorithm is utilized to iteratively update the PID controller's parameters to produce the greatest possible system response. The fitness function of each particle is calculated, the swarm's position and velocity are updated, the PID controller's parameters are altered based on the swarm's ideal position, and the system's reaction is looped. We gauge the algorithm's journey towards convergence by keeping an eye on either the count of iterations or the performance of the objective function. The HB-PSO algorithm's iterative procedure enables an efficient search for the best PID controller parameters to minimize the objective function and increase system performance.

Assessing the relative merits of Zeigler-Nichols method (ZNM) [24] and HBPSO algorithms necessitates analyzing the parameters of a particular control or optimization issue. The Zeigler-Nichols technique is a well-known manual adjustment method due

Fig. 6. HB-PSO algorithm steps of evaluation of PID controller parameters

to its usability and heuristic quality. It may lack precision and grapple with complex problems, but it may be effective for relatively simple systems. However, hybrid optimization algorithms are the best option for automating optimization because they employ multiple optimization techniques. Although they may require more time and processing capacity, they are superior at discovering optimal or near-optimal solutions to challenging problems. Before making a final decision, you should consider the advantages and disadvantages of both human tuning and automated optimization, as well as the complexity of the control system, the level of precision required, the available resources, etc. Zeigler-Nichols may suffice when computing resources are limited, and the problem is straightforward. Complex systems that require high precision may find a HBPSO algorithm beneficial despite its higher computational expense. The HBPSO is most efficient method for enhancing dynamic stability of GPSS-SMIB system.

3.2 Development of GPSS-SMIB Power System

Single Line Diagrams are simplified visual representations of electrical systems, such as SMIB systems as shown in (See Fig. 7). Engineers and researchers use SLDs to analyze system behavior, identify problems, and devise control solutions. Such systems are accurately simulated using the HPM model, which accounts for the dynamic interactions between mechanical and electrical components. Using this model, improve the reliability and resiliency of power systems in the face of failures by studying voltage stability, transient reactions, and system performance.

Integrating the mathematical HPM model into simulation software enables the accurate modeling of a SMIB. Engineers and researchers can now simulate and analyze the dynamic behavior of the SMIB system due to this connection. They can investigate system responses, evaluate performance, and develop control methods by creating a simulation, defining parameters, and conducting experiments within the simulated environment. By following these methods, we can more easily comprehend complex power systems, increase their dependability, and execute virtual experiments.

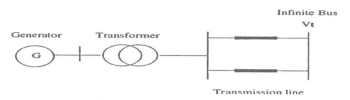

Fig.7. Single line diagram of SMIB power system.

(See Fig. 8) depicts significant progress has been made in power system analysis through the integration of a HPM model-based GPSS with a SMIB system. This system uses the mathematical profundity of the HPM model to investigate the SMIB system across a broad spectrum of inputs in great detail. It is essential for research into control techniques, system resilience enhancements, and power system performance optimization, all of which improve electrical engineering and grid dependability.

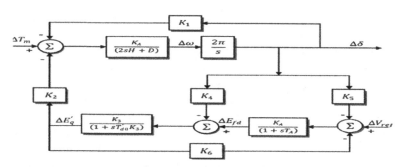

Fig. 8. HPM based GPSS connected SMIB system

3.3 Procedural Steps to Achieve PID Parameter of GPSS-SMIB Model Using the HB-PSO Algorithm

By simulating a GPSS-connected SMIB power system, the proposed investigation intends to enhance transient stability analysis. Utilizing a PID controller to manage the generator's stimulation voltage is essential to this upgrade, as it enhances the system's transient responsiveness. Utilizing optimization techniques to fine-tune the PID controller's parameters for optimal performance is standard practice. The HBPSO algorithm is a ground-breaking strategy that incorporates elements of the boa and PSO methods, and it stands out in this context. The primary objective of this system is to maintain the electrical grid's frequency within an acceptable range under a wide variety of operating conditions. The HBPSO algorithm's rigorous objective of locating optimal PID controller parameter configurations within the GPSS-SMIB model necessitates a number of crucial following operational procedures for the study's success.

In First phase, you must explicitly define the problem you're attempting to address by stating that you wish to reduce the disparity between actual and optimal results.

In Second phase, we will create a MATLAB/SIMULINK model of the SMIB-GPSS interface. Using the information provided in the system definition section, build an equation-based model of the SMIB system. Next, evaluate this model using simulation software such as MATLAB/Simulink.

In Third phase, PID Controller Design by modifying the generator's excitation voltage, a PID controller helps maintain the frequency stability of the system.

In Fourth phase is to initiate the HBPSO algorithm. Set the initial controller settings obtained in Step 3 as the algorithm's inputs. For an algorithm to operate effectively, its parameters must be determined. Population size, maximal number of iterations, and convergence criteria are among these parameters.

In Fifth phase, apply the objective function defined in Step 1 to the particles in the swarm and assess their fitness.

In sixth phase, change particle position and motion as required, move and rotate the elements.

In seventh phase is to fine-tune the PID controller parameters for the optimal position of the swarm.

In eighth phase is to evaluate the system's response using the simulated values of the modified PID controller.

In ninth phase, convergence validation, consider convergence conditions, such as a limited number of iterations or a certain objective function tolerance.

If the convergence conditions **in tenth phase** are not met, the iterative procedure will repeat fifth phase through ninth phase until convergence is achieved.

In eleventh phase, it is validation and testing, in which the optimized PID controller is put through its tests under a variety of real-world conditions, such as varying loads and power grid disruptions. Test the system's reaction time and compare it to your original PID controller setup and other conventional adjusting methods. Success is achieved when the optimized PID controller outperforms the original design or conventional approaches in terms of overshoot, settling time, and steady-state error.

3.3.1   Fitness Function for PID Controller Using HBPSO Algorithm

The fitness function for the PID controller is given by Eq. (8), and we use the HB-PSO algorithm to tune the controller's gains appropriately (see Fig. 1).

$$f(d_v) = \int_0^t |(d_r - d_v)| * dt \tag{8}$$

We can represent the "variable control parameter (v)" using the Eq. (9), which is indicated shown below,

$$v = \left\{ K_p, K_i, K_d \right\} \tag{9}$$

In analogous circumstances, v may also be assigned. To reach the optimal condition where dv = 0, the minimum value of f (dv) must be determined. This fitness function is defined within the framework of ITAE. This research work investigates the speed and orientation of the rotor under three distinct failure conditions and operational modes. Simulation, as well as linear and nonlinear programming, are utilized to analyse the power grid exhaustively. In addition to lowering the frequency of oscillations in rotor speed and rotor angle, nonlinear research indicates that PID-PSS increases time-response parameters such as "overshoot and settling time."

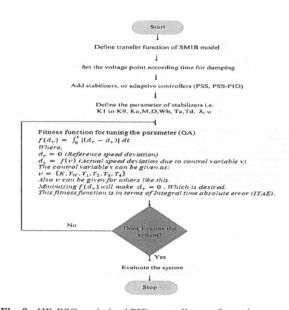

Fig. 9. HB-PSO-optimized PID controller configurations movement.

As depicted in (See Fig. 9), the HBPSO algorithm is employed in a repetitive optimization strategy to fine-tune the PID controller's settings in an effort to attain optimal system responsiveness. Throughout this iterative process, the fitness function of each particle is calculated, the swarm's position and velocity are updated, the PID controller's parameters are adjusted based on the optimal swarm position, and the system's performance is continuously monitored. We monitor the number of iterations or the effectiveness of the objective function to determine how close the algorithm is to convergence. By iteratively seeking for the optimal PID controller settings, the HBPSO algorithm minimizes the objective function and optimizes system performance.

The flexibility and versatility of HBPSO make it ideal for companies and researchers. HBPSO optimizes complicated processes, improves efficiency, and addresses dynamic situations in industries, improving operational performance and cost-effectiveness. Researchers in power systems, control theory, and artificial intelligence may use HBPSO to find new answers. Its hybrid particle swarm-butterfly method balances exploration and exploitation, making it suitable for many optimization problems.

This model's optimal performance and flexibility make it a promising choice for both new ventures and established systems. It lays the groundwork for entrepreneurs to optimize their processes and allocate resources effectively. Revitalization and improved efficiency may save operating expenses in existing systems. The HBPSO method finds the particle with the lowest fitness value as the optimal solution. When it comes to optimizing the GPSS-SMIB system's PID controller constants, the HBPSO method is superior to both the BOA and PSO algorithms since it merges their strengths.

4 Simulation Results

Here, we will discuss the outcomes of network stability experiments conducted on the SMIB system. Using the HBPSO optimization method, the parameters of a PID controller were fine-tuned to produce a robust power system stabilizer (PSS) with enhanced stability across various operating conditions. Using eigenvalues, damping ratios, and Eigenvalues, the strength of the power system is evaluated, and the results include tables of system parameters and evaluations of performance (peak overshoot and settling time) for both existing and novel PSS controllers. The SMIB system was developed using MATLAB/SIMULINK.

The excitation controller has significantly increased the system's efficiency and consistency compared to its unregulated predecessor. This improvement enables the implementation of significant damping coefficients, accelerating system reaction times and reducing static errors, resulting in increased precision. The capability of the excitation controller to effectively attenuate electromechanical oscillations has immensely improved the transient regimes as a whole. The quality of transient responses for all system parameters has been significantly enhanced, and the system now exhibits remarkable transient stability, especially when using the PID controller. Even in the most pressing situations, such as the station returning to its dormant state (Under stimulated), the system's precision and speed are on full display, requiring only a few seconds to set up.

The presented Table 1 provides parameters for a control system, including proportional, integral, and derivative gains (K_1 to K_6), as well as other characteristics such as time constants and damping ratios. By using these system parameters, this work enhances dynamic stability of the controller. The values assigned to each parameter significantly influence the system's behavior. The provided Table 2 enumerates proportional (K_P), integral (K_I), and derivative (K_D) gains for a control system. These values are crucial in determining the response characteristics of the system, with K_P influencing the immediate response to errors, K_I addressing accumulated errors over time, and K_D mitigating rapid changes. The high proportional gain (K_P) suggests a system that strongly reacts to current errors, while the relatively small integral gain (K_I) implies a cautious approach to accumulated errors over time. The substantial derivative gain (K_D) indicates a sensitivity to rapid changes, contributing to stability and damping oscillations. The effectiveness of these parameters, however, depends on the specific dynamics and requirements of the controlled process. Further insights into the nature of the system and its performance objectives would be necessary for a more precise analysis and potential optimization.

Table 1. System parameters

Constant Parameters	Torque in N-M	Other Parameters
$K_1 = 1.4479$	$T_A = 0.05$	$M = 4.74$ Kg-m^2
$K_2 = 1.3174$	$T_F = 1.0$	$w = 377$ rad/sec
$K_3 = 0.3072$	$T_d' = 5.9$	$D = 0$
$K_4 = 1.805$	$T_E = 0.95$	
$K_5 = 0.0294$		
$K_6 = 0.5257$		
$K_A = 400$		
$K_F = 0.025$		
$K_E = -0.17$		

Table 2. Optimized parameters using HBPSO

Parameters	Values
K_P	98.244
K_I	2.6946
K_D	97.3093

(See Fig. 10: a, b, c) indicates the MATLAB/SIMULINK based HPM model, SMIB implementation, and proposed SMIB. The prototype equations are formulated, a simulink model is constructed to represent the system graphically, system parameters are input, simulation duration and time step are specified, the simulation is run to analyze dynamic behavior, control strategies are tested, parameters are fine-tuned, various operating scenarios are evaluated, and the results are documented. This method is advantageous because it provides a unified setting for analyzing power systems, optimizing control techniques, and measuring responses to various disruptions.

Simulations are frequently used in power system studies for stability analysis and control. Model initialization consists of A Simulink model in MATLAB that can accurately represent the synchronous generator, excitation system, and load to describe the SMIB system. Include in the model the PID controller component. During PID constants are defined, and specified initial values. Optimization techniques are used to determine the optimal values for these parameters. Conduct simulations under varying loads and fault conditions. Consider the PID controller's transient stability and voltage regulation in these circumstances (see Fig. 10(d)). Using key performance indicators such as overshoot, settling time, and steady-state error to evaluate the effectiveness of the PID controller. These measurements can be plotted and analyzed with ease in MATLAB.

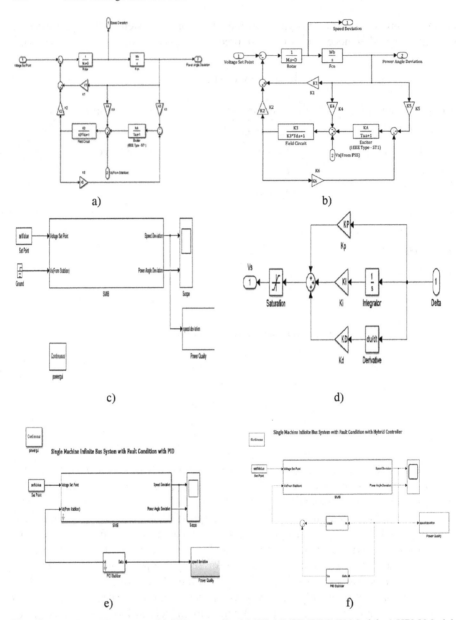

Fig. 10. GPSS-SMIB system with PID controller MATLAB/SIMULINK Model: a) HPM Model b) SMIB Implementation c) Proposed SMIB d) PID Controller e) SMIB with PID f) Hybrid Controller

Using a PID Controller to simulate the SMIB, developed the model further, add a PID controller to the existing SMIB Simulink model. The PID controller is connected to the generator's excitation circuit to achieve this (see Fig. 10(e)). When designing a controller, we are considered the PID controller's ability to maintain stability by modulating the generator's excitation voltage. Adjust the PID controller's settings for optimal performance with this task. Analyzed the SMIB system's stability by simulating it in various environments, both with and without disruptions. Evaluated the PID controller's ability to reduce oscillations and maintain steady-state conditions.

Third, as (see Fig. 10(f)), a hybrid controller simulation, the SMIB model give benefit from a hybrid controller that combines characteristics of multiple control strategies. It has a PID controller and an additional control scheme, such as a Power System Stabilizer (PSS). This work is ensured that the hybrid controller's interaction with the generator's excitation system and the remaining SMIB model components function correctly. Also, evaluated the efficacy of the hybrid controller by simulating its performance against a conventional PID controller.

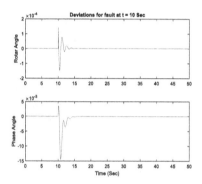

Fig. 11. Rotor and phase angle distortion of Hybrid model

Critical clearing time (recovery of power system stability following a disturbance) and absolute integral time error will be used to evaluate controller performance. This comparison investigates how much the PSS-PID controller enhances stability compared to the PSS and PID controllers alone. In addition, it will explore how optimization strategies influence controller performance. The study's findings will be discussed to enhance the stability of the proposed model.

Generator speed variances are (see Fig. 11) as a result of the PSO-PID controller's reaction to an impulsive malfunction at t = 5 s. This inaccuracy in deviation is picked up by the PID controller at the subsequent sampling time, at which point a correction signal is generated. As shown in (see Fig. 11) the PSO-PID controller can effectively offset the effects of the malfunction and quickly restore regular system functioning. This demonstrates the controller's prowess in preserving stability and transient responsiveness despite sudden errors, ultimately leading to better performance and faster system recovery.

(See Fig. 12) depicts the PSO-PID controller's phase angle and rotor angle responses at t = 10 s when an impulsive defect occurs. The problem persists for 50 (fifty) seconds without a controller but vanishes after only one sample time when PSS and PID controllers are implemented. The generator's rotor deviates from its constant pace first.

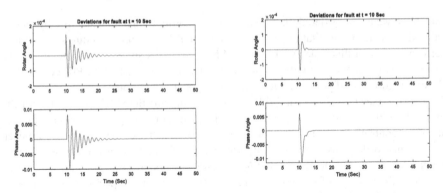

Fig. 12. Rotor and phase angle distortion of Hybrid model (PID-PSS)

If the deviation is more significant than zero, the PID controller will issue a compensation signal at the next sampling period. After approximately 4 s, the PSS controller's variations average out to zero, according to the data.

(See Fig. 13) illustrates the composite approach's response to a transient impulsive defect at t = 10 s. After a single sample, the issue is resolved. When the generator's rotor deviates from a constant speed, the PSS detects a deviation error and generates a compensation signal. As evidenced by the data, the HBPSO algorithm plays a crucial role in optimizing PSS and PID gains, resulting in a more rapid onset of system stability. As the research progresses, it becomes evident how much superior the system is when excitation controllers such as PSS, PID, and Hybrid are present as opposed to when they are absent. In critical states such as station resting (under-stimulated), these controllers' introduction of significant damping coefficients results in faster reaction times, decreased static errors, increased precision, and improved transient regimes. The system as a whole is more stable, accurate, and responsive due to its rapid recovery periods and low static error rates.

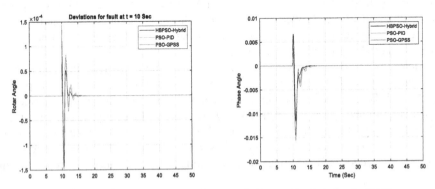

Fig.13. Correlative assessment of rotor and phase angle deviation in SMIB

The examination of stability in the SMIB system is conducted through incremental load changes of 5%, 10%, and 15%. The evaluation of PSSs designed using the HBPSO

Table 3. Stability analysis for various controllers

Load Changes	Optimized controller	Eigen value	Damping Ratio
5% step decreases	HBPSO-PID-PSS	$-1.59 \pm j4.34$	0.298
	BOA-PID-PSS	$-0.74 \pm j3.91$	0.198
	PSO-PID-PSS	$-0.49 \pm j3.37$	0.174
10% step decreases	HBPSO-PID-PSS	$-1.28 \pm j4.21$	0.213
	BOA-PID-PSS	$-0.56 \pm j3.54$	0.151
	PSO-PID-PSS	$-0.26 \pm j2.46$	0.124
15% step decreases	HBPSO-PID-PSS	$-1.14 \pm j2.74$	0.196
	BOA-PID-PSS	$-0.43 \pm j2.13$	0.132
	PSO-PID-PSS	$-0.19 \pm j1.93$	0.105

technique and PID controller is performed under these load conditions. Table 3 presents the stability analysis, focusing on eigenvalues and damping of the electromechanical modes. The outcomes demonstrate that the proposed controller adeptly shifts the eigenvalues of electromechanical modes towards the left side of the S-plane, indicative of enhanced damping characteristics for improved stability.

Hybrid butterfly particle swarm optimization may improve power system dynamic stability. Combining particle swarm optimization with the butterfly algorithm, this optimization method is adaptable and effective for fine-tuning control parameters and optimizing power system performance. This technique may solve complex and dynamic power system situations by effectively using the hybrid algorithm's adaptive and exploratory characteristics. Thus, system stability and resilience may increase significantly. This novel technique might improve power system management tactics, making them more robust and optimal under varied situations and disruptions.

5   Conclusion and Future Work

By utilizing the Hybrid Butterfly-Particle Swarm Optimization (HBPSO) technique, this research paper introduces the HBPSO-PID-GPSS method. In particular, its objective is to enhance the dynamic stability of power systems as a Heffron-Phillips model modification. By employing the secondary bus voltage of the generator side transformer as a point of reference, the proposed Multi-Parameter Self-Tuning System (MPSS) design presents an alternative approach that utilizes local information rather than the external system data used by conventional systems. The damping performance is considerably enhanced in comparison to traditional MPSS methods through the utilization of the HBPSO algorithm to optimize the MPSS parameters and PID controller gains. This is evidenced by the reduction in peak length and settling time. Eigenvalue analysis offers additional confirmation that the HBPSO-based PID-MPSS design is effective by illustrating a positive transition of unstable eigenvalues to the target stable zone. The findings of this research indicate that the proposed methodology exhibits considerable potential in enhancing the dynamic stability of power system management across various operational conditions.

Power system stability will be further advanced in future endeavours by integrating Fractional Order PID (FOPID) control with a PID-based Power System Stabilizer (PID-PSS) employing nature-inspired metaheuristic optimization algorithms. This approach harnesses the flexibility and precision of FOPID and PID-PSS to mitigate low-frequency oscillations and uphold generator synchronization. It incorporates adaptive tuning, fault tolerance, remote monitoring, and control capabilities, making it suitable for deployment across extensive areas of the power grid to ensure optimal operation under varying conditions.

Acknowledgements. The authors would like to express their gratitude to Department of Electrical and Electronics Engineering, Oriental University, Indore, Madhya Pradesh for all of their assistance and encouragement in carrying out this research and publishing this paper.

Conflicts of Interest. The authors declare no conflict of interest.

References

1. Elmenfy, T.H.: Design of velocity PID-fuzzy power system stabilizer using particle swarm optimization. WSEAS Trans. Syst. **20**, 9–14 (2021)
2. Mishra, A., Singh, N., Yadav, S.: Design of optimal PID controller for varied system using teaching–learning-based optimization. In: Sharma, H., Govindan, K., Poonia, R.C., Kumar, S., El-Medany, W.M. (eds.) Advances in Computing and Intelligent Systems. AIS, pp. 153–163. Springer, Singapore (2020). https://doi.org/10.1007/978-981-15-0222-4_13
3. Kamal, T., et al.: Novel improved adaptive neuro-fuzzy control of inverter and supervisory energy management system of a microgrid. Energies (MDPI). **13**, 1–20 (2020)
4. Abdul-Ghaffar, H.I., Ebrahim, E.A., Azzam, M.: Design of PID controller for power system stabilization using hybrid particle swarm-bacteria foraging optimization. WSEAS Trans. Power Syst. **8**(1), 12–23 (2021)
5. Gu, Y., Green, T.C.: Power system stability with a high penetration of inverter-based resources. In: Proceedings of the IEEE. (2022)
6. Banga-Banga, T.W.P.P.: Model reference adaptive control algorithm for power system inter-area oscillations damping (Doctoral dissertation, Cape Peninsula University of Technology) (2022)
7. Benbouzid, M.: Design, Control and Monitoring of Tidal Stream Turbine Systems. Dokumen Pub (2023). https://dokumen.pub/design-control-and-monitoring-of-tidalstream-turbine-systems-1839534206-9781839534201.html
8. Joseph, S.B., et al.: Metaheuristic algorithms for PID controller parameters tuning: review, approaches and open problems. Heliyon **8**, 1–29 (2022)
9. Tandan, N., Swarnkar, K.K.: PID controller optimization by soft computing techniques. Int. J. Hybrid Inf. Technol. **8**(7), 357–362 (2015)
10. Ramshanker, A., Chakraborty, S.: Maiden application of skill optimization algorithm on cascaded multi-level neuro-fuzzy based power system stabilizers for damping oscillations. Int. J. Renew. Energy Res. (IJRER) **12**(4), 2152–2167 (2022)
11. Saleem, B., Badar, R., Manzoor, A., Judge, M.A., Boudjadar, J., Islam, S.U.: Fully adaptive recurrent Neuro-fuzzy control for power system stability enhancement in multi machine system. IEEE Access **10**, 36464–36476 (2022)
12. Sedaghati, A., Malik, O.P.: Efficient Self-tuned fuzzy logic based power system stabilizer. Electric Power Compon. Syst. **49**(1–2), 79–93 (2021)

13. Ekinci, S., İzci, D., Hekimoğlu, B.: Implementing the Henry gas solubility optimization algorithm for optimal power system stabilizer design. Electrica **21**(2), 250–258 (2021)
14. Shahgholian, G.: Review of power system stabilizer: application modeling analysis and control strategy. Int. J. Tech. Phys. Prob. Eng. **5**(3), 41–52 (2021)
15. Khatir, A., Bouchama, Z., Benaggoune, S., Zerroug, N.: Indirect adaptive fuzzy finite time synergetic control for power systems. Electr. Eng. Electro-Mech. **1**, 57–62 (2023)
16. Chaib, L., Choucha, A., Arif, S.: Optimal design and tuning of novel fractional order PID power system stabilizer using a new metaheuristic Bat algorithm. Ain Shams Eng. J. **8**(2), 113–125 (2022)
17. Saini, M., Djalal, M.R., Yunus, A.S.: Optimal coordination PID-PSS control based on craziness particle swarm optimization in sulselrabar system. In: IEEE 2022 5th International Seminar on Research of Information Technology and Intelligent Systems (ISRITI), pp. 695–699 (2022)
18. Silaa, M.Y., Barambones, O., Derbeli, M., Napole, C., Bencherif, A.: Fractional order PID design for a proton exchange membrane fuel cell system using an extended grey wolf optimizer. Processes **10**(3), 450 (2022)
19. Naresh, G., Raju, M.R., Narasimham, S.V.L.: Application of harmony search algorithm for the robust design of power system stabilizers in multi-machine power systems. J. Electr. Eng. **13**(2), 9–19 (2022)
20. Arora, S., Singh, S.: Butterfly optimization algorithm: a novel approach for global optimization. Soft. Comput. **23**, 715–734 (2019). https://doi.org/10.1007/s00500-018-3102-4
21. Yuan, S., Lv, M., Baldi, S., Zhang, L.: Lyapunov-equation-based stability analysis for switched linear systems and its application to switched adaptive control. IEEE Trans. Autom. Control **66**(5), 2250–2256 (2020)
22. Ray, P.K., Das, S.R., Mohanty, A.: Fuzzy-controller-designed-PV-based custom power device for power quality enhancement. IEEE Trans. Energy Convers. **34**(1), 405–414 (2021)
23. Selim, F., Attia, A.F.: Power system stabilizer with self-tuning based on hierarchical fuzzy logic controller. In: IEEE 23rd International Middle East Power Systems Conference (MEPCON), pp. 1–6 (2022)
24. Patel, V.V.: Ziegler-Nichols tuning method. Resonance **25**, 1385–1397 (2020)

Enhancing Student Welfare: A Comprehensive Analysis of the User Interface for a University Mental Health Counselling App

Rahil Parikh[1]($\boxtimes$), Himanshu Nimonkar[2], Saikrishna Karra[1], Ashwini Dalvi[2], and Irfan Siddavatam[2]

[1] Department of Computer Engineering, K. J. Somaiya College of Engineering, Mumbai, India
`{r.parikh,s.karra}@somaiya.edu`
[2] Department of Information Technology, K. J. Somaiya College of Engineering, Mumbai, India
`{h.nimonkar,ashwinidalvi,irfansiddavatam}@somaiya.edu`

Abstract. The critical relevance of mental health cannot be understated. A sizeable portion of university students face barriers to accessing counselling assistance. Many students hesitate to seek the crucial support they need for their mental health issues because of a lack of accessibility and practical problems connected with conventional counselling methods. This study presents a creative application called "Mento-peace" which is intended to successfully address this pervasive problem by offering an intuitive, cost-effective and easily available online system for counselling which is especially suited to the requirements of university students. This application includes a wide range of essential rehabilitative assets in addition to the system's main attributes, such as online discussions, reflective evaluation services, and cooperative mental health networks. A critical analysis of the effectiveness of this application and its impact on student mental health welfare will be analyzed through a survey conducted among university students. Our innovative project aims to transform the environment for university students by providing everyone with unrestricted access to expert advice when they require it. Out of the university students who responded to the survey question concerned with seeking counselling services, it was observed that a majority of 87.4% are willing to opt for such services, if made available to them through the proposed application.

Keywords: College counselling · mental health · User Interface (UI) · student welfare · survey analysis

1 Introduction

University students face a wide range of difficulties, including the demands of their academic work and the complexities in their private lives. This combination of pressure frequently results in a variety of mental health issues, such as mood disorders and anxiousness which can hurt both academic success and overall wellbeing in general. Unfortunately, given the prevalent prejudice surrounding the field, numerous students are reluctant to get help regarding their mental health issues, which can create an obstacle which prevents individuals from getting the help they require.

S. Rajagopal et al (Eds.): ASCIS 2023, CCIS 2040, pp. 194–203, 2024.
https://doi.org/10.1007/978-3-031-59107-5_13

There exists an urgent need to provide students with the necessary resources to support their mental health. The examination of the frequency of causes of mental health issues within this population is the basis of this research. Research has shown how common illnesses like insomnia and anxiety affect many university students. The effectiveness of programs designed to promote the mental well-being of university students has been the subject of such competing research. The array of solutions includes conventional counselling tools, online systems, and peer groups. These investigations have conclusively shown that such counselling sessions are effective in easing the manifestations of mental health issues as well as bringing about a general improvement in the mood of people. Parallel to this, scholarly research has focused on identifying the barriers that university students face while seeking professional mental health care. These obstacles involve personal bias, a lack of knowledge about the resources that are accessible, and other practical problems. To overcome such obstacles, the proposed research work explores and analyzes the responses of survey participants to satisfy its primary objective of evaluating the effectives of the "Mento-peace" application.

Throughout the sections that follow, the proposed study explores the related research which will help outline the approach, and ultimately come up with a conclusion that demonstrates the growing significance of treating the mental health of university students.

2   Related Work

Booc et al. [1] highlight the disturbing worldwide frequency of mental health problems and suggest an application for smartphones. Danowitz and Beddoes et al. [2] researched mental health conditions throughout Western American universities. Their study reveals an elevated chance of identifiable mental health disorders amongst university students using verified questionnaires. This research digs further into statistical divisions while it finds greater incidences across previously marginalized communities of color. Their results highlight the critical need for specialized assistance systems among these students by highlighting issues regarding mental health that need to be addressed. Xu [3] introduces an innovative technique for examining mental health issues among students. This research categorizes datasets using the C4.5 technique for information extraction and identifies key elements influencing university students' mental health. This study provides views on different mental conditions and demonstrates the possibilities for improving mental health awareness among university students via decision tree structures with 2018 institution statistics.

Wang et al. [4] offer an extensive approach to boosting mental health teaching among university students using technology. The research addresses combining Massive Open Online Courses along with classroom flipping assets for a better standard of instruction and using WeChat websites alongside associated internet pages to encourage mental well-being. Lim et al. [5] emphasize how difficult it may be to maintain one's mental well-being through adolescence, an issue that's frequently overlooked. The proposed Buddy application uses Firebase along with Airtable for storage capabilities whilst building its UI with Figma along with Bravo Studio to incorporate straightforwardness and durability. Teles et al. [6] aim to classify the present state of cellphone applications that are specifically geared towards treating sadness, stressing the critical need to address such problems.

Mendis et al. [7] explore possibilities for making an app for smartphones that will help natives from Sri Lanka recognize and treat mental health problems that are becoming more common among students residing there. The study makes an important improvement towards our understanding of technology-assisted mental health care by using well-established measures along with predictive modelling techniques. Rosario et al. [8] illuminate the fascinating nexus between technological innovation as well as mental wellness. The team's research presents SmileTeq, a cell phone application that can offer critical help to students struggling with depressive symptoms and anxiousness. Xia and Lin [9] stress on the importance of improving student mental wellness literacy while noting numerous studies on this subject. This paper examines current behavioral problems affecting students as well as crucial functions using information extraction technologies. Liu and Mai [10] highlight the significance of computers in college-level mental health instruction. The mental health document organization tool with its supplementary mental health training environment is the focus of the investigation. With testing as well as assessing in handheld devices, the cognitive document administration program uses various software, whereas the cognitive assistance education portal makes use of other software with increased practicality. The paper highlights that by utilizing such developments in technology, it is possible to improve the convenience, effectiveness, and intelligence of the psychological instruction provided to undergraduates.

3   Methodology

The "Mento-peace" app seeks to improve the mental state of university students by working to remove obstacles in academic and social counselling, dispelling false beliefs about mental health, and smoothly incorporating professional counselling into the college syllabus. Although counselling programs are widely available at educational institutions, there is a glaring lack of full coverage of these assets in the course curriculum. Instead, details on counselling facilities frequently get lost on the primary website of the university.

To assess how well students comprehend the variety of counselling programs offered on campus, a detailed survey was created. An extensive survey named "Understanding College Student Mental Health" was conducted to see how informed students were about the university's counselling programs. The survey was designed in a manner such that it contains sequential domain-specific questions for participants to answer. The survey contains 106 responses, which serve as a reliable sample size. This sample size is sufficient to represent a diverse population of people and their varied views on mental health. The results from the survey are representative of a broader view held by students about mental health, which can be generalized and applied to other universities to evaluate the awareness of mental health among their corresponding student populations. Upon analyzing the responses, it becomes evident that a significant proportion (94.3%) of the respondents were between the ages of 18 and 24, and primarily composed of undergraduate students. Notably, 94.3% of all respondents exhibited awareness of mental health, however, a mere 28.3% actively sought assistance for their mental well-being.

These statistics underscore the prevailing struggle among most students concerning navigating the challenges and pressures within this age range.

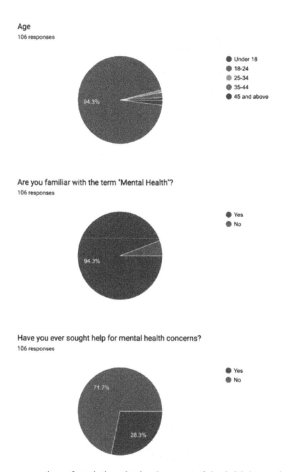

Fig. 1. Visual representation of statistics obtained as part of the initial questions of the survey.

The statistics represented in Fig. 1 provide an insight into the age demographic of the people surveyed and the basic awareness of mental health. The responses of the survey were collected using Google Forms specifically tailored to address questions related to mental health. Out of 106 respondents, 91.5% of respondents indicated that they did not utilize any mental health resources provided by the university. Despite 55.7% of respondents experiencing mental health challenges during their time at university, 56.6% were unaware of the mental health resources being provided by their university.

The mental health statistics depicted in Fig. 2 show that while a majority of the people have faced mental health challenges during their time at a university a vast amount of people are not aware of the different mental health facilities offered by the college.

The data in Fig. 3 shows that a total of 65% of people find the UI of the proposed application appealing to a certain extent. Only 12.6% of 95 respondents are reluctant to

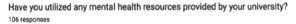

Have you utilized any mental health resources provided by your university?
106 responses

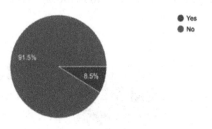

Are you aware of the mental health resources available on your campus?
106 responses

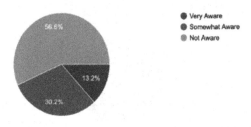

Have you experienced mental health challenges during your time in university?
106 responses

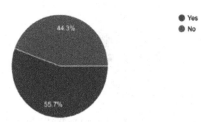

Fig. 2. Numerical figures of mental health questions in the form of a pie chart

seek counselling through the proposed application, whereas a large majority of 78.9% people believe that the overall experience offered through the "Mento-peace" application in terms of counselling will be more effective than other counselling applications or traditional counselling methods.

Figure 4 and Fig. 5 show the user interface of the proposed "Mento-peace" application. It consists of a welcome page, a login page and a register page at the beginning. Once user authentication and verification are completed a home page is displayed from which the user can view and select different activities to be performed to improve their mental health. The other options include a dashboard, a custom-curated playlist, a quiz, messaging for friends, specialized interaction with a counsellor and the About Us page.

How visually appealing do you find the UI of our application?
106 responses

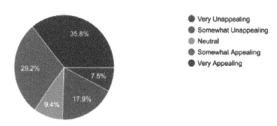

Will you be willing to seek counselling if it is readily accessible through such an application?
95 responses

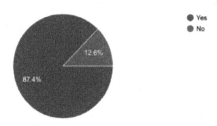

Will you think overall counselling experience from our app will be effective enough or better compared to other apps and conventional methods that you know of?
95 responses

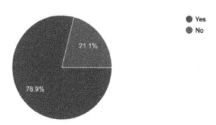

Fig. 3. Graphical representation of the favorable reception of the "Mento-peace" app among students

The user can listen to their favorite songs, speak to their close friends in times of crisis and have meaningful and therapeutic sessions with their counsellor. This would help increase mental health awareness among different friend groups and social circles and drastically reduce the negative consequences associated with mental health problems. The research answers a critical question regarding the efficacy of the proposed application. As evident from the results of the survey, a majority of the respondents are of the opinion that the user interface of the proposed application is comparable to or better than

Fig. 4. Proposed application User Interface (UI)

conventional approaches and other applications. This indicates that the proposed application has achieved its objective of being an effective and reliable source for university students to seek mental health counselling.

Fig. 5. Proposed application user interface for different pages

4 Conclusion

In conclusion, the proposed methodology has shown the complexity of the mental health issues that university students experience. Due to the widespread societal prejudices associated with various types of disorders including anxiety and depression, such problems frequently go unrecognized. The presented methodology aims to offer doable alternatives which reduce the prejudice associated with counselling, eventually improving students' general state of mind. Additionally, universities may be crucial in tackling such issues. To enhance the mental health of university students, a comprehensive strategy that breaks down prejudice along with one that promotes candid communication is needed. Institutes of higher learning have the potential to serve as revolutionary accelerators by fostering a culture in which psychological wellness is prioritized. 78.9% of 95 respondents believe that the proposed application is superior as compared to other similar applications. Moreover, 87.4% of these 95 respondents are willing to seek mental health counselling made available through the proposed application. This indicates that the user interface of the "Mento-peace" application has produced the intended results and that such an application would be highly beneficial in addressing the mental health problems of university students. The impact of this research goes outside academics, repeating the need for more public awareness and comprehension. This signals a time in which psychological wellness is not just a private battle, but rather a communal dedication to wellness.

References

1. Booc,C.E.R., San Diego, C.M.D., Tee, M.L., Caro, J.D.L.: A mobile application for the campus-based psychosocial wellness program. In: 2016 7th International Conference on Information, Intelligence, Systems & Applications (IISA), Chalkidiki, Greece, 2016, pp. 1–4 (2016). https://doi.org/10.1109/IISA.2016.7785426
2. Danowitz, A., Beddoes, K.: A snapshot of mental health and wellness of engineering students across the Western United States. In: IEEE Frontiers in Education Conference (FIE). Uppsala, Sweden 2020, pp. 1–5 (2020). https://doi.org/10.1109/FIE44824.2020.9273885
3. Xu,J.: Design and application of college students' psychological data mining and analysis system. In: 2020 13th International Conference on Intelligent Computation Technology and Automation (ICICTA), Xi'an, China, 2020, pp. 461–464 (2020). https://doi.org/10.1109/ICICTA51737.2020.00104
4. Wang, G., Zhou, W., Zhang, Y.: Using information technology to improve the Mental Health Education of University Students. In: 2015 7th International Conference on Information Technology in Medicine and Education (ITME), Huangshan, China, 2015, pp. 723–726 (2015). https://doi.org/10.1109/ITME.2015.61
5. Lim, O.O., Hareva, D.H., Steven, E., Sentausa D., Abineno, F.A.: Companion: mental health mobile applications for students. In: 2022 1st International Conference on Technology Innovation and Its Applications (ICTIIA), Tangerang, Indonesia, 2022, pp. 1–6 (2022). https://doi.org/10.1109/ICTIIA54654.2022.9935882
6. Teles, A., et al.: Mobile Mental Health: a review of applications for depression assistance. In: IEEE 32nd International Symposium on Computer-Based Medical Systems (CBMS), Cordoba, Spain 2019, pp. 708–713 (2019). https://doi.org/10.1109/CBMS.2019.00143
7. Mendis, E.S., Kasthuriarachchi, L.W., Samarasinha, H.P.K.L., Kasthuriarachchi, S., Rajapaksa, S.: Mobile application for mental health using machine learning. In: 2022 4th International Conference on Advancements in Computing (ICAC), Colombo, Sri Lanka, 2022, pp. 387–392 (2022). https://doi.org/10.1109/ICAC57685.2022.10025036

8. Rosario, D.F.T.D., Mariano, A.E.D., Samonte, M.J.C.: SmileTeq: an assistive and recommendation mobile application for people with anxiety, depression or stress. In: 2019 International Conference on Information and Communication Technology Convergence (ICTC), Jeju, Korea (South), 2019, pp. 1304–1309 (2019). https://doi.org/10.1109/ICTC46691.2019.8940036

9. Xia, Y., Lin, Z.: College students' mental health education system based on data mining technology. In: 2021 International Symposium on Advances in Informatics, Electronics and Education (ISAIEE), Germany, 2021, pp. 106-109 (2021). https://doi.org/10.1109/ISAIEE55071.2021.00033

10. Liu, F., Mai, Y.: Application of computer technology in college students' mental health education. In: 2022 3rd International Conference on Education, Knowledge and Information Management (ICEKIM), Harbin, China, 2022, pp. 1019–1024 (2022). https://doi.org/10.1109/ICEKIM55072.2022.00222

Leveraging Business Intelligence and Student Feedback for Enhancing Teaching and Learning in Higher Education

Hemant S. Sharma$^{(\boxtimes)}$ and Hiren D. Joshi

Department of Computer Science, Gujarat University, Ahmedabad, Gujarat, India
{hemantsharma,hdjoshi}@gujaratuniversity.ac.in

Abstract. The main objective of this study is to examine data, improve teaching quality, and accelerate ongoing development in higher education through the use of Business Intelligence (BI) tools and the incorporation of student feedback. Business Intelligence and other forms of technology play a critical role in improving the efficiency, effectiveness, and individualization of educational services. Higher education has a serious problem due to the lack of a well-defined plan to incorporate student feedback and data analytics into the classroom. Due to its absence, the potential to gain insightful information and improve educational experiences is hindered. A machine learning hybrid model is trained and proposed known as Convolution Neural Network (CNN) + Long-Short Term Memory (LSTM) model to predict student feedback. The investigation reveals that students provide feedback in various forms, encompassing positive, negative, and neutral responses concerning faculty performance. The proposed hybrid model achieves an accuracy of 90.34% and a loss of 0.285 in classifying the sentiment analysis of the students. Also, the proposed hybrid model performs better as compared with other conventional approaches.

Keywords: Business Intelligence · academic feedback system · learning management system · sentimental analysis

1 Introduction

The higher education sector is characterized by an ongoing endeavor to achieve excellence in educational approaches and methods of knowledge acquisition. The forces of globalization and the rapid advancements in information and communication technology (ICT) have not only reshaped competition among businesses but have also reverberated within the higher education sector. This impact is particularly evident in leading universities across the United States, Australia, and Western Europe, where the imperative to sustain a competitive edge has prompted a proactive embrace of innovative management practices and cutting-edge pedagogical methods [1].

Within this context, the adoption of Information and Communication Technologies (ICTs) has become integral to nearly every facet of modern life, extending its reach into institutional processes vital to the very survival of universities. These technologies

S. Rajagopal et al (Eds.): ASCIS 2023, CCIS 2040, pp. 204–224, 2024.
https://doi.org/10.1007/978-3-031-59107-5_14

permeate both administrative management, which underpins universities' operational efficiency, and academic administration [2]. A notable exemplar of ICTs in academic management is the ubiquitous Learning Management System (LMS), which facilitates online interactions between educators and students [3].

However, there arise occasions where a more targeted infusion of ICTs is required to address overarching challenges in education. It is in these contexts that ICTs can serve as catalysts for the implementation of innovative pedagogical models and novel approaches to teaching and learning.

Among these technologies, Business Intelligence (BI) stands out as a powerful tool renowned for facilitating informed decision-making across diverse industries. BI empowers users with the ability to visualize insights through reports, maps, ad hoc queries, dashboards, and benchmarking, ultimately contributing to enhanced organizational efficiency and strategic planning [4]. Notably, BI software has played an instrumental role in shaping modern business strategies since the advent of fully functional BI software by pioneers like IBM and Siebel (now owned by Oracle) between 1970 and 1990 [5].

The Indian educational system, integral to the country's economic prospects on the global stage, is no exception to the integration of ICTs. To navigate this complexity effectively, there is a growing need for software solutions that can effectively represent data in ways comprehensible to a diverse workforce. Collaborations between technology companies, universities, and businesses have resulted in the utilization of BI solutions such as Tableau, Board, Domo, QlikView, BI360, and Yellowfin to enhance academic performance and mitigate managerial conflicts [6].

In our proposed system, we introduce an innovative approach where users are presented with a series of questions, and their responses are used to draw meaningful conclusions. These questions are generated through various survey feedback forms and the Minnesota Multiphasic Personality Inventory-2 (MMPI-2), with users responding to formats such as Yes/No, Agree/Disagree, and True/False [7]. Each question offers four possible responses, enabling users to earn points and reflect upon their choices through the system.

The purpose of this investigation is to use data analysis to better the quality of instruction and aid in the institution's continuous progress, tapping into the potential of BI technologies in higher education and developing an advanced machine learning model for forecasting student feedback. This model will be able to shed light on student attitudes and preferences. By contrasting the results of this model with those of more established sentiment analysis tools, this study aims to verify the model's reliability for usage in academic contexts. The study's overarching goal is to improve higher education by presenting a strategic framework that does more than just improve data analysis techniques; it also proactively incorporates feedback into broader institutional decision-making processes, with the hope of improving teaching and learning.

1.1 Importance of BI in Education

In an era characterized by rising expectations for accountability, performance, and cost-effectiveness in the education sector, the role of Business Intelligence (BI) has never been more crucial. The advent of online educational resources has necessitated better decision-making and accurate monitoring to meet the demands of today's learners.

The BI education portal, an invaluable resource, offers access to a rich repository of materials, including in-depth case studies, interactive BI demonstrations, education-specific solution overviews, and more, all tailored to address the challenges and opportunities faced by educators and the technology they employ [8].

- Self-service, open-source BI has empowered a new medical school at Commonwealth Medical College, enabling users to access both pre-made and custom reports, minimizing overhead.
- The University of Lucknow has harnessed BI to upgrade its student information system, capitalizing on its scalability, user-friendliness, and speed for comprehensive data management.
- Leading providers of Learning Management System (LMS) solutions have harnessed BI technology to reduce time-to-market for their offerings.
- Internationally recognized providers of education management software are democratizing BI, making it more accessible to faculty members worldwide [8].

This article is structured as follows: Sect. 1 discusses the introduction part and then Sect. 2 presents a comprehensive literature review of pertinent prior research; Sect. 3 provides the background context of prior relevant studies, while Sect. 4 outlines the problem at hand and presents the proposed solution, in Sect. 5 the research objectives of the study are mentioned. In Sect. 6, the methodology employed in our study is elucidated. Section 7 reveals the study's results, and in Sect. 8, we present our concluding remarks.

2   Literature of Review

This section contains a review of literature in the field of identifying BI parameters for academic feedback systems for the university.

Quadir et al., (2022) [9] expressed in terms of learning objectives, obstacles to learning, and methods for analyzing large datasets. Ineffectiveness in detecting academic and behavioral modeling and waste of resources; inappropriate curricula and teaching strategies; failures in quality assurance; privacy and ethical concerns; are the four main concerns that have emerged as a result of the identification of the most mentioned educational problems. According to the results, educational data mining is the best method for checking the quality of education and offering possible solutions to problems like failing to recognize student behavior patterns and wasting money.

Cardoso and Su (2022) [10] introduce the Higher Education-Business Intelligence and Analytics (HE-BIA) Maturity Model (MM), which is a version of the BIA MM tailored to the university sector. This research presents a design science methodology for creating and assessing two artifacts: the maturity model (MM) and the maturity assessment technique. Higher education institutions found the HE-BIA model assessment to be i) appropriate for their purposes and (ii) helpful in understanding the current state of their BIA environment. This helped to highlight the fact that BIA is both a technological endeavor and an organizational development.

Hamad et al., (2021) [11] examined the people who work at the reference desks of Jordanian universities to see business intelligence. In addition, both the potential and the obstacles that come along with it are reviewed and investigated. Based on the findings, it's clear that the information department staff thinks BI is a good thing for the library's decision-makers to have at their disposal so that they can make the best possible choices in the shortest amount of time. The findings also highlight the need to invest in the right infrastructure before rolling out BI in Jordan's academic libraries.

Khatibi et al., (2020) [12] provided a paradigm for using BI to monitor indicators in higher education and predict future trends by bringing together disparate internal and external data sources. The goal of the established system is to provide a holistic assessment of Iran's higher education system about those of its regional neighbors. The findings highlight that although Iranian higher education is a standard bearer in the scientific community, especially in the fields of science and engineering, the brain drain is expanding at an alarming pace.

Villegas-Ch et al., (2020) [13] described a strategy for deciding on factors that could influence the growth of learning by combining a data mining model and methodology inside a BI architecture. As a proof of concept for the suggested technique, a case study is provided in which students are recognized and categorized based on the data they contribute across the various information systems at a university.

Bojorque and Pesántez (2019) [14] introduced a machine-learning and retrieval-based Artificial Intelligence (AI) auditing strategy for scholarly materials. The authors conducted the research using actual data from a Latin American university's courses, grades, and online material. It concludes that utilizing AI approaches reduces decision support time, permits comprehensive data analysis rather than a data sample, and uncovers trends not previously found in the case study universities.

Boulila et al., (2018) [15] provided a BI solution for Taibah University's academic needs. SQL Server Data Tools are used to conduct the experiments. The SQL Server tools SQL Server Integration Services (SSIS), SQL Server Analysis Services (SSAS), and SQL Server Reporting Services (SSRS) are described in depth. Numerous statistical and predictive indications useful for scholastic endeavors are made available by the suggested method.

Hamed et al., (2017) [16] showed that ideas from data mining and BI can be utilized to back up decision-making at Arabic universities. There is a growing awareness of the need to use the voluminous amounts of data kept in academic systems to create smarter systems. So, this study is a real help in improving the standard of education.

Sujitparapitaya et al., (2012) [17] investigate the impact of a wide range of factors on the uptake of BI in academic settings, therefore adding to the body of knowledge on the topic of innovation adoption in academic administration. Results were broadly comparable with those for corporate organizations, but there were a few surprise findings as well. Private rather than public institutions of higher education were less likely to use BI. The study's results are reviewed, along with their practical and theoretical ramifications. Table 1 indicates the comparison table of the literature review.

Table 1. Comparison table of literature of review

Authors	Techniques Used	Outcomes
Quadir et al., (2022) [9]	Data mining	According to the results, educational data mining is the best method for checking the quality of education and offering possible solutions to problems like failing to recognize student behavior patterns and wasting money
Cardoso and Su (2022) [10]	Domain-specific BIA MM	The results demonstrated that a more detailed explanation and communication during gap analysis was enabled by the fact that the concepts, circumstances, and systems applied to the participants' normal working environment
Hamad et al., (2021) [11]	BI	The findings highlighted the necessity for higher management to recognize the value of BI in libraries
Khatibi et al., (2020) [12]	BI	The findings highlight that although Iranian higher education is a standard bearer in the scientific community, especially in the fields of science and engineering, the brain drain is expanding at an alarming pace
Villegas-Ch et al., (2020) [13]	ICT	Current educational impetus has allowed students to coordinate career and educational pursuits via ICT
Bojorque and Pesántez (2019) [14]	AI	High levels of accuracy in predicting course status were found in terms of precision (0.912), recall (0.903), and fallout (0.709), respectively

(continued)

Table 1. (*continued*)

Authors	Techniques Used	Outcomes
Boulila et al., (2018) [15]	SSIS, SSAS, SSRS	This analysis yielded a set of indicators that can help users of the proposed solution on different scales (from the University president to the student)
Hamed et al., (2017) [16]	DM and BI	The outcome details the courses with a failure rate of more than 15% every semester, as well as the variations in success rate for each course over terms
Sujitparapitaya et al., (2012) [17]	BI	The results indicate that several critical characteristics are positively linked with BI adoption in IHEs, including organizational legitimacy and absorptive ability

3 Background Study

BI plays a crucial role in gaining a market edge in almost every industry, including higher education. Massive databases including information on students, faculty, staff, and university resources (such as libraries and laboratories) are commonplace at universities. It's possible that the information stored in these databases could prove to be game-changing. In this research, the authors outline a data mining strategy as one of the BI approaches that could be employed in academic settings. The model's significance stems from the fact that it adopts a systemic perspective on managing universities, treating the institution as input, processing, output, and feedback, and then employing a variety of BI tools and techniques at each stage of the process to improve business decision-making. In addition, a case study from the Arab International University is presented as an example of the proposed concept in action [18].

4 Problem Formulation

Students are provided with a statement of their learning as well as recommendations on how to improve the system via the use of feedback, which is the most significant component of assessment in the teaching process. Most educational establishments, including educational establishments such as universities, still rely on an antiquated, labor-intensive, and inflexible paper-based approach to evaluate the effectiveness of their faculty members. Today's universities are up against significant challenges in terms of the formulation of their regulations. Considering the shifting landscape of the educational processes, universities are engaged in fierce competition to determine what makes them stand out from the crowd and to choose the students who are most suited for their programs. The most prestigious academic institutions in every part of the globe are going to need to implement BI strategies to address the difficulties and take advantage of the new possibilities.

5 Research Objectives

- To examine data, improve teaching quality, and accelerate ongoing development in higher education through the use of Business Intelligence (BI) tools and the incorporation of student feedback.
- To design a machine learning model to predict the feedback of the students.
- To prove the robustness of the model, it is compared with other conventional sentiment analysis tools.

6 Research Methodology

In this section, the author will identify BI parameters for the academic feedback system for the university. This section described a model for BI in higher education.

6.1 Business Intelligence System (BIS)

The term Business Intelligence (BI) encompasses strategic planning and managerial initiatives aimed at transforming raw data into actionable insights for corporate analysis and decision-making [19]. To comprehensively address specific subjects of interest, such as business trends, BI employs technical concepts and methodologies tailored for processing unstructured data.

BI comprises a suite of decision support tools designed to gather, access, and analyze data, aiding corporate users, including executives, managers, and analysts, in making more informed and expedited business decisions [20]. It signifies a comprehensive grasp of all factors influencing a company's operations. Effective and high-quality business decisions necessitate a deep understanding of elements like customers, competitors, business partners, economic conditions, and internal processes. Business analytics tools are instrumental in facilitating such decisions within organizations, enabling swift and accurate data processing by executives, managers, and analysts [21]. For a visual representation, please refer to Fig. 1, which illustrates the typical architecture of BI.

Following are a few of BIS's benefits.:

- **Manufacturing:** BIS aids industry leaders in locating technical, environmental, and economic data useful at different points in the production process. In terms of value creation, from product concept to final product, it can help lower unforeseen expenses. The study of material use made possible by BIS helps to shorten the manufacturing lead time and improve product quality[23].
- **Production Planning and Control:** BIS allows production and control team members to evaluate resources and shifts, inventory components and supplies, evaluate quality and supplier concerns, generate sales strategies and projections, and guide

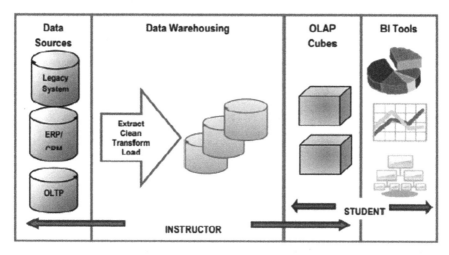

Fig. 1. Typical BI architecture [22].

new product changes or upgrades based on seasonal swings. Using Key Performance Indicators (KPIs) and metrics, BIS can analyze, regulate, and monitor production plans, issuing automatic warnings if a critical scenario develops or a threshold is passed [23].

- **Finance Management:** Finance data analysis in the Data Warehouse (DW) leads to better financial reporting and more educated business decisions. Market analysis, horizontal and vertical analysis, and ratio analysis that compares provisions, risk assessment charges, and the actual cost of promotional activities are only some of the cost analysis approaches used by BIS to assist budgeting using analytical models. Cost increases from different angles are analyzed through Online Analytical Processing (OLAP)[24].

- **Sales/Distributions:** Optimization research of physical warehouses in particular locations allows inventory managers to effectively handle stock shortages and return orders[25]. Inventory managers and merchandisers could reduce the amount of out-dated and unsold textiles and clothing in stock and better meet the needs of customers. The ability to combine and integrate data sets from many information systems and sources is made possible by BIS, allowing decision-makers to get accurate data on the ever-changing supply chain, customer base, and market. The objective is to improve supply chain and inventory management[26].

Data warehousing, Online Analytical Processing (OLAP), and knowledge discovery, mostly helped by data mining methods, are the three data management technologies defined by its architecture. This data is rounded out by the elements shown in Fig. 2 from Olszak and Ziemba[27].

ETL Tools	Data Warehouses	OLAP Tools
•Responsible for data transfer from operational /transaction systems to data warehouses.	•Provide space for thematic storing of aggregated and analysed data.	•Allow users access to data; •Enable analysis and model business problems; •Share information stored in data warehouses.

Data Mining Tools	Reporting Tools	Presentation Layers
•Determine patterns, generalisations, regularities and rules in data resources.	•Allow the creation and use of reports.	•Provide users with the information in a comfortable and accessible way.

Fig. 2. BI System Key Components

6.2 Convolution Neural Network (CNN) and Long-Short Term Memory (LSTM)

A Convolutional Neural Network (CNN) with Long Short-Term Memory (LSTM) architecture is a strong way to classify sentiments. The LSTM is great at understanding sequential information and catching long-term dependencies, while the CNN is great at capturing local patterns and features in the textual data [28]. CNN is good at finding important words or phrases in the feedback in this situation, and LSTM is good at looking at the general context and sentiment flow. The model learns from a primary generated dataset that pairs feedback examples with different types of sentiments, such as positive, negative, or neutral. The CNN + LSTM model learns to generalize and make accurate predictions based on student input that it hasn't seen yet [29].

6.3 Data Collection

The dataset that is used in this research is generated through primary sources. A Graphical User Interface (GUI) is used to collect the data. A questionnaire containing questions is filled out by the university students. Students responded to a series of questions about various aspects of the courses, including class time, relevancy of content, teaching quality, and difficulty levels. The free-text comments capture a wide variety of sentiments, from criticisms exposing inefficiencies, boredom, and misunderstanding to accolades for industrious instructors and well-taught, high-quality courses. The dataset contains the feedback report of 1000 students in the engineering domain as they provide feedback related to teacher and their related subjects. This data is further pre-processed before training the proposed hybrid machine learning model. Figure 3 shows the GUI interface through which feedback is collected from 1000 students for different subjects. This GUI interface is designed in Python using Tkinter. The present study incorporates a comprehensive evaluation of the graphical user interface (GUI) interface, which has been developed by the author and holds potential for future utilization in gathering feedback.

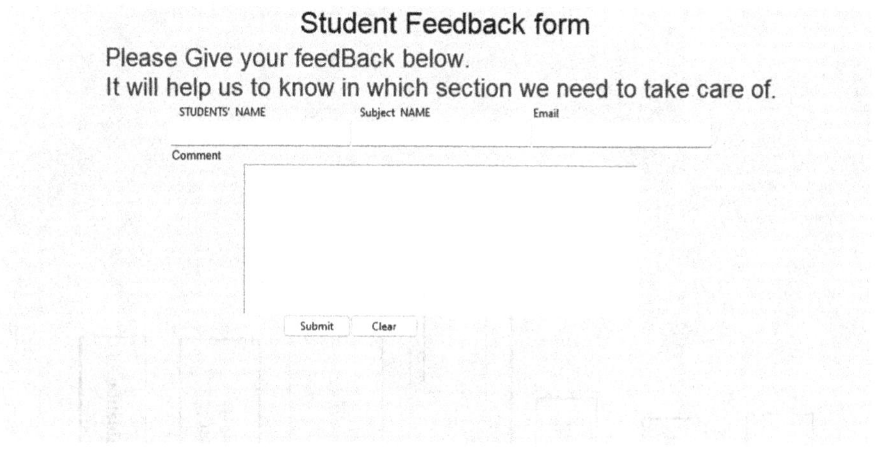

Student Feedback form

Please Give your feedBack below.
It will help us to know in which section we need to take care of.

STUDENTS' NAME   Subject NAME   Email

Comment

Submit   Clear

Fig. 3. GUI interface

6.4 Proposed Methodology

The author utilized a dataset response supplied by students as feedback for a certain professor in this section. There are four categories in the feedback form: behavior and discipline, subject command, teaching methodology, and student interaction. Each section has between four and five questions, and responses are recorded as a number from one to five, with two being a strong disapproval and seven a strong agreement. Figures 4 and 5 show the proposed algorithm and process of creating reports from the perspective of both students and administrators when using the feedback form.

Students View

Step 1: Every student will be sent a one-of-a-kind link to the feedback form through email. The form is divided into four pieces, and each area includes between three and five questions.

Step 2: Students can offer feedback on each part by typing their thoughts into the corresponding comment box after reading it.

Step 3: The form has a single psychometric section with a total of 22 questions after the remark box for input from the user. Users only have 5–10 s to respond to each question in this section.

Step 4: All the feedback that is provided by the students would be entered into a database along with a unique identifier for the input, the choice that was chosen by the students, and any remarks it could well have provided.

Administrator View

Step 1: At this stage, the administrative staff requests the development of reports from a specific faculty member for a certain subject that has been provided by the students.

Step 2: When an administrator requests a report or an exact output of the feedback that students have provided, all the information that is recorded in the database will be fetched and sent to the server.

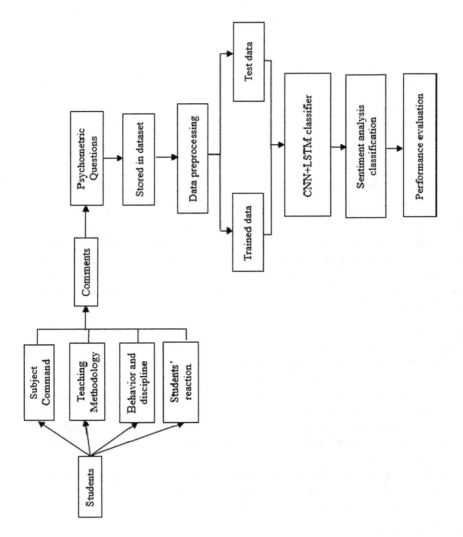

Fig. 4. Proposed algorithm.

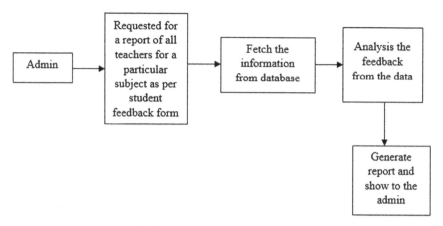

Fig. 5. Admin view of feedback form

Step 3: After retrieving the data, it is sent to the analysis module for processing. The analysis Module would sift through the feedback provided and provide constructive topic recommendations to the faculty. Suggestion extraction, best and worst faculty case scenarios, graph creation, emotive models, and many more are all part of the analysis module. This evaluation would show teachers where they can work to improve.

Step 4: If the administrator requests a report, it would be created on the front end of the system and sent to them through the feedback form.

Step 5: After the data collection the next step is data preprocessing, in data preprocessing the data is cleaned and normalized.

Step 6 In this step the pre-processed data is further split into train and test data. The CNN + LSTM classifier is trained using trained data and further, the model is used for sentiment analysis.

Step 7: Based on the classification the performance of the classifier is evaluated using performance metrics i.e., accuracy and loss.

6.5 Evaluation Metrics

The performance of the proposed model is evaluated using performance metrics. In this research, the performance metric is known as accuracy. Table 2 shows the hardware and software configuration and the tool used for implementation.

i) Accuracy

The proportion of true positive and negative values relative to the total number of values [30].

$$TP = \frac{TP + TN}{TP + TN + FP + FN} \tag{1}$$

TP = True Positive
FP = False Positive

TN = True Negative
FN = False Negative

Table 2. System configuration

System	Configuration
Tool	Google Colab
Computer	Windows 10 pro
Processor	Intel core i5 2.70GHz
RAM	8 + 8 GB
Type	X64 based processor

7 Results and Discussion

In this section, the results that are obtained after the implementation of the proposed model are discussed in detail. Figures 6 (a) and 6 (b) show the accuracy and loss of the proposed CNN + LSTM model during training and validation. From Fig. 6 (a) it is seen, as the no. of epochs increases the accuracy of the proposed CNN + LSTM model increases, and finally at 40 epochs, it becomes constant to 90.34% similarly, in loss from 40–50 epochs the lowest value of the loss is achieved i.e., 0.285 as seen in Fig. 6 (b) Table 3 shows the hyperparameters of the proposed CNN + LSTM model.

Table 3. Hyperparameters settings

Hyperparameters	Value
Learning rate	0.001
Optimizer	Stochastic gradient descent
Momentum	0.9
No. of epochs	50
Batch size	32
Loss function	Cross entropy
No. of LSTM nodes	100
Filters	128
Kernel size	3
Activation function	ReLu
Dropout	0.2

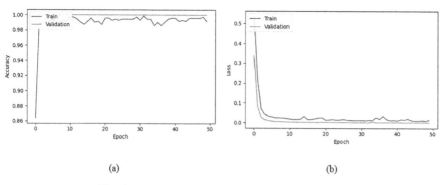

(a)   (b)

Fig. 6. (a) Model accuracy and Fig. 5 (b) Model loss

Sample student comments from the dataset are shown in Table 4. As a result of student feedback, authors can expect to hear both positive and negative assessments, as well as a few neutral assessments. In addition, it should guide the analysis of which feedback was necessary and which was superfluous.

Table 4. Sample comments for students' feedback from the dataset

No. of students	Student feedback analysis	Sentiment Labels		
		Positive	Negative	Neutral
1	The timing is quite strange. Such classes should not be provided at such late hours since programming requires a fresh mind. We are all lifeless, exhausted, and drowsy till our class time	–	–	Yes
2	Inefficient, boring, confusing	–	Yes	–
3	She is a very hardworking lecturer who assists us much, however, the course is just too irrelevant for students	Yes	–	–
4	Very well-taught, high-quality course. It's easy to follow along in both class and lab, and the professor provides clear explanations. Still, the difficulty level can be too low	Yes	–	–
5	Increase the number of programming assignments and raise the difficulty level to reflect the demands of the field of computer science	–	–	Yes

In Figs. 7 and 8, the authors see a visual representation of the data collected from student evaluations on the instructor's topic command and the quality of their interaction with the student. The answer to the question posed to the class can be calculated from the output and numerical value of the relevant question and section. In addition to that, both the best- and worst-case scenarios for it should be laid out. Authors recognize that there is a wide range of student opinions about the value of faculty.

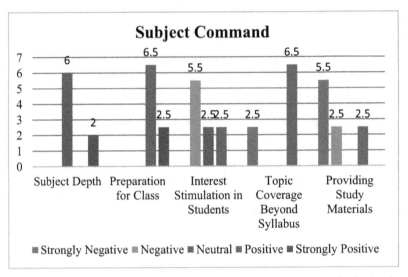

Fig. 7. Graphical analysis of the 'Subject Command' Section based on feedback given by Students.

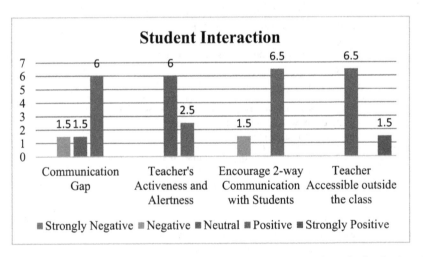

Fig. 8. Graphical analysis of the 'Student interaction' Section based on feedback given by Students.

Table 5 shows the feedback of 1000 students related to various subjects of their courses. Based on the teachers' teaching skills, their attitude, behavior, and many more parameters considering these criteria the student feedback is classified as positive and negative, and most of the students are neutral in their feedback. Figure 9 shows the feedback of students as positive, negative, and neutral in a graphical manner.

Table 5. Students' feedback related to different subjects.

Feedback			
Subject	Positive	Negative	Neutral
Programming language	350	430	220
Cloud computing	508	327	165
Operating system	476	314	210
Software reliability	205	608	187

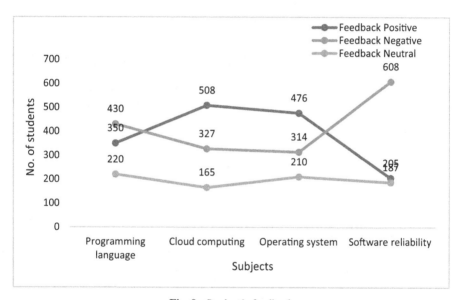

Fig. 9. Student's feedback

Table 6 provides examples of test datasets, showcasing actual sentiment labels along-side predicted ones. The model accurately predicted sentiment for feedback 1 and 3. However, for feedback 2, a notable observation was made: the model struggled to appro-priately handle negation, as the relevant word did not fall within a window of size 3, unlike a window of size 2. Consequently, this led to an incorrect prediction. In our methodology, we encountered instances where neutral feedback was misclassified as either positive or negative. This outcome can be attributed to the limited availability of training samples representing the neutral class.

Table 6. Predicted and actual sentiment labels of selected student feedback

S. no.	Student Feedback	Actual Sentiment Label	Predicted Sentiment Label
1	Useless course	Negative	Negative
2	The course isn't all that fascinating	Negative	Positive
3	The instructors were quite useful in that they clarified the prior understanding	Positive	Positive
4	She or he is an excellent educator. Sometimes she or he has trouble seeing the relevance of ideas	Neutral	Positive

7.1 Comparative Analysis

The proposed technique for analyzing student comments was compared to various online sentiment analysis tools in addition to the one it described. In this section, the authors compare the proposed methodology to several existing sentiment analysis methods. Table 7 and Fig. 10 show the results of a comparison between the suggested method and existing techniques for sentiment analysis.

Table 7. Comparative analysis of proposed approaches with others

Approaches	Accuracy
LSTM	66.50%
Aylien Text API	67.03%
Artificial Neural Network [31]	88.2%
Proposed CNN + LSTM model	90.34%

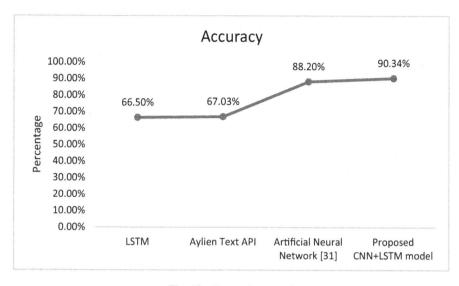

Fig. 10. Comparison graph

8 Conclusion

The author has determined an important metric for the university's academic feedback system based on data gathered from BI tools. Universities are being pressured to alter their long-held pedagogical tenets, which have relied mostly on the personal experiences of faculty members to impart their expertise to students. Improvements in teaching methods that teach pupils anything new are part of this shift. These factors have driven universities to actively seek a solution that empowers them to extract data from diverse information systems and convert it into actionable knowledge to improve learning outcomes. The findings indicated the emotive interpretation of student feedback in three forms: positive, negative, and neutral. Further, a machine learning model known as CNN + LSTM is used for sentiment analysis, achieving an accuracy of 90.34% and a loss of 0.285. It helps the faculty prepare an overall report that includes the feedback made by students as well as a graphical representation of each component. Assessing faculty performance is beneficial for the administration as it allows them to identify effective teachers and those in need of improvement, ultimately leading to an overall enhancement in teaching quality. It is also discovered that the proposed CNN + LSTM model outperforms the other methods. The study also has some limitations that are stated below:

- The study focuses on analyzing student feedback, it doesn't address how faculty members react to such feedback whether it is positive or negative. The lack of information on whether faculty members adjust or enhancements in response to the feedback restricts the capacity to fully comprehend the feedback loop and how student input affects teaching strategies.

- The feedback gives a brief acknowledgment of the system's potential to improve faculty members' handling of negative feedback, it does not go into great detail on the particular processes or tactics used to manage negative feedback.
- The hybrid design of the proposed CNN + LSTM model has certain limitations when it comes to identifying changing sentiment patterns since it struggles to capture long-term relationships inside feedback sequences.
- The complexity of managing different sentence lengths in student feedback raises additional issues that can affect the model's capacity for generalization.

In the future, the project's academic feedback system has been designed in such a way that the user's future needs are addressed. The project is adaptable enough to accommodate adjustments while maintaining the current system. In the future, there could be a provision to change the questions and enhance the faculty's negative feedback in the educational system. Also, data augmentation techniques are employed to artificially increase the variety of the training dataset, and transfer learning techniques can be used to pre-train the model on big datasets to boost performance. This can improve the model's ability to generalize to different sentence lengths and linguistic phrases seen in student feedback.

Ethical Consideration. This research paper ensures the confidentiality and anonymity of student feedback provided on various subjects to mitigate potential biases and safeguard the ethical integrity of the research process.

References

1. Kabakchieva, D.: Business intelligence systems for analyzing university students' data. Cybern. Inf. Technol. **15**(1), 104–115 (2015)
2. Ferguson, R.: Learning analytics: drivers, developments, and challenges. Int. J. Technol. Enhanced. Learn. **4**, 304 (2013)
3. Comendador, B.E.V., Rabago, L.W., Tanguilig, B.T.: An educational model based on Knowledge Discovery in Databases (KDD) to predict learners' behavior using classification techniques. In: Proceedings of the IEEE International Conference on Signal Processing, Communications and Computing, Conference Proceedings, Hong Kong, China, 5–8 August 2016, pp. 1–6 (2016)
4. A review of the state of the art in business intelligence software2021G Srivastava, M S, R Venkataraman, K V, P N10.1080/17517575.2021.1872107Enterprise Information Systems
5. SubhadraNamana, U.D.V.: Business intelligence software for educational institutions (2012). http://www.diva-portal.org/smash/get/diva2:1080950/FULLTEXT01.pdf
6. Kumar, S., Sharan, H.O.: Evaluation of business intelligence software for education system in India. Ilkogretim Online **19**(1), 700–712 (2020)
7. Minnesota Multiphasic Personality Inventory (MMPI). https://psychcentral.com/lib/minnesota-multiphasic-personality-inventorymmpi
8. Ashish, J., Jagadale, V.: (2016) http://www.iraj.in/journal/journal_file/journal_pdf/14-234-1458366974183-188.pdf
9. Quadir, B., Chen, N.-S., Isaias, P.: Analyzing the educational goals, problems, and techniques used in educational big data research from 2010 to 2018. Interact. Learn. Environ. **30**(8), 1539–1555 (2022)

10. Cardoso, E., Xiaomeng, S.: Designing a business intelligence and analytics maturity model for higher education: a design science approach. Appl. Sci. **12**(9), 4625 (2022)
11. Hamad, F., Al-Aamr, R., Jabbar, S.A., Fakhuri, H.: Business intelligence in academic libraries in Jordan: Opportunities and challenges. IFLA J. **471**, 37–50 (2021)
12. Khatibi, V., Keramati, A., Shirazi, F.: Deployment of a business intelligence model to evaluate Iranian national higher education. Soc. Sci. Hum. Open **2**(1), 100056 (2020)
13. Villegas-Ch, W., Palacios-Pacheco, X., Luján-Mora, S.: A business intelligence framework for analyzing educational data. Sustainability **12**(14), 5745 (2020)
14. Bojorque, R., Pesántez-Avilés, F.: Academic quality management system audit using artificial intelligence techniques. In: Ahram, T. (ed.) AHFE 2019. AISC, vol. 965, pp. 275–283. Springer, Cham (2020). https://doi.org/10.1007/978-3-030-20454-9_28
15. Boulila, W., Al-Kmali, M., Farid, M., Mugahed, H.: A business intelligence-based solution to support academic affairs: the case of Taibah University. Wireless Networks 1–8 (2018)
16. Hamed, M., Mahmoud, T., Gómez, J.M., Kfouri, G.: Using data mining and business intelligence to develop decision support systems in Arabic higher education institutions. In: Marx Gómez, J., Aboujaoude, M.K., Feghali, K., Mahmoud, T. (eds.) Modernizing academic teaching and research in business and economics. SPBE, pp. 71–84. Springer, Cham (2017). https://doi.org/10.1007/978-3-319-54419-9_4
17. Sujitparapitaya, S., Shirani, A., Roldan, M.: Business intelligence adoption in academic administration: an empirical investigation. Issues Inf. Syst. **13**(2), 112–122 (2012)
18. Alzoabi, Zaidoun, Faek Diko, and Saiid Hanna. "Suggested Model for Business Intelligence in Higher Education. In: Business Intelligence and Agile Methodologies for Knowledge-Based Organizations: Cross-Disciplinary Applications, pp. 223–239. IGI Global (2012)
19. Raisinghani, M.S.: Business Intelligence in the digital economy: opportunities, limitations, and risks. Hershey, PA: Idea Group Pub (2004)
20. Obeidat, M., North, M., Richardson, R., Rattanak, V., North, S.: Business intelligence technology, applications, and trends. Int. Manag. Rev. **11**(2), 47–55 (2015)
21. Yeoh, W., Koronios, A.: Critical success factors for business intelligence systems. J. Comput. Inf. Syst. Pp. 23–32 (2010)
22. Mrdalj, S.: Would cloud computing revolutionize teaching business intelligence courses? Issues Inf. Sci. Inf. Technol. **8**, 209–217 (2011)
23. Ahmad, S., Miskon, S.: The adoption of business intelligence systems in textile and apparel industry: case studies. In: Saeed, F., Mohammed, F., Gazem, N. (eds.) IRICT 2019. AISC, vol. 1073, pp. 12–23. Springer, Cham (2020). https://doi.org/10.1007/978-3-030-33582-3_2
24. Rostek, K.: Business Intelligence for Insurance Companies. Found. Manag. **1**, 65–82 (2009)
25. Ahmad, S., Miskon, S., Alabdan, R., Tlili, I.: Exploration of influential determinants for the adoption of business intelligence system in the textile and apparel industry. Sustainability **12**(18), 7674 (2020)
26. Ahmad, S., Miskon, S., Alkanhal, T.A., Tlili, I.: Modeling of business intelligence systems using the potential determinants and theories with the lens of individual, technological, organizational, and environmental contexts—a systematic literature review. Appl. Sci. **10**, 3208 (2020)
27. Olszak, C., Ziemba, E.: Approach to building and implementing business intelligence systems. Interdiscip. J. Inf. Knowl. Manag. **2**, 135–148 (2007)
28. Wang, J., Yu, K., Lai, R., Zhang, X.: Dimensional sentiment analysis using a regional CNN-LSTM model. In: Proceedings of the 54th Annual Meeting of the Association for Computational Linguistics (volume 2: Short papers), pp. 225–230 (2016)
29. Alayba, A.M., Palade, V., England, M., Iqbal, R.: A combined CNN and LSTM model for Arabic sentiment analysis. In: Holzinger, A., Kieseberg, P., Tjoa, A.M., Weippl, E. (eds.) CD-MAKE 2018. LNCS, vol. 11015, pp. 179–191. Springer, Cham (2018). https://doi.org/10.1007/978-3-319-99740-7_12

30. Mishra, A.: Metrics to evaluate your machine learning algorithm" published in Towards Data Science, Feb 24, 2018. https://towardsdatascience.com/metrics-to-evaluate-your-machine-learning-algorithmf10ba6e38234
31. Katragadda, S., Ravi, V., Kumar, P., Jaya Lakshmi, G.: Performance analysis on student feedback using machine learning algorithms. In: 2020 6th International Conference on Advanced Computing and Communication Systems (ICACCS), pp. 1161–1163. IEEE (2020)

Raspberry Pi-Driven Affordable Image-To-Braille Converter for Visually Impaired Users

Ananya Kulkarni[(⊠)] [ID], Maitri Shah[ID], Nivedita Thakur[ID], Srushti Pednekar[ID], and Viral H. Shah[ID]

Department of I.T., Dharmsinh Desai University, Nadiad, Gujarat, India
ananyakulkarni2103@gmail.com, viralshah.it@ddu.ac.in

Abstract. Addressing the growing demand for affordable assistive technology for the visually impaired, this paper introduces an innovative system for real-time image-to-Braille conversion, utilizing optical character recognition and Raspberry Pi 4 technology. The system captures text from images and converts it into Braille characters, embossed by solenoids for tactile reading. The research aims to enhance inclusivity in education and daily life for visually impaired individuals, with a particular focus on developing countries like India.

Keywords: Assistive Device · Refreshable Braille Display · Optical Character Recognition · IoT · Raspberry Pi · Actuators · Braille Cell

1 Introduction

Vision impairment is a global challenge, affecting nearly 2.2 billion people world-wide, with profound implications for social inclusion and academic advancement, particularly among children [8]. Students with low vision often face formidable challenges in reading and writing despite employing aids like optical tools. Combining these aids with technology, such as screen enlargers and speech synthesizers, has the potential to significantly alleviate these challenges [8]. This demonstrates the critical role assistive technology plays in ensuring inclusivity in education, underscoring the importance of teachers' proficiency with these tools.

A systematic review conducted by Elizabeth Hoskin [11] underscores the effectiveness of technology in braille literacy education for children. The study sheds light on the pivotal role that technology can play in enhancing the literacy skills of visually impaired students, making content engaging, and ultimately improving their quality of life This aligns with the perspectives of surveyed teachers, as highlighted in research conducted by Alves [4], where 84.2% of educators stressed the significance of assistive technology in improving the skills and accessibility of visually impaired students. These findings underscore the growing need for cost-effective assistive devices to meet the unique educational requirements of the visually impaired population as shown by Gupta [13].

S. Rajagopal et al (Eds.): ASCIS 2023, CCIS 2040, pp. 225–242, 2024.
https://doi.org/10.1007/978-3-031-59107-5_15

Similarly reviews highlighted by Mukhiddinov [17] show the challenges and progress in creating affordable touch displays, data for teaching computers, and creating touch graphics for visually impaired individuals. These graphics are crucial for learning science and math, and include 3D models, interactive graphics, QR codes, and augmented reality. Popular tools include the Tactile Pro tablet and software like TactileView and QuickTac. Challenges include cost reduction, smooth audio integration, and improving touch graphics. Researchers are using machine learning and augmented reality to enhance these technologies.

The legacy of Louis Braille, with his 3x2 matrix of raised dots, continues to be the standard language for blind education [8]. This underlines the enduring importance of Braille as a means for visually impaired individuals to access knowledge [13]. However, as suggested by Baciero [6], innovation in the field of assistive technology is continuously expanding the horizons of accessibility and tactile perception. The research introduces TouchScope, a passive-haptic device designed to investigate tactile perception using a refreshable Braille display, offering new avenues for enhancing tactile learning experiences.

In a rapidly evolving technological landscape, automatic tactile graphics generation has gained prominence. A systematic literature review conducted by Sarkar [20] emphasizes the significance of tactile graphics in science, technology, engineering, and mathematics (STEM) education for visually impaired students. The review highlights the progress made in the field of automatic tactile graphics generation and the challenges that remain, such as the high cost of refreshable tactile displays.

Russomanno [19] also highlights the importance of tactile feedback in Braille reading for visually impaired individuals. Despite e-publishing expanding accessibility, challenges like complex content handling and high costs remain. Restricted tactile cues can lead to errors in Braille recognition, especially at higher speeds. The'Body-Braille' system uses micro vibrators across various body surfaces and offers diverse interaction and communication options for visually impaired individuals, enhancing Braille information accessibility.

A survey conducted by Lavanya Gupta [12] suggests that wearable devices, particularly head-mounted displays and clip-on devices, are gaining popularity. Aira AR Smart Glasses and MyEye2 are examples of assistive technologies designed for reading, recognizing faces, and identifying currency. The Intelligent Reader for the Visually Handicapped uses Raspberry Pi technology to interpret text from images. However, these devices often address specific challenges and can be expensive, requiring multiple devices for various tasks. Improving these technologies, such as using IoT for wireless detection, could enhance their effectiveness.

Moreover, the research by Sana Shokat [21] delves into the analysis and evaluation of Braille-to-text conversion methods, offering insights into the evolving methods of rendering Braille content in digital formats. In a parallel development, Gupta [13] presents the design and implementation of an Arduino-based Refreshable Braille Display Controller, showcasing the potential for innovation and affordability in the development of Braille technology.

In the context of touchscreen devices, Mrim Alnfiai and Srinivas Sampalli [3] introduce BrailleEnter, a touch screen Braille text entry method for the blind. Their research explores how innovative interaction methods can make smartphones and tablets more accessible for visually impaired individuals, emphasizing the importance of user-centric design.

Research by Frances [10] provides insights into the preferences and practices of students who read Braille and use assistive technology. It demonstrates the changing landscape of assistive tools and the importance of allowing students to make choices regarding tools and strategies to efficiently complete their school tasks.

The paper by Ramos-Garca [18] presents an IoT Braille Display aimed at assisting visually impaired students in Mexico. Their work illustrates the potential of IoT technology to provide affordable and accessible Braille solutions, particularly in regions with limited resources.

1.1 Braille System

Braille, a tactile encoding system, serves as a vital method for individuals with visual impairments to read and write in a specific language through touch. Originating from the adaptation of a nonverbal communication system created by French army captain Charles Barbier, Braille was refined by Louis Braille in the late 1800s, laying the groundwork for the contemporary Braille code [24].

Six dot positions make up each braille character or cell. These dot positions form a rectangle composed of 2 columns with 3 dots in each column, where first column is numbered from 1 to 3 and second column is numbered from 4 to 6. A single dot or any combination of dots may be raised at any of the 6 positions. Counting spaces, in which no dots appear, there are 64 English braille combinations in total. When referencing a braille character, one may describe the positions where dots are raised. Each dot within a cell has a number. Starting in the upper left and moving down, the dots are universally numbered 1 through 6 as seen in the Fig. 1 below [5].

Fig. 1. The Braille Cell

The Braille notation for alphabets are shown in Fig. 2. For capital sign, dot 6, placed before a letter, makes it a capital letter. The numeral sign, dots 3, 4, 5, 6, placed before a character, makes it a number and not a letter as shown in Fig. 3. Braille punctuation marks are formed by using dots in the lower part of the cell as shown in Fig. 4 [23].

This research paper seeks to propose a comprehensive solution to simplify the learning process for individuals with visual impairments, especially considering the challenges faced in resource-limited regions such as India. Recognizing that not all books are available in Braille and producing audio files for every book is impractical, the focus is on developing a cost-effective and efficient assistive device. This device, designed

⠁	⠃	⠉	⠙	⠑	⠋	⠛	⠓	⠊	⠚
a	b	c	d	e	f	g	h	i	j
⠅	⠇	⠍	⠝	⠕	⠏	⠟	⠗	⠎	⠞
k	l	m	n	o	p	q	r	s	t
⠥	⠧	⠺	⠭	⠽	⠵				
u	v	w	x	y	z				

Fig. 2. The Braille Alphabet

⠂	⠆	⠒	⠲	⠢	⠖	⠶	⠦	⠔	⠴
1	2	3	4	5	6	7	8	9	0

Fig. 3. The Braille Numbers

⠂	⠆	⠒	⠲	⠖	⠶	⠦	⠦⠄	⠔	⠄	⠤
,	;	:	.	!	()	? "	*	"	'	-

Fig. 4. Common Punctuation Marks

to be compact, affordable, and user-friendly, aims to cater to individuals with limited technical knowledge. The ultimate goal is to introduce Braille at an early age, the device can be used to bridge the gap between individuals with and without disabilities. By introducing such solutions from childhood, the research aims to contribute to not only reduce the accessibility gap but also enhance literacy rates among the visually impaired, ultimately improving their quality of life in both educational and daily activities.

2 Literature Survey

In the realm of assistive technologies, refreshable Braille cells play a pivotal role in enhancing the lives of visually impaired individuals by providing realtime access to information. Among these technologies, Braille Displays stand out as indispensable tools, offering dynamic interfaces that convert digital text into Braille characters. This transformation allows users to perceive and interact with content in a tactile form, fostering literacy and facilitating communication for the visually impaired.

2.1 Actuators

Piezoelectric Actuators: Piezoelectric actuators rely on the piezoelectric effect, where certain materials generate an electric charge in response to mechanical stress. These actuators are known for their high-speed operation and low power consumption. However, their reliability may face challenges in extended matrices of Braille cells [15].

Electromagnetic Linear Actuators: These actuators use an electromagnetic coil to generate a force for moving objects. They offer relatively high reliability and power but can be bulky and consume a moderate amount of power. Challenges may arise in miniaturization for applications in Braille displays [15].

Electroactive Polymers (EAP): EAP actuators are constructed from electroactive polymers, showcasing a simple design and low power consumption. They are suitable for extended displays; however, improvements may be needed for widespread use in Braille displays [15].

Electro-Rheological Actuators: These actuators utilize an electro-rheological fluid, changing viscosity under an electric field. They are compact, capable of generating significant force, but may be costly and consume a moderate amount of power. They find suitability for compact displays [15].

Thermo-Pneumatic Actuators: Thermo-pneumatic actuators use heated gas to expand and contract a diaphragm. They have a straightforward design and are compact, but they may be slower and consume a considerable amount of power. They are suitable for applications like Braille displays [15].

Shape Memory Alloy (SMA) Actuators: SMA actuators use a metal that can revert to its original shape when heated. They are compact, powerful, but can be expensive and have high power consumption. These actuators are deemed suitable for Braille displays, but cost considerations may be a factor in their adoption [15].

2.2   Existing Systems

The exploration of innovative methodologies in aiding visually impaired individuals is evident in various research endeavors. In one instance, a research paper outlines a method for automatically extracting salient objects from images, with a particular focus on generating tactile graphics for the benefit of the visually impaired. Through the combination of local adaptive thresholding and Grab-Cuts, the approach addresses challenges posed by varying lighting conditions in natural scene images. Despite demonstrating promising accuracy, particularly in evaluations on the MSRA 10k dataset, it is crucial to acknowledge a potential limitation. The reliance on image-based features may pose difficulties in handling complex scenes or images with intricate details, potentially leading to inaccuracies in salient object extraction [1].

Another research initiative introduces a 2D multiarray braille display and eBook reader designed to enhance mobile braille devices and improve reading continuity for visually impaired individuals. Notably, the system supports industry standards like DAISY and EPUB, ensuring compatibility with a wide range of eBooks. Additionally, the inclusion of a wireless mirroring function for smartphone interaction adds a layer of accessibility. However, the paper highlights a significant drawback - user discomfort with the 3D haptic device. This discomfort raises concerns about the practicality and overall user acceptance of the technology, emphasizing the need for further refinement [14].

Addressing the challenge of making visual artworks accessible to the blind and visually impaired, another research initiative introduces an Interactive Multimodal Guide

(IMG). This innovative system combines tactile and audio modalities, featuring a 2.5-dimensional bas-relief model and an Arduino-based control board for a comprehensive solution. While the IMG demonstrates considerable potential, occasional inconsistencies in prototype performance, especially with touch gestures, emerge as a limitation. These inconsistencies may impact the reliability of the interactive experience, calling for improvements in the system's robustness [9].

In a distinct context, a paper details the development of an Arabic Optical Braille Recognition (OBR) system, aiming to digitalize Braille content in Arabic documents. The workflow involves several processing stages, such as image conversion, frame cropping, thresholding, and Braille cell recognition. While proficient in recognizing Arabic Braille, the system exhibits limitations in language specificity. Additionally, uncertainties arise concerning its performance across different document qualities and Braille codes. The lack of comparative evaluations with existing software further underscores the need for a more comprehensive assessment [2].

Introducing an Optical Braille Recognition (OBR) algorithm for Hindi documents, another research initiative demonstrates practical potential in translating scanned Hindi text to Braille. However, the algorithm faces challenges in accurately distinguishing specific Hindi characters during segmentation and matching. This limitation impacts the precision of the conversion process, emphasizing the importance of addressing character recognition issues for improved accuracy [7].

The educational realm for visually impaired children is a focal point in another paper, which presents BraillePlay games designed to enhance Braille literacy. Emphasizing education, accessibility, and skill-level adaptation, games like VBReader and VBWriter leverage simple gestures and high contrast. Despite positive feedback on improved Braille understanding, a longitudinal study identifies challenges in effectively assessing learning outcomes and maintaining sustained engagement in blind children when using the BraillePlay games. This recognition of challenges emphasizes the ongoing need for refinement and adaptation in educational technology for visually impaired individuals [16].

2.3 Comparative Analysis

This comparative analysis delves into a variety of assistive technologies designed for individuals with visual impairments. The focus is on understanding the strengths and weaknesses of each tool, ranging from those creating tactile graphics to braille displays and educational games. By examining these technologies side by side, the goal is to discern their effectiveness and areas for improvement. This comparison, presented in a Table 1, serves as a valuable resource for researchers and developers, aiding in the refinement of solutions that best cater to the needs of visually impaired individuals.

Comparative analysis of actuators aims to shed light on various types of actuators, emphasizing their distinct advantages and challenges. Actuators are crucial components in devices such as haptic interfaces, braille displays, and other tactile feedback systems designed to enhance the sensory experience of users. Table 2 shows comparative analysis for actuators.

Table 1. Comparative Analysis of Assistive Technologies for the Visually Impaired

Technology	Strengths	Weaknesses
Salient Object Extraction	High accuracy in image processing	Limited by image-based features in complex scenes
2D Multiarray Braille Display	Supports broad eBook compatibility	Users may experience discomfort with the 3D haptic device
Interactive Multimodal Guide	Utilizes a multimodal approach with tactile and audio modalities	Inconsistencies in prototype performance, especially with touch gestures
Arabic OBR System	Proficientinrecognizing Arabic Braille	Lacks language specificity; No comparative evaluations
Hindi OBR Algorithm	Demonstrates practical potential in translating Hindi text	Faces challenges in character segmentation accuracy
BraillePlay Games	Positive feedback on enhancing Braille literacy	Challenges in effectively assessing learning outcomes

Table 2. Comparison of Different Actuators for Braille Rendering

Actuator Type	Reliability	Speed	Power Consumption	Dimensions
Piezo Actuators	Reasonable	Fast	Low	Suitable for single row, challenges in extended matrices
Electromagnetic Linear Actuators	-	-	Moderate	Challenges in miniaturization
ElectroActive Polymers (EAP)	Simple construction, Low	-	Low	Suitable for extended displays, improvements needed
Electro Rheological Actuators	Moderate	Compact	Moderate	Suitable for compact displays
Thermo pneumatic Actuators	Simple design, Compact	-	High	Compact, suitable for Braille
ShapeMemory Alloy(SMA) Actuators	Compact, Controlled	-	High	Compact, suitable for Braille

3 Proposed System

3.1 Model Overview

The device aims to be an affordable, computer-independent, portable reader. It works on the concept of optical character recognition; whereby it captures an image using a Raspberry Pi 4 camera, and sends it to Raspberry Pi 4, the heart of the system, where the text-to-braille conversion happens. The Pi 4 controls the solenoids and moves them according to the braille mapping. The braille text thus produced is understood by the user by touching the solenoid pins. This facilitates the very easy and fast conversion of any kind of text into braille. The Fig. 5 shows how the model would turn out.

3.2 Hardware

The hardware components of our system are essential for its functionality, as depicted in the block diagram presented in Fig. 6. Here is an overview of the key hardware components:

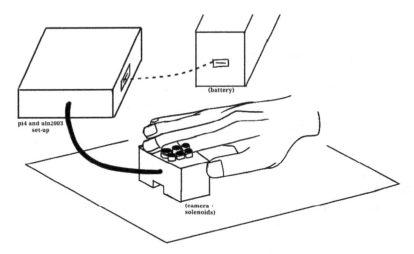

Fig. 5. Model of Proposed System

1. **Raspberry Pi 4 Model B:** The Raspberry Pi 4 Model B comes with Gigabit Ethernet, dual-band 2.4GHz and 5GHz wireless LAN, Bluetooth 5.0, and multiple USB ports (2x USB 3.0, 2x USB 2.0), facilitating various connections and peripherals. It operates using a 5V USB-C power supply. Here in this model it serves as the central processing unit, the Raspberry Pi 4 controls the solenoid plunger through the ULN2003 relay driver.
2. **LM2596:** LM2596 is a widely used and reliable voltage regulator IC that offers efficient step-down voltage regulation, making it valuable for numerous electronic applications requiring stable and adjustable DC power supplies. It accepts a wide

range of input voltages, often between 3V and 40V, depending on the specific variant. The output voltage can be adjusted within a certain range, typically from around 1.25V to 37V, by using external components like resistors or potentiometers. Over here it converts the input voltage (likely higher than 12V) to a stable 5V supply for powering the Raspberry Pi.

3. **ULN2003:** The ULN2003 is a versatile and widely used IC that simplifies the interface between microcontrollers or logic circuits and inductive loads, providing a convenient and efficient way to drive high-current devices while offering protection against voltage spikes. Here it interfaces with the Raspberry Pi's GPIO pins to control the solenoid plunger, providing electrical isolation.

4. **Solenoid Plunger:** The plunger is typically a ferromagnetic material, which means it can be magnetized when exposed to a magnetic field. When the solenoid is energized, the generated magnetic field pulls or pushes the plunger towards or away from the center of the coil. When the electrical current is turned off, the magnetic field collapses, and the plunger returns to its initial position due to either a spring mechanism or other restoring forces in the system. Here in this model on receiving the current the solenoid plunger moves up and down to convert simple text of the captured image to braille.

5. **Schottky Diode:** These diodes are placed in parallel with each solenoid to protect the circuit from voltage spikes when the solenoid turns off.

6. **Rasberry Pi Camera Rev 1.3:** The Rev 1.3 version typically utilizes a 5-megapixel fixed-focus sensor. The sensor captures light and converts it into digital image data. The camera module is controlled and configured using software libraries and commands provided in the Raspberry Pi OS. Users can access the camera using Python or terminal commands to capture images, record videos, adjust settings (such as resolution, frame rate, and exposure), and perform various image processing tasks.

7. **Rechargeable 12 V Battery:** Battery is used to provide power to the circuit.

The proposed design intends for the entire processing unit, including Raspberry Pi, ULN2003, LM2959, and Schottky diode, to be enclosed within a 3D- printed structure that can be easily carried or even worn on the arm. The pictures.

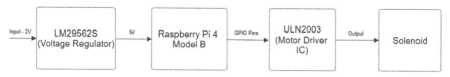

Fig. 6. Block Diagram

demonstrate how the solution suggested in the research has been put into action. Figure 7a shows the actual implementation of the proposed solution and Fig. 7b shows how pins of solenoid act when a character is detected.

3.3 Software

The software component of our system plays a pivotal role in image processing, text recognition, and controlling the Braille representation, as illustrated in the flowchart presented in Fig. 8. Below, we provide an overview of the software implementation:

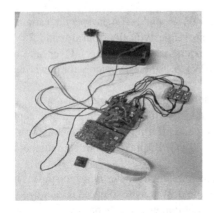

(a) Circuit Implementation   (b) A Braille cell.

Fig. 7. Hardware Implementation

Programming Language and Libraries: The system is implemented using the Python programming language. Libraries such as Picamera, OpenCV, and Tesseract are utilized for image capture, preprocessing, and optical character recognition.

Image Capture: Picamera library is employed for capturing images using the Raspberry Pi camera. The resolution is set to 640x480 pixels, though it can be adjusted based on specific requirements.

Image Preprocessing: OpenCV is utilized for image preprocessing tasks. Preprocessing steps include converting the image to grayscale, applying Gaussian blur, and thresholding to obtain a binary image.

Optical Character Recognition (OCR) Tesseract OCR engine is integrated for extracting text from the captured image. The OCR process involves a series of steps, including adaptive thresholding and connected component analysis, enhancing accuracy.

GPIO Control for Braille Representation: The program interfaces with the Raspberry Pi's GPIO (General Purpose Input Output) pins to control the solenoids responsible for Braille representation. GPIO pins serve as a communication interface, sending signals to activate specific solenoids based on detected Braille patterns.

Character to Braille Mapping: A mapping function converts detected characters to their corresponding binary Braille representations. Braille patterns are determined based on a predefined lookup table or character mapping. The Table 3 shows the character mapping done.

Motor Activation for Braille Output: Motors (solenoids) are activated sequentially to create Braille characters following the binary representation. The activation process is timed, ensuring a synchronized and controlled display of Braille characters.

This software enables real-time image processing and Braille character embossing, making our system an efficient tool for the visually impaired.

Table 3. Mapping of Each English Character to Braille String

Character	Mapping
A	100000
B	110000
C	100100
D	100110
E	100010
F	110100
G	110110
H	110010
I	010100
J	010110
K	101000
L	111000
M	101100
N	101110
O	101010
P	111100
Q	111110
R	111010
S	011100
T	011110
U	101001
V	111001
W	010111
X	101101
Y	101111
Z	101011

3.4 Working Mechanism

Our system operates through the following steps:

1. The process starts with the capture of an image when a push button is pressed.
2. After capturing the image, the Tesseract OCR engine is employed to extract text from it.
3. Once the text is recognized, it is separated into individual characters for further processing.
4. Each character is mapped to its corresponding binary Braille representation.

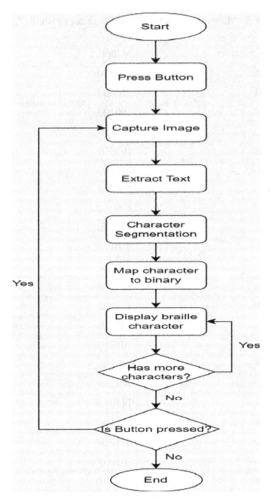

Fig. 8. Flowchart for program

5. A circuit connection is established to control the solenoids for Braille dot representation. This involves:
   (a) Connecting the LM2596 voltage regulator's output (regulated 5V) to the
       Raspberry Pi's 5V and GND pins.
   (b) Using the Raspberry Pi's GPIO pins to connect to the input pins of the ULN2003
       relay driver.
   (c) Connecting the output pins of the ULN2003 to the terminals of the solenoids.
   (d) Including a Schottky diode in parallel with each solenoid, with its cathode con-
       nected to the positive terminal of the solenoid and its anode connected to the
       negative terminal.
   (e) Ensuring that the power supply to the solenoids is maintained at 12V, with the
       LM2596 regulating higher input voltages down to 5V for the Raspberry Pi.

6. The binary Braille representation is transmitted from the Raspberry Pi to the solenoids through the circuit connections. This controls the raising and lowering of solenoids to create Braille characters.
7. The Braille characters are displayed sequentially by raising or lowering the corresponding solenoids, following the binary representation.

The described system exclusively recognizes alphabets and numbers in a given text, disregarding any other characters like symbols or whitespace. Moreover, it operates in a case-insensitive manner, treating uppercase and lowercase letters equivalently.

4 Result Analysis

The experimental results reveal significant insights into character recongnition performance across a spectrum of fonts and text variations. The primary focus was on the input text "HELLO WORLD," explored in different fonts, alongside additional experiments involving distinct texts such as "GOOD MORNING" and "DDU," all with a fixed font size of 72.

Console Output
The console outputs (Fig. 9) visually present the system's interpretations of "HELLO WORLD" (Font Size = 72) and "GOOD MORNING" (Font Size = 72).

Each output provides a snapshot of the system's recognition of the input text. Figures in 9 show console output.

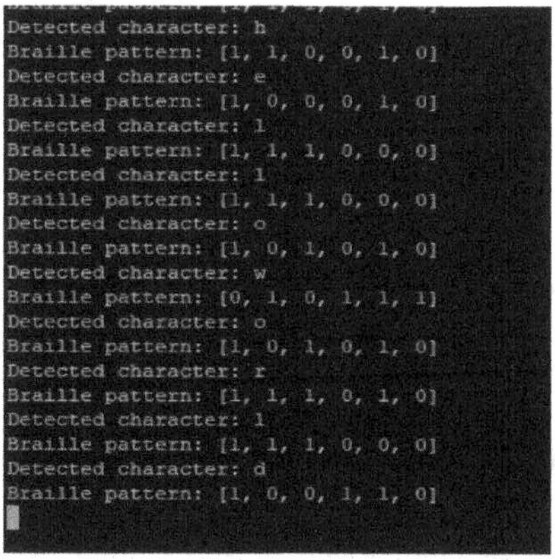

| (a) Output 1 | (b) Output 2 |

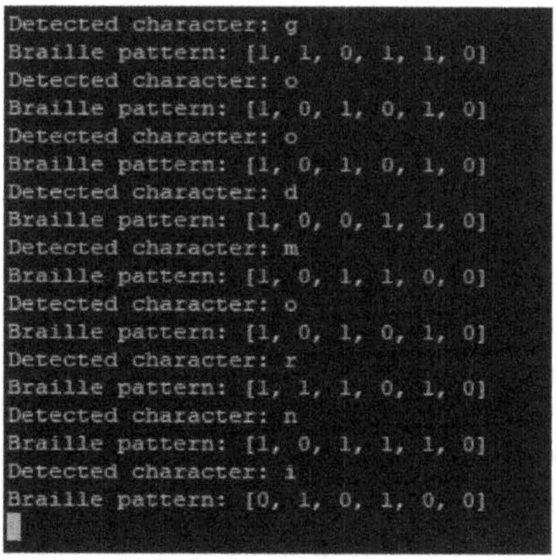

Fig. 9. Console Output

Character Recognition Metrics

Two Tables 4 and 5 outline character recognition metrics for "HELLO WORLD" at various font sizes. Metrics include characters read, characters not read, and accuracy percentage. Notably, font size 26 poses challenges, with only a 20% accuracy due to difficulties in recognizing characters.

Table 4. Character Recognition Metrics for Different Texts and Fonts

Text	Characters Read	Characters not read	Accuracy %
Hello World-Font Size = 72	h, e, l, l, o, w, o, r, l, d	-	100
Good Morning Font Size = 72	g, o, o, d, m, o, r, n, i, n, g	-	100
DDU Font Size = 72	d, d, u	-	100

Table 5. Character Recognition Metrics for "Hello World" at Various Font Sizes

Text	Font Size	Characters Read	Characters not read	Accuracy %
Hello World	72	h, e, l, l, o, w, o, r, l, d	-	100
Hello World	48	h, e, l, l, o, w, o, r, l, d	-	100
Hello World	36	h, e, l, l, o, w, o, r, l, d	-	100
Hello World	28	h, e, l, l, o, w, o, r, l, d	-	100
Hello World	26	h, e	l, l, 0, w, o, r, l, d	20

Moreover, the recognition process dissects "HELLO WORLD" into individual characters, with each character H, E, L, L, O, W, O, R, L, D identified separately, contributing to the overall accuracy assessment. The system is case-insensitive and does not consider any special characters.

The Braille mapping Table 6 delineates the corresponding Braille representation for each letter in the phrase "Hello World." This mapping is instrumental in understanding how recognized characters translate into Braille patterns.

The graphical representation facilitates a quick comparison of recognition performance under distinct font conditions, aiding in the identification of trends or peculiarities.

To visually convey accuracy fluctuations across diverse font sizes, a grouped bar graph is fitting. The x-axis represents font sizes, while the y-axis denotes accuracy percentages. Each group of bars on the graph signifies the accuracy of character recognition for different texts ("Hello World," "Good Morning," and "DDU") at specific font sizes. The grouped nature of the bars allows for a clear.

comparison between different texts and their recognition accuracy across various font sizes. The Fig. 10 shows comparison graph.

Table 6. Braille Mapping for "Hello World"

Letter	Braille Mapping
h	110010
e	100010
l	111000
o	101010
w	010111
r	111010
d	100110

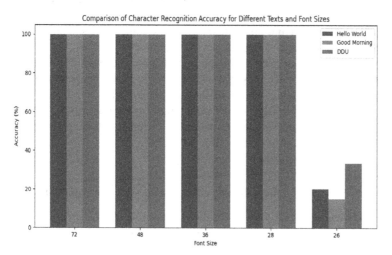

Fig. 10. Comparison Bar Graph

5 Challenges Encountered and Solutions

5.1 Challenges

In the pursuit of enhanced accessibility for the visually impaired, our research has identified several challenges that need careful consideration:

1. **Complex Content Handling:** E-publishing has improved accessibility, but handling complex technical texts remains a challenge [22].
2. **Costly Refreshable Braille Displays:** Existing refreshable braille displays are often expensive, necessitating the exploration of more affordable alternatives [19].
3. **Bulky Braille Cells:** The size of actuators, specifically push-pull solenoids measuring 5x5x5cm each, collectively creates a bulky braille cell.
4. **Piezo Actuator Limitations:** While piezo actuators fulfill Braille requirements with reasonable reliability, their cost and suitability for single-line displays pose limitations [15].

5. **Battery Weight and Portability:** The weight of the battery diminishes the device's portability, highlighting a significant concern for users.

5.2 Solutions

To address these challenges, following solutions can be implemented in future:

1. **Actuator Modification:** Explore alternative actuators that are smaller in size, lighter, and more cost-effective.
2. **Cooling Fan Addition:** Integrate a cooling fan to address any heating issues related to extended camera and solenoid usage.
3. **Dual Raspberry Pis Implementation:** Use two Raspberry Pis to optimize performance, distributing the computational load efficiently.
4. **Target Audience Consideration:** Clearly define the target audience to tailor the device's functionalities and design to specific user needs.
5. **Extension of Camera and Solenoids:** Extend the camera and solenoids to eliminate size and weight issues, ensuring the device remains portable.
6. **Switch or Android Connectivity:** Replace push buttons with more effective switches or explore Android connectivity options for improved user interaction. It would also enable continuous reading, enhancing the user experience.
7. **Buzzer Integration for Alerts:** Include a buzzer to alert users when text has been successfully read, addressing the limitations of the push-button approach.

6 Future Developments

Looking forward, envision the following advancements for future iterations:

1. **Android Integration:** Explore the seamless integration of Android technology to provide a more user-friendly interface, enhancing the overall accessibility and usability of the system.
2. **Wireless Capability:** Implement wireless connectivity, potentially through Wi-Fi, to untether the device and offer users greater flexibility and mobility.
3. **Storage and Line Detection Algorithm:** Incorporate storage capabilities for offline functionality and introduce a robust line detection algorithm to elevate text recognition accuracy. This enhancement aims to make the system more versatile and reliable.
4. **PDF Reading Functionality:** Enhance the system to include the capability to read text from PDF files. This feature adds value by allowing users to access content from PDFs in Braille, contributing to the system's compatibility and utility.
5. **Multilingual Braille Conversion:** Extend the system's capabilities to support multilingual Braille conversion, catering to a diverse user base and promoting inclusivity.

7 Conclusion

A new device has been developed to assist visually impaired people. By utilizing optical character recognition technology and the Raspberry Pi 4, it can seamlessly translate text into Braille. This device is both compact and affordable, making it an ideal tool for educational and everyday use. By capturing text from images and processing the conversion to Braille within the Raspberry Pi 4, users can easily access Braille characters through solenoid pins. In the future, the device may include external storage for additional text files and a speech input-output system to enhance self-learning mechanisms. These advancements aim to promote inclusivity and enhance the quality of life for visually impaired individuals, particularly in developing countries such as India. The paper emphasizes the significance of assistive technology in improving the lives of visually impaired individuals while acknowledging the difficulties of handling complex content and affordability. Future enhancements include multilingual Braille conversion and the development of an app that allows text files like PDFs to be converted into Braille by connecting with the user's phone.

References

1. Abdusalomov, A., Mukhiddinov, M., Djuraev, O., Khamdamov, U., Whangbo, T.K.: Automatic salient object extraction based on locally adaptive thresholding to generate tactile graphics. Appl. Sci. **10**(10) (2020). https://doi.org/10.3390/app10103350. https://www.mdpi.com/2076-3417/10/10/3350
2. Al-Salman, A., AlOhali, Y., AlKanhal, M., AlRajih, A.: An arabic optical braille recognition system, April 2007
3. Alnfiai, M., Sampalli, S.: Brailleenter: A touch screen braille text entry method for the blind. Procedia Comput. Sci. **109**, 257–264 (2017). https://doi.org/10.1016/j.procs.2017.05.349, https://www.sciencedirect.com/science/article/pii/S1877050917310189 8th International Conference on Ambient Systems, Networks and Technologies, ANT- 2017 and the 7th International Conference on Sustainable Energy Information Technology, SEIT 2017, 16-19 May 2017, Madeira, Portugal
4. Alves, C., Monteiro, G., Rabello, S., Gasparetto, M., Monteiro de Carvalho, K.: Assistive technology applied to education of students with visual impairment. Revista panamericana de salud pblica = Pan Am. J. Public Health **26**, 148–52 (08 2009). https://doi.org/10.1590/S1020-49892009000800007
5. Authority, B.: Learn About Braille — Braille Authority of North America — brailleauthority.org. https://www.brailleauthority.org/learn-about-braille. Accessed 18 Nov 2023
6. Baciero, A., Perea, M., Duabeitia, J.A., Gmez, P.: Touchscope: a passive-haptic device to investigate tactile perception using a refreshable braille display. J. Cognition **6**, 21 (2023). https://doi.org/10.5334/joc.271
7. Beg, U., Parvathi, K., Jha, V.: Text translation of scanned Hindi document to braille via image processing. Indian J. Sci. Technol. **10** (09 2017). https://doi.org/10.17485/ijst/2017/v10i33/112335
8. Bhanushali, B., Dhoot, A., Gandhi, P., Mehta, K.: Refreshable braille displays. Int. J. Comput. Appl. **180**(37), 1–4 (2018). https://doi.org/10.5120/ijca2018916914. http://www.ijcaonline.org/archives/volume180/number37/29303-2018916914
9. Cavazos Quero, L., Iranzo Bartolom, J., Cho, J.: Accessible visual artworks for blind and visually impaired people: Comparing a multimodal approach with tactile graphics. Electronics **10**(3) (2021). https://doi.org/10.3390/electronics10030297. https://www.mdpi.com/2079-9292/10/3/297
10. D'Andrea, F.M.: Preferences and practices among students who read braille and use assistive technology. J. Visual Impairment Blindness **106**(10), 585–596 (2012). https://doi.org/10.1177/0145482X1210601003

11. Elizabeth R. Hoskin, Morag K. Coyne, M.J.W.S.C.D.D.T.C.D., Pinder, S.D.: Effectiveness of technology for braille literacy education for children: a systematic review. Disability and Rehabilitation: Assistive Technol., 1–11 (2022). https://doi.org/10.1080/17483107.2022.207 0676, https://doi.org/10.1080/17483107.2022.2070676

12. Gupta, L., Varma, N., Agrawal, S., Verma, V., Kalra, N., Sharma, S.: Approaches in Assistive Technology: A Survey on Existing Assistive Wearable Technology for the Visually Impaired, pp. 541–556. Springer, June 2021. https://doi.org/10.1007/978-981-16-0965-7.42

13. Gupta, R., Singh, P., Bhanot, S.: Design and implementation of arduino based refreshable braille display controller. Indian J. Sci. Technol. 9, Sept 2016. https://doi.org/10.17485/ijst/2016/v9i33/99593

14. Kim, S., Ryu, Y., Cho, J., Ryu, E.S.: Towards tangible vision for the visually impaired through 2d multiarray braille display. Sensors 19(23) (2019). https://doi.org/10.3390/s19235319, https://www.mdpi.com/1424-8220/19/23/5319

15. Leonardis, D.D., Loconsole, C., Frisoli, A.: A survey on innovative refreshable braille display technologies. In: International Conference on Applied Human Factors and Ergonomics (2017). https://api.semanticscholar.org/CorpusID:195957974

16. Milne, L., Bennett, C., Azenkot, S., Ladner, R.: Brailleplay: educational smart-phone games for blind children. In: ASSETS14 - Proceedings of the 16th International ACM SIGACCESS Conference on Computers and Accessibility, pp. 137–144, October 2014. https://doi.org/10.1145/2661334.2661377

17. Mukhiddinov, M., Kim, S.Y.: A systematic literature review on the automatic creation of tactile graphics for the blind and visually impaired. Processes 9(10) (2021). https://doi.org/10.3390/pr9101726. https://www.mdpi.com/2227-9717/9/10/1726

18. Ramos-Garca, O.I., et al.: An iot braille display towards assisting visually impaired students in Mexico. Eng. Proc. 27(1) (2022). https://doi.org/10.3390/ecsa-9-13194, https://www.mdpi.com/2673-4591/27/1/11

19. Russomanno, A., OModhrain, S., Gillespie, R.B., Rodger, M.W.M.: Refreshing refreshable braille displays. IEEE Trans. Haptics 8(3), 287–297 (2015). https://doi.org/10.1109/TOH.2015.2423492

20. Sarkar, R., Das, S.: Analysis of different braille devices for implementing a cost-effective and portable braille system for the visually impaired people. Int. J. Comput. Appl. 60, 1–5 (2012). https://doi.org/10.5120/9717-3073

21. Shokat, S., Riaz, R., Rizvi, S.S., Khan, K., Riaz, F., Kwon, S.J.: Analysis and evaluation of braille to text conversion methods. Mob. Inf. Syst. 2020, 3461651:1–3461651:14 (2020). https://api.semanticscholar.org/CorpusID:221048542

22. Velzquez, R., Hernndez, H., Preza, E.: A portable piezoelectric tactile terminal for braille readers. Appl. Bionics Biomechanics 9, 45–60 (01 2012). https://doi.org/10.1155/2012/637851

23. Works, B.: Braille Alphabet - Braille Works — brailleworks.com, Jan 2022. https://braillewo rks.com/braille-resources/braille-alphabet/. Accessed 18 Nov 2023

24. Works, B.: What is Braille? [Your Guide to Braille] - Braille Works — braille- works.com, Jan 2022. https://brailleworks.com/braille-resources/what-is-braille/. Accessed 18 Nov 2023

Improved Genetic Algorithm Based k-means Cluster for Optimized Clustering

F. Mohamed Ilyas[1]([⊠]) and S. Thirunirai Senthil[2]

[1] Department of M.C.A. (Ph.D.), Bharath Institute of Higher Education and Research (BIHER), Chennai, Tamil Nadu, India
`2012edu@gmail.com`
[2] Department of M.C.A, Faculty of Arts and Science, Chennai, Tamil Nadu, India

Abstract. The Human Freedom Index (HFI) is an annual evaluation that measures a variety of factors, such as the rule of law, security, religion, expression, and regulation, to determine the degree of human freedom. On the basis of these considerations, relationships between social and economic factors have been developed. Several agents of intelligent software are frequently utilizing clustering techniques in filtering, extracting, categorizing materials that are already present on the World Wide Web since clustering approaches deal with the enormous volume of information. Dataset involved in this research is HFI at 2022 which involves 3464 observations and 141 features. The great sensitivity of the initial cluster centers, which may cause the K-Means method to become trapped in the local optimum is one of the major issues. The proposed work Genetic Algorithm (GA) using density method to address the drawbacks of K means cluster includes clustering numbers, as well as local optimization. In contrast to the initial cluster centroids that are chosen at random using the Improved Genetic Based K Means (IGBKM) clustering technique introduced for utilized chromosomes in creating cluster centroids. The KMeans clusters have commenced with the best cluster centers suggested using GA which maximize the fitness functions. In comparison to traditional k-means clustering technique, the results reveal in improving the K Means performance through genetic based by sensible selection for initiating the cluster centroids.

Keywords: Human Freedom · k means Clustering · Genetic Algorithm · Fitness Function · Optimization

1 Introduction

In order to enhance policies, offer answers, and potentially develop decision-making abilities while creating social, civic, and economic solutions on the basis of any industry has to forecast future trends, hypothesize current data trends, and build relationships between indicators. Generating predictions, improving decisions, and enriching global policies for the next generation is done by estimating and analyzing historical and contemporary conditions are the scenarios that utilize the ideas of data science. The HFI evaluates the degree of human freedom for 165 nations as well as territories in 2021 have accounted for

98.1% of world's population. It is a broad-based index that takes into account both financial and personal freedom in accordance with different characteristics and requirements. The HFI compiles a substantial amount of data published jointly by the Cato Institute, the Fraser Institute, and the Heritage Foundation. The main problem for researchers is handling this volume and amount of streaming data. The problem here is to cope with high-dimensional, large-volume big data sources that change frequently. The so-called data streams are enormous, unrestricted streams of data that come in and go out continuously and the data unavailable for access and future treatment. The database in the data stream may include supervised and unsupervised data, which are the fundamental methodologies used in ML algorithms. Clustering algorithms are frequently used to identify related data groupings based on the dataset's hidden structures, which may also be regarded as a key component of data science [1].

In unsupervised ML, data clustering is regarded as a challenging and complicated topic [2]. Kmeans cluster is certainly the most fashionable and significant cluster technique because of its efficiency and simplicity [3]. There are several clustering algorithms available. K means is involved with various issues such as sensitivity to the initial population of cluster center, converging to a local optimum, as well as difficulties figuring out the clusters count [4]. A number of clustering techniques are proposed to address these drawbacks. Finding starting seeds that are of greater quality compared to the randomized initial seeds in which K means selects has been suggested for a number of existing techniques [5]. For instance, utilizing density-based initial seeds has demonstrated an effective K-means clustering filtering approach that proposed quick density clustering methods based on K-means. Furthermore, enhanced k means cluster is frequently employed for addressing the sensitivity of the initially chosen seed selection for K-means. Only the enhanced k means have unable in recognizing the distribution states of data points, leading to seeds with a dissimilar distribution and repeated calculations. In spite of the quality of the original seeds, the clustering of k means has struggled to discover an optimal solution worldwide. Therefore, a number of GA-based Kmeans is created recently in an effort to increase the k means cluster performance and efficiency. Compared to straightforward K-means or straightforward GA-based clustering, these clustering methods deliver better cluster outcomes. K-means minimum problems can be avoided by combining GA with K-means. Furthermore, the primary function of a Self Organizing Map (SOM) is to convert the input data to topological attributes that the map will retain. In order to determine the final clustering outcome for the healthcare business, the data is processed and the ideal number of segments is determined. Figure 1 modified information is then fed into the GA K-Means [6].

The major clustering goal has organized the data into groups of objects that substantially comparable to one another yet distinct from one another [7]. Finding the most homogeneous clusters are substantially distinct from various clusters has focused on the clustering technique. The use of various clustering approaches, including partitioning strategies, hierarchical techniques, density-based techniques, model-based techniques and grid-based techniques [8], uses different approaches to categorize the data in various manners. The partitioning clustering techniques have the benefits of efficiency and low computing cost. The main disadvantages are a high degree of reliance on the initial parameters and the potential for becoming trapped in a specific optimal condition [9]. It

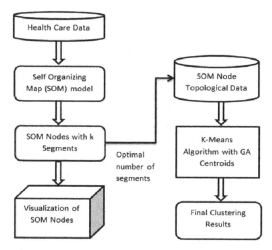

Fig. 1. Framework of GA with K-Means using SOM

is frequently difficult to choose the best clustering algorithm that has been utilized due to its algorithms typically require a number of input parameters which can impact the extent to which the algorithm performs. Although it is straightforward, reliable, and effective, the K-Means cluster has utilized frequently with partition clustering technique [10, 11]. Nevertheless, it is quite sensitive during first cluster centers were chosen, and when the initial centroids are chosen at random, and merely remain at the local optimum [12]. By supplying the necessary parameters for clustering methods, evolutionary methods are frequently used to optimize them. Clustering algorithms are optimized using techniques like Ant Colony Optimization (ACO), GA, Particle Swarm Optimization (PSO), etc.

2   Literature Review

The main difficulty in applying the K-Means method is figuring out how many clusters there will be additional to their initial centers. The initial centers have been selected at random and do not ensure a high-quality clustering for different K-Means may result in various outcomes when applied to the same data set. Furthermore, such a process can end up with less than ideal partitions.

Lin Wei-Chao et al. have employed the DIARETDB0 data set and two clustering algorithms. The initial strategy has utilized cluster centers in presenting the majority class, but the subsequent strategy used cluster centers of nearest neighbors. The dataset is made up of 89 color photos that were collected at the Kuopio University Hospital [13]. Furthermore, a Decision Tree (DT) has employed classifier in identifying the data sets with the best performances for both large and small datasets. Shrivastava et al. [14] utilized clustering of big data in which the evolutionary technique steps are applied in order to construct an estimated MapReduce architecture. They used the idea of GA to solve the issue of clustering local optimal in Kmeans with big data. Chen et al. [15] utilized eight genes as the data set for creative gene selection techniques, which relied on clusters. It introduced the Kernel-Based Clustering technique for Gene Selection

(KBCGS), a novel approach. Six features from the cancer dataset were compared using SVM and KNN in classifying the accuracy. To provide noise immunity and membership change, Lei et al. [16] used the Fuzzy C Means (FCM) cluster method for morphological reconstruction. The distance among pixels for the neighbors of local spatial as well as cluster centers determined how the data was partitioned in this case. Their research demonstrated the FCM algorithm's speed and strength, particularly when used for image segmentation. Fast generalized FCM technique employing unique factors as a local degree of likeness has been proposed by Cai et al. [17] attempted to minimize noise from images as well as eliminate deal with on trial adjusted parameters (α) that are necessary in the En-FCM algorithms [17].

The GA is a stochastic and population-based technique that is employed to solve optimization issues. Each solution has been defined as a chromosome and describes a gene to every parameter. This method is applied to a chromosome population that is selected at random by determining the chromosomal structures. Chromosomes that demonstrate an improved approach to the target issue than others received a higher chance of reproducing. Kanungo and Shukla [18] proposed technique can determine the global optimum to a particular issue by keeping the best answers in each generation and also used for developing other solutions. High-fitness individuals in the population are selected to grow, and a new population is produced through crossover and mutation involving these individuals. Hence, the Individuals might become more adapted to their setting in the newly formed population.

In order to maximize the lifetime of the network, Barekatain et al. [19] proposed hybrid GA and K-means. Through the application of the K-means algorithm, this technique improved dynamic clustering in the network environment and GA, reducing or minimizing energy consumption and lengthening the network life. The recommended approach reduces energy usage by using enhanced GA to identify the ideal range of Cluster Head (CH) nodes. The k-means-based approach constantly clusters the network employed to maintain stable distribution strength. The outcome shows that using a genetic algorithm in conjunction with hierarchical clustering is a practical and scalable strategy that can be applied to a wide range of nodes using different base station configurations and node deployment methods. Barekatain et al. [20] proposed technique is more reliable for clustering, according to the results of the NS2 simulation. This plan was to select the initial clusters using a GA rather than randomly, as this could result in a reduction in the level of clustering error complexness for the traditional K means technique as well as better solutions. Al Malki et al. [21] presented a hybrid GA with the Kmeans cluster algorithm for addressing the shortcomings of the K-means clustering method, including the possibility of empty clusters based on the initial cluster centers, the inclination to converge to local optimum values, and the potential inability to provide a comprehensive solution to complicated problems with a reasonable investment of computational time.

3   Research Methodology

The HFI measures have economic freedom like freedom in trading as well as it seizure the degree in which people is free to enjoy the main freedom that related to civil liberties in the countries. Moreover, this measure finds out the indicators for law rule, legal discrimination, and freedom movement against the equivalent sex relationships. However, this research focus on identify the optimal cluster that assist the organization to prior the ranking based on the index available in the variables with less time consumption and less storage consumption. The approach utilized to manage genetic operations is primarily covered in this section.

- An improved GA for density based method for estimating gene amount of each chromosome rearrangement technique is used.
- The number of cluster in each chromosome is assigned to perform best k means cluster.

This is typically the adaptive genetic operation as described.

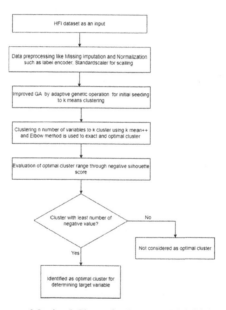

Fig. 2. Architecture of Optimal Cluster by Improved GA based k Means Cluster

The proposed IGBKM technique is a high quality with initial seeding that improves the strength of k means cluster by improved GA through adaptive genetic operations is shown in Fig. 2. There are several density based methods that applied widely in clustering research. This proposed architecture has empowers density based method for initializing GA populations from best chromosomes with various shape and sizes of k means cluster. Moreover, the process of seed lust assist the traditional GA to provide radius setup that placed in the dataset in accomplishing density distribution amount of each data point in each cluster and determines the density based on each cluster data point in the radii are removed from dataset.

3.1 Dataset Collection

The dataset consists of 141 attributes and 3464 observations have been taken in HFI that includes 164 countries details related to civil liberties, religion, rule of law and legal discrimination against similar sex relationship shown in Fig. 3. The countries involved in this dataset comes under 10 different region in the world namely, East Asia, North America, Caucasus and Central Asia, Eastern Europe, Western Europe, North America, Latin America and the Caribbean, Oceania, South Asia, Middle east and North Africa as well as Sub-Saharan Africa. Moreover, this dataset has involved woman based freedom which illustrated in several categories of the index.

```
In [2]: df = pd.read_csv(r'C:\Users\home\Desktop\arivu\hfi_cc_2022.csv')
        df.head()
```

Out[2]:

	year	countries	region	hf_score	hf_rank	hf_quartile	pf_rol_procedural	pf_rol_civil	pf_rol_criminal	pf_rol_vdem	...	ef_regulation_business_adm	ef_re
0	2020	Albania	Eastern Europe	7.67	47.0	2.0	5.903741	4.725831	4.047825	7.194198	...	5.651538	
1	2020	Algeria	Middle East & North Africa	5.13	154.0	4.0	4.913311	5.503872	4.254187	5.461189	...	4.215154	
2	2020	Angola	Sub-Saharan Africa	5.97	122.0	3.0	2.773262	4.352009	3.478950	5.306895	...	2.937894	
3	2020	Argentina	Latin America & the Caribbean	6.99	74.0	2.0	6.824288	5.679943	4.218635	6.748978	...	2.714233	
4	2020	Armenia	Caucasus & Central Asia	8.14	26.0	1.0	NaN	NaN	NaN	7.204175	...	5.170406	

5 rows × 141 columns

Fig. 3. Dataset for Human Freedom Index (HFI) at 2022 [22]

3.2 Working of Improved GA

This research discusses the method of maintaining the genetic operations for improving the gene arrangement based on usage of cosine and the probability adapted for providing and preventing convergence to the local optimal with no genetic defined genetic parameters.

3.3 Population Initialization

Based on the dataset involved, the density based technique is introduced for estimating the gene amount of each chromosome. With respect to the input dataset, the setting of density radii is defined and also estimating the amount of gene in each chromosome that rely on population size. Each chromosome sizes and shapes are not equal in length as well as different in population have basically determined from users. This research concentrated for enriching the initial population diversity as well as the population size amount of chromosomes are randomly produced. When the density value $DR_x > 1$, then the DR_x required to be normalized within the range 0 to 1. Hence, the seeded outcome of each chromosome has been initialized through improved GA for enhanced k means cluster as an initial population is generated.

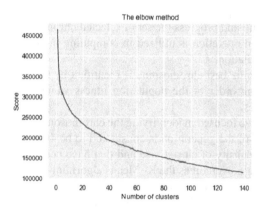

Fig. 4. Elbow Method for IGBKM Cluster for Finding Optimal Cluster

The enhanced k means cluster is an improved k means algorithm in which advanced and developed performance using initialization with best choices for the cluster centroids shown in Fig. 4. The shortest distances covered with the best chromosome for the respective number of cluster and gene are considered to be the initial seeds. Thus the terminal condition required to be provided and calculated. The fitness function of each chromosome is measured by Sum of Squared Error (SSE) and the k mean operation complexity is measured through time and memory. Moreover, the population size of gene chromosome is chosen with respect to the fitness value of descending order. The selection operation of improved GA is considered as top best GA fitness. The algorithm of IGBKM is discussed below.

Algorithm of IGBKM:

Input: dataset with density radii (DR_x), normalization data $D_{Norm} = \{D_1, D_1, \ldots, D_n\}$.

Output: Selection operation of population in improved GA with K means

Step 1: Initialize the population with DR_x, provided dataset dimension (m) and normalize the dataset of the given dataset.

Step 2: Let initialize the population matrix with DbM and threshold as T for population size 1 to N by user in which the $DRx = DRpopulation$ size

Step 3: Computing the distance among data points using D_{Norm} which estimate the density fitness and outcome is stored in DM.

Step 4: If the $DR_x < T$, then chromosome is generated for population size 1 to N else execute the next DR_x value till the value of DR_x become null.

Step 5: Computing the number of seeds S_{ix} and $ix = 1, 2, \ldots, N$ for each chromosome (CH_x) and $x = 1, 2, \ldots, N$ which have taken a seed randomly from a chromosome CH_x.

Step 6: Take a new seed S_{ix} from the uniform chromosome and select the gene with DR_x as probability in which function of seed selection for initializing seed for each chromosome.

Step 7: CH_x denotes chromosome of initial seed uniformly and repeat the operation till the population size obtained and randomly generate chromosome and selection of seed in each chromosome is random.

Step 8: Defining adaptive GA by initializing the parameter m and number of iteration as G. Initially set null and progress the set of selected chromosome.

Step 9: Selection operation is utilized in computing the each chromosome fitness from the initial population.

Step 10: Finally the best chromosome is identified by maximum fitness value and sorted by descending order of the population fitness value for computing similarity among chromosomes.

This research have focused in identifying the chromosome with population size with generation and size of the generation is considered to be 40 by mapping the offspring with respect to the density of cluster size and that have been evaluated. The proposed IGBKM algorithm has overcomes the K- Means algorithm limitation by measuring the centroid number in the data. IGBKM justify the k-clusters number. Hence, the centroids are based on GA that makes definite that the centroids don't overlap. The centroids from various subspaces after IGBKM builds diverse segments measured through python in which GA is inbuilt in this model. The accumulative Euclidean distance for each pattern is measured from the seed of each chromosome and sum of each chromosome has focused in capturing the top 10 best chromosome shown in Fig. 5. Therefore, the

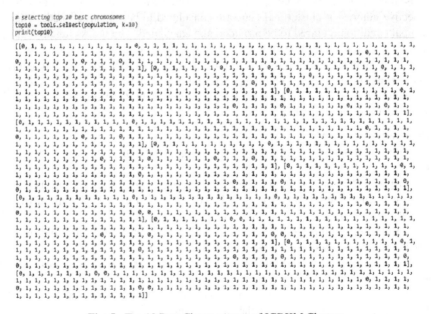

Fig. 5. Top 10 Best Chromosomes of IGBKM Cluster

application of k means cluster for each chromosome with distinct cluster using different data partitions.

Moreover, there are six '0' identified in the first best chromosome in IGBKM but in k means seven '0' has been identified. Therefore, this proposed IGBKM cluster has improved the accuracy as well as the speed of convergence in K-Means cluster. Thus, the randomly initialized cluster centroids has ability to overcome the stuck in local optimum using IGBKM cluster model which initially determined the population density using DbM of GA. Finally, these values are given to k means cluster for initializing the value of cluster's center distance to starting cluster distances using selection operations of best chromosomes.

4 Experimental Results

This experimental research has influenced to solve the complexity in the large and unsupervised data through proposed IGBKM cluster using DbM. This proposed clustering method assist in resolving complex and large dataset as well as minimize the time consumption and memory consumptions. This research has addressed the evaluation of IGBKM cluster benefits through evaluating parameters such as silhouette average score, peak memory and time consumed is compared with existing k-means cluster technique. The silhouette average score is basically obtained with negative value and positive value but the negative value of each cluster with less number is considered to be the best cluster. From cluster 15 is considered because of elbow curve and consider till cluster 29. The cluster 24 has least number of negative value as 343 followed by cluster 16and 29 as 346 shown in Fig. 6.

```
This Many Clusters: 15 | Number of Negative Values: 443
This Many Clusters: 16 | Number of Negative Values: 346
This Many Clusters: 17 | Number of Negative Values: 458
This Many Clusters: 18 | Number of Negative Values: 431
This Many Clusters: 19 | Number of Negative Values: 471
This Many Clusters: 20 | Number of Negative Values: 467
This Many Clusters: 21 | Number of Negative Values: 392
This Many Clusters: 22 | Number of Negative Values: 516
This Many Clusters: 23 | Number of Negative Values: 428
This Many Clusters: 24 | Number of Negative Values: 343
This Many Clusters: 25 | Number of Negative Values: 353
This Many Clusters: 26 | Number of Negative Values: 359
This Many Clusters: 27 | Number of Negative Values: 347
This Many Clusters: 28 | Number of Negative Values: 403
This Many Clusters: 29 | Number of Negative Values: 346
```

Fig. 6. Number of Negative Values for various Clusters

Figure 7 illustrates the negative values counts which assist in defining the best cluster in to determine the information from the unsupervised data. These clusters discusses the negative value counts in which the cluster 22 has high negative value as 516. The cluster 24 with very least negative values is 343 followed by cluster 16 and 29 with least negative value is 346. Fitness of the IGBKM is declared through the negative value count with mapping the offspring of genetic populations. The less negative value count with mapping the offspring of genetic population is considered as the best fitness.

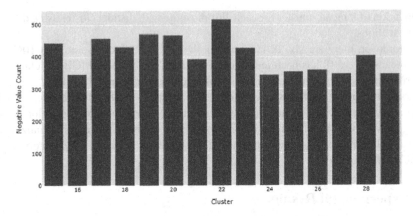

Fig. 7. Number of Negative Value Counts for Various Clusters

Figure 8 has illustrate the silhouette average score for proposed IGBKM cluster algorithm in which the average score of silhouette is 0.0953 comparatively higher than traditional k-means method is 0.0935 respectively. This determines proposed method can able to accomplish better information through number of cluster but in elbow method we have obtain only through range of cluster because of nonlinear in the range of 13 to 30. In the case of k-means, the nonlinear line is obtained in the range 15 to 30.

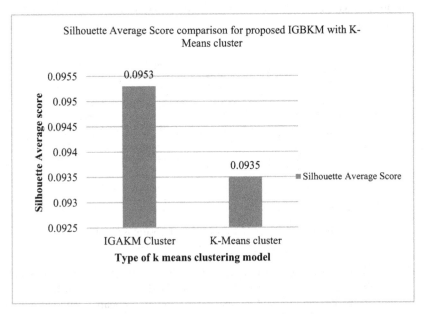

Fig. 8. Comparison of Silhouette Average Score for various K-means

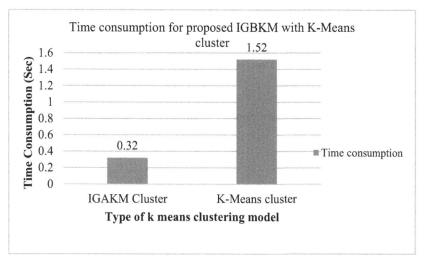

Fig. 9. Comparison of Time Consumption for various K-means

Figure 9 has illustrate the time consumption for proposed IGBKM cluster algorithm in which the time take is 0.32 s comparatively lesser than traditional k-means method is 1.52 s respectively. This is due to better understanding in selection operation of IGBKM algorithm using DbM.

Figure 10 has illustrate the peak memory used for proposed IGBKM cluster algorithm in which the peak memory used is 241.83 MiB comparatively lesser than traditional k-means method is 253.57MiB respectively.

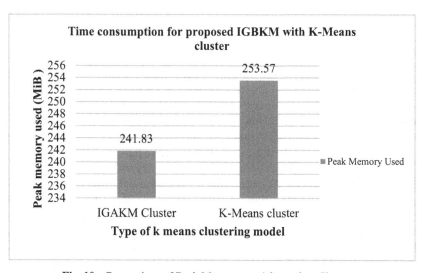

Fig. 10. Comparison of Peak Memory used for various K-means

Figure 11 has illustrates the number of negative value for proposed IGBKM cluster is compared with K-Means cluster in which the lowest negative value present in the IGBKM is 343 and optimal cluster is 24 is determined. In the case of K-Means, the number of negative value is 355 and obtained optimal cluster is 25.

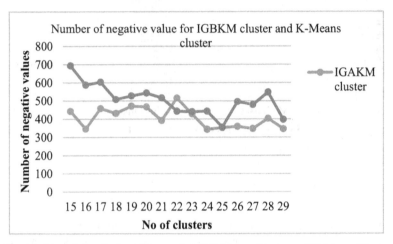

Fig. 11. Identifying Optimal Clusters in MBK-Means Cluster and K-Means Cluster

The optimal cluster obtained for IGBKM clustering method is 24with least negative value count but the traditional k mean algorithm has influences more negative values count. Hence, the 343 variable is converted in to 24 cluster which can able to provide efficient information present in the HFI dataset.

5   Conclusion

K-means clustering is the best traditional unsupervised clustering technique which selects randomly over an initial centroid and also uses a lot of memory and processing time. The proposed IGBKM cluster algorithm has outperformed conventional clustering in terms of cluster performance. However, it is very important to build the cluster with a consistent set of initial centroids to minimize the iteration number. Therefore, the segregated data is used to choose starting centroids that require the fewest iterations while still being successful. The complexity of the Kmeans cluster algorithm is inversely correlated with the number of iterations. As a result, the performance and characteristics of the proposed IGBKM clustering algorithm are better than those of existing techniques. This is evaluated through Silhouette score method which is 0.0953 and even consumed less runtime and peak memory is 0.32 s and 241.83 MiB than traditional k-means clustering as 1.52 s and 251.53 MiB correspondingly that demonstrated the advantages of the suggested approach. Additionally, the proposed IGBKM cluster performs better, producing less negative values of 343 in the best cluster 24 as the answer to the HFI dataset.

References

1. Sarker, I.H.: Data science and analytics: an overview from data-driven smart computing, decision-making and applications perspective. SN Comput. Sci. **2**(5), 1–22 (2021)
2. Bai, L., Cheng, X., Liang, J., Shen, H., Guo, Y.: Fast density clustering strategies based on the k-means algorithm. Pattern Recogn.Recogn. **71**, 375–386 (2017)
3. Huang, D., Wang, C.D., Wu, J.S., Lai, J.H., Kwoh, C.K.: Ultra-scalable spectral clustering and ensemble clustering. IEEE Trans. Knowl. Data Eng.Knowl. Data Eng. **32**(6), 1212–1226 (2019)
4. Nguyen-Trang, T., Nguyen-Thoi, T., Truong-Khac, T., Pham-Chau, A.T., Ao, H.: An efficient hybrid optimization approach using adaptive elitist differential evolution and spherical quadratic steepest descent and its application for clustering. Scientific Programming, pp. 1–15 (2019)
5. Cai, Y., Tang, C.: Privacy of outsourced two party k-means clustering. Concurrency Comput. Practice Exp. **33**(8), 1–12 (2021)
6. Alsayat, A., El-Sayed, H.: Efficient genetic K-Means clustering for health care knowledge discovery. In: IEEE 14th International Conference on Software Engineering Research, Management and Applications (SERA), pp. 45–52. IEEE, Towson, MD, USA (2016)
7. Keyvanpour, M., Serpush, F.: ESLMT: a new clustering method for biomedical document retrieval. Biomed. Eng./Biomedizinische Technik **64**(6), 729–741 (2019)
8. Irfan, S., Dwivedi, G., Ghosh, S.: Optimization of K-means clustering using genetic algorithm. In: International Conference on Computing and Communication Technologies for Smart Nation (IC3TSN), pp. 156–161. IEEE, Gurgaon, India (2017)
9. Aljarah, I., Mafarja, M., Heidari, A.A., Faris, H., Mirjalili, S.: Clustering analysis using a novel locality-informed grey wolf-inspired clustering approach. Knowl. Inf. Syst.. Inf. Syst. **62**, 507–539 (2020)
10. Yu, S.S., Chu, S.W., Wang, C.M., Chan, Y.K., Chang, T.C.: Two improved k-means algorithms. Appl. Soft Comput.Comput. **68**, 747–755 (2018)
11. Aggarwal, S.: Singh, P: Cuckoo and krill herd based k means++ hybrid algorithms for clustering. Expert. Syst. **36**(4), 1–10 (2019)
12. Jothi, R., Mohanty, S.K., Ojha, A.: DK-means: a deterministic k-means clustering algorithm for gene expression analysis. Pattern Anal. Appl. **22**, 649–667 (2019)
13. Lin, W.C., Tsai, C.F., Hu, Y.H., Jhang, J.S.: Clustering-based undersampling in class-imbalanced data. Inf. Sci. **409**, 17–26 (2017)
14. Shrivastava, P., Sahoo, L., Pandey, M., Agrawal, S.: AKM—augmentation of K-means clustering algorithm for big data. In: Intelligent Engineering Informatics: Proceedings of the 6th International Conference on FICTA, pp. 103–109. Springer, Singapore (2018)
15. Chen, H., Zhang, Y., Gutman, I.: A kernel-based clustering method for gene selection with gene expression data. J. Biomed. Inform. **62**, 12–20 (2016)
16. Lei, T., Jia, X., Zhang, Y., He, L., Meng, H., Nandi, A.K.: Significantly fast and robust fuzzy c-means clustering algorithm based on morphological reconstruction and membership filtering. IEEE Trans. Fuzzy Syst. **26**(5), 3027–3041 (2018)
17. Cai, W., Chen, S., Zhang, D.: Fast and robust fuzzy c-means clustering algorithms incorporating local information for image segmentation. Pattern Recogn.Recogn. **40**(3), 825–838 (2007)
18. Kanungo, S., Shukla, A.: A novel clustering framework using farthest neighbour approach. International Conference on Computing, Communication and Automation (ICCCA), pp. 164–169. IEEE, Greater Noida, India (2017)
19. Aibinu, A.M., Salau, H.B., Rahman, N.A., Nwohu, M.N., Akachukwu, C.M.: A novel clustering based genetic algorithm for route optimization. Eng. Sci. Technol. Int. J. **19**(4), 2022–2034 (2016)

20. Barekatain, B., Dehghani, S., Pourzaferani, M.: An energy-aware routing protocol for wireless sensor networks based on new combination of genetic algorithm & k-means. Procedia Comput. Sci. **72**, 552–560. Elsevier (2015)
21. Al Malki, A., Rizk, M.M., El-Shorbagy, M.A., Mousa, A.A.: Hybrid genetic algorithm with K-means for clustering problems. Open J. Optim.Optim. **5**(02), 71–83 (2016)
22. Freedom index. https://www.kaggle.com/datasets/gsutters/the-human-freedom-index

WSN Based Alert Architecture for Object Intrusion Detection and Fire Detection in Agricultural Farms in India

Dinesh Kumar Kalal$^{(\boxtimes)}$ and Ankit Bhavsar

FCAIT, GLS University, Ahmedabad, India
{dinesh.kalal,ankit.bhavsar}@glsuniversity.ac.in

Abstract. The crops on farms are frequently destroyed by local wildlife such as buffaloes, cows, goats, birds, and fire, amongst other things. This results in significant financial losses for the farmers. It is not feasible for farmers to fence off entire fields or to be on the land around the clock in order to provide security for it. As a result, the following is our proposal for an WSN based automatic crop protection architecture against animals and fire. This is a Wireless sensor based architecture that makes use of a microcontroller and is based on an Arduino Uno. Both an ultrasonic sensor and a smoke sensor are utilized by this architecture. The ultrasonic sensor is used to identify objects that are approaching the area, and the smoke sensor is utilized to detect fires. In such a scenario, the sensor sends a signal to the microcontroller instructing it to do an action.

The microcontroller will now sound an alarm to scare the animals away from the field. It will also send an alert message to the farmer to know about the problem and allow him to travel to the location in the event that the animals do not flee in response to the alarm. If it detects smoke, it will switch the motor on as soon as possible and also send an alert message to the farmer to know about the fire in the field. Because of this, the crops are completely protected from both animals and fire, minimizing the risk of loss to the farmer.

Keywords: Agriculture · Wireless Sensor Network (WSN) · Crop Protection · Animal Attack · Fire Protection

1 Introduction

The agricultural industry in India has exhibited remarkable progress and achievements over the course of the last six decades. Following a prolonged period of reliance on imports, which was further exacerbated by significant droughts in the mid-1960s, a sequence of governmental measures and technological advancements were implemented, resulting in a substantial increase in agricultural output and enabling India to achieve self-sufficiency in key commodities such as wheat, rice, sugar, and animal proteins. The implementation of the "green revolution" in India showcased the potential for significant enhancements in agricultural production through the appropriate implementation of policies, utilization of technology, and allocation of investments.

© The Author(s), under exclusive license to Springer Nature Switzerland AG 2024
S. Rajagopal et al (Eds.): ASCIS 2023, CCIS 2040, pp. 257–267, 2024.
https://doi.org/10.1007/978-3-031-59107-5_17

Agriculture continues to be one of the most significant and prosperous sectors in India, contributing over 17% to GDP. In India, agriculture provides a living for about 58% of the people. Agriculture generates roughly 10% of all export revenue in addition to providing high-quality raw materials for processing to regional industry. Agriculture will need to contribute more to value addition, productivity improvement, high-quality goods, and skilled workforce to successfully meet these difficulties in order to sustain the spectacular Indian economic growth in the upcoming years [2].

The technology of wireless sensor networks (WSNs) is increasingly being recognized as a highly promising solution for enhancing overall reliability, primarily due to its capacity to provide continuous and precise environmental monitoring. Wireless sensor nodes are commonly characterized by their affordability, energy efficiency, compact size, and constrained functionalities in terms of sensing, data processing, wireless communication, and power provision. The utilization of wireless sensor networks (WSNs) is employed, wherein a substantial quantity of cooperative sensor nodes may be installed. Wireless Sensor Networks (WSNs) have emerged as a notable advancement in comparison to conventional sensors, owing to the convergence of micro-electro-mechanical (MEMS) technology, wireless communications, and digital electronics. The rapid advancement of Wireless Sensor Network (WSN) technology has significantly expedited the progress and implementation of diverse innovative wireless sensor variants.

2   Indian Farms

2.1   Agriculture in India

India is widely recognized as a prominent worldwide player in the agricultural sector. India holds the distinction of being the foremost global producer of milk, pulses, and spices. Additionally, it boasts the largest cow herd, specifically buffaloes, and possesses the most extensive agricultural land dedicated to cultivating wheat, rice, and cotton. The country in question holds the distinction of being the second most significant contributor to the global production of rice, wheat, cotton, sugarcane, farmed fish, fruit, vegetables, and tea. The nation possesses around 195 million hectares of land dedicated to agricultural cultivation, with approximately 63 percent, or nearly 125 million hectares, relying on rainfall for irrigation, while the remaining 37 percent, equivalent to 70 million hectares, are irrigated. Moreover, it is worth noting that forests include over 65 million hectares of India's land. Agriculture is the backbone of the Indian economy, employing a large percentage of the population and contributing significantly to the country's GDP. However, Indian agriculture is faced with numerous challenges, including animal intrusion, which leads to significant losses in crop productivity and food security. According to the United Nations' latest population estimates and projections, China may soon lose its long-held title as the world's most populous nation. India's population is anticipated to reach 1,425,775,850 people in April 2023, tying and eventually exceeding that of mainland China [2].

The agricultural sector in India has had a gradual drop in its contribution to the overall economy, accounting for less than 17%. This decline can be attributed to the rapid growth of the industrial and services sectors. However, it is important to recognize that the significance of agriculture in India extends beyond this quantitative measure, as it plays a crucial role in the country's economic and social framework. Firstly, it is noteworthy that a significant proportion, approximately 75%, of households in India rely on incomes derived from rural areas. Furthermore, it is worth noting that a significant proportion of India's impoverished population, approximately 770 million individuals or almost 70 percent, primarily reside in rural regions. Furthermore, the food security of India is contingent upon the cultivation of cereal crops, alongside the imperative to enhance the production of fruits, vegetables, and milk in order to adequately cater to the needs of a burgeoning population characterized by escalating earnings. In order to achieve this objective, it is imperative that an agricultural sector characterized by productivity, competitiveness, diversification, and sustainability is established in a rapid and efficient manner (Fig. 1).

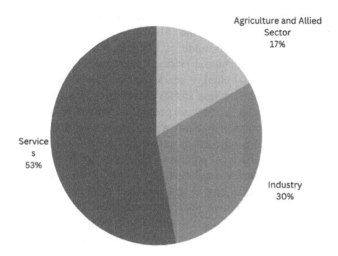

Fig. 1. Contribution of Various sector in Indian Economy.

2.2 Problems Faced by Indian Farmer

Animal intrusion is a significant problem faced by Indian farmers, particularly in regions where open grazing is common. This problem is exacerbated by the large population of stray animals, including cows, buffaloes, and goats, which roam freely and cause damage to crops. For example, in July 2021, farmers in the state of Uttar Pradesh reported significant losses due to a swarm of locusts that destroyed crops such as maize, soybean, and sugarcane. Similarly, in June 2020, a herd of elephants destroyed crops in several villages in the state of Odisha, causing losses to farmers. Apart from the animal attack fire in the farm field is main.

2.3 Agriculture Damages Due to Animal Attack

There is so much research that has been done analyzing the crop and plant damages caused by animal attacks in different parts of the country, According to a survey conducted by E. A. Jayson of Kerala Forest Research Institute Peechi Thrissur, It was found that (20%) twenty per cent of the farm production was damaged by the animal attack [3]. Twenty different species of animals were seen in the region throughout the study. The most instances of Gaur (207) were seen, then Chital. Gaur herds averaged 18 animals, with a male-to-female ratio of 1:3 [3].

In Himachal Pradesh Piyush Mehta of Dr YS Parmar University of Horticulture & Forestry studied that with the score of 4.5 farmers strongly agrees that quantity of crop production is reduced because of crop raiding by wild animals. Author also concluded that due to crop damage by wild animals, the average per capita income of the farmers also affected [4].

According to Vijay Kumar, Animal-related damage has recently been India's biggest hazard to the fields of crops in locations close to forests or protected areas. Nilgai, wild boars, monkeys, and stray cattle have caused havoc among the farming population in India's North-West Himalayan area. Nilgai, an antelope revered by Hindus, has increased in population outside of protected regions [5].

According to the National Institute of Disaster Management, monkeys caused Himachal Pradesh to lose agricultural products valued at $2,200 crore between 2007 and 2012. Similar to this, wild monkey attacks caused 250 villages in the Jammu area to lose agriculture production totaling 15,596 acres for Rs 33 crore per year [6].

The author studies the conflict between people and animals in the region of northern Gujarat. The primary objectives of the study were to locate areas that are prone to conflict, describe the many types of conflicts that occur there, and assess the economic damage that these conflicts do to the local populace. The region of North Gujarat is entirely agricultural land with a human population. Conflict between humans and carnivores may result in more widespread crop destruction, as has already been observed in this region. It was reported that animals including sloth bears, blue bulls, wild boars, and wild asses routinely harmed standing crops in the area, resulting in significant losses for the farmers [7].

2.4 Existing Method of Farm Protection

Livestock Fences
A popular and long-lasting wild animal deterrent is fencing. Agricultural fences are a very successful technology for protecting wild animals. However, the use of fences is frequently prohibited. Certain types of fences may be prohibited or restricted by some municipal and governmental organizations. Therefore, it's crucial to review local laws and ordinances before choosing a proper fence.

Organic Deterrents
Instead of employing mechanical or chemical protective methods, some farmers opt to use natural resources. There are several strategies to reduce agricultural damage from wild animals, such as: Smoke, Emulsion, beehive fencing, Castor Oil and chemicals.

In addition to the above listed methods, some farmers use scarecrows, firecrackers, bright lights, fire, thumping drums, and dogs. The most prosperous farmers would check their crops as frequently as possible in addition to using specific crop protection techniques. After all, the only way to guarantee that everything on the field happens according to plan is to constantly watch it.

3 Wireless Sensor Network

Wireless Sensor Networks (WSNs) can be defined as networks consisting of small and simple devices called nodes. These nodes have the ability to sense the surrounding environment and transmit the collected information from the monitored area. The data collected can be sent directly or through multiple intermediate nodes to a central point called a sink. The sink can then utilize the data locally or connect to other networks, such as the internet, through gateway nodes [1].

The primary constituents of a sensor node include a sensing unit, a processing unit, a transceiver, and a power unit, as depicted in Fig. 2. The sensing device is responsible for detecting the physical amount, which is subsequently converted into a digital representation using an Analog to Digital converter (ADC). Subsequently, the processor is employed for subsequent computational tasks, while the transceiver is utilized for the transmission and reception of data from other nodes or the Base Station. The power unit holds significant prominence within a sensor node. In the context of unattended applications, it is important to note that once the battery has been depleted, it is not possible to replace it.

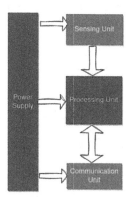

Fig. 2. Architecture of Wireless Sensor Node

4 Related Works

In this paper we had studied the research paper [7–14] out of the listed paper we summarized the outcome of the following papers.

8. Harneet et al.: Author of this paper proposed an IOT based system that can be used to elaborately emphasize a cumulative strategy that applies "Internet of Things" technology, conventional agricultural practices, and strategies to prevent crop loss.

9. Mohit et al.: Author of this paper proposed a system in which when an animal reaches the agricultural area in the suggested project. While PIR sensors are utilized to identify an animal's location, vertically positioned LDRs assist us determine an animal's size.

10. Balkrishna et al.: According to the author, in order to prevent animals from trespassing on crops, IOT and machine learning are utilized. Animal intrusion poses a significant threat to agricultural productivity, which affects food security and reduces farmer earnings. The suggested model's solutions to this problem are being developed using the Internet of Things and machine learning approaches.

11. Nandat et al.: According to the study of the author, there is a smart irrigation and crop security system powered by IOT. Perceptive agriculture will be implemented utilizing an integrated technique in the IIOT sector that is moving forward with the arrangements employing open source software and low-power hardware.

12. Stefano Giordano et. al: In this research, Author provided an integrated method for smart agriculture using open source software and low power hardware in the Internet of Things space.

5   Proposed Architecture for Object Instruction Detection and Fire Detection

As was stated in the last section of this article, there are a variety of conventional techniques for defending farm fields from animal assault. However, these conventional methods have a number of drawbacks, such as wire fences that may be damaging to animals (Fig. 3).

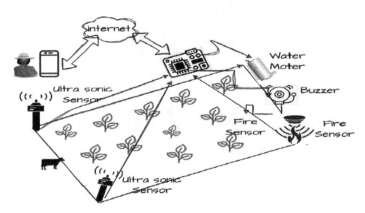

Fig. 3. Architecture of Agriculture Farm Protection

In addition, this approach necessitates a continuous eye on the farm. Due to the shortcomings of conventional techniques, this paper presents a new approach to agricultural land protection that makes use of information technology. In this paper we are going to use a microcontroller known as nodemcu, ultrasonic sensor, Fire Sensor, buzzer and blink app mobile application. In the proposed modern solution we are implanting various sensors on the farm field like an ultrasonic sensor which is capable of detecting any motion in the farm field at the distance of 5 m, and smoke sensor which can detect any fire in the farm field. This sensor sends data to the nodemcu (microcontroller board) which takes action against data received from the sensor. If it finds any object in the field it activates the buzzer sound for deviating animals from the field as well as it sends alert messages to the farmers mobile. Smoke sensors sense fire in the field then also it automatically sends the message to the farmers (Fig. 4).

Fig. 4. Prototype of WSN based Farm Protection

6 Prototype Implementation

An example of the installation of a smart crop protection system is shown in the picture that is provided above. This system integrates a wide variety of sensors, including an ultrasonic sensor and a fire sensor, among others. A fire sensor is strategically placed inside the agricultural field in order to detect the presence of fire, and an ultrasonic sensor is deployed in order to identify obstacles within a certain portion of the field. In addition, a buzzer is utilized in order to provide humans with auditory notifications. One of the ultrasonic sensors that is currently being used is the HC-SR04. The device is made up of a component that is capable of measuring distances as well as a buzzer that generates an auditory signal if it detects an obstruction. The capacity to detect the presence of fire inside an agricultural area is one of the capabilities of a fire sensor. A selected guardian can get location information thanks to the GSM module, which provides this feature. A direct current (DC) of 12 V (V) is converted into a decreased direct current (DC) of 5 V (V) by the regulated power supply, which is entrusted with taking on this responsibility. An infrared (IR) sensor, an ultrasonic sensor, and a latency detection and response (LDR) sensor are the three input devices that are included in the controller's configuration. Following that, the data that was obtained is processed, which ultimately results in the development of output in the form of a buzzer, an LED, and a GSM. Light-dependent resistors, also known as LDRs, infrared sensors, also known as IR sensors, and ultrasonic sensors are included into the input modules. A buzzer, a GSM module, an LED indication, and an LCD indicator are all included in the output modules collection. In this specific scenario, the employment of an Arduino microcontroller and a controlled power source are components that are absolutely necessary.

6.1 Sensor

UltraSonic Sensor: An ultrasonic sensor is an electronic apparatus utilized for measuring the distance of a target item (Fig. 5).

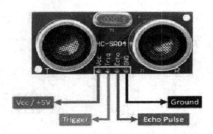

Fig. 5. Ultrasonic Sensor

Fire Sensor
A fire / flame sensor can be defined as a specialized detector designed to identify and respond to the presence of a fire or flame (Fig. 6).

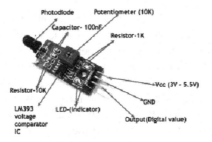

Fig. 6. Ultrasonic Sensor

Microcontroller
The Nodemcu is an open-source development board used to create embedded and WSN applications. Nodemcu is made up of hardware based on the ESP-12 module and firmware that runs on Espressif Systems' ESP8266 Wi-Fi SoC (Fig. 7).

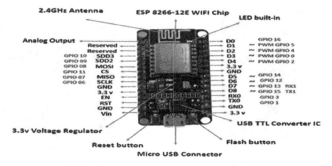

Fig. 7. Micro Controller (Nodemcu)

6.2 Block Diagram

(See Fig. 8).

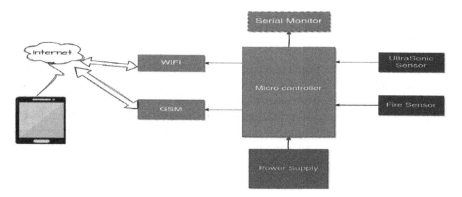

Fig. 8. Block diagram of WSN Based Farm Protection

6.3 Result Analysis

Figure 9 demonstrates the functioning of an ultrasonic sensor in an agricultural farm. Upon the detection of an object entering the farm field, the sensor activates a sound device, thereby deterring the thing from entering. Additionally, the sensor transmits an alarm message to the farmer's mobile application. In addition to the ultrasonic sensor, a fire sensor is also installed in the farm. This sensor is designed to detect any fire incidents that may occur in the farm field. Upon detection, the fire sensor transmits the relevant data to the microcontroller, which promptly initiates appropriate actions. Furthermore, a fire warning message is sent to the mobile phone of the farmer, ensuring timely notification.

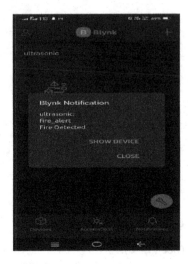

Fig. 9. Alert Message on Farmer Mobile Screen

7 Conclusion

The implementation of a Wireless Sensor Network (WSN) based alert architecture for the purpose of object incursion detection and fire detection has the potential to significantly decrease the amount of human labor required in farm fields. The implementation of the suggested architecture has the potential to mitigate agricultural product loss by effectively detecting animals and fire occurrences in the field. Additionally, this technology is capable of transmitting alarm messages to the farmer's mobile device, therefore eliminating the necessity for continuous human monitoring around the clock.

References

1. Gulati, A., Juneja, R.: Transforming Indian agriculture. In: Chand, R., Joshi, P., Khadka, S. (eds.) Indian Agriculture Towards 2030. India Studies in Business and Economics. Springer, Singapore (2022). https://doi.org/10.1007/978-981-19-0763-0_2
2. United Nations: Department of Economic and Social Affairs, Population Division. World Population Prospects 2022: Summary of Results (2022). UN DESA/POP/2022/TR/NO. 3
3. Veeramani, A., Jayson, E.A.: A survey of crop damage by wild animals in Kerala. Indian Forester **121**, 949–953 (1995)
4. Mehta, P., Negi, A., Chaudhary, R., Yasmin, J., Thakur, P.: A study on managing crop damage by wild animals in Himachal Pradesh. Int. J. Agric. Sci. **10**, 6438–6442 (2018)
5. Kumar, V., Attri, V., Rana, D.S., Chauhan, S.K.: Crop raiding': farmers perspectives in Shiwalik hills of North-Western Himalayas, India. J. Int. Wildl. Law Policy **25**(4), 301–313 (2022). https://doi.org/10.1080/13880292.2022.2146851
6. Reddy, M.D.: Monkey menace, its management. Int. J. Manage. Technol. Eng. **8**, 5904 (2018)
7. Nishith, D.: Evaluation & assessment of man-animal conflicts with special reference to human injury & crop damage by wildlife in North Gujarat. Technical Report (2012). https://doi.org/10.13140/RG.2.2.34629.70889

8. Mohite, R.B., Chinchawade, A.J., Waghmode, U.P., Thorat, Z.V., Mane, V.B., Pawar, V.E.: Smart farm protection system using IoT. In: 2023 4th International Conference on Signal Processing and Communication (ICSPC), Coimbatore, India, pp. 158–162 (2023). https://doi.org/10.1109/ICSPC57692.2023.10125709
9. Korche, M., Tokse, S., Shirbhate, S., Thakre, V., Jolhe, S.P.: IoT based smart agriculture and animal detection system. Int. J. Latest Eng. Sci. **04**(04), 2581–6659 (2021). https://doi.org/10.51386/25816659/ijles-v4i4p101
10. Balakrishna, K., Mohammed, F., Ullas, C.R., Hema, C.M., Sonakshi, S.K.: Application of IOT and machine learning in crop protection against animal intrusion. Global Trans. Proc. **2**(2), 169–174 (2021)
11. Nanda, I., Sahithi, C., Swath, M., Maloji, S., Shukla, V.K.: IIOT based smart crop protection and irrigation system. In: 2020 Seventh International Conference on Information Technology Trends (ITT), pp. 118–125. IEEE (2020)
12. Giordano, S., Seitanidis, I., Ojo, M.: IoT solutions for crop protection against wild animal attacks. IEEE Int. Conf. Environ. Eng. (2018). https://doi.org/10.1109/EE1.2018.8385275
13. Akyildiz, I.F., Weilian, S., Sankarasubramaniam, Y., Cayirci, E.: A survey on sensor networks. IEEE Commun. Mag. **40**(8), 102–114 (2002)
14. Sohraby, K., Minoli, D., Znati, T.: Wireless Sensor Networks, Second Edition. Wiley Publications (2006)
15. Jha, K., Doshi, A., Patel, P., Shah, M.: A comprehensive review on automation in agriculture using artificial intelligence. Artif. Intell. Agriculture **2**, 1–12 (2019)
16. García, L., Parra, L., Jimenez, J.M., Lloret, J., Lorenz, P.: IoT-based smart irrigation systems: an overview on the recent trends on sensors and IoT systems for irrigation in precision agriculture. Sensors **20**(4), 1042 (2020)
17. Kour, V.P., Arora, S.: Recent developments of the internet of things in agriculture: a survey. IEEE Access **8**, 129924–129957 (2020)
18. Gubbi, J., Buyya, R., Marusic, S., Palaniswami, M.: Internet of things (IoT): a vision, architectural elements, and future directions. Future Gener. Comput. Syst. **29**(7), 1645–1660 (2013)
19. Shabadi, L.S., Biradar, H.B.: Design and implementation of IOT based smart security and monitoring for connected smart farming. Int. J. Comput. Appl. **975**, 8887 (2008)
20. Balaji, S., Nathani, K., Santhakumar, R.: IoT technology, applications and challenges: a contemporary survey. Wireless Pers. Commun. **108**(1), 363–388 (2019)
21. Bhatia, S., Chauhan, A., Nigam, V.K.: The internet of things: a survey on technology and trends. Inf. Syst. Front. **17**, 261–274 (2016)
22. Tiwary, A., Mahato, M., Chandrol, M.K.: Internet of things (IoT): research, architectures and applications. Int. J. Future Revolution Comput. Sci. Commun. Eng. **4**, 2454–4248 (2018)

Decentralized Disruptive Crypto Landscape: How Digital Currencies Are Shaking up Finance?

Manish Dadhich[1]([✉]), Anurag Shukla[1], Manvinder Singh Pahwa[2], and Ashish Mathur[3]

[1] Sir Padampat Singhania University, Udaipur, India
manish.dadhich@spsu.ac.in
[2] Dr. Harisingh Gour University, Sagar, India
[3] Central University of Haryana, Jant-Pali, India

Abstract. Cryptocurrency has introduced significant disruptions. It also poses challenges and risks that must be addressed, such as regulatory concerns, market manipulation, scalability issues, and environmental impact. The paper aims to explore the long-term impact of Cryptocurrency on the financial market, which will depend on how these challenges are addressed and how technology continues to evolve. The rise of cryptocurrencies has prompted central banks to explore the development of their digital currencies. CBDC (Central Bank Digital Currency) aims to leverage blockchain technology for faster, cheaper, and more secure transactions while maintaining central bank control over monetary policy. This development could potentially reshape the traditional banking system. The study has attempted cryptocurrencies that have the potential to provide financial services to unbanked or underbanked populations worldwide. With access to the internet and a digital wallet, individuals can participate in the global economy and send and receive funds quickly, even in areas with limited banking infrastructure. The paper may be helpful for FinTech experts, bankers, investors, and administrators to get inside financial markets and disruption.

Keywords: Disruption · FinTech · CBDC (Central Bank Digital Currency) · Capital Gain · Cryptocurrency · BTC

1 Introduction

Cryptographic money is computerized cash, an elective installment made utilizing encryption calculations (Purohit et al., 2022; Shrimali & Patel, 2021). Cryptocurrencies have gained significant importance and have the potential to bring about various transformative impacts. These currencies are typically based on decentralized blockchain technology, which removes the need for intermediaries like banks or governments to facilitate transactions. This decentralization allows for peer-to-peer transactions, reducing reliance on central authorities and increasing financial inclusivity. Cryptocurrencies can provide financial services to individuals who may not have access to traditional banking systems. People in underserved regions without proper identification documents

S. Rajagopal et al (Eds.): ASCIS 2023, CCIS 2040, pp. 268–282, 2024.
https://doi.org/10.1007/978-3-031-59107-5_18

can securely participate in the cryptocurrency ecosystem, storing, sending, and receiving value (Kappert et al., 2021; Krishnapriya & Sarath, 2020). Security and privacy are a great concern for the crypto market, and these currencies employ cryptographic techniques to secure transactions and ensure users' privacy. Using public and private keys, encryption, and digital signatures adds layers of security, making it difficult to tamper with transactions or steal funds. Further, cryptocurrencies facilitate seamless and near-instantaneous cross-border transactions. Traditional financial systems often involve lengthy processes, high fees, and currency conversions. Cryptocurrencies eliminate these barriers, enabling individuals and businesses to transact globally easily.

With cryptocurrencies, individuals have direct control over their funds. They can store and manage their digital assets without relying on third parties. This financial sovereignty empowers individuals to be their bank, reducing the risk of funds being frozen, seized, or subject to capital controls (Gaurav Kumar Singh, 2022). The total market share of Cryptocurrency refers to the combined value of all cryptocurrencies in circulation. As of my knowledge cutoff date of September 2022, the total market share of Cryptocurrency was estimated to be around USD 2.5 trillion (Dadhich, Pahwa, et al., 2021; Kappert et al., 2021; Rodenburg & Pappas, 2017). However, it is essential to note that the market share of Cryptocurrency can be highly volatile and subject to significant fluctuations. The cryptocurrency market is influenced by various factors, including global economic conditions, regulatory developments, and investor sentiment, which can all impact the market share of cryptocurrencies.

Compared to recent mechanisms in the decentralized disruptive crypto landscape, digital currencies represent a seismic shift in the financial landscape. These innovative mechanisms challenge conventional financial systems by introducing decentralized technologies like Blockchain, which ensures transparency, security, and immutability of transactions (see Table 1).

Table 1. Mechanism Evolved FinTech Landscape

Mechanism	Description
Decentralized Finance (DeFi)	Utilizes smart contracts for lending, borrowing, and trading without traditional intermediaries; enhances financial inclusion and accessibility
Non-Fungible Tokens (NFTs)	Represents unique digital assets, often used for ownership and provenance of digital art, collectibles, and real estate; empowers creators and artists
Central Bank Digital Currencies (CBDCs)	Government-backed digital versions of national currencies; aim to improve payment system efficiency and provide a digital alternative to traditional fiat

(*continued*)

Table 1. (*continued*)

Mechanism	Description
Layer 2 Scaling Solutions	Addresses blockchain scalability issues with solutions like Optimistic Rollups and zk-Rollups; enhances transaction throughput and reduces fees
Cross-Chain Compatibility	Enables interoperability between different blockchains using blockchain bridges and protocols like Polkadot and Cosmos; fosters collaboration across ecosystems
Tokenization of Assets	Digitizes real-world assets (e.g., real estate, commodities) to allow fractional ownership and increased liquidity; uses security tokens for traditional financial instruments
Stablecoins	Cryptocurrencies pegged to fiat currencies or commodities provide a stable value store and facilitate seamless transitions between traditional and digital finance

The purpose of the study is to comprehensively investigate and analyze the transformative impact of decentralized cryptocurrencies on the traditional financial landscape. The research aims to uncover digital currencies' underlying mechanisms, opportunities, and challenges, particularly those utilizing decentralized blockchain technology, by exploring the evolving relationship between decentralized cryptocurrencies and new-age financial institutions. The purpose is to contribute a nuanced understanding of how digital currencies reshape the financial sector and influence various stakeholders, including consumers, investors, policymakers, and financial institutions. The scope of the study encompasses a multidimensional analysis of the decentralized disruptive crypto landscape, emphasizing its significance within the broader financial ecosystem. The study holds profound significance in the context of sustainable development and developing countries. The potential for digital currencies to enhance financial privacy and security is particularly relevant in regions with concerns about surveillance, contributing to the protection and empowerment of individuals. This study sheds light on the disruptive nature of digital currencies and emphasizes their potential to contribute positively to sustainable economic development in developing countries.

2   Central Bank Digital Currency (CBDC)

CBDCs are intended to be a digital representation of a country's physical currency and are designed to be used as a medium of exchange for goods and services (Shrimali & Patel, 2021). CBDCs differ from other digital currencies like cryptocurrencies because they are issued and regulated by central banks, whereas cryptocurrencies are decentralized and operate independently of any central authority (Kappert et al., 2021). CBDCs are still in the experimental phase in many countries, with several major banks worldwide exploring the potential benefits and challenges of issuing their digital currencies. Some potential benefits of CBDCs include increased efficiency and security of payments, improved financial inclusion, and greater control over monetary policy. However, there are concerns about privacy and surveillance and the potential impact on traditional banking systems and financial stability (Pahwa et al., 2022).

Global Cryptocurrency Market, 2021-

2028 ($ Bn)

Country Share For North America

Region- 2021 (%)

Fig. 1. Global share of Cryptocurrency[1]

Figure 1 represents information about the dominance of different cryptocurrencies, worldwide 4.06 billion $ in 2028, in which BTC has the largest market share. Ethereum is also a fast-growing coin with an overall CAGR of 12.5%.

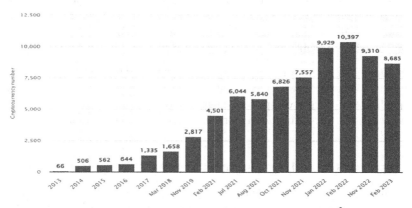

Fig. 2. Number of Cryptocurrencies worldwide, 2013–23[2]

Figure 2 condenses the information related to the number of cryptocurrencies worldwide, 2013–23, which depicts the augmented trend from the last decade. Thus, certain features of these Cryptocurrencies made them so popular in the recent past:

Decentralized Mechanism: Experts contend that BTC's success can be attributed to blockchain technology. The primary objective of the design of the blockchain network was to make it possible for BTC transactions to take place without the involvement of

---

[1] https://www.skyquestt.com/report/cryptocurrency-market.

[2] https://www.statista.com/statistics/863917/number-crypto-coins-tokens/.

any third parties. As a result, it transforms it into a decentralized mechanism that enables the quick transaction, data transparency, and anonymity that users desire (Croutzet & Dabbous, 2021).

Facilities for Distant Trading: Remote trading capabilities of such currencies are a major factor in increasing the masses' prominence. Most trading platforms accept these currencies as a payment method because they are easy to transact. New digital currencies that have just come onto the market haven't yet been deemed trustworthy and reliable for conducting transactions. Who might want to remain in a long line in this digitalized world must be observed.

Energetic Highlights: Protocols are not the only factor contributing to the global adoption of BTC and other currencies. Despite its inherent complexity, Cryptocurrency is quite user-friendly and straightforward to manage. BTC dividing is an uncommonly planned program to work with this interaction (Ren et al., 2022).

Efficacy of Use: It's important to know that using new-age currencies to purchase or trade is relatively straightforward. In alignment with this notion, BTC facilitates a quick transaction process and has no third parties as intermediaries (Vinod Ramchandra et al., 2022).

Security: A proper and robust security mechanism is necessary for digital currencies. BTC didn't get much response from the market in its early days because it was criticized for having a fragile security system. However, since the introduction of Blockchain, a new layer of security has been added to the entire system. As a result, it now provides the most sophisticated and advanced security features, ensuring that digital currencies are kept as safe as possible (Dadhich, Pahwa, et al., 2021).

Trade Worth: It is vital while investing in cryptocurrencies in the FinTech market in the present scenario. Notwithstanding, the justification behind this is that the market is unpredictable, which accompanies the gamble of huge misfortunes. Therefore, it is always prudent to proceed cautiously for trading purposes (Gaurav Kumar Singh, 2022).

2.1 Approaches Towards Cryptographic Money and Security

Cryptocurrency and security-related methods are essential components underpinning the trust and reliability of decentralized financial systems. Cryptographic security serves as the cornerstone, ensuring the confidentiality and integrity of digital transactions. Using public and private key pairs, cryptographic hash functions, and advanced encryption techniques safeguards sensitive information and prevents unauthorized access. The decentralized nature of cryptocurrencies, coupled with consensus mechanisms like Proof of Work (PoW) or Proof of Stake (PoS), mitigates the risk of a single point of failure, enhancing overall network security. Security audits, penetration testing, and regulatory compliance measures are pivotal in identifying and addressing vulnerabilities within the cryptocurrency ecosystem. Regular security assessments help maintain a proactive stance against potential threats, ensuring developers can promptly implement necessary updates and improvements (Babu et al., 2023). Moreover, education and user awareness programs are crucial in preventing social engineering attacks. Informed users are less susceptible to scams and phishing attempts, contributing to an overall more secure environment (Erukala Suresh Babu, Amogh Barthwal, 2023; Li et al., 2019). Collaboration within the cryptocurrency community, information sharing about emerging threats, and continual improvement, including the development of quantum-resistant cryptography, collectively fortify the resilience of digital currencies against evolving challenges (M Baritha Begum, N. Deepa, Mueen Uddin, Rajesh Kaluri, Maha Abdelhaq, 2023; Patel et al., 2023).

3   Research Methodology

The study employed secondary research, which included gathering information and data from existing sources, such as books, academic journals, reports, and online databases. This type of research is conducted by analyzing and interpreting information already collected by others rather than conducting original research. The technical aspects of various cryptocurrencies, including taxation challenges in investing in crypto, were also evaluated from reliable sources. Focus on information that provides insights into the trends in the global crypto-market, trading & regulatory developments were also pillars of the secondary research that have been incorporated in this study. Moreover, investigating market trends, including the growth of decentralized finance (DeFi), the emergence of new financial instruments, and the impact on traditional banking systems, is vital to discuss. By combining these research methods strategically, researchers can develop a comprehensive and well-rounded understanding of the opportunities and challenges presented by digital currencies. This approach enhances the robustness and reliability of findings, making the research more valuable and applicable to the rapidly evolving landscape of digital currencies.

4   Discussion and Analysis

4.1   Taxation on Cryptocurrency in India and Abroad

The taxation of Cryptocurrency varies by country and jurisdiction, but cryptocurrencies are generally treated as property for tax purposes. This means that any profits (not losses) made from buying, selling, or trading cryptocurrencies are subject to capital gains tax, like the tax treatment of stocks and other investment assets (Dadhich, Poddar, et al., 2022; Kouam & Asongu, 2022). In many countries, including the United States, taxpayers are required to report any gains from cryptocurrency transactions on their tax returns. The specific tax rates and reporting requirements can vary depending on the country and the taxpayer's eligibility. Crypto-investors and traders must keep accurate records of their transactions, including the purchase price, sale price, and associated fees or expenses (Schulz & Feist, 2021). This can help ensure that they accurately report their gains or losses and avoid potential penalties or fines for non-compliance with tax regulations. Additionally, some countries have introduced specific tax regulations related to Cryptocurrency, such as requiring cryptocurrency exchanges to report transaction data to tax authorities or imposing taxes on cryptocurrency mining activities. As such, it is important for investors to stay informed about the tax regulations in their country or jurisdiction and to seek professional advice if necessary (Dadhich, Doshi, et al., 2022; Milian et al., 2019).

In India, the taxation of Cryptocurrency is regulated by the Income Tax Act 1961, which treats cryptocurrencies as assets for tax purposes. This means that any profits or gains from the sale or exchange of cryptocurrencies are subject to capital gains tax. The specific tax rates and reporting requirements depend on the cryptocurrency transaction type and holding period. Short-term capital gains, which are gains from the sale of cryptocurrencies held for less than 36 months, are subject to tax at the taxpayer's applicable income tax rate (Luo et al., 2022). Long-term capital gains, which are gains from the sale of cryptocurrencies held for 36 months or more, are subject to tax at a lower rate of 30%. Crypto-investors and traders in India must keep accurate records of their transactions, including the purchase price, sale price, and associated fees or expenses (Ding et al., 2022). They must also report cryptocurrency gains on their income tax returns. Additionally, in March 2020, the Supreme Court of India overturned a ban on cryptocurrency trading by the RBI, which had previously prevented banks from providing services to cryptocurrency businesses. Since then, the Indian government has been exploring the regulation of cryptocurrencies in the country, including the possibility of introducing a specific tax framework for cryptocurrencies. Generally, the taxation of Cryptocurrency in India is still evolving, and investors and traders need to stay up-to-date with the latest developments and seek professional advice (Ding et al., 2022). Initially, the Indian government's position on cryptocurrencies was one of caution. However, the government recently responded to the enormous popularity and trading volume generated by cryptocurrencies and virtual digital assets (VDAs), resulting in cryptocurrency tax regulations that distinctly outline the tax effects on digital asset management. The Finance Minister of India announced the cryptocurrency tax in the Union Budget 2022 at a flat rate of 30% on any income from the transfer of VDAs. Additionally, it was announced that another section, 194S would address how TDS would be handled if a VDA was transferred (Dadhich, Hiran, et al., 2022; Huang & Lee, 2022).

4.2 Challenges in Investing Crypto

Investing in crypto carries several risks, including capital loss, government regulations, fraud, and cyberattacks. This study names a few of them as follows:

Loss of Money: Investing in crypto can have inherent risks. As it is known fact that the crypto market is recognized for its price fluctuations, and many people have experienced losses and gains. There are some common reasons why people may incur losses in such transactions. (i) Cryptocurrencies are highly volatile, with prices capable of experiencing significant fluctuations within short periods. Sudden market shifts can lead to substantial losses if investments are not well-timed or properly managed. (ii) Insufficient understanding of the crypto market and specific projects can result in poor investment decisions. Failing to research the fundamentals, technology, team, and prospects of a cryptocurrency can lead to investing in projects with little value or potential, increasing the likelihood of losses (Le, 2021; M. Dadhich, R. Doshi, S. Mathur, R. Meena, 2021).

Unofficial Laws: Endicott College professor of financial planning Michael Collins, CFA, says that many governments haven't fully regulated the management and trading of cryptocurrencies, making it hard to know what legal and financial risks to expect. Some prominent financial analysts advocate for prohibiting cryptocurrencies in United

States and Europe. They also emphasized making a black and white legal draft to promote such transactions.

Fraud: The crypto sphere is fraught with fraud, just like any other industry that is not regulated. The lack of governing oversight of the industry left many thousands of stakeholders out of the pinch, which, in turn, caused fraud to soar. Crypto fraud encompasses various threats, from phishing attacks and Ponzi schemes to exchange hacks and market manipulation. Users must exercise caution against fake wallets, apps, and fraudulent ICOs, emphasizing the importance of utilizing reputable platforms and conducting thorough research. The risk of insider trading highlights the need for regulatory oversight and ethical standards (Jacoby et al., 2023).

Hacks: Cryptocurrency hacks can take various forms, including exploiting weaknesses in software code, conducting phishing attacks to trick users into revealing private keys or login credentials, or employing malware to compromise security. These breaches can result in the theft of users' funds, disruption of exchange operations, or manipulation of market prices. Security measures such as two-factor authentication, hardware wallets, and regular code audits are crucial to mitigate the risk of hacks and enhance the overall security of the cryptocurrency ecosystem. More than \$3.5 billion worth of Cryptocurrency was sneaked in 2021, a serious concern for the fintech market. Even though many exchanges provide private insurance, they cannot get the crypto back (Chang et al., 2022).

4.3   Could Crypto Become the New Global Currency?

Cryptocurrency, such as Bitcoin, Ethereum, and others, has gained significant attention and popularity over the past few years. However, it is still a relatively new concept, and there is much debate about whether it could become the new global currency (Quayson et al., 2021). Additionally, crypto offers fast and low-cost transactions globally. This feature is especially useful for international trade and cross-border payments, which can be time-consuming and costly with traditional banking systems. However, several challenges must be addressed before crypto becomes the new global currency. One of the main challenges is the high volatility of crypto prices, which makes it difficult to use as a stable currency for everyday transactions. Moreover, crypto adoption still faces regulatory and legal challenges in many countries, which could limit its potential as a global currency (Ren et al., 2022). Both potential advantages and significant challenges mark the prospect of cryptocurrencies becoming the new global currency. Proponents emphasize the decentralized nature, borderless transactions, financial inclusion, and reduced cryptocurrency costs. However, skeptics point to volatility, regulatory uncertainties, scalability issues, and security concerns as obstacles to widespread adoption. The realization of cryptocurrencies as a global currency hinge on addressing these challenges, regulatory developments, technological advancements, and evolving societal attitudes toward digital assets (Dadhich, Manish, Shalendra Singh Rao, Renu Sharma, 2021; Vinod Ramchandra et al., 2022).

4.4 Cryptocurrency Trading

Buying and selling cryptocurrencies via an exchange is one of the most popular ways to trade cryptocurrencies. A cryptocurrency exchange is a platform where users can buy and sell cryptocurrencies for fiat or other cryptocurrencies (Marqués et al., 2021). To buy cryptocurrencies on an exchange, the users must first create an account and verify their identity. Once the account is verified, funds can be deposited in a specific cryptocurrency at a certain price. If there is a matching sell order on the exchange, the trade will be executed, and the user will receive the Cryptocurrency in the exchange wallet (Dadhich, Pahwa, et al., 2021). To sell cryptocurrencies on an exchange, users should have the Crypto coin in their exchange wallet and can then place a sell order for them at a certain price. If there is a matching buy order on the exchange, the trade will be executed, and users will receive the fiat currency in their exchange account. It is important to note that cryptocurrency exchanges may charge fees for buying and selling cryptocurrencies, which can vary depending on the exchange and the trading volume (Robert Mwiinga, 2022). Additionally, exchanges may have different security measures and policies, so it is essential to research and choose a reputable exchange that suits your needs. Buying and selling cryptocurrencies via an exchange is a straightforward process that involves creating an account, depositing funds, placing buy or sell orders, and executing trades. However, it is important to consider the exchange's fees, security, and reputation before trading cryptocurrencies (Liu et al., 2023).

Contracts for Difference (CFD) trading on cryptocurrencies allows traders to speculate on the price movements of cryptocurrencies without owning the underlying asset. CFD allows traders to profit from the price movements of an asset without owning it. When trading CFDs on cryptocurrencies, traders can go long or short on the price movements of the underlying asset. If a trader believes that the price of Bitcoin, for example, will rise, they can open a long position on a Bitcoin CFD. If the price of Bitcoin does rise, the trader will make a profit. On the other hand, if the trader believes that the price of Bitcoin will fall, they can open a short position on a Bitcoin CFD. If the price of Bitcoin falls, the trader will make a profit. One of the advantages of CFD trading on cryptocurrencies is that traders can benefit from the high volatility of the cryptocurrency market without actually owning the underlying asset (Manish Dadhich, Manvinder Singh Pahwa, Vipin Jain, 2021). CFD trading also allows traders to use leverage, which means they can control a larger position in the market with a smaller amount of capital. It is also important to note that CFD trading on cryptocurrencies is a speculative activity involving significant risks, including losing your entire investment (Brotsis et al., 2021).

5 Limitations

While cryptocurrencies have many potential benefits, several limitations need to be considered:

Price Volatility: It's important to note that while price volatility presents opportunities for significant gains, it also carries inherent risks, including the potential for substantial losses. Therefore, it is crucial to exercise caution, conduct thorough research, and use risk management strategies when investing in cryptocurrencies.

Limited Acceptance: While cryptos are becoming more widely accepted, they are still not accepted as widely as traditional currencies. This can limit their usefulness for everyday transactions, making them less appealing to some investors. Crypto mining, necessary for creating and verifying new blocks on a blockchain, requires significant computing power and energy. This can have negative environmental impacts and contribute to climate change. Some cryptocurrencies, such as Bitcoin, have limited scalability due to their design. This can result in slow transaction times and high fees during periods of high network activity.

Scalability: Some cryptocurrencies, such as Bitcoin, face scalability challenges. As transaction volumes increase, the processing time and fees can also increase. This scalability issue limits the widespread adoption of cryptocurrencies for everyday transactions, especially during peak usage periods.

Regulatory Uncertainty: The regulatory landscape for cryptocurrencies is still evolving in many jurisdictions. The lack of consistent regulations and differing approaches can create uncertainty for businesses, investors, and users. Regulatory actions can impact the cryptocurrency market and introduce compliance challenges.

Security Concerns: While cryptocurrencies employ cryptographic techniques to secure transactions, security concerns remain. The responsibility of safeguarding private keys and ensuring cryptocurrency holdings falls on the users. Hacking incidents, phishing attacks, and vulnerabilities in exchanges or wallets have resulted in substantial losses for individuals and organizations.

Adoption and Acceptance: Although cryptocurrencies have gained popularity, their adoption is not yet widespread. They are still considered niche assets and are not universally accepted as payment. Limited acceptance by merchants and businesses can hinder cryptocurrencies' mainstream adoption and utility.

Energy Consumption: Some cryptocurrencies, such as Bitcoin, rely on energy-intensive mining processes. The mining operations require substantial computational power, contributing to significant energy consumption and environmental concerns.

Lack of Regulation: The decentralized nature of cryptocurrencies means there is limited oversight and consumer protection compared to traditional financial systems. Scams, fraudulent schemes, and market manipulation can expose investors to risks without adequate recourse.

User Experience: Cryptocurrency wallets and transactions can be complex for non-technical users. The user experience needs improvement to make cryptocurrencies more accessible and user-friendly, particularly for mainstream adoption (Leng et al., 2022).

6   Road Ahead of Cryptocurrency

The road ahead for cryptocurrencies is uncertain, but several trends and developments may shape the future of this emerging asset class.

Increased Adoption: Crypto adoption has been steadily growing over the past few years, with more businesses and individuals accepting cryptocurrencies as payment. This trend is likely to continue as more people become aware of the benefits of cryptocurrencies, including fast and low-cost transactions, global accessibility, and decentralization (Manish Dadhich; Himanshu Purohit; Ritesh Tirole; Sumit Mathur; Aman Jain, 2023).

Regulation: Governments worldwide are working to establish regulatory frameworks for cryptocurrencies to address money laundering, tax evasion, and consumer protection concerns. While regulations may slow down the growth of the cryptocurrency industry in the short term, they could also provide more legitimacy and stability to the market in the long term.

Institutional Adoption: Large financial institutions and corporations are starting to invest in cryptocurrencies and blockchain technology, which could boost the market and drive mainstream adoption. Institutional investment could also help address some of the liquidity issues and price volatility that have plagued the cryptocurrency market.

Integration with Traditional Finance: Cryptocurrency and conventional finance are starting to converge, with more companies offering cryptocurrency-related products and services, such as cryptocurrency debit cards, crypto-backed loans, and stablecoins. This integration could help bridge the gap between Cryptocurrency and the traditional finance world and make it easier for more people to use and invest in cryptocurrencies (G. K. Singh, M. Dadhich, 2021).

Technologies and Innovations: Cryptocurrency is a rapidly evolving industry, and new technologies and innovations that could transform the market are constantly being developed. For example, advancements in blockchain technology could improve scalability and reduce transaction costs, while new cryptocurrency projects could offer unique features and use cases (Aggarwal et al., 2019).

Thus, the future of Cryptocurrency is uncertain, but several trends and developments could shape the industry in the coming years. Increased adoption, regulation, institutional investment, integration with traditional finance, and new technologies and innovations are all factors to watch as the cryptocurrency market evolves. The result of the study was somewhat similar to previous research (Abdollahi et al., 2022; Dadhich, Rao, et al., 2021; Golovianko et al., 2023). The outcomes of the study are anticipated to offer valuable insights into the transformative impact of decentralized cryptocurrencies on the financial landscape, which is aligned with Detailed insights into the influence of digital currencies on traditional financial markets. The study may reveal patterns of market capitalization, volatility trends, and the evolving role of decentralized finance (DeFi) in shaping investment strategies and market behavior. The study also identified challenges and opportunities associated with the decentralized disruptive crypto landscape. This could include obstacles to adoption, potential regulatory hurdles, and the innovative potential of decentralized technologies in addressing financial needs.

7   Conclusion

The decentralized and disruptive nature of the crypto landscape is undeniably reshaping the traditional financial paradigm. Digital currencies, with their decentralized blockchain technology, challenge the existing systems by providing increased transparency, reducing reliance on intermediaries, and facilitating borderless transactions. While traditional financial systems have long been entrenched, the rise of cryptocurrencies highlights the potential for a more inclusive and efficient global financial infrastructure. However, challenges such as regulatory uncertainties, scalability issues, and the need for broader societal acceptance underscore the ongoing evolution required to integrate digital currencies fully into the financial mainstream. The comparison of results between decentralized cryptocurrencies and existing systems reveals both the transformative promise and the need for continued innovation and adaptation in the ever-changing finance landscape. Cryptocurrency has been associated with the issue of black money, as it has been used for illicit activities such as money laundering, tax dodging, and illegal communication. This is because cryptocurrency transactions are often anonymous and difficult to trace, making them attractive to those seeking to conceal their financial activities. However, it is essential to note that Cryptocurrency is not inherently illicit, and most cryptocurrency transactions are legitimate. In fact, many legitimate businesses and individuals use Cryptocurrency for payment or investment. To address the issue of black money, many countries have implemented regulations to ensure that cryptocurrency exchanges and transactions are subject to the same anti-money laundering (AML) and KYC regulations as traditional financial institutions. This has helped to increase transparency and reduce the use of Cryptocurrency for illicit activities. Eventually, while Cryptocurrency may have been used for illicit activities in the past, it is essential to recognize that it has the potential to be a legitimate and valuable tool in the financial system if proper regulations and safeguards are put in place.

References

Abdollahi, A., Sadeghvaziri, F., Rejeb, A.: Exploring the role of blockchain technology in value creation: a multiple case study approach. Qual. Quant. 2, 1–25 (2022)

Aggarwal, S., Chaudhary, R., Aujla, G.S., Kumar, N., Choo, K.K.R., Zomaya, A.Y.: Blockchain for smart communities: applications, challenges and opportunities. J. Network Comput. Appl. 144, 13–48 (2019). https://doi.org/10.1016/j.jnca

Babu, E.S., Rao, M.S., Swain, G., Nikhath, A.K., Kaluri, R.: Fog-Sec: secure end-to-end communication in fog-enabled IoT network using permissioned blockchain system. Int. J. Network Manage 33(5), 1–15 (2023). https://doi.org/10.1002/nem.2248

Brotsis, S., Limniotis, K., Bendiab, G., Kolokotronis, N., Shiaeles, S.: On the suitability of blockchain platforms for IoT applications: architectures, security, privacy, and performance. Comput. Networks 191, 1–29 (2021). https://doi.org/10.1016/j.comnet.2021.108005

Chang, V., Minh, L., Doan, T., Di, A., Sun, Z.: Digital payment fraud detection methods in digital ages and industry 4.0. Comput. Electr. Eng. 100(December 2021), 107734 (2022). https://doi.org/10.1016/j.compeleceng.2022.107734

Croutzet, A., Dabbous, A.: Do fintech trigger renewable energy use? Evidence from OECD countries. Renewable Energy 179, 1608–1617 (2021). https://doi.org/10.1016/j.renene.2021.07.144

Dadhich, M., Singh Rao, S., Sharma, R., Meena, R.: Analytical study of stochastic trends of non-performing assets of public and private commercial banks in India. In: 2021 3rd International Conference on Advances in Computing, Communication Control and Networking (ICACCCN) Analytical, pp. 71–76 (2021). https://doi.org/10.1109/ICAC3N53548.2021.9725463

Dadhich, M., Doshi, R., Rao, S.S., Sharma, R.: Estimating and predicting models using stochastic time series ARIMA modeling in emergent economy. In: Kumar, R., Ahn, C.W., Sharma, T.K., Verma, O.P., Agarwal, A. (eds.) Soft Computing: Theories and Applications, pp. 295–305. Springer, Singapore (2022). https://doi.org/10.1007/978-981-19-0707-4_28

Dadhich, M., Hiran, K.K., Rao, S.S., Sharma, R.: Impact of COVID-19 on teaching-learning perception of faculties and students of higher education in Indian purview. J. Mobile Multimedia 18(4), 957–980 (2022). https://doi.org/10.13052/jmm1550-4646.1841

Dadhich, M., Pahwa, M.S., Goswami, S., Rao, S.S.: Analytical study of financial wellbeing of selected public and private sector banks: a CAMEL approach. In: 2021 IEEE International Conference on Emerging Trends in Industry 4.0, ETI 4.0 2021, pp. 1–6 (2021). https://doi.org/10.1109/ETI4.051663.2021.9619424

Dadhich, M., Poddar, S., Hiran, K.K.: Antecedents and consequences of patients' adoption of the IoT 4.0 for e-health management system: a novel PLS-SEM approach. Smart Health 25, 100300 (2022). https://doi.org/10.1016/j.smhl.2022.100300

Dadhich, M., Rao, S.S., Sethy, S., Sharma, R.: Determining the factors influencing cloud computing implementation in library management system (LMS): a high order PLS-ANN Approach. Library Philosophy and Practice, 6281 (2021). https://digitalcommons.unl.edu/libphilprac/6281

Ding, N., Leilei, G., Peng, Y.: Fintech, financial constraints and innovation: evidence from China. J. Corp. Finan. 73, 102194 (2022). https://doi.org/10.1016/j.jcorpfin.2022.102194

Babu, E.S., Barthwal, A., Kaluri, R.: Sec-edge: trusted blockchain system for enabling the identification and authentication of edge based 5G networks. Comput. Commun. 199(1), 10–29 (2023)

Singh, G.K., Dadhich, M., Chouhan, V., Sharma, A.: Impact of big data analytics & capabilities on supply chain management (SCM) - an analysis of Indian cement industry. In: 3rd International Conference on Advances in Computing, Communication Control and Networking (ICAC3N), Greater Noida, India, pp. 313–318 (2021). https://doi.org/10.1109/ICAC3N53548.2021.9725531

Dadhich, M., Singh, G.K.: Assessment of multidimensional drivers of blockchain technology (BoT) in sustainable supply chain management (SSCM) of Indian cement industry: a novel PLS-SEM approach. Int. J. Logistics Syst. Manage. 1(1), 1 (2022). https://doi.org/10.1504/IJLSM.2022.10045308

Golovianko, M., Terziyan, V., Branytskyi, V., Malyk, D.: Industry 4.0 vs. industry 5.0: co-existence, transition, or a hybrid. Procedia Comput. Sci. 217, 102–113 (2023). https://doi.org/10.1016/j.procs.2022.12.206

Huang, S.Y.B.., Lee, C.J.: Predicting continuance intention to fintech chatbot. Comput. Hum. Behav. 129, 107027 (2022). https://doi.org/10.1016/j.chb.2021.107027

Jacoby, G., Liao, C., Xiaomeng, L., Wan, F.: The effect of fraud experience on investment behavior. Emerg. Markets Rev. 55, 101007 (2023). https://doi.org/10.1016/j.ememar.2023.101007

Kappert, N., Karger, E., Kureljusic, M.: Quantum computing – the impending end for the blockchain? In: PACIS 2021 Proceedings, June, pp. 1–14 (2021)

Kouam, J.C., Asongu, S.A.: Effects of taxation on social innovation and implications for achieving sustainable development goals in developing countries: a literature review. Int. J. Innov. Stud. 6(4), 259–275 (2022). https://doi.org/10.1016/j.ijis.2022.08.002

Krishnapriya, S., Sarath, G.: Securing land registration using blockchain. Procedia Comput. Sci. 171, 1708–1715 (2020). https://doi.org/10.1016/j.procs.2020.04.183(2020)

Le, M.T.H.: Examining factors that boost intention and loyalty to use fintech post-COVID-19 lockdown as a new normal behavior. Heliyon **7**(8), e07821 (2021). https://doi.org/10.1016/j. heliyon.2021.e07821

Leng, J., et al.: Industry 5.0: prospect and retrospect. J. Manuf. Syst. **65**, 279–295 (2022). https:// doi.org/10.1016/j.jmsy.2022.09.017

Li, C., Yinsong, X., Tang, J., Liu, W.: Quantum blockchain: a decentralized, encrypted and distributed database based on quantum mechanics. J. Quantum Comput. **1**(2), 49–63 (2019). https://doi.org/10.32604/jqc.2019.06715

Liu, Y., Li, Z., Nekhili, R., Sultan, J.: Forecasting cryptocurrency returns with machine learning. Res. Int. Bus. Finan. **64**, 101905 (2023). https://doi.org/10.1016/j.ribaf.2023.101905

Luo, S., Sun, Y., Yang, F., Zhou, G.: Does fintech innovation promote enterprise transformation? Evidence from China. Technol. Soc. **68**, 101821 (2022). https://doi.org/10.1016/j.techsoc.2021. 101821

Dadhich, M., Doshi, R., Mathur, S., Meena, R.K., Gujral, P.D.: Empirical study of awareness towards blended e-learning gateways during COVID-19 lockdown. In: 2021 International Conference on Computing, Communication and Green Engineering (CCGE), Pune, India, pp. 1–6 (2021). https://doi.org/10.1109/CCGE50943.2021.9776386

Baritha Begum, M., Deepa, N., Uddin, M., Kaluri, R., Abdelhaq, M., Alsaqour, R.: An efficient and secure compression technique for data protection using burrows-wheeler transform algorithm. Heliyon **9**(1), 1–20 (2023)

Dadhich, M., Pahwa, M.S., Jain, V., Doshi, R.: Predictive models for stock market index using stochastic time series ARIMA modeling in emerging economy. In: Manik, G., Kalia, S., Sahoo, S.K., Sharma, T.K., Verma, O.P. (eds.) Advances in Mechanical Engineering: Select Proceedings of CAMSE 2020, pp. 281–290. Springer Singapore, Singapore (2021). https://doi.org/10. 1007/978-981-16-0942-8_26

Dadhich, M., Purohit, H., Tirole, R., Mathur, S., Jain, A.: Industry 40 revolution towards a future-ready society and manufacturing excellence. AIP Conference Proceedings **2521**, 040026 (2023). https://doi.org/10.1063/5.0113614

Marqués, J.M., et al.: Policy report on fintech data gaps. Latin Am. J. Central Bank. **2**(3), 100037 (2021). https://doi.org/10.1016/j.latcb.2021.100037

Milian, E.Z., de Mauro, M., Spinola de Carvalho, M.M.: Fintechs: a literature review and research agenda. Electron. Commer. Res. Appl. **34**, 100833 (2019). https://doi.org/10.1016/j.elerap. 2019.100833

Pahwa, M.S., Dadhich, M., Saini, J.S., Saini, D.K.: Use of artificial intelligence (AI) in the optimization of production of biodiesel energy. In: Vyas, A.K., Balamurugan, S., Hiran, K.K., Dhiman, H.S. (eds.) Artificial Intelligence for Renewable Energy Systems, pp. 229–238. Wiley (2022). https://doi.org/10.1002/9781119761686.ch11

Patel, A., Ajaykumar Kethavath, N.L., Kushwaha, A.N., Jagadale, M., Sheetal, K.R., Renjith, P.S.: Review of artificial intelligence and internet of things technologies in land and water management research during 1991–2021: a bibliometric analysis. Eng. Appl. Artif. Intell. **123**, 106335 (2023). https://doi.org/10.1016/j.engappai.2023.106335

Purohit, H., Dadhich, M., Ajmera, P.K.: Analytical study on users' awareness and acceptability towards adoption of multimodal biometrics (MMB) mechanism in online transactions: a two-stage SEM-ANN approach. Multimedia Tools Appl. **82**(9), 14239–14263 (2022). https://doi. org/10.1007/s11042-022-13786-z

Quayson, M., Bai, C., Sarkis, J.: Technology for social good foundations: a perspective from the smallholder farmer in sustainable supply chains. IEEE Trans. Eng. Manage. **68**(3), 894–898 (2021). https://doi.org/10.1109/TEM.2020.2996003

Ren, Y.S., Ma, C.Q., Kong, X.L., Baltas, K., Zureigat, Q.: Past, present, and future of the application of machine learning in cryptocurrency research. Res. Int. Bus. Finan. **63**, 101799 (2022). https:// doi.org/10.1016/j.ribaf.2022.101799

Mwiinga, R., Dadhich, M.: Empirical investigation of the drivers of 5G and the mediating role of users' attitudes to achieving word of mouth and willingness: a case study of the microfinance institutions of Zambia. 5G, Cybersecurity and Privacy in Developing Countries, p. 22. River Publishers (2022). https://doi.org/10.1201/9781003374664

Rodenburg, B., Pappas, S.P.: Blockchain and quantum computing. Mitre Technical Report (Issue December) (2017). https://doi.org/10.13140/RG.2.2.29449.13923

Schulz, K., Feist, M.: Leveraging blockchain technology for innovative climate finance under the green climate fund. Earth Syst. Gov. 7, 100084 (2021). https://doi.org/10.1016/j.esg.2020. 100084

Shrimali, B., Patel, H.B.: Blockchain state-of-the-art: architecture, use cases, consensus, challenges and opportunities. J. King Saud Univ. Comput. Inf. Sci. 34(9), 6793–6807 (2022). https://doi.org/10.1016/j.jksuci.2021.08.005

Ramchandra, M.V., Kumar, K., Sarkar, A., Kr, S., Mukherjee, K.A.: Assessment of the impact of blockchain technology in the banking industry. Mater. Today Proc. 56, 2221–2226 (2022). https://doi.org/10.1016/j.matpr.2021.11.554

Multiplatform Mobile App for Multilingual OCR Based Translator for Tamil (MMOT)

Pooja Ramesh, S. Rahul Kumar, Kumar Rishi, and Vallidevi Krishnamurthy[(✉)]

School of Computer Science and Engineering, Vellore Institute of Technology, Chennai, India
{pooja.ramesh2020,rahulkumar.s2020,
kumar.rishi2020}@vitstudent.ac.in, vallidevi.k@vit.ac.in

Abstract. In an increasingly interconnected world, language barriers can pose significant challenges for communication and cultural understanding. This is particularly true for tourists from revolving around Tamil region, who may find it difficult to communicate with people in other parts of India or abroad. To address this issue, we have developed a Multiplatform application (Eke et al. 2019) using Kotlin (Moskala et al. 2017) that uses machine learning to identify text in images and translate it to Tamil (Nedumaran et al. 2009). The app leverages the power of the Google ML Kit and the Google Translate API to provide accurate and reliable translations in real-time. It is designed to be user-friendly and intuitive, with various features that make it a valuable tool for tourists and anyone who needs to communicate with Tamil speakers or understand written Tamil text. Additionally, the app includes the ability to change its language to Tamil and uses a 3rd party library for taking pictures either from the gallery or camera, with editing capabilities. The app was evaluated through testing with a group of users and in a hackathon, where it demonstrated its effectiveness in translating text to Tamil. The motive behind choosing this project was to help Tamil oriented people freely roam and experience cultures without feeling any language barrier. In this paper, we describe the design and development of the application, discuss our methodology for evaluating its performance, and present our results and future work.

Keywords: Language barriers · Cultural understanding · Machine learning

1 Introduction

The world today is becoming increasingly interconnected, and people are more mobile than ever before. As people travel to various parts of the world, they often encounter language barriers, which can be a significant hindrance to their ability to communicate and understand the cultures they encounter. This problem is particularly acute for tourists from revolving around Tamil region, who may find it difficult to communicate with people in other parts of India or abroad. To help address this issue, we have developed a Multiplatform application that uses machine learning to identify text in images and translate it to Tamil. To produce precise and trustworthy translations in real-time, the programme makes use of machine learning and natural language processing. It uses the

© The Author(s), under exclusive license to Springer Nature Switzerland AG 2024
S. Rajagopal et al (Eds.): ASCIS 2023, CCIS 2040, pp. 283–295, 2024.
https://doi.org/10.1007/978-3-031-59107-5_19

Google ML Kit, a ready-to-use machine learning SDK, to identify text in images captured using the device's camera or selected from the device's gallery. The identified text is then passed through the Google Translate API, which then translates it into Tamil. The app supports many popular languages, including Hindi (Khakare et al. 2021), English, Gujarati, Marathi, German, and French.

The app is designed to be user-friendly and intuitive, with a simple and easy-to-use interface that allows users to quickly capture or select images and receive translations in Tamil. These features make the app a valuable tool for tourists from Tamil region, as well as for anyone who needs to communicate with Tamil speakers or understand written Tamil text. For this project, some related works in the market are also there where Optical Character Recognition (OCR) technology (Selvakanmani et al. 2020) has been widely used in various applications to extract text from images and documents. Many OCR applications have been implemented on Applications, which leverages the power of ML and natural language processing to provide accurate and reliable text recognition. Some of the examples are Google ML SDK itself, CamScanner, Adobe PDF Scanner, there are several examples that have been thoroughly described.

One example is Google's ML Kit, which provides a set of tools for implementing machine learning on Android and iOS devices. The ML Kit includes an OCR feature that allows developers to easily integrate text recognition into their Mobile applications. The ML Kit's OCR feature is easy to use and provides accurate text recognition for a wide range of languages. Another example of an OCR implementation on Android is CamScanner, a popular document scanning app that includes OCR capabilities. CamScanner uses OCR technology to extract text from scanned documents and images, allowing users to easily convert scanned pages into editable text.

There are few more that have OCR integrated. One popular OCR application is Adobe Acrobat's OCR feature, which uses advanced recognition technology to accurately extract text from scanned documents and images. The OCR recognition process accounts for language and structure and corrects words that it sees as being spelled incorrectly. Its spell-checking technology allows for the most accurate information to be conveyed to users. Another popular OCR operation is Nanonets, an AI- grounded OCR software that automates data capture for intelligent document processing of checks, bills, ID cards, and more. Nanonets uses advanced OCR, machine literacy image processing, and Deep Learning (Singh et al. 2020) to prize relevant information from unshaped data. It is fast, accurate, easy to use, and allows druggies to make custom models for their specific requirements.

In comparison to these existing OCR applications, our proposed app offers several advantages. Firstly, it is specifically designed to extract text from images and translate it to Tamil, making it a valuable tool for Tamil-speaking tourists. Secondly, it leverages the power of the Google ML Kit and Google Translate API to provide accurate and reliable translations in real-time. Finally, it is designed to be user-friendly and intuitive, with distinct features that make it easy to use. In comparison to these existing OCR implementations on Mobile App (Zhou et al. 2008), Our suggested mobile app has various advantages. To begin with, it is particularly developed to extract text from photographs and translate them into Tamil, making it a useful tool for Tamil-speaking tourists. Second, it makes use of the Google ML Kit and Google Translate API to produce accurate and trustworthy real-time translations. Lastly, it is user-friendly and straightforward, with various capabilities that make it simple and convenient to use. The app is constantly being updated and improved, with new features and enhancements being added regularly to improve its performance and usability.

2 Literature Survey

While both our research and (Chigali et al. 2020)'s app share the goal of extracting and translating text from images, the approaches differ in a few key technical aspects. Our research focuses solely on Android development using Kotlin and Google's ML Kit for optical character recognition. This provides tight integration with Android APIs for selecting images and leveraging on-device machine learning models. In contrast, (Chigali et al. 2020) built a cross-platform app using Flutter and relied on the open source Tesseract OCR engine. A Flutter implementation allows for iOS support in addition to Android. However, it may lack some of the performance and optimization benefits of a native Android app. Both utilize Google Translate for text translation. In summary, our research prioritizes an Android-first implementation leveraging Google ML Kit, while they focus on cross-platform support even if it meant using an open source OCR engine. These represent tradeoffs between native platform optimization and portability. The rapid growth of mobile devices and networks around the world is creating new opportunities and challenges for supporting content in local languages such as Tamil. Nedumaran et al. 2009 provides an overview of Tamil content delivery on mobile platforms, focusing on delivery methods, device support, and case studies. Short Message Service (SMS) has limitations in supporting Tamil text due to the 160 character limit per message, but notes that concatenation and compression methods can help. For richer content delivery, mobile data networks like GPRS and 3G provide more flexibility. The Sellinam system developed by the authors uses a mix of SMS and mobile data access. Major device vendors like Nokia and Samsung have started incorporating Indian language capabilities into low-end models. For advanced smartphones that lack native Tamil support, the Sellinam application implements its own Tamil rendering using Java ME.

Optical character recognition (OCR) of handwritten Devanagari script is an active research area given the diversity of writing styles. Khakare et al. 2021 provides an overview of deep learning techniques for Devanagari OCR. The biggest challenges include the diversity of writing styles and the need for large datasets. Khakare et al. 2021 proposes a system architecture with stages for preprocessing, segmentation, feature extraction, and recognition. They evaluated several CNN architectures and found that Inception V1 provides high accuracy without requiring as much computational effort as VGG. Transfer learning aims to enable training with fewer samples. Rohira et al. 2019 presents a mobile application for optical character recognition (OCR) and translation of text in images. It helps travelers understand foreign language texts by recognizing and translating words in real-time. The authors provide background information on the challenges of interpreting unfamiliar signs, customs, and characters when traveling abroad. The proposed system architecture includes image processing, character recognition using a convolutional neural network (CNN), and a translation API. The CNN layers used include convolutional layers, ReLU activation layers, max pooling layers, and fully connected layers. The results demonstrate that images with text can be captured, characters recognized, and translated into the language of your choice in real time on a mobile device. An accessible user interface allows you to select source images and target language from drop-down menus.

Oliveira et al. 2020 uses a mixed methods study to investigate the adoption of Kotlin for Android development. Kotlin was announced as an officially supported language by Google in 2017. The authors conduct a qualitative analysis of his Stack Overflow posts using topic modeling to uncover common problems that developers face with Kotlin. We also conducted semi-structured interviews with Android developers about their experiences implementing Kotlin. Key findings indicate developers find Kotlin concise, null-safe, and interoperable with Java which aids adoption. However, developers face challenges with optional types, tooling, and overuse of functional programming idioms. The paper provides an empirical assessment of Kotlin's adoption tradeoffs on Android, highlighting benefits like conciseness and interoperability as well as pitfalls around null-safety and functional programming usage. The mixed-methods approach combines social Q&A data with developer interviews to evaluate a new language. Gromov et al. 2021 describes integrating Kotlin multiplatform projects with Swift Package Manager dependencies. Kotlin Multiplatform provides a cross-platform development approach that allows you to reuse code across mobile, web, and desktop. Apple platforms currently use CocoaPods for dependency management. However, Swift Package Manager is becoming increasingly popular. The author provides an overview of current Kotlin multiplatform limitations regarding CocoaPods dependencies. They are proposing an extension to integrate Swift Package Manager dependencies into Kotlin projects and create Kotlin libraries available via Swift Packages in Xcode. Key contributions include Kotlin build logic and Gradle plugins for Swift dependency resolution, framework building, and Kotlin binding generation. This paper demonstrates the feasibility of natively supporting Swift Package Manager in Kotlin multiplatform for Apple platform development. This is expected to provide more flexibility in dependency management compared to CocoaPods. This work will contribute to the further development of Kotlin Multiplatform as a cross-platform solution.

Harizi et al. 2022 developed text recognition with convolutional neural networks (CNNs) that explores text interpretation in natural scene images. Traditional optical character recognition (OCR) methods struggle with scene text due to diverse challenges in font, scale, orientation, and imaging conditions. CNNs have emerged as superior solutions, replacing older machine learning techniques. They introduced CNNs to scene text recognition, followed by efforts focusing on character-level recognition and sequence modeling using recurrent neural networks. To address the need for large datasets, research emphasizes synthetic data generation and augmentation. Recent methods employ encoder-decoder architectures like CRNNs and attention networks, while post-processing with lexicons and language models enhances accuracy. The paper proposes a CNN-based system for character and word recognition, demonstrating superior performance on standard datasets like ICDAR 2003 and Chars74K. It concludes that CNNs, coupled with lexicons, effectively interpret scene text in challenging real-world images, suggesting future work in text detection enhancement and multi-orientation training data integration. Boros et al. 2022 investigated the impact of optical character recognition (OCR) errors on multilingual event detection in digitized historical documents. The authors evaluate two event detection approaches on datasets in six languages - an unsupervised discourse-level system (Daniel-sys) and a convolutional neural network (CNN) model. They introduce noise to simulate OCR errors and analyze how detection performance changes across noise types like blurring and character errors. Key findings show detection is more affected by dataset imbalance, annotation style, and language characteristics than OCR noise. The discourse-level system is more robust to OCR errors than the CNN model. The study provides a novel analysis of how OCR quality influences event extraction on multilingual digitized text. Ultimately, this research underscores the importance of considering various linguistic factors alongside OCR quality when developing event detection systems for digitized historical documents. By emphasizing the strengths of discourse-level approaches over neural network models in handling OCR-induced noise, this study offers valuable insights for improving multilingual event extraction from diverse, imperfect textual sources.

Kim et al. 2022 proposed an end-to-end OCR-free model for visual document understanding called Donut. Current methods rely on OCR engines to extract text from document images before understanding. Donut uses a Transformer architecture to directly map images to structured outputs without separate OCR. A simple pretraining scheme teaches the model to read text by predicting words. The model is flexible to new languages via synthetic training data generation. Experiments on document classification, information extraction, and QA tasks show Donut matches or exceeds OCR-based methods in accuracy and speed. The work demonstrates the feasibility of an OCR-free pipeline for document understanding. Removing the OCR dependency provides efficiency and flexibility gains. Extensive experimentation across document classification, information extraction, and question-answering tasks reveals that Donut achieves parity or surpasses OCR-dependent methods in both accuracy and processing speed. This pioneering work not only validates the viability of an OCR-free pipeline for document understanding but also highlights the efficiency and adaptability benefits attained by eliminating the OCR bottleneck. Hwang et al.'s 2022 developed a landscape of anything-to-text recognition (XTR) technologies in language learning research across 2011–2020. Their review, based on 48 relevant articles from scholarly databases, uncovers a predominant focus on English language learning, leveraging speech-to-text and image-to-text recognition primarily among university student participants, emphasizing listening skills. They propose an XTR framework encompassing multimedia representations, recognition accuracy, and learning effects tailored to learner needs. In a parallel vein, Kim et al. (2022) introduces 'Donut,' an innovative OCR-free model for visual document understanding. By leveraging a Transformer architecture, Donut directly processes document images to structured outputs, bypassing the drawbacks associated with OCR engines such as cost, inflexibility, and error propagation. Demonstrating superior accuracy and speed in document tasks like classification, information extraction, and question answering, Donut signifies the potential of an OCR-free approach, promising efficiency and adaptability gains while transforming document understanding pipelines. Cascianelli et al. 2022 proposed a methodology using deformable convolutions to improve handwritten text recognition (HTR) on both modern and historical documents. HTR is a challenging image understanding task that can boost digitization of handwritten texts. State-of-the-art approaches couple convolutional neural networks (CNNs) for visual feature extraction with recurrent neural networks (RNNs) for sequence modeling, and use connectionist temporal classification (CTC) for decoding (Puigcerver, 2017; Bluche & Messina, 2017). However, standard CNN kernels have fixed grids and weights, disregarding variability in shape, scale, and orientation of handwritten characters. To address this, deformable convolutions learn content-dependent, non-rigid grids that better adapt to geometric variations. After reviewing related work, the authors design CRNN and 1D-LSTM architectures using deformable convolutions and evaluate on modern (IAM, RIMES) and historical (ICFHR14, ICFHR16, Leopardi) datasets. Results show deformable convolutions consistently improve over standard convolutions, with more layers enhancing robustness to background noise. This demonstrates deformable convolutions are well-suited for HTR with free-layout and degraded historical documents.

Robby et al. 2019 implemented optical character recognition (OCR) to recognize Javanese script characters using the Tesseract OCR engine. They extracted 5880 characters from digital fonts as well as handwritten sources. They preprocessed the characters using image enhancing techniques. The dataset was trained using separate bounding boxes for main body and diacritics as well as a single bounding box. Testing was done on 780 characters from digital and handwritten sources. The highest accuracy (97.5%) was obtained by combining the training methods on the digital font test data. It was difficult to differentiate between sets of 'e' and 'i' characters. Overall, this work makes a novel contribution by creating the first public dataset of Javanese script for training OCR models. Good accuracy was obtained on the digital data, but there is a need for improvement on handwritten data. The use of more advanced deep learning methods may further boost accuracy for this challenging task of recognizing non-Latin scripts. Dhanikonda et al. 2022 proposed an efficient deep learning model called Interrelated Tagging Prototype with Segmentation for Telugu Text Recognition (ITP-STTR) for optical character recognition of Telugu text. They collected a dataset of Telugu characters including vowels, consonants and modifiers. The images were pre-processed and segmented into sub-images for feature extraction. They built a CNN model with convolution, pooling and fully connected layers to perform character recognition. He proposed model achieved the highest accuracy (97.5%) compared to the existing methods. Key contributions of this paper include the creation of an annotated set of Telugu text datasets, application of segmentation techniques for improved feature learning, and the demonstration of high-accuracy OCR for a difficult non-Latin script, although good results were obtained on printed data, the applicability of the model can be improved by extending it to handwritten text. All in all, this paper makes significant progress in OCR for Indian languages using deep learning.

Ma et al. 2022 proposed a novel text translation enhanced end-to-end text image translation model. The researchers curated synthetic and real-world datasets for text image translation in three language pairs: English-Chinese, English-German, and Chinese-English. The model comprises a spatial transformer image encoder, a text embedding encoder, a shared transformer encoder-decoder, and task-specific decoders. To leverage large-scale text parallel corpus, multi-task learning is employed with machine translation as an auxiliary task. The optimization is further enhanced through joint multi-task learning with optical character recognition. Through extensive experiments, the proposed method demonstrates superior performance compared to existing end-to-end models by effectively incorporating external data. Notably, it outperforms cascade models in terms of accuracy, parameters, and speed. The key contributions include leveraging easily accessible translation data, highlighting the complementarity of translation and recognition tasks, and advancing the state-of-the-art in low-resource text image translation. Potential future directions involve extending the model to multi-lingual translation and incorporating visual context. Qaroush et al. 2022 proposed an omnifont printed Arabic character recognition method using explicit segmentation and convolutional neural networks. They developed a hybrid segmentation approach using projection profiles, connected components, and baseline removal to handle overlapping characters. The method achieved 95% segmentation accuracy on the APTID-MF dataset covering 10 fonts. The extracted segments were then input to a LeNet-5 CNN for feature extraction and classification. With the incorporation of data augmentation, the CNN achieved an impressive recognition accuracy of 99.97%. Notably, the overall approach achieved a recognition accuracy of 95% without relying on font recognition or post-processing. This work contributes significantly to Arabic Optical Character Recognition (OCR) by introducing an effective segmentation technique and showcasing the application of deep learning for omnifont recognition. Future research could aim at refining segmentation techniques and exploring more advanced deep neural networks.

3 Methodology

In this section, we describe the methodology used to develop our App application for extracting and translating text from images to Tamil. Our approach involved using Kotlin, a contemporary programming language for Multiplatform development, and the Google ML Kit framework.

Kotlin was chosen as the programming language for our application due to its conciseness, safety, and interoperability with Java. Kotlin's concise syntax allows developers to write more readable and maintainable code, while its safety features help prevent common programming mistakes such as null pointer exceptions. Additionally, Kotlin's interoperability with Java allows developers to use existing Java libraries and frameworks in their Kotlin code. The Google ML Kit framework was chosen for its powerful machine learning capabilities and ease of use. The ML Kit provides a set of ready-to-use machine learning models that can be easily integrated into Mobile applications. These models include text recognition, language identification, and translation, among others.

MMOT allows users to capture images using the device's camera or select images from the device's gallery. Once an image has been selected, the ML Kit's text recognition model is used to identify any text within the image. The improved feature is the moment we click or select pictures, there is no extra option for extraction after selection of image, it will automatically scan and give the extracted text, then for the identified text is then passed to the Language Identifier model to determine its language. Once the language of the text has been identified, it is provided to the Google Translate model for translation to Tamil. The Google Translate model supports translations from a wide variety of languages and provides accurate and reliable translations in real-time.

Figure 1 depicts the architecture diagram of MMOT. The mobile app initializes necessary variables and objects like binding, identifiers, flags, progress dialogs, and text

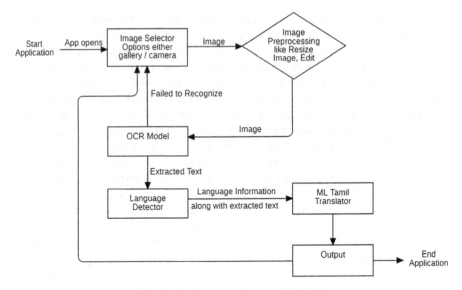

Fig. 1. Architecture diagram of MMOT

recognizers for basic OCR functionality. The content view is set using binding to link layout instances. A toggle button allows switching the UI text between languages. When the add image button is clicked, an input dialog gives options to select an image from camera or gallery which is then automatically extracted into the recognize text field using OCR. Clicking translate gets the recognized text, detects the language using LanguageIdentification, and sets a flag if Hindi is found to trigger devanagari scripts. For Hindi, the text is translated to Tamil using a HindiToEnglishTranslator object. Otherwise, TranslatorOptions are created to specify source and target languages and initialize a Translation object, downloading models if needed. The Translation object's translate() method is then used on the recognized text to output translated text to the translated text field. This overall workflow allows multilingual image-based text extraction and translation in the mobile app. To evaluate the performance of our application, we conducted user testing with a group of various language pictures in the hackathon. We were asked to use the app to capture or select images containing text in various languages and evaluate the accuracy and reliability of the translations provided by the app. We tested the application's performance on a dataset of 20 photos with text in various languages. We carefully checked the correctness of the translations offered by the programme and discovered that 18 of the 20 photos were correctly translated.

Overall, MMOT methodology involved using contemporary tools and technologies such as Kotlin and the Google ML Kit to develop a Mobile application that leverages the power of machine learning to extract and translate text from images to Tamil. Our approach was validated through user testing, which demonstrated the effectiveness of our app in providing accurate and reliable translations.

Table 1. A brief comparison with existing product features and MMOT

S. No	App or Model	Features they have	Accuracy**	Feature Difference
1	Cam Scanner or Adobe Scan	Scanning the various type of image and converting to pdf	Only for scanning - −20%	Unlike Cam Scanner Our App provide the feature of extracting the text from the images, however in selecting image they provide filtering also including edits, while our app provides only edit option to recognize the text in a best manner
2	Google Lens	Complete Web based actions, in the app we can click pictures and rest whatever we want from picture it is redirecting us to google platform, however they provide the feature of scanning and extracting the image at once only	For Scanning – 0 For translating to Tamil - +20%	Unlike Lens, our app can extract the text and translate within the app itself

** *The higher the accuracy value, the better our goods. Negative accuracy implies that the relevant product outperforms our product in a certain attribute, and its value indicates how big of a difference there is.*
0 indicates there were equal.

4 Results and Discussion

In Table 1, Accuracy is being defined as

$$A = \left(\frac{n1}{t1}\right)$$

A = Accuracy.
n1 = No of pictures got corrected for the activity, t1 = No. Of Images gathered

$$A_{diff} = \left(\frac{(A_{mmot} - A_{com})}{A_{com}}\right) \cdot 100$$

A_{com} = Accuracy of compared product, A_{mmot} = Accuracy of our product, A_{diff} = Difference in Accuracy.
*On an average 10 photos have been observed (Fig. 2).

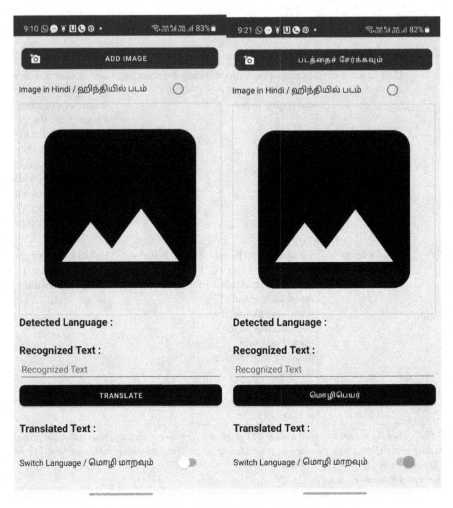

Fig. 2. (a)&(b) Design of Main UI (User Interface) of the App

Our evaluation results demonstrate that the application performs well in identifying text in images and translating it to Tamil. However, there is still room for improvement, particularly in terms of accuracy in low-quality images or complex scripts. One approach to improving accuracy would be to switch to an online version of the Google ML Kit, which may provide more up-to-date and accurate models (Figs. 3 and 4).

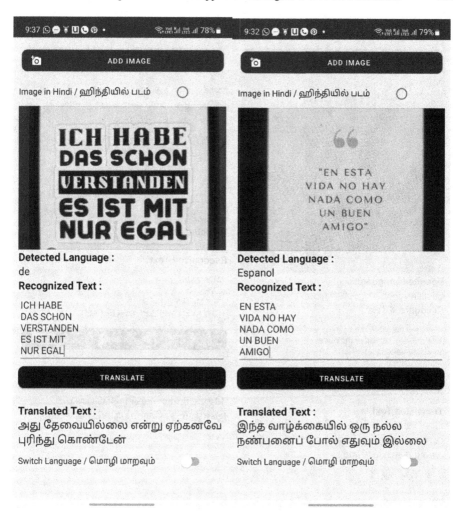

Fig. 3. (a) Translation from German to Tamil (b) Translation from Spanish to Tamil

Another potential area for improvement is the user interface of the application. While we designed the application with simplicity in mind, it may be useful to conduct user testing to identify any areas for improvement or features that users may find helpful.

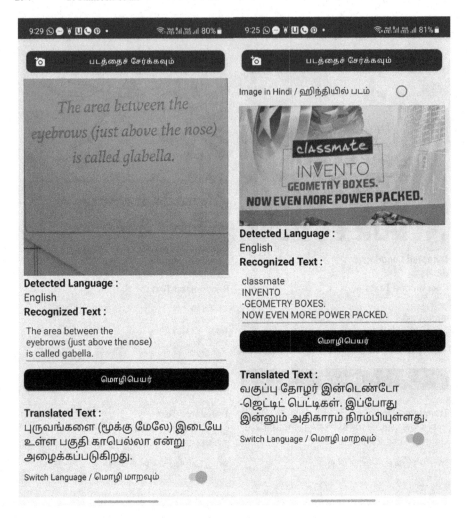

Fig. 4. (a)&(b) Translation from English to Tamil

5   Conclusion

The application provides a simple and effective way for Tamil-speaking tourists to translate text from various languages into Tamil. The use of Google ML Kit's pre-trained models and SDK allowed for a streamlined development process. Future work includes improving the accuracy of the application in low light conditions, as well as expanding the number of supported languages. Additionally, incorporating user feedback would be beneficial in improving the overall user experience. Overall, this application demonstrates the potential for machine learning to facilitate communication and access to information in diverse language settings.

References

Chigali, N., Bobba, S.R., Vani, K.S., Rajeswari, S.: OCR assisted translator. In: 2020 7th International Conference on Smart Structures and Systems (ICSSS), pp. 1–4. IEEE, July 2020

Nedumaran, M.: Tamil on mobile devices. In: Conference Papers, p. 187 (2009)

Khakare, R.S., Lomte, V.M., Pawar, R.N., Makawne, R.T., Pawar, S.N.: Survey on Devanagari character recognition using deep learning techniques (2021)

Rohira, A., Shah, R., Sadarangani, O., Shinde, M., Therese, S.: Word detection and translation. In: 2nd International Conference on Advances in Science & Technology (ICAST), April 2019

Selvakanmani, S., Chandrashekar, T., Federick, N.D., Jaffar, A.M.: Optical character recognition based text analyser: a case study (2020)

Zhou, S.Z., Gilani, S.O., Winkler, S.: Open-source OCR framework using mobile devices. In: Multimedia on Mobile Devices 2008, vol. 6821, pp. 30–35. SPIE, February 2008

Moskala, M., Wojda, I.: Android Development with Kotlin. Packt Publishing Ltd. (2017)

Oliveira, V., Teixeira, L., Ebert, F.: On the adoption of Kotlin on android development: a triangulation study. In: 2020 IEEE 27th International Conference on Software Analysis, Evolution and Reengineering (SANER), pp. 206–216. IEEE, February 2020

Gromov, P., Chernyshev, Y.: Integration of Kotlin multiplatform projects with swift package manager dependencies. In: Conference of Open Innovations Association, FRUCT, no. 29, pp. 451–454. FRUCT Oy (2021)

Eke, D.: Design and development of a multi-platform software development kit of a mobile medical device (2019)

Singh, A., Bhadani, R.: Mobile Deep Learning with TensorFlow Lite, ML Kit and Flutter: Build Scalable Real-World Projects To Implement End-to-End Neural Networks on Android and iOS. Packt Publishing Ltd. (2020)

Harizi, R., Walha, R., Drira, F., Zaied, M.: Convolutional neural network with joint stepwise character/word modeling based system for scene text recognition. Multimedia Tools Appl., 1–16 (2022)

Boros, E., Nguyen, N.K., Lejeune, G., Doucet, A.: Assessing the impact of OCR noise on multilingual event detection over digitised documents. Int. J. Digit. Libr.Libr. 23(3), 241–266 (2022)

Kim, G., et al.: OCR-free document understanding transformer. In: Avidan, S., Brostow, G., Cissé, M., Farinella, G.M., Hassner, T. (eds) ECCV 2022. LNCS, vol. 13688, pp. 498–517. Springer, Cham (2022). https://doi.org/10.1007/978-3-031-19815-1_29

Hwang, W.Y., Nguyen, V.G., Purba, S.W.D.: Systematic survey of anything-to-text recognition and constructing its framework in language learning. Educ. Inf. Technol. 27(9), 12273–12299 (2022)

Cascianelli, S., Cornia, M., Baraldi, L., Cucchiara, R.: Boosting modern and historical handwritten text recognition with deformable convolutions. Int. J. Doc. Anal. Recogn. (IJDAR) 25(3), 207–217 (2022)

Robby, G.A., Tandra, A., Susanto, I., Harefa, J., Chowanda, A.: Implementation of optical character recognition using tesseract with the Javanese script target in android application. Procedia Comput. Sci. 157, 499–505 (2019)

Dhanikonda, S.R., et al.: An efficient deep learning model with interrelated tagging prototype with segmentation for telugu optical character recognition. Sci. Programm. (2022)

Ma, C., et al.: Improving end-to-end text image translation from the auxiliary text translation task. In: 2022 26th International Conference on Pattern Recognition (ICPR), pp. 1664–1670. IEEE, August 2022

Qaroush, A., Awad, A., Modallal, M., Ziq, M.: Segmentation-based, omnifont printed Arabic character recognition without font identification. J. King Saud Univ.-Comput. Inf. Sci. 34(6), 3025–3039 (2022)

Analyzing EEG Signals While Doing Various Psychological Tasks

T. Manoj Prasath$^{(\boxtimes)}$ and R. Vasuki

Department of Biomedical Engineering, Bharath Institute of Higher Education and Research,
Chennai 73, India
mprasath.t@gmail.com, hod.bme@bharathuniv.ac.in

Abstract. Stress is becoming a threat to a person's prosperity regardless of how old they are. The current way of life has made life so miserable that both mental and physical health is destroyed. Each of these have been seen as benefiting from yoga, which is also widely believed to be a method for reducing stress. We looked explored how the Electroencephalogram (EEG) responded to intensive, high-impact yoga with low power after finishing a mental activity while paying attention to sound in order to gauge the recovery effect of severe yoga on the EEG. When mentally calculating numbers or possibly paying attention to a 5 kHz unpleasant tone, the low-alpha wave's average sufficiency (8–10 Hz). Particularly, the mean adequacy in the low-alpha wave demonstrated a quantitatively vast difference between resting before pressure testing and psychological number juggling while standing and listening to the 5 kHz tone. Yet, after 20 min of rigorous yoga, the low-alpha wave was stabilised; the average abundance exceeded up to 29% of the sufficiency in the before focused on relaxing. Comparable Theta wave findings were attained. However, under test settings, other EEG rhythms with higher recurrence the outcomes and progress of the various stages was done in view of the information acquired from the estimations. At long last, the general progress of the proposed calculation was assessed and the qualities and shortcomings of the picked approach were examined. The determined qualities were contrasted with those from the headband with check whether the "eSense" calculation matches techniques in view of conventional methodologies.

Keywords: EEG · yoga · mental task · stress · eSense

1 Introduction

Theta and alpha oscillations are described as small frequency bands representing the activity of multifunctional neural networks, according to current research [6]. They have varying degrees of associations with processing that is cognitive, emotive, and oriented. An electroencephalogram (EEG) is a technique for visualising the brain that captures electrical activity on the scalp's surface [1]. EEG often takes the form of scalp electrodes containing a number of sensors that are intended to adhere to the surface of the skull. When one is in a meditative state, where focused internalised attention results in an emotionally satisfying "blissful" experience, one can identify and characterise the brain

© The Author(s), under exclusive license to Springer Nature Switzerland AG 2024
S. Rajagopal et al (Eds.): ASCIS 2023, CCIS 2040, pp. 296–308, 2024.
https://doi.org/10.1007/978-3-031-59107-5_20

regions involved by measuring the EEG spectral power and coherence in the individually defined delta, theta, and alpha bands [3] (Fig. 1).

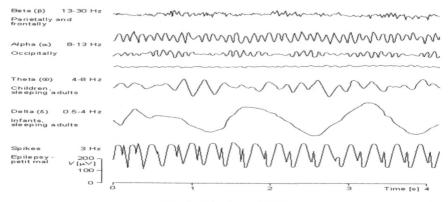

Fig. 1. Waveform of EEG

By and large as far as brain research it is said and followed that any activity or response like sharpness, tension, profound solidness, instincts, compassion, responses and recognition is because of the tangible reactions falls inside the mind from their everyday movement. Subliminal, the term begat during 18 - nineteenth is a strong memory working profound the reason for our responses. It records the occasions and act to it appropriately. This is the essential brain science. In our social living, each individual gets different mental lucidities over his everyday practice and from the general public. Wandering the steady level and their work insight, very personage has their own mental way of behaving which might reflect in their way of life as well as in wellbeing. Life examples are the essential area of realizing with regards to brain research.

It is likewise one of the essential parts of knowledge. Consideration or fixation relies upon the seeing individual and furthermore on the climate in which the subject is found. Debilitating of consideration can happen while tired, fortifying can be brought about by the innovation of the article, and the surprise of the peculiarity, creative mind consideration can be isolated into purposeful and accidental. At the point when conscious, the subject sees boosts or occasions in a deliberate manner, and a specific measure of exertion is expected to keep up with it. It partakes in two mental exercises - carefulness (the work to notice the whole perceptual field for a more drawn out time of focus) and search (the dynamic movement itself).

Furthermore, it's critical to understand that the classification process aims to be able to use particular metrics to identify the signals' origin and the variables that impact various patterns in order to model or classify the signals and include them into a BCI [17]. Any research challenge's most difficult and complicated step is choosing the measurements that will be used [6]. This information is known as features, and the extraction of these features is a current research topic [15, 16]. In many situations when a range of characteristics must be used to accomplish an efficient classification, the most popular approaches for extracting characteristics are mainly tied to time-frequency domain transformations to identify the frequency magnitudes. Further related work is described in [7], which builds a disease recognition model using deep convolution networks based on leaf image categorization. It is given in a way that places an emphasis on instruction and the strategy used to promote the use of a suitable system in actual practice. The developed model is able to distinguish between plant leaves and their surroundings and can spot different plant diseases in healthy leaves. The authors used "Google Net," which is recognized as a trustworthy deep learning architecture, to recognize various sorts of illness. Using transfer learning [8], the pre-trained model has been enhanced. Using the exact opposite of what they should be doing, it is a way for getting someone to do something. This happens in our daily lives, instigating a revolution that attacks our society through unfavorable forces. Using biological brain signals to identify human emotions is gaining popularity. A reliable and affordable tool used to assess brain activity is electroencephalography (EEG). To meet the requirements of a brain-computer interface, several procedures must be carried out sequentially in order to detect emotion using EEG signals (BCI) [9]. These procedures typically start with the removal of artifacts from the EEG signals, followed by the extraction of temporal or spectral information from the time or frequency domain of the EEG signal, respectively, and ultimately the creation of a multi-class classification approach. The emotion classification strategy's accuracy is significantly improved by feature quality. There is constant electrical activity in the brain, as shown by electrical recordings taken from the surface of the brain or even the outside of the head. The level of excitation of various brain regions brought on by sleep, waking, or brain disorders like epilepsy or even psychoses determines both the intensity and the patterns of this electrical activity. Brain waves are the oscillations in the recorded electrical potentials, and the complete record. Deep neural network (DNN) has excelled in the fields of image, audio, and natural language processing over the last several years [18–20]. With the help of successive non-linear transformations built on hierarchical representations and mapping, the features can be automatically extracted from the input data. EEG decoding based on DNN has gained popularity because of its capacity to reduce the interference of redundant information and non-linear feature extraction [9]. To ensure the robustness and generalizability of DNN, large-scale dataset support is one of the prerequisites for obtaining the desired results.

2   Literature Survey

Gannouni, S., Aledaily, A., Belwafi, K., Aboalsamh, H.: Emotion detection using electroencephalography signals and a zero-time windowing-based epoch estimation and relevant electrode identification. Scientific Reports 11(1), 1–17(2021).

It was hypothesised that persistent physical activity and internally focused attention are combined with mind-body exercises like yoga to produce a fleeting experience of self-contemplation [5]. Which contributes to activating the neurohormonal processes that improve health by the reduction in sympathetic activity. Hence, it lessens stress and anxiety, enhances the functioning of the autonomic and higher neurological centres, and even, as demonstrated in certain research, enhances the physical well-being of cancer patients.

Suhaimi, N.S., Mountstephens, J., Teo, J.: EEG-based emotion recognition: A state-of-the-art review of current trends and opportunities. Computational intelligence and neuroscience, 2020(8875426), 1–19(2020).

According to the trials that have been done [10], yogic practises may significantly enhance a number of indices that are crucial for managing DM2, such as lipid levels, body composition, and glycaemia control. Also, it lowers blood pressure and oxidative stress, improves pulmonary and neurological system function, promotes mood, sleep, and quality of life, and causes persons with DM2 to take fewer medications.

Sharma, G., Sharma, N., Singh, T., Agrawal, R.: A Detailed Study of EEG based Brain Computer Interface. In First International Conference on Information Technology and Knowledge Management (ICITKM), 137–143(2017).

The study [11] of Heart rate variability during cyclic meditation and supine rest with 42 male volunteers has shown activation of predominantly sympathetic during yoga posture phase and parasympathetic dominance increase after cyclic medication. Three classification procedures were used to assess the effectiveness of the quadratic classifier (QDC) method in a novel approach to emotion recognition utilising EEG signals. The accuracy of detecting emotions increased by 2.37%, 11.22%, and 5.64%.

Salama, E.S., El-Khoribi, R.A., Shoman, M.E., Shalaby, M.A.W.: EEG-based emotion recognition using 3D convolutional neural networks. International Journal of Advanced Computer Science and Applications 9(8), 329–337.

An another combination of two algorithm PCA and Relief algorithm [17] used to conduct the textual & EEG signal based detection of emotion [12]. Where feature extraction as been done based on time and frequency domain. At last, SVM was trained to detect the emotion, which resulted recognition of emotion with multi-channel feature fusion method.

Indurani, P., Firdaus Begam B.: A Detailed Analysis of EEG Signal Processing in E-healthcare Applications and Challenges, International Journal of Innovative Research in Science, Engineering and Technology (IJIRSET) 10(1), 635–642(2021).

Indurani et al. [13] concentrated on aspects of human psychology that relate to decisions, planning, anger, grief, joy, fear, and other human mental states. Biosensor data, such as EEG readings from ambient assisted living, are used to record the mental states of patients (ALL). In this study, modifications to energy, wavelet entropy, and the classifiers SVM, QDA, and k-nearest neighbour have been made. Using four electrodes from the EEG database, this method is tested based on the "DEAP" method.

Ma, Q., Wang, M., Hu, L., Zhang, L., Hua, Z.: A novel recurrent neural network to classify EEG signals for customers' decision-making behavior prediction in brand extension scenario. Frontiers in Human Neuroscience, 15(610890), 1–13(2021).

It was crucial to forecast customer behaviour in terms of market judgement. Nonetheless, individual variations and the complex, non-linear structure of the EEG signals made it difficult to distinguish the electroencephalogram (EEG) signals and predict consumers' decisions using conventional classification methods. In order to solve the aforementioned difficulties, the current study developed a recurrent t-distributed stochastic neighbour embedding (t-SNE) neural network to classify the EEG signals in the planned brand extension paradigm and forecast the participants' judgements (whether to accept the brand extension or not). The recurrent t-SNE neural network had two steps. In the initial stage, features were extracted from EEG recordings using the t-SNE approach. Second, a recurrent neural network with layers based on long short-term memory (LSTM) [14].

3 Methodology

3.1 Portable EEG Machine

High quality range of portable EEG machine Maximums 32 is been used to acquire EEG signals from the subject. It has 24 channels, USB powered machine, 32 channel video EEG and long time monitoring. Ten-fold cross validation, a method of subject-independent experimentation, is the method we use. Male and female individuals from each of the 10 trials were chosen (Fig. 2).

A research was completed with engine reactions of the EEG signal during changes in the condition of cognizance in light of various measurements of the medication Propofol. The target of this work was to confirm a potential endeavour at an engine response during a system utilizing the sedative Propofol, where the individual would know about the technique, yet would not be able to play out the development because of neuromuscular blockers. In this work, 12 solid subjects were assessed. Primer tests, first and foremost, are completed with each volunteer where they are approached to move with practically no sort of Propofol application. From this test, classifiers in light of calculated relapse are made, ordering non-movement and development and the attributes utilized depend on Power Ghostly Thickness (PSD) utilizing the Welch strategy. Hence, a similar test is completed with each worker, however with two measurements of Propofol, 0.5 and 1.0 ug/ml.

3.2 Placement of Electrode System

The International 10–20 standard for electrode placement was followed for recording EEG data utilising a 19-channel electrode cap and linked-ears montage. Reveals the order of the chosen channels (FP1, FP2, F3, F4, C3, C4, P3, P4, F7, F8, T3, T4, T5, T6, FZ, CZ, PZ, O1, and O2). The EEG signals were amplified using MITSAR gear and then passed through a mixed - signal converter. The signals were recorded at a sample rate of 500 Hz (Fig. 3).

Using PSYTASK Software A three-minute pause was taken between each of the two portions of the experiment. Six categories were shown in the first section, and in the second section, the same categories were still shown in the same sequence for all participants. A total of 360 photos were shown to each person during the trial. Each category had 30 photographs, 15 of which were linked to the topic at hand and 15 of which were not related at all but were drawn at random from other categories. Each participant only saw the photographs once, and their orders were never revealed. Presentation of stimuli in both the both auditory and visual (on the monitor screen) (using the sound card and speakers) evaluating the velocity of reaction. You can use a keyboard and mouse to measure overall reaction time.

3.3 Attention Exercises

In the first attention exercise, the participant is asked to repeat a series of numbers using a numbered pad in the exact same order as they were displayed. Another set of numbers is then displayed, but this time the participants are asked to report the numbers

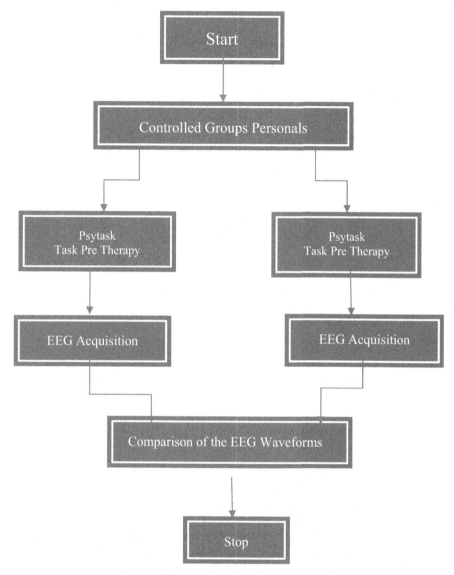

Fig. 2. Workflow Flow Chart

in reverse. Shows how the participant interacts with the activity by using the numerical pad. Participants in the second attention exercise must click the space bar on the keyboard each time they see the letter "A" while viewing a series of letters on the Pystask software monitor (one letter per second).

Each sign conveys data, however few out of every odd snippet of data is applicable to the end client. The futile sign is then alluded to as clamor. By the term recurrence examination it mean the utilization of different strategies to track down the recurrence parts of the info signal, of which it is made. It tends to be a ceaseless or discrete sign

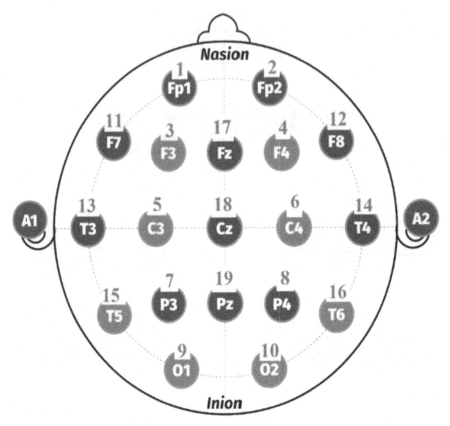

Fig. 3. 19 channels of electrodes were utilized to record EEG signals.

and is normally described by its plentifulness and recurrence, as well as the start and end regarding time. For recurrence examination, the fundamental objective is to decide the sufficiency and recurrence size of individual sign parts. While in transient examination deciding the event of the sign part inside the time axis is significant. The two standards can't be accomplished simultaneously, however finding a reasonable trade off arrangement with respect to the use is consistently conceivable. The most often involved contraption for recognizing some part is the supposed change. They can be partitioned according to a few perspectives, one of the essential divisions is for constant or discrete signal handling. The easiest way to deal with describing waves is to track down the recurrence of convergence of the nonexistent x-pivot (for example while plotting the time course of the wave). In the event that an estimation season of 60 s and count is thought of, for instance, 800 changes.

3.4 EEG Signal Modelling

$$E = Q/Cm$$

where Q is expressed in terms of coulombs/cm^2, Cm is a measure of the membrane's capacity in terms of farads/cm^2, and E is expressed in terms of volts. It is necessary to mathematically connect the action potentials are reproduced by the stimulating current entering the cell through the stimulating electrodes to the amount of charge Q+ on the inner surface (and Q on the outer surface) of the cell membrane (APs). The electrical potential, sometimes referred to as the electrical force, E, is then calculated.

3.5 Prediction Method

$$y(n) = -\sum_{K-1}^{P} ak\ y(n-k) + x(n)$$

where n stands for the discrete sample time normalised to unity, ak, k = 1, 2,..., p, are the linear parameters, and x(n) represents the noise input. Each sample is obtained in an autoregressive moving average (ARMA) linear predictive model based on a variety of its prior input and output sample values.

3.6 Coherence of Wavelet Transform

At a particular scale, wavelet coherence (WC) is a qualitative estimate that demonstrates how links between signals vary over time. The wavelet transform of a signal is a representation of frequency and time that results from the conviction of the signal with a particular wavelet family. ψt, f(u):

$$\int_{-\infty}^{-\infty} x(u).^{\varphi}t, F(u)du$$

3.7 Result and Analysis of EEG Waveforms

Rms EEG machine was used to analyse brain waves at post yoga. The advantage of the analysis is that persons can perform the task very easily by having good concentration. The stress occurred during various activities also reduced by doing yoga which was analysed by us in Rms EEG machine .In this section, a comparison with the prior investigations, as represented in Table 1, has been carried out. Four emotions—happy, scared, furious, and pleasant—were utilised to suggest a real-time emotion monitoring system. During recording the EEG signals, individuals were invited to listen to music with their eyes closed.

Psychological Task and Pre-Yoga EEG

A programme called PSYTASK is used to organise and carry out psychophysiology tests. The PSYTASK application operates on the primary PC, while WinEEG works on the secondary PC. WinEEG programme provides a simultaneous boosts show with EEG securing and sends synchronisation codes to PSYTASK programme to regulate its work.

Table 1. Pre and Post Yoga Analysis Data

Name	Condition							
	Pre yoga Analysis				Post analysis			
	Go	No go	Commission	Omission	Go	No go	Commission	Omission
Mythile	88	97	77.5	22.5	90	87	89.5	10.5
Kandeepan	86	92	69.1	30.9	96	82	81.2	18.8
Kayalvizhi	83	89	56.3	43.7	93	79	66.3	33.7
Martina	69	79	54.0	46.0	89	76	62.8	37.2
Riya	84	89	79.3	20.7	94	69	89.3	10.7

The recoded data can be used to compute and analyse event-related probabilities (ERP) and event-related desynchronization (ERD).

Psychological Task and Post-Yoga EEG

The same group of controlled subjects are been used as experimental subjects [4]. The experimental subjects are subjected to do yoga. After that again the same psychological test is been given to them and EEG is been taken. To evaluate all of the experiments in our research for arousal or valence, classification accuracy was utilised. Classification-EEG signal is produced autonomously of outside feeling and might be completely and uninhibitedly directed by the person. It is likewise useful for patients with neurological issues as it takes into consideration more regular and unconstrained connections in light of the fact that the neuroprosthesis is consequently controlled Numerous physiological benefits of yoga practise include increased pulse variability (HRV), decreased circulatory strain, increased respiratory rate, increased bar reflex responsiveness, and balance of autonomic sensory (ANS) Parasympathetic activity is increased while intentional movement is decreased [2]. Previous studies have shown that yoga activities significantly influence the focal sensory system's performance and help people enhance their attention, focus, and other mental capacities' pipes (Fig. 4).

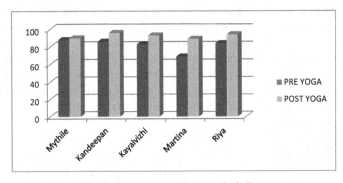

Fig. 4. Pre and Post Yoga Analysis Data

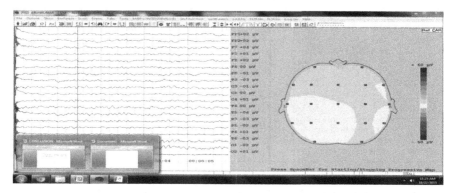

Fig. 5. Tomography map while doing yoga

The analysis revealed that the regular practice of yoga can able to increase the performance of the brain which was analysed frequency during week. The outcomes, as talked about in the past segment, appears to demonstrate that the component extraction process had the option to recognize certain assortments in the EEG signal which are excellent for a particular kind of imagined improvement. The best method for taking apart these assortments and to get a prevalent understanding of what is genuinely happening inside the brain, the event related conceivable outcomes (Fig. 6).

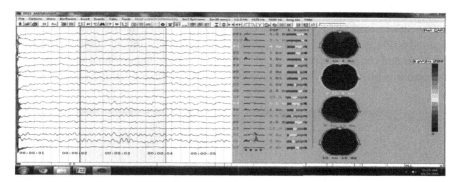

Fig. 6. Frequency Analysis

Till now, what has been seen is that, there are assortments in the EEG signal toward the start of an imagined improvement. Furthermore, these assortments themselves vary in view of the district of the head from where the EEG signals we rerecorded. To get a predominant perception of the assortments in the EEG, a close to examination of the EEG signals has been done using time-repeat examination of the event related conceivable outcomes. The assessment has been done among EEG signals for a wide range of imagined improvements among different subjects and moreover among EEG signals from different head spots of a similar subject (Fig. 7).

We presently need to fall the data of the two circumstances by contrasting them. One chance is to take the contrast between the circumstances: we deduct the two power

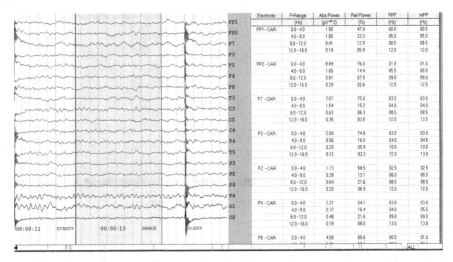

Electrode	F-Range (Hz)	Abs Power (µV**2)	Rel Power (%)	PPF (Hz)	MPF (Hz)
FP1 - CAR	0.0 - 4.0	1.50	47.9	00.0	00.5
	4.0 - 8.0	1.05	33.3	05.0	05.0
	8.0 - 12.0	0.41	12.9	08.5	08.5
	12.0 - 16.0	0.19	05.9	12.0	12.0
FP2 - CAR	0.0 - 4.0	8.69	76.0	01.0	01.0
	4.0 - 8.0	1.65	14.4	05.5	05.5
	8.0 - 12.0	0.81	07.0	09.0	09.0
	12.0 - 16.0	0.29	02.6	12.0	12.5
F7 - CAR	0.0 - 4.0	7.57	75.0	03.5	03.0
	4.0 - 8.0	1.54	15.2	04.0	04.0
	8.0 - 12.0	0.63	06.3	08.0	08.5
	12.0 - 16.0	0.35	03.5	12.0	13.5
F3 - CAR	0.0 - 4.0	2.60	74.8	03.5	03.0
	4.0 - 8.0	0.56	16.0	04.0	04.5
	8.0 - 12.0	0.20	05.9	10.5	10.0
	12.0 - 16.0	0.12	03.3	12.0	13.0
FZ - CAR	0.0 - 4.0	1.73	58.5	02.5	02.5
	4.0 - 8.0	0.39	13.1	06.0	05.5
	8.0 - 12.0	0.64	21.6	08.0	08.5
	12.0 - 16.0	0.20	06.9	12.0	12.5
F4 - CAR	0.0 - 4.0	1.21	54.1	03.0	03.0
	4.0 - 8.0	0.37	16.4	04.0	05.5
	8.0 - 12.0	0.48	21.6	09.0	09.0
	12.0 - 16.0	0.18	08.0	13.0	13.0
F8 - CAR	0.0 - 4.0	4.06	68.6	00.5	01.0

Fig. 7. Time Domain Frequency values

spectra and afterward partition them by their aggregate - this standardizes the distinction by the normal action. The obtained EEG signals are for the most part of multi-channel nature. To characterize these signs, for instance, we have two options: to work on a subset of channels chosen in view of specific standards or to deal with all channels [5]. Figure 5 gives a representation for the general course of EEG signal grouping in view of channel determination. In this sign handling setting, lessening the quantity of channels is required on the grounds that the arrangement cycle with an enormous number of channels is tedious and causes subject bother. Also, it adds to the computational intricacy of the framework, which is expected to be low in specific applications (Fig. 8).

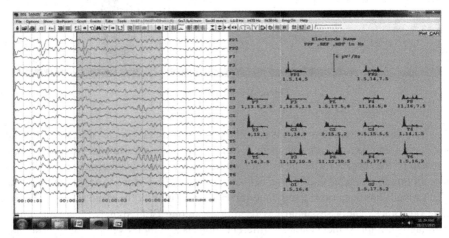

Fig. 8. Amplitude waveform maps

As discussed already, for each subject, there are two restricted regions in the head whose EEG signals showed different properties. The terminals were picked so they address one from each get-together the cathode position whose EEG signal has been dissected It will in general be seen that there are assortments in the EEG signals right when a singular endeavours to imagine a sort of improvement. These assortments are different for different kinds of advancements imagined too concerning different regions of the head. Moreover, the assortments furthermore vary for same sort of improvements at whatever point pondered against different subjects. Expecting the event related potential outcomes of EEG signals recorded from a comparative spot of the head likewise, for a comparable kind of imagined improvement is taken a gander at for different subjects, finding a shared trait exceptionally hard among the assortments of the EEG signals.

4 Conclusion

The paper has attempted to investigate the varieties in the EEG signal that come about because of envisioning different kinds of engine developments. Electroencephalography has a place with electro biological imaging devices broadly utilized in clinical and research regions.EEG estimates changes in electric possibilities brought about by enormous number of electric dipoles framed during brain excitations. EEG signal comprises of various cerebrum waves reflecting cerebrum electrical movement as indicated by anode positions and working in the adjoining cerebrum locales. Intensifiers with generally intensification gain between 100–100,000, with input impedances somewhere around 100 Super Ohms, what's more, typical mode dismissal proportion something like 100 dB. Simple channels coordinated in the unit with high pass channel with cut-off recurrence in the scope of 0.1–0.7 Hz and low pass channel with remove recurrence short of what one portion of the inspecting rate. In reality, frequencies over 50 Hz are seldom required as they contribute irrelevantly to control range of EEG. The gadget is single channel which is both a benefit and hindrance since it is straightforward yet it likewise restricts the degree of examination. Improved outcome can be noticed if the nature of the anodes is gotten to the next level.

References

1. Sengupta, P.: Health impacts of yoga and pranayama: a state-of-the-art review. Int. J. Prev. Med. **3**(7), 444–458 (2012)
2. Ross, A., Thomas, S.: The health benefits of yoga and exercise: a review of comparison studies. J. Altern. Complement. Med.Altern. Complement. Med. **16**(1), 3–12 (2010)
3. Sarang, P., Telles, S.: Effects of two yoga based relaxation techniques on heart rate variability (HRV). Int. J. Stress. Manag.Manag. **13**(4), 460–475 (2006)
4. Jacobs, J., Kahana, M.J.: Direct brain recordings fuel advances in cognitive electrophysiology. Trends Cogn. Sci.Cogn. Sci. **14**(4), 162–171 (2010)
5. Gannouni, S., Aledaily, A., Belwafi, K., Aboalsamh, H.: Emotion detection using electroencephalography signals and a zero-time windowing-based epoch estimation and relevant electrode identification. Sci. Rep. **11**(1), 1–17 (2021)
6. Garcia-Garcia, J.M., Penichet, V.M., Lozano, M.D.: Emotion detection: a technology review. In: Proceedings of the XVIII International Conference on Human Computer Interaction, vol. 8, pp. 1–8. Association for Computing Machinery, New York, NY, United States (2017)

7. Nawaz, R., Cheah, K.H., Nisar, H., Yap, V.V.: Comparison of different feature extraction methods for EEG-based emotion recognition. Biocybernetics Biomed. Eng. **40**(3), 910–926 (2020)
8. Struck, A.F., et al.: Comparison of machine learning models for seizure prediction in hospitalized patients. Ann. Clin. Transl. Neurol. **6**(7), 1239–1247 (2019)
9. Qing, C., Qiao, R., Xu, X., Cheng, Y.: Interpretable emotion recognition using EEG signals. IEEE Access **7**, 94160–94170 (2019)
10. Suhaimi, N.S., Mountstephens, J., Teo, J.: EEG-based emotion recognition: a state-of-the-art review of current trends and opportunities. Comput. Intell. Neurosci.. Intell. Neurosci. **2020**(8875426), 1–19 (2020)
11. Sharma, G., Sharma, N., Singh, T., Agrawal, R.: A detailed study of EEG based brain computer interface. In: First International Conference on Information Technology and Knowledge Management (ICITKM), pp. 137–143 (2017)
12. Salama, E.S., El-Khoribi, R.A., Shoman, M.E., Shalaby, M.A.W.: EEG-based emotion recognition using 3D convolutional neural networks. Int. J. Adv. Comput. Sci. Appl. **9**(8), 329–337 (2018)
13. Indurani, P., Firdaus, B.B.: A detailed analysis of EEG signal processing in E-healthcare applications and challenges. Int. J. Innov. Res. Sci. Eng. Technol. (IJIRSET) **10**(1), 635–642 (2021)
14. Ma, Q., Wang, M., Hu, L., Zhang, L., Hua, Z.: A novel recurrent neural network to classify EEG signals for customers' decision-making behavior prediction in brand extension scenario. Front. Hum. Neurosci.Neurosci. **15**(610890), 1–13 (2021)
15. Liu, Y., Fu, G.: Emotion recognition by deeply learned multi-channel textual and EEG features. Future Gener. Comput. Syst **119**, 1–6 (2021)
16. Rahman, M.A., Hossain, M.F., Hossain, M., Ahmmed, R.: Employing PCA and t-statistical approach for feature extraction and classification of emotion from multichannel EEG signal. Egypt. Inf. J. **21**(1), 23–35 (2020)
17. Li, Z., et al.: Enhancing BCI-based emotion recognition using an improved particle swarm optimization for feature selection. Sensors **20**(11), 1–16 (2020)
18. Pion-Tonachini, L., Kreutz-Delgado, K., Makeig, S.: ICLabel: an automated electroencephalographic independent component classifier, dataset, and website. Neuroimage **198**, 181–197 (2019)
19. Batbaatar, E., Li, M., Ryu, K.H.: Semantic-emotion neural network for emotion recognition from text. IEEE access **7**, 111866–111878 (2019)
20. Issa, D., Demirci, M.F., Yazici, A.: Speech emotion recognition with deep convolutional neural networks. Biomed. Signal Process. Control **59**(101894), 1–11 (2020)

"Obstacles in the Way of Digital Payment" – An Analytical Study

Vishal Ramaiya[✉], Neeraj Kumar Dubey, and Pramod Goyal

Faculty of Management Studies, Marwadi University, Rajkot, India
vishalramaiya13@gmail.com

Abstract. In the current highly competitive landscape, leading organizations find it increasingly challenging to maintain a competitive edge against global rivals in a world characterized by increasing interconnectedness. Electronic payments, encompassing a spectrum of financial transactions conducted devoid of traditional paper-based documents, have gained prominence. These transactions include the use of debit cards, credit cards, smart cards, e-wallets, e-cash, electronic cheques, and more. However, the acceptance and utilization of e-payment systems exhibit substantial variations across the globe, with some methods enjoying widespread adoption while others languish with lower utilization rates. This study is designed with the objective of meticulously identifying the multifaceted issues and challenges that confront electronic payment systems. Additionally, we will present potential solutions to enhance the digital payment system. It's important to note that while digital payment systems offer numerous opportunities, they also bring along lots of potential threats and challenges.

The Rajkot District is the focus of the study, with 104 participants. Convenience-based sampling was used to choose the participants. Interview schedules and a Google form were used to collect primary data. The data was analyzed and interpreted using simple percentage analysis and the Likert scale. The study's findings highlight the region's persistent reliance on cash transactions. As a result, there is a clear need for increased customer awareness programs targeted at teaching customers about the convenience and benefits of digital payment channels as a replacement for cash transactions.

Keywords: Digital Payment · E- Banking · Demonetization · e-commerce · NEFT · RTGS · IMPS

1 Introduction of Digital Payment System

The payment system within any nation must meet the stringent criteria of safety, security, reliability, efficiency, and accessibility. In today's ever-evolving landscape, the adoption of electronic payment systems varies across countries, each at its own pace. Electronic

---

Supplementary Information The online version contains supplementary material available at https://doi.org/10.1007/978-3-031-59107-5_21.

S. Rajagopal et al (Eds.): ASCIS 2023, CCIS 2040, pp. 309–325, 2024.
https://doi.org/10.1007/978-3-031-59107-5_21

payment systems, a component of e-commerce transactions, facilitate electronic payments for the exchange of goods or services over the internet. In essence, these systems enable users to conduct online payments for a variety of purposes, with all transactions occurring digitally. This method offers instant convenience and employs enhanced encryption features, fostering transparency in the economy by diminishing issues such as corruption, tax evasion, and illicit funding of terrorism.

It has been said that every disruption creates opportunities and one such disruption was the announcement of demonetization by Prime Minister Mr. Narender Modi on 08 November 2016. Demonetization created huge growth opportunity for digital payment in India and the digital wallet companies garbed the opportunities with both the hands to expand their market share (Saravanan, April 2019), Post demonetization, and COVID-19 era people have started accepting and welcoming digital mode of payment. From small business owners to big merchants everyone has started using digital payments. The payment is done through different digital mode of payment like – E-Wallets, Unified Payment Interface (UPI), Cards, NEFT, RTGS, IMPS, Unstructured Supplementary Service Data (USSD), etc. [6].

The Reserve Bank persistently pursued its goal of establishing a cashless society through the widespread adoption of digital payment methods across the nation. Amidst the growing array of electronic payment systems, the bank placed a paramount emphasis on ensuring the security and safety of digital transactions. to this end, the bank dedicated its efforts to fortifying a sturdy and reliable technology infrastructure, ensuring the seamless operation of critical and systemically significant methods for payments and settlements throughout the nation.

The payment and settlement systems recorded a robust growth of 57.8 per cent in terms of transaction volume during 2022–23 on top of the expansion of 63.8 per cent recorded in the previous year. In value terms, the growth was 19.2 per cent in 2022–23 as against 23.1 per cent in the previous year, mainly due to growth in the large value payment system, viz., Real Time Gross Settlement (RTGS). The share of digital transactions in the total volume of non-cash retail payments increased to 99.6 per cent during 2022–23, up from 99.3 per cent in the previous year [13].

However, it's essential to recognize that the opportunities presented by the new digital payment ecosystem come with inherent risks. Challenges range from cybersecurity and privacy concerns to the impact of outdated technology and the emergence of new competitors. Navigating this evolving landscape is far from straightforward for organizations aiming to establish themselves in the future payments marketplace.

In response to government initiatives aimed at transforming India into a digital economy, along with private companies and payment banks securing licenses from the RBI, the financial landscape is witnessing a profound transformation. "Faceless, Paperless, Cashless" is a pivotal theme of Digital India, emphasizing various digital payment methods while addressing the challenges and providing solutions that align with the current context.

2 Significance of the Study

The central theme of the "2025 Payments Vision" document revolves around the concept of '4Es': enabling e-payments for everyone, everywhere, and every time. Within the framework of this vision, the Reserve Bank of India (RBI) has outlined five key objectives in the Payments Vision 2025 document, which are integrity, inclusion, innovation, institutionalization, and internationalization. To realize these objectives, Vision 2025 will concentrate on four strategic pillars, encompassing with responsive regulation, strong infrastructure, efficient supervision, and a customer-centric approach, in light of the challenges discussed, concerted efforts are being made to address them, with a particular focus on enhancing digital transactions. These enhancements encompass improved security features, streamlined transactional processes, and cost reduction measures, all of which hold substantial potential for advancing the state of digital payment processing. This study is anticipated to stimulate interest and foster discussions on this pressing issue. Furthermore, it serves as a fundamental reference point for future research endeavors, encouraging further exploration and innovation in response to the changing nature of the digital payment landscape.

3 Scope of the Study

This study is extensive due to the myriad opportunities digital transactions offer in the future. India's rapid emergence as a formidable economy necessitates factors like enhanced transparency and corporate governance for sustainable development. However, these advancements can only materialize when the populace adopts digital payments and transactions. Although multiple studies have explored digital payment systems, none have delved into the perspectives of customers in the Rajkot district. Thus, this study concentrates on assessing the challenges, issues, and customer perceptions concerning e-payment systems in the Rajkot district, filling a critical research gap.

4 Objectives

1. To understand and analyze the growth patterns in digital payment.
2. To determine how well-informed male and female users are about digital payments and to examine how frequently they use them.
3. To identify the awareness level of customers towards digital payment
4. To investigate how users' level of education affects their level of trust in electronic payment systems.
5. To assess the difficulties, face by customers in digital transaction.

5 Hypothesis

1. Ho1: There is no significant relationship across Gender users of digital payment and their frequency of using digital payment.
2. H02: There is no significant relationship among different educational level users of digital payment and their frequency of using digital payment.
3. Ho3: There is no significant relationship across different age groups digital payment and their frequency of using digital payment.

6 Literature Review

Shah Z. A. (2017) In his study, "Digital Payment System: Prospects and Problems", the author looks at India's infrastructure and the difficulties that the country's whole economy is facing as it moves toward becoming a cashless society. According to the report, a sizable portion of transactions still involve cash, especially in rural areas. This indicates that a fully cashless economy is still a long way off for India.

Md. Shakir Ali et al. (2017) in his research "digital payments for rural India - challenges and opportunities", emphasizes the critical role of digital payments in India's economic development. Improved transparency, corporate governance, and increased rural adoption of digital payments are key factors for the nation's progress. To fully unlock the rural potential, it's essential to address the challenges associated with digital payment solutions. Accompanied by policy measures aimed at narrowing the digital divide and reinforcing ICT infrastructure, this approach can pave the way for sustainable growth.

Renu devi (2019) In her article titled "challenges of Indian e-payment system", the author's conclusion emphasizes that the effective implementation of an electronic payment system is contingent upon several critical factors. These factors encompass robust security measures, well-established infrastructure, prompt responses to combat fraud, stringent protection of personal banking details, the implementation of targeted awareness programs for older age groups, and effective communication regarding the advantages of the e-payment system throughout the entire economy. These combined efforts aim to enhance user trust and bolster market confidence in the Indian E-payment system.

Bhaskaran Anish. B. (2019) In his article "A Study on Problems and Challenges on Digital Payment System as an Ease of Payment Mechanism among Customers in E-Commerce Scenario with Special Reference to Kottayam District" the author emphasizes the importance of promoting electronic payment methods in India while promoting via means of other practical alternatives to credit and debit cards. In order to improve the system, it is essential to lower transaction costs, make the internet more accessible, streamline business procedures, boost security, and support ecosystems that are centered around the needs of customers. India's government and people must work together to overcome obstacles and increase faith in digital technologies in order for the country to become a cashless society.

Revathi. P. (2019): stated in her article title "digital banking challenges and opportunities in India in today's digital age", banking and financial services are undergoing significant transformation. While convenience is a primary driver behind integrating technology into banking, transparency and security remain crucial. Customers are increasingly using mobile and online platforms, creating opportunities for banks to offer unique digital services. However, to harness the full potential of digitization, several challenges must be addressed.

Gupta Deepak et al. (2020) In his article titled "problems and prospects of digital payments: an empirical study of Haryana", the author's findings indicate that a substantial portion of the respondents face difficulties when trying to employ digital payment methods. These difficulties predominantly revolve around inadequate acceptance infrastructure, a limited selection of digital payment alternatives, insufficient digital literacy, and inadequate internet connectivity. While digital payments constitute a noteworthy progression, it is imperative for governmental reforms to address these challenges and foster the integration of individuals who are presently contending with these impediments in their adoption of digital payment systems.

Sudiksha Shree (2020) concludes in his article titled "Digital payments and consumer experience in India: a survey-based empirical study" that this research provides insights into the intricate dynamics of perception, convenience, and demographic factors that influence the uptake of digital payment methods. The study emphasizes the necessity for continued research and policy adaptations to ease the shift toward digital payments in a financial environment that is continually evolving.

Malusare Lalita (2021) in her article titled "Digital Payment Methods in India: A Study of Problems and Prospects", how much is digital literacy among the Indian population remains relatively low, which has hindered the widespread development and adoption of digital payment systems across the country. Notably, social and infrastructural barriers have played an important part in limiting the usage of digital payment systems. However, it is observed that mobile banking has been gaining popularity in India due to its ease of use and accessibility. Enhancing digital literacy among the population is deemed essential. Furthermore, concerns regarding risks and security issues in digital payments persist.

Jain Vipin (2021) In his article titled "Digital Banking: A Case Study of India", the conclusions drawn emphasize the profound influence of digitalization on India's banking sector. These findings underscore the potential prospects and obstacles that the digital banking landscape may encounter in the future.

Kumar Suresh K. (2022) Concludes in the article titled "UPI - the growth of cashless economy in India" that there is a strong indication of increased adoption of digital transactions among Indians in the future. The expanding banking sector is actively promoting the use of credit and debit cards, making plastic money a common possession among most Indians. The shift towards making online payments and purchases has created a growing necessity for Indians to embrace cashless transactions as a part of their daily lives. The government's efforts, including the impact of demonetization, have been instrumental in driving India toward a digital economy by reducing the reliance on physical currency and encouraging the use of BHIM-UPI. The realization of a cashless economy hinges on the widespread acceptance of plastic money, online banking, and electronic wallets by users.

Sharma Bhavna (2022) stated in her article title: "DIGITAL BANKING: A NEED OF TIME" The digital transformation of the banking sector is a global phenomenon characterized by the automation of processes and the use of advanced technologies. In India, this transformation has evolved significantly, with mobile devices now playing a central role in banking services. While digital banking has greatly improved the customer experience, several challenges must be addressed. These include ensuring widespread internet connectivity, managing digital risks, and fostering collaboration between stakeholders. How these challenges are tackled will determine the pace and direction of India's digital banking journey.

7 Research Methodology

Research Design: The research adopted a descriptive and exploratory approach and utilized an online survey through a Google Forms questionnaire. The questionnaire included a mix of open-ended and closed-ended questions, as well as checkboxes. Additionally, both face-to-face and telephone interviews were conducted as part of the data collection process.

Population: Respondents of Rajkot district.

Sample Size: 104.

Sampling Technique: Convenience cum Judgement Sampling technique is used for selecting appropriate samples of users for the collection of data.

Tools for Analysis:

- **Simple tools:** The researcher will use for verifying the validity of data in the study like tables, figures, percentage and Likert scale analysis.
- **Statistical tools:** The researcher will use standard statistical metrics like mean, standard deviation, variance, correlation, p-value and ANOVA

8 Data Analysis and Interpretation: (Growth of Digital Payment)

Payment system infrastructure continued to see significant expansion and evolution in the fiscal year 2022–2023. In comparison to other digital payment methods, the Real-Time Gross Settlement (RTGS) system showed impressive growth, with a substantial increase of 16.7% in transaction volume. RTGS showed a corresponding increase of 16.5% in transaction value. Similar high increases were seen in transactions made via the National Electronic Funds Transfer (NEFT) system, which saw a 30.8% increase in volume and a 17.4% gain in value. In line with the general development of economic activity, these trends show a greater involvement of huge firms in high-value transactions (Table 1.).

As of the end of March 2023, a vast network of 1,65,390 Indian Financial System Code (IFSC) units belonged to 243 member institutions and provided access to RTGS services, while 1,66,544 IFSC units belonged to 230 member banks and provided access to NEFT services.

Additionally, during the fiscal year, there were notable changes in the card-based transaction sector. An amazing growth of 47.3% in value and 30.1% in volume was seen in credit card transactions. Debit card transactions, on the other hand, saw a reduction, with volume and value both down by 13.2% and 1.4%, respectively. Transaction volumes and values for prepaid payment instruments (PPIs) rose by 13.5% and 2.9%, respectively, demonstrating positive growth.

Table 1. Payment System Indicators - Annual Turnover (April-March)

Item	Volume (lakh)					
	2020–21	2021–22	2022–23	2020–21	2021–22	2022–23
1	2	3	4	5	6	7
A. Settlement Systems						
CCIL Operated Systems	28	33	41	1,619.43	2,068.73	2,587.97
B. Payment Systems						
1. Large Value Credit Transfers – RTGS	**1,592**	**2,078**	**2,426**	**1,056.00**	**1,286.58**	**1,499.46**
Retail Segment						
2. Credit Transfers	**3,17,868**	**5,77,935**	**9,83,695**	**335.04**	**427.28**	**550.12**
2.1 AePS (Fund Transfers)	11	10	6	0.01	0.01	0.00
2.2 APBS	14,373	12,573	17,898	1.11	1.33	2.48
2.3 ECS Cr	0	0	0	0.00	0.00	0.00
2.4 IMPS	32,783	46,625	56,533	29.41	41.71	55.85
2.5 NACH Cr	16,465	18,758	19,267	12.17	12.82	15.44
2.6 NEFT	30,928	40,407	52,847	251.31	287.25	337.20
2.7 UPI	2,23,307	4,59,561	8,37,144	41.04	84.16	139.15
3. Debit Transfers and Direct Debits	**10,457**	**12,189**	**15,343**	**8.66**	**10.34**	**12.90**
3.1 *BHIM Aadhaar* Pay	161	228	214	0.03	0.06	0.07
3.2 ECS Dr	0	0	0	0.00	0.00	0.00
3.3 NACH Dr	9,646	10,755	13,503	8.62	10.27	12.80
3.4 NETC (Linked to Bank Account)	650	1,207	1,626	0.01	0.02	0.03
4. Card Payments	**57,787**	**61,783**	**63,345**	**12.92**	**17.02**	**21.52**
4.1 Credit Cards	17,641	22,399	29,145	6.30	9.72	14.32
4.2 Debit Cards	40,146	39,384	34,199	6.61	7.30	7.20
5. Prepaid Payment Instruments	**49,366**	**65,783**	**74,667**	**1.97**	**2.79**	**2.87**
6. Paper-based Instruments	**6,704**	**6,999**	**7,088**	**56.27**	**66.50**	**71.63**
Total - Retail Payments (2 + 3 + 4 + 5 + 6)	4,42,180	7,24,689	11,44,138	414.86	523.94	659.04

(*continued*)

Table 1. (*continued*)

Item	Volume (lakh)					
	2020–21	2021–22	2022–23	2020–21	2021–22	2022–23
Total Payments (1 + 2 + 3 + 4 + 5 + 6)	4,43,772	7,26,767	11,46,563	1,470.86	1,810.52	2,158.50
Total Digital Payments (1 + 2 + 3 + 4 + 5)	**4,37,068**	**7,19,768**	**11,39,476**	**1,414.58**	**1,744.01**	**2,086.87**

Source: RBI

The substantial growth in electronic payments can be attributed to the greater accessibility of acceptance infrastructure and the Payments Infrastructure Development Fund's (PIDF) program's launch in January 2021, which has a substantial driving force. Until March 2023, the count of Point of Sale (PoS) terminals, a vital component of this infrastructure, had surged by 28.3%, reaching 77.9 lakh. Furthermore, the utilization of Bharat Quick Response (BQR) codes experienced a 6.7% uptick, accumulating to 53.8 lakh in the same time period. Additionally, the Unified Payments Interface Quick Response (UPI QR) codes observed an impressive surge of 48.4%, totalling 25.64 crore by March 2023. The network of automated teller machines (ATMs) also expanded to 2.59 lakh by the end of March 2023, compared to 2.52 lakh in the previous fiscal year. These developments collectively signify the evolving landscape of digital payment systems, highlighting their growing integration into the daily lives of consumers and businesses.

Demographic Factors for the Study in Percentage
(See Figs. 1, 2, 3, 4 and 5).

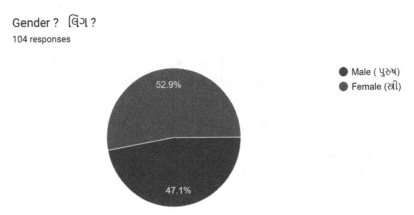

Gender ? લિંગ ?
104 responses

● Male (પુરુષ)
● Female (સ્ત્રી)

52.9%

47.1%

Fig. 1. Gender Distribution Among Survey Respondents: A pie chart illustrating the breakdown of 104 respondents, revealing that 52.9% are female and approximately 47.1% are male".

What is your Age (in years) ? તમારી ઉંમર કેટલી છે (વર્ષમાં) ?

104 responses

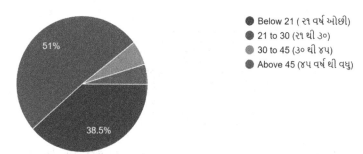

Fig. 2. "Age Distribution of Survey Respondents: This chart reveals a predominant presence of individuals aged 21 to 30 years old, with significant representation among those aged 21 and below. Smaller proportions are observed in the older age groups, indicating a younger-leaning demographic within the surveyed population".

What is your Educational qualifications ? તમારી શૈક્ષણિક લાયકાત શું છે ?

104 responses

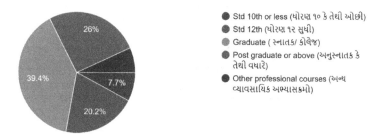

Fig. 3. Educational Qualifications of Survey Respondents: This data provides insights into the educational qualifications of the respondents, showing a diverse range of educational backgrounds among the surveyed population. The majority of respondents are graduates, followed by postgraduates, while smaller proportions have completed education up to the 12th standard, pursued other professional courses, or have education up to the 10th standard or below.

What is your Occupation ?   તમારા વ્યવસાય શું છે ?

104 responses

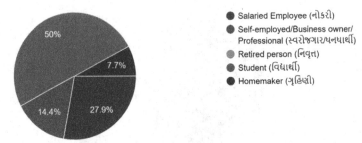

Fig. 4. Occupational Diversity of Digital Payment Users: The data provides valuable insights into the occupational diversity of digital payment users. It highlights the prominent presence of students and salaried employees as active users of digital payment methods, while self-employed individuals and homemakers also make up a portion of the user base. The absence of retired individuals in this survey suggests a potential gap in digital payment adoption among this demographic.

How frequently do you use digital payment methods (e.g., mobile wallets, online banking, contactless payments, etc.)?   તમે કેટલી વાર ડિજિટલ પે...ોવેટ્સ, ઓનલાઇન બેંકિંગ, કોન્ટેક્ટલેસ પેમેન્ટસ વગેરે)?

104 responses

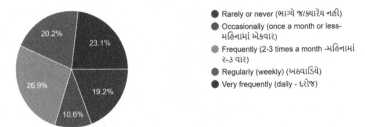

Fig. 5. Frequency of usage of digital platform for payments: This data provides valuable insights into how frequently people use digital payments among the surveyed population. It indicates that a significant portion of respondents uses digital payments frequently, with a notable daily usage rate. However, there are also respondents who use digital payments less frequently or rarely, highlighting a range of payment behaviour within the sample.

Users Trust in Digital Payment
(See Fig. 6).

Is digital payment a trustworthy and secure method of conducting financial transactions in today's digital age? શું તમને લાગે છે ડિજીટલ પેમેન્ટ એ આજના...વહાર કરવા માટેની ભરોસાપાત્ર અને સુરક્ષિત પદ્ધતિ છે ?
104 responses

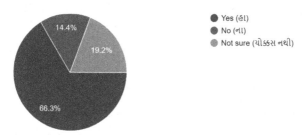

Fig. 6. **Diverse Perspectives on Digital Payments:** These responses illustrate the diverse range of perspectives held by the surveyed individuals concerning digital payments. While a significant portion trusts these methods, there are also those who harbour reservations or uncertainties regarding their security and reliability. These findings suggest that there may be room for improving and addressing concerns related to trust and security in the digital payment landscape to further enhance user confidence.

Users Experience While Using Digital Payment
(See Fig. 7).

How satisfied are you with the overall user experience when making digital payments? ડિજિટલ ચૂકવણી કરતી વખતે તમે એકંદર વપરાશકર્તા અનુભવથી કેટલા સંતુષ્ટ છો?
104 responses

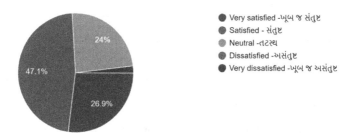

Fig. 7. **Positive Sentiment Towards Digital Payments:** The survey results indicate a predominantly positive sentiment among respondents regarding their digital payment experiences. The majority of users are either very satisfied or satisfied with the overall user experience, while a smaller portion remains neutral, and only a minimal fraction expresses dissatisfaction. These findings suggest that digital payment systems have generally succeeded in providing satisfactory user experiences to a large segment of the surveyed population.

Hypothesis Testing
(See Table 2.).

Table 2. Hypothesis Testing for the Relationship between Gender and Frequency of Digital Payment Usage

Gender/ frequency	Rarely or never	Occasionally	Frequently	Regularly	Very frequently	Chi-square test	df	P-value
MALE	04	02	15	13	15	14.2108	4	0.0067
FEMALE	16	09	12	10	08			

1. Null Hypothesis (Ho): There is no significant relationship across gender users of digital payment users and their frequency of using digital payment.

Alternative Hypothesis (H1): There is a significant relationship across gender of digital payment users and their frequency of using digital payment.

"Hypothesis Testing Results: The null hypothesis (Ho) states that there is no significant relationship between gender and the frequency of using digital payment methods, while the alternative hypothesis (H1) suggests otherwise. Conducting a Chi-Square Test for Independence, the null hypothesis is rejected, indicating a statistically significant correlation between gender and digital payment frequency within the research group. The findings reveal a chi-square statistic of 14.2108 and a p-value of 0.006652, meeting the conventional significance threshold of $p < 0.05$" (Table 3.).

Table 3. Hypothesis Testing for the Relationship Between Educational Level and Frequency of Digital Payment Usage

Education/ frequency	Rarely or never	Occasionally	Frequently	Regularly	Very frequently	Chi-square test	df	p-value
Std 10th or less	1	1	3	1	2	23.372	16	0.1
Std 12th	9	3	5	1	3			
Graduate	8	4	7	9	13			
Post graduate or above	2	3	10	6	6			
Other professional courses	0	0	2	4	1			

2. Null Hypothesis (Ho): There is no significant relationship among different educational level users of digital payment and their frequency of using digital payment.

Alternative Hypothesis (H1): There is a significant relationship among different educational level users of digital payment and their frequency of using digital payment.

Hypothesis Testing Results: The results, with a chi-square test statistic of 23.372 and a p-value of 0.1, do not fulfill the criteria for statistical relevance at the customary level of p 0.05. The results of this investigation do not allow us to rule out the null hypothesis. This shows that there isn't enough evidence to support the assertion that, within the scope of this study, people with different educational levels exhibit noticeably different rates of using digital payments (Table 4.).

Table 4. Hypothesis Testing for the Relationship Between Age and Frequency of using Digital Payment

Age/ Frequency	Rarely or never	Occasionally	Frequently	Regularly	Very frequently	Chi-square test	df	p-value
Below 21	11	5	12	3	9	19.456	12	0.078
21 to 30	7	4	13	14	15			
30 to 45	1	1	0	4	0			
Above 45	1	1	2	0	1			

3. Null Hypothesis (Ho): There is no significant relationship across different age groups digital payment and their frequency of using digital payment.

Alternative Hypothesis (H1): There is a significant relationship across different age groups digital payment and their frequency of using digital payment.

Hypothesis Testing Results: There was initially no strong correlation between age groups and the frequency of using digital payments, according to the null hypothesis (Ho). On the basis of the test results, however, we lack sufficient data to rule out the null hypothesis. A p-value of 0.078 was obtained using the Chi-Square statistic, which came to 19.456. The calculated p-value does not drop below the significance level, which was set at 0.5. As a result, we lack the statistical evidence necessary to draw the conclusion that the frequency with which the examined population uses digital payments is significantly correlated with age (Table 5.).

Table 5. Difficulties face by customers while using digital payment:

	Strongly Agree	Agree	Neutral	Disagree	Strongly disagree	Weighted score	Rank
Lack of awareness	25	41	25	6	7	25.53	1
Insufficient Point of Sale (PoS) devices, QR codes, and internet connectivity	17	40	27	16	4	24.13	4
Instability of the mobile network	20	46	21	11	6	25	2
Digital transactions are unsafe and risky	18	26	33	16	11	22.4	7
Take more time for payment/ payment failure	11	29	33	22	9	21.3	8
digital frauds and Lack of effective Redressal mechanism	22	46	17	10	9	24.93	3
Additional fees or hidden charges	16	30	30	22	6	22.66	6
Insufficient customer support	18	31	30	17	8	23.06	5

The table presents the difficulties faced by customers while using digital payment methods: ranked according to weighted scores derived from survey responses. Lack of awareness and instability of the mobile network emerge as the top concerns, while safety-related issues rank lower, indicating a moderate level of confidence in transaction security among respondents.

Findings of the Study:

1. Digital Payment Growth Patterns:
    The study revealed a significant expansion and evolution of the payment system infrastructure, particularly in digital transactions. The Real-Time Gross Settlement (RTGS) system exhibited remarkable growth, with a 16.7% increase in transaction volume and a corresponding 16.5% rise in transaction value. Similar positive trends were observed in transactions through the National Electronic Funds Transfer (NEFT) system, indicating a surge in high-value corporate transactions.
2. Gender Influence on Digital Payment Usage:
    The research found a statistically significant relationship between gender and the frequency of using digital payment methods. The Chi-Square Test for Independence indicated that gender plays a role in influencing how frequently individuals use digital payment methods. This insight can be valuable for businesses and policymakers aiming to tailor services to different gender-specific preferences and needs.
3. Education Level and Digital Payment Usage Frequency:
    Contrary to the hypothesis, the study did not find a significant relationship among users with different educational levels and their frequency of using digital payments. The results suggest that, within the scope of this study, people with different educational backgrounds do not exhibit noticeably different rates of using digital payments.
4. Age Groups and Digital Payment Frequency:
    The analysis did not provide sufficient evidence to reject the null hypothesis regarding the correlation between age groups and the frequency of using digital payments. Therefore, among the study participants, age does not appear to be a significant factor impacting how frequently they use digital payments.
5. Customer Concerns in Digital Transactions:
    The survey responses highlighted notable concerns among respondents regarding digital payments. Lack of awareness and mobile network instability emerged as significant issues, whereas safety and risk-related concerns ranked lower in importance. These findings provide valuable insights for developing strategies to address concerns and encourage the adoption of digital payment techniques.

The Following are Ideas and Suggestions for Enhancing the Digital Payment System:

1. Initiate comprehensive awareness campaigns aimed at educating the public about the advantages and security aspects of digital payments.
2. Expand the digital payment infrastructure by increasing the availability of Point of Sale (PoS) machines and enhancing internet access in underserved regions.
3. Enhance security protocols by implementing multi-factor authentication and robust fraud detection mechanisms to safeguard user interests.
4. Ensure the design of user-friendly interfaces and streamlined transaction processes to simplify the digital payment experience.

5. Establish responsive customer support channels dedicated to addressing the concerns and queries of digital payment users.
6. Enforce stringent data privacy regulations to protect user information and enhance trust in digital payment systems.
7. Drive continuous innovation in digital payment methods and technologies to meet evolving user expectations and preferences.
8. Actively collect user feedback to identify and promptly address any issues or preferences, thereby enhancing the overall digital payment experience.

Conclusion

The study recognizes the pivotal role of digital payments in the context of India's broader economic development. It aligns with the Reserve Bank of India's "Payments Vision 2025", emphasizing integrity, inclusion, innovation, institutionalization, and internationalization as key objectives. As India strives to become a digital economy, addressing the challenges identified in this study will be essential for sustainable growth in a rapidly evolving world. The use of digital payments has become a transformative force in the financial landscape. However, different locations and populations have varying degrees of adoption and acceptance of digital payment systems. This analytical study, focusing on Rajkot District, has explored the multifaceted challenges that hinder the widespread adoption of electronic payment systems in the region.

The results of this study highlight how important cash transactions are in Rajkot District, where conventional payment methods are still the norm. The survey shows that there is a definite need for increased awareness campaigns that inform consumers about the advantages of using digital payment methods instead of cash. The region needs to make significant efforts to close the awareness gap and promote the benefits of digital payments if it is to move toward a cashless society.

The research also examines demographic factors, such as gender and education level, to understand their influence on digital payment usage and trust. The findings show a substantial correlation between gender and how frequently people use digital payments, suggesting gender-specific preferences in adoption patterns. However, the study did not find significant evidence to support a relationship between different educational levels or age groups and digital payment usage frequency among the study participants. The study's findings indicate that obstacles like lack of awareness and mobile network instability are the most pressing concerns for digital payment users in Rajkot District. These insights can guide efforts to address these challenges and enhance user confidence in digital payment systems.

In conclusion, this research helps us better understand the barriers to the widespread use of digital payments. In order to encourage digital payments in Rajkot District and, by extension, in other similar regions, it offers useful insights for decision-makers, financial institutions, and companies. The area can create the conditions for a future that is more inclusive and digitally empowered by addressing these issues and raising awareness.

Future Scope of the Study

- This research can be further enhanced by employing advanced parametric tests or statistical methodologies.
- This study relies on a limited sample size therefore, it would be advantageous to expand the research to include more villages, cities, or different states.
- There is scope to study at the state level and national level in this area.

References

1. Akhtar, S., et al.: Digital payments for rural India - challenges and opportunities. Int. J. Manage. Appl. Sci. 35–40 (2017)
2. Sharma, B., et al.: Digital banking: a need of time. Int. J. Adv. Appl. Res. **9**, 504–513 (2022)
3. Deepak, G., et al.: Problems and prospects of digital payments: an empirical study of Haryana. J. Crit. Rev. 4665–4675 (2020)
4. Shree, S., et al.: Digital payments and consumer experience in India: a survey based empirical study. J. Bank. Financ. Technol. (2021)
5. Devi, R.: Challenges of Indian e-payment system. J. Emerg. Technol. Innov. Res. 668–677 (2019)
6. Jain, S.A.: A study on challenges faced by the consumers and its impact on usage of digital mode of payments in the city of Mumbai. Int. J. Creat. Res. Thoughts (IJCRT) 896–906 (2022)
7. Jain, V., et al.: Digital banking a case study of India. Solid State Technol. **63**, 19980–19988 (2020)
8. Kumar, S., et al.: UPI - the growth of cashless economy in India. Arab. J. Bus. Manage. Rev. 36–40 (2022)
9. Malusare, L.: Digital payments methods in India: a study of problems and prospects. Int. J. Sci. Res. Eng. Manage. (IJSREM) **3**, 1–7 (2019)
10. Revathi, P.: Digital banking challenges and opportunities in India. EPRA Int. J. Econ. Bus. Rev. **7**, 20–23 (2019)
11. Saravanan, A., et al.: A study on problems and challenges on digital Payment System as an ease of payment mechanism among customers in E-Commerce scenario with special reference to Kottayam District. Cikitusi J. Multidisc. Res. 115–129 (2019)
12. Shah, Z.A.: Digital payment system: problems and prospects. EPRA Int. J. Econ. Bus. Rev. **5**, 194–201 (2017)
13. https://m.rbi.org.in/scripts/AnnualReportPublications.aspx?Id=1380. Accessed 28 Sept 2023

Smart Computing

Implementation of a Novel, Secure Module-Based Architecture for Blockchain-Based Real Estate Transaction Processing

Vishalkumar Langaliya$^{(\boxtimes)}$ [ID] and Jaypalsinh A. Gohil [ID]

Department of Computer Application, Marwadi University, Rajkot 360003, Gujarat, India
vishalkumar.langaliya111484@marwadiuniversity.ac.in,
jaypalsinh.gohil@marwadieducation.edu.in

Abstract. Purpose: This study suggests organizing real estate transactions in a decentralized manner by using private blockchain technology. The writers point out the main problems with India's present transactional procedures and advocate for the application of blockchain technology as a fix. The study's ultimate conclusion is that the recommended approach might be able to enhance transaction processes in Indian government offices, encouraging increased effectiveness, openness, and a decrease in dishonest behavior.

Methods/Design/Methodology: The present transaction procedure and the centralized technology are inspected at the government office using a physical observation method. The next step involves questioning a large number of people to recognize the main areas where the process is tense. Utilizing the insights from the talks, a blockchain solution addressing the issues raised is created. Interviewees are asked for their approval of the predicted model after the design.

Practical Implications: To streamline the real estate transaction process at the Indian government office, a private blockchain application is developed. The seller, the purchaser's property, and the payment are all entered into a single, intricate front end, and the sensitive data is stored in an appropriate database. When the required information has been subjected to the smart business logic, the data is sent to the isolated blockchain for ultimate execution. To verify the proposed system, one artificial effectiveness is made that places a significant load on it and measures the load trashing. To validate the proposed system, a massive amount of sample data is generated.

Originality/Value: Current studies specify that blockchain technology can increase transaction process confidence by improving efficiency, transparency, security, and data accessibility. Therefore, the proposed application is beneficial for the real estate transaction process in India going forward.

Keywords: Blockchain Technology · Smart contracts Algorithms · Real Estate Documents Processing · Smart Contract Design · Smart Contract Implantation

S. Rajagopal et al (Eds.): ASCIS 2023, CCIS 2040, pp. 329–348, 2024.
https://doi.org/10.1007/978-3-031-59107-5_22

1 Introduction

1.1 Blockchain and Its Architecture

Blockchain isn't simply a bit of technology; it's also a set of business functions and application cases. It is also linked with financial ideas in its cryptocurrency implementations. Many businesses by now understood that they must be blockchain-ready to maintain their market states [1]. The birth of Bitcoin in 2008 uncovered the world to an innovative concept that is now poised to transform society as a whole. It is something that has the potential to affect every area, including the financial sector, government, journalism, law, and the arts, to name a few [2]. If we go back over the last few years, we can see that in 2013, certain concepts emerged that proposed the use of blockchain for purposes other than cryptocurrency [3]. A blockchain is made up of three different technologies. The following are the three ingredients. Peer-to-peer networking, for starters, allows a group of computers to connect without relying on a single central authority, preventing a single point of failure. Second These computers use asymmetric cryptography to send encrypted messages to predetermined recipients, allowing anybody to verify the sender's identity while limiting access to the message's contents to the designated recipients [4]. Asymmetrical encryption is used in Bitcoin and Ethereum to build a set of determinations for your account, making sure that only you can transfer tokens. Third issues The normal order of transactions is preserved in both Bitcoin and Ethereum using the Merkle tree data structure, which is then encrypted into a "fingerprint" that the computers on the network can use to compare one another and swiftly synchronize. This makes it possible to compare big datasets quickly and provides a safe way to confirm that the data hasn't been altered [5] (Refer to Fig. 1).

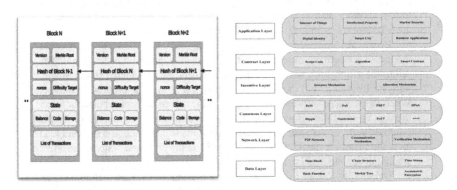

Fig. 1. Construction of Blockchain   Fig. 2. Architecture of Blockchain

The six main layers of a blockchain architecture are the application layer, contractual layer, incentives layer, agreement layer, network layer, and data layer. The architectural components of each tier are depicted in the diagram below (Refer to Fig. 2).

1.2 Indian Real Estate Sector

Residential, business, manufacturing, undeveloped land, and distinct use are the five main partitions of real estate. A real estate investment is the purchase of a home, a rental property, or land. Property rights contribution proprietorship of the land, enhancements, and natural assets like minerals, plants, animals, water, etc. organizations in the real estate sector that manage, buy, sell, invest in, and develop real estate, including land, houses, and other buildings. Numerous real estate firms also help their clients select the appropriate home, resolve price disagreements, and handle the sale or leasing procedure. India's Gross Domestic Product (GDP) is strongly influenced by the real estate industry. Construction, real estate transactions, housing financing, and other associated services are just a few of the sector's direct and indirect economic impacts, which significantly boost national output. Real estate development is a direct indicator of economic expansion and activity. Tax revenue: Through tax income, the real estate sector supports the economy. On real estate transactions, the government receives taxes in the form of property revenue taxes, sales taxes, and income taxes [6].

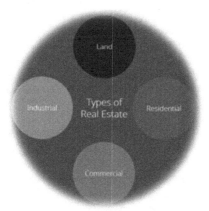

Fig. 3. Types of Real Estate

Residential, business, manufacturing, raw land, and specialized uses are the five main partitions of real estate. A real estate investment is the purchase of a home, a place to rent, or land. It is possible to create secondary real estate investments through real estate pooled investments [7] (Refer to Fig. 3).

1.3   The Value of Blockchain Technology for the Indian Real Estate Industry

Blockchain accelerates rental collects and repayments to property proprietors, permits innocuous data sharing, and proposals top-notch due diligence throughout the range. This improves operational effectiveness and enables time- and money-saving opportunities. The 17 real estate blockchain businesses listed below leverage the booming technology to expand their clientele. Blockchain speeds up transactions, decreases the need for intermediaries, minimizes fraud, and makes real estate more efficient, safe, and transparent. Blockchain enables tokenization and fractional ownership of real estate assets. Owners of real estate can establish digital tokens that represent their smaller shares by dividing the assets they own into smaller ones. Overall, blockchain technology in real estate remains in its infancy, but the advantages are huge. Blockchain technology has the probability to revolutionize the real estate sector as more firms use it, enhancing transparency, cutting costs, and boosting consumer confidence in the entire transaction process.

2 Comprehensive Analysis of Related Works

Authors	Blockchain Application Domain	Problem Statement	Research Method	Solution	The solution is tested?	Deployment or Implementat ion
Fahim Ullah et al [2021]	Deals in smart city real estate	Real estate transactions in smart cities will use blockchain smart contracts.	conceptual framework	a novel smart contract architecture that is suitable for real estate transactions	Yes	Yes
Adarsh Kumar et al. [2020]	Innovative Healthcare 4.0 Smart Processes	Utilise Blockchain 3.0 to develop a smart healthcare system.	conceptual framework	Blockchain version 3.0 interoperability and integration with Healthcare 4.0	Yes	Yes
Mayank Raikwar et al [2018]	Insurance Processes	Design an experimental prototype on Hyperledger fabric	Design Experimenta l Prototype	Prepare a model for processing insurance-related transactions	Yes	No
Hoai Luan Pham et al [2018]	Secure Remote Healthcare System	suggested powered by blockchain Ethereum-based remote health care system	Design of Experimenta l Processing mechanism	created and evaluated an online healthcare system built on a blockchain smart contract.	Yes	Yes
Toqeer Ali et al [2020]	Property Registration System	a Permissioned Blockchain-based Property Registration System.	Use case-based study and design framework.	Smart Model was designed for the Property Registration System	No	No
Olawande Daramola et al [2020]	Electronic Voting in National Elections	to better comprehend the benefits, risks, and difficulties associated with an electronic voting system based on blockchain for national elections.	Architecture Trade-off Analysis Method (ATAM)	demonstrated how to use the framework trade-of-analysis technique (ATAM) to facilitate election	No	No
Valentina Gatteschi et al [2018]	Insurance Processes	To aid the insurance sector, while it may be easily adapted to other fields.	SWOT Analysis	Outline the benefits and drawbacks.	No	No

Fig. 4. (a) Comparative and Comprehensive Analysis [8–21]

Authors	Blockchain Application Domain	Problem Statement	Research Method	Solution	The solution is tested?	Deployment or Implementation
Sujit Biswas et al [2020]	E-Healthcare Systems.	To gain a better understanding of establishing a blockchain solution for e-healthcare systems	Literature Survey	analyse and describe how commercial blockchain can be applied to the healthcare industry.	No	No
Friorik P. Hjalmarsson et al [2018]	E-Voting System	creating a blockchain-based electronic voting system	Design of experimental framework	suggested a system for voting electronically based on blockchain	Yes	Yes
Tanesh Kumar et al. [2018]	healthcare systems	to list the problems and challenges with implementing blockchain technology in medical centres.	Literature survey	The medical sector blockchain's smart contract is presented.	No	No
Ioannis Karamitsos et al [2018]	Real Estate System	offer a blockchain-based method for creating smart contracts.	Conceptual framework	For a particular use case, state finite operations and procedures are offered.	Yes	Yes
Rohan Bennett et al [2021]	Land Administration	Hybrid Strategies for Smart Contracts in Land Management that are Being Proposed	Comparative analysis	A framework for maturity for the application of smart contracts and blockchain to real estate transactions.	Yes	Yes
Vinay Thakura et al [2019]	Land Titling System	Blockchain documentation for India's adoption of title titling	Conceptual framework and design of system	a method created to put in place a land ownership system	Yes	Yes

Fig. 4. (*continued*)

The investigation study is intensive on a comprehensive literature assessment of current research investigations conducted between 2015 and 2021. The analysis being conducted now involves a thorough assessment of blockchain applications across several industries. According to this study, only a minor amount of application areas, including the real estate, healthcare, insurance, and electronic voting industries, have been investigated for the use of blockchain technology. Future uses of smart contacts and blockchain technology could include numerous underrepresented industries (Refer to Fig. 4(a) and 4(b)).

3   Proposed Methodology

Independent trust, security, and integrity are only a few of the issues in the IREDP domain that would be addressed by the suggested architecture. Government agencies would handle and store IREDP data using the suggested Hyperledger fabric, which is a permission blockchain to procedure paperwork like sale deeds and mortgages. Contributors include the seller, the buyer, the mortgage company, and the insurance authority, while peers include the registration authority, the district magistrate (collector), the court, and the municipal authority. Because the IREDP documentation and data are private, we are employing permission blockchain as opposed to blockchain. Real estate sales and purchases may be conducted directly between the seller and the buyer. They can start blockchain transactions. One smart contract with business logic for real estate registration was created, along with three other basic smart contracts. To store processed documents, we suggest using the IPFS (Inter Planetary File System). The suggested model stores characteristics including truthfulness, safety, and secrecy. It also removes the possibility of a solitary point of letdown.

3.1   Core Architecture and Components

The three primary fundamental components of the projected framework are as follows.

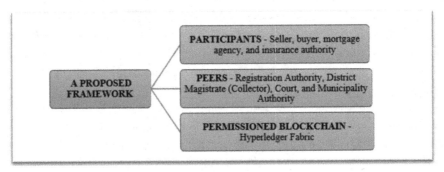

Fig. 5. Components of A Projected Framework

The primary four counterparts that control the transactional process are the authorized characteristics of the property being inspected by the district magistrate. For example, while registering an apartment, the municipal authorities validate that the unit is ended and prepared for registration. They also approve the type of property and its condition (Refer to Fig. 5). Any vendor or purchaser participates in the proposed framework as a direct user. It is a permission blockchain, which restricts network involvement. As an outcome, the administration's call for oversight over blockchain network contribution is met. However various organizations have control over the data. The blockchain, which is based on Hyperledger Fabric, maintains data about real estate transactions and makes it available to users using smart contracts (chain code) [22] (Refer to Fig. 6). The InterPlanetary File System (IPFS), a peer-to-peer network and distributed file system protocol, enables data storage and delivery. Data and transactions are kept apart in IPFS, which reduces computational and transmission costs while maintaining privacy [23]. Due to the harmless storage method offered by the IPFS protocol, it's a feasible option for storing sale deed records.

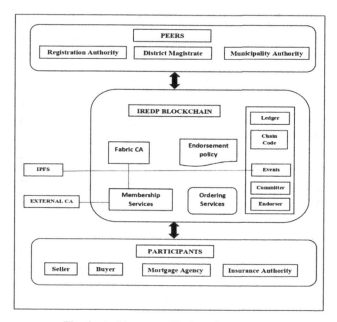

Fig. 6. Architecture of Projected Framework

3.2 Process Flow for Transactions

The critical next step in finalizing Indian real estate documentation is the suggested framework is focused on the Property Registration Process. Participation in the property's registration is agreed upon between the seller and the buyer. This transaction will be recorded at the registration office using the appropriate legal documentation. The regulatory bodies will authorize the selling deed documents following a review of the documentation and payment of the necessary stamp duty fees (Refer to Figs. 7 and 8).

3.3 Proposed Four-Step Verification Secure Logic for Property Registration Process

The four-step verification logic that is applied when transaction information is relocated to the blockchain system was the main focus of the research project (Refer to Fig. 9(a), 9(b) and 9(c)).

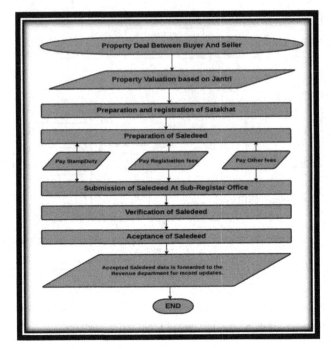

Fig. 7. Property Registration Process Flow

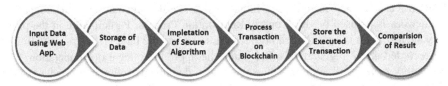

Fig. 8. Process Flow of Proposed Property Registration System

4　Implementation

4.1　Set up of Front-End Application

We created the front end to accept data from the buyer and accept information about the buyer, seller, property, registration, stamp duty, and payment. The created application accepts the data and sends it for verification before transferring it to the blockchain network for execution (Refer to Figs. 10, 11, 12, 13, 14, 15, 16, 17, 18, 19, 20, 21).

```
// Participant verification and authentication
function Verification (enroll-no, sign)
{
      if(enroll-no-exists=false) then
            abort request;
      end if
      if (sign_valid=false) then
            abort request;
      end if
}
end function

// Access Verification of Participants
function access_privilege(enroll-no, Smart-Contract-id)
{
      if (enroll-no having the ability to invoke-Smart-Contract-id=false)
then
            REJECT-TRANSACTION.
      end if
}
end function

//Examining the format and looking for duplicates Transaction
function check_proposal_format(transaction-proposal)
{
      Verify_whether_proposal_is_in_desired_format;
}
end function

function Verify_transaction_originality(transaction-proposal)
{
      Verify_whether_transaction_is_Duplicate_or_Original;
}
end function

//Approval for New Property Registration Transaction  from all
authorities.
function Property_Registration_transaction_approval(owner-info, property-
info, property-completion-info)
{
      // Approval from the Municipal Authority
      if (peer-name=Municipal-Authority) then
      {
            if(property-owner-info-is- valid ==False) then
                  REJECT-TRANSACTION
            else
            if (property-plan-verified==False) then
                  REJECT-TRANSACTION
            else
            if (property-construction-completion-certificate-
issued==False)  then
                  REJECT-TRANSACTION
            else
                  transaction-approved-by-Municipal-Authority=True;
```

Fig. 9. (a) Algorithm for property registration process

```
                    modify world_state; (Key value: Municipal-Authority-
Validation=True)
            end if
            end if
        end if
        }
        else
            REJECT-TRANSACTION;
        end if

        // Approval from the District-Megistrate-Authority
        if (peer-Is-District-Megistrate-Authority) then
            {
                    if(Any-pettion-against-subjected-property==true) then
                        REJECT-TRANSACTION

                else
                        transaction-approved-by-District-Megistrate-
Authority=True;
                        modify world_state; (Key value: District-
Megistrate-Authority-Validation=True)
                    end if
                    end if
                end if
            }
            else
                REJECT-TRANSACTION;
        end if
        // Approval from the District-Court-Authority
            if (peer-Is-District-Court-Authority) then
                {
                        if(Any-Stay-order-against-subjected-
property==true) then
                            REJECT-TRANSACTION

                    else
                            transaction-approved-by-District-Court-
Authority=True;
                            update world_state; (Key value: District-
Court-Authority-
                            Validation=True)
                        end if
                        end if
                    end if
                    }
                    else
                        REJECT-TRANSACTION;
            end if
            // Approval from the Registration-Authority
            if (peer-Is-Registration-Authority) then
            {
                if(owner-validation=FALSE) then
                    REJECT-TRANSACTION
```

Fig. 9. (*continued*)

```
               else if(Saledeed-transact-property-amount > owner-property-
amount) then
                          REJECT-TRANSACTION
               else if(property-valuation=FALSE) then
                          REJECT-TRANSACTION
               else if(Stampduty-paid=True || Stampduty-paid-
amount=evaluated-fee) then
                          transaction-approved-by-Registration-
Authority=True
                          modify world_state;
                          (Key value: Registration-Authority-
Validation=True, Fee-paid=True,
                          owner=new-owner)
                          Insert transaction to the distributed ledger;
               else
                          REJECT-TRANSACTION;
               end if
               end if
               end if
       }
       else
               REJECT-TRANSACTION
       end if
}
end function

// Final Saledeed transaction execution
function Final-SaleDeed-transaction-Execution (transaction-no,
world_state)
{
       if (peer-Registration-Authority==true) then
       {
       if key-value (Registration-Authority- Validation=True , Municipal-
       Authority-Validation=True, District-Court-Authority-
Validation=True,
       District-Megistrate-Authority-Validation=True,Fee-paid=True,
owner-new-owner) then
          {
               Issue-saledeed and store it to IPFS;
                IPFS-address=reference of saledeed on IPFS;
                Calculate hash_saledeed=hash(Issued-saledeed);
               Modify world_state (key-value: hash_saledeed =
hash_transaction,
               IPFS_saledeed_location = IPFS-address);
          }
          else
               REJECT-TRANSACTION
       }
       else
               REJECT-TRANSACTION
       end if
       end if
}
end function
```

Fig. 9. (*continued*)

Fig. 10. Login Screen for Purchaser to Make Application for Document.

Fig. 11. Screen to enter Purchaser-related information.

Fig. 12. Screen to enter seller-related information.

Fig. 13. Screen to enter Property-related information.

Fig. 14. Screen to enter Payment related information.

Fig. 15. Screen to enter Stamp duty fee and Registration fee-related information.

Fig. 16. Screen to summarize information about document information.

Fig. 17. Approval Screen for Data Verification Officer.

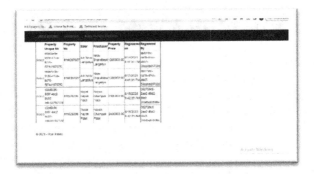

Fig. 18. Approval Screen for District Magistrate.

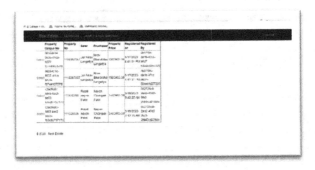

Fig. 19. Approval Screen for Nagar Palica Officer

4.2 Setup of Permissioned Blockchain

1. Setup of the Communication Channel

Any system relies on communication to function properly. Furthermore, in the commercial sector, effective communication skills are crucial [24]. Working with the Hyperledger fabric necessitates mentioning the communication channel. We categorize the network into three distinct channels.

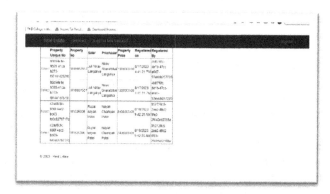

Fig. 20. Approval Screen for Registrar

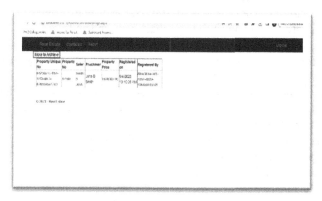

Fig. 21. Final Approval Screen for Admin

C-1: This channel comprises the seller, the buyer, the Registrar Authority, the District Magistrate, and the Municipality Authority, all of whom are involved in the registration of new property. In this channel, we proposed a smart contract that would be auto-initialized throughout the registration process for new properties.

C-2: This is the network's second communication channel, which includes the Registrar Authority, Mortgage Agency, Property Owner, and Insurance Agency. The smart contract for the channel is used to query for property information and register for a mortgage.

C-3: The Registrar Authority, District Magistrate, Municipality Authority, and Court made up the network's third channel. This channel is used to communicate between the authorities mentioned above. They communicate in a private manner that is not visible to others.

2. Setup Membership Services

To participate in the system, you must be a member of the distributed network. The Membership Service Provider (MSP) provides this functionality. Fabric-CA or External CA can issue membership in the proposed system, which can be used to initiate transactions, validate them, and sign them. Fabric's default MSP implementation supports common PKI methods for digital signature authentication and can accommodate commercial certification authorities (CAs). Fabric also includes Fabric-CA, which is a stand-alone CA [25].

3. Identification Management

In the literature, identity management is sometimes known as identity and access management (IAM). Identity management, in general, refers to a set of rules and technologies that ensure that only authorized persons have access to an organization's resources [26, 27]. The government authorities function as peers in the proposed system, while other players work as participants. At the level of the participating organization's MSP, their identities would be managed. An identification and enrolment certificate will be issued to each user in the fabric network. A private key and signed certificate are included in the enrolment certificate. The user's private key is used to digitally sign the transaction and is kept private.

4. Setup Endorsement Policy

Every chain code has an authorization strategy that stipulates the number of nobles on a network who must execute chain code and endorse the outcomes for the transaction to be measured as valid. These endorsement regulations specify which administrations must "endorse" the implementation of a proposal (by their peers) [28]. The peers, Registrar Authority, Court Authority, Municipal Authority, and District Magistrate are all required to sign the endorsement in our proposed framework, and they are all expected to run Smart Contracts that are made in such a way that they will run different approaches depending on the business logic requirements. Every Chain code includes an endorsement strategy that requires the number of peers on a channel who must run the Chain code and endorse the outcomes for the transaction to be measured as valid [29].

5. Tools and Technology

We constructed a dummy micro basic form of the model with the lowest configuration utilizing some replica test data to implement the given framework and analysis. We used the following technical Specification for deployment purposes. Hyperledger Fabric (version: 1.4), Ubuntu version: 16.04.6 LTS. Hyperledger Fabric requires the following prerequisites: SDK - Node.js - v12.3.1, curl - v7.47.0, Docker - v19.03.0, Docker-compose - v1.24.0, Go - v1.12 NPM - v6.10.3 Python-2.7.

4.3 Execution of Transaction on the Blockchain Network

We created the front-end report so that admins could see the final performed transaction (Refer to Fig. 22).

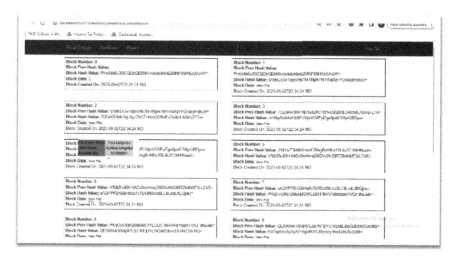

Fig. 22. Report of Executed Transaction for Admin

5   Result Analysis

5.1   Outcome Analysis of Proposed System

The Dumay dataset, which consists of 5000 documents and information exchanged on the blockchain network to evaluate the scalability, efficiency, and performance of the transaction processing capacity, is developed to analyze the proposed system on a wide scale. Based on the results, we have prepared the analysis that follows (Refer to Table 1).

Table 1. Performance Analysis

No of Transaction	Time Taken for Execution (In Second)
1-500	10.125
501-1000	11.025
1001-1500	10.489
1501-2000	11.345
2001-2500	10.236
2501-3000	10.489
3001-3500	10.687
3501-4000	10.258
4001-4500	10.651
4501-5000	10.478

5.2 Comparative Analysis of Proposed System with Existing System

During the duration of the research, the front-end (web app) creation and data loading into the appropriate schema are completed. After implementing the recommended algorithms, all of the data was then transmitted to the blockchain platform for finishing touches. The final result is visualized using blockchain technology. This term also makes a comparison to the existing system (Refer to Fig. 23).

Features	Exiting Indian Real Estate Document Processing	Proposed Indian Real Estate Document Processing	Research Contribution
Type of Network	Centralized Network	Distributed Peer-to-Peer Network	Set up the Blockchain-based network
Transaction Status	Variable	Immutable	Implementation of SHA-256 Hash code for Block Encryption
Transaction Security	Less	Greater	Applied a stage verification Algorithm
Transaction Visibility	Opaque	Transparent	By using the distributed Ledger Technology
Transaction Controller	Single and Central authority	No single authority	Due to a Distributed network and Algorithm flow, it involved a group of people.
Transaction Traceability	Less	Greater and Fast	Due to local availability and a unique hash code system

Fig. 23. Comparative analysis of proposed and existing systems.

6 Conclusion

Blockchain and other upcoming technologies are thoroughly explained at the beginning of the text. The beginning section of the paper also discusses the real estate sector and its significance. Additionally emphasized is blockchain's beneficial effect on the Indian real estate market. The review section offers a tabular format for a thorough and comparative study of the many research projects that have been completed between 2015 and 2022, demonstrating the glaring research gap that may be addressed using blockchain for the processing of Indian real estate documents. The article's suggested methodology section includes a detailed explanation of the fundamental components, proposed system architecture, property Registration process flow, and overall system flow. To increase the security of real estate transactions, a four-step verification method is also described and executed at the deployment stage. The front-end design with screenshots is shown during the implementation stage, and the setting up of the blockchain and the final real estate transaction execution are also detailed. The result analysis section, which is a graphical depiction of the outcome result and exhibits the suggested system scalability at a large scale, is at the end of the article. This section also compares the current system with the suggested system and also mentions the successful completion of the research goals.

References

1. Singhal, B., Dhameja, G., Panda, P.S.: Beginning Blockchain a beginner's guide to building blockchain solutions-bikramaditya singhal gautam dhameja priyansu sekhar panda (2018)
2. Sarmah, S.S.: Application of blockchain in cloud computing. Int. J. Innov. Technol. Explor. Eng. **8**(12), 4698–4704 (2019). https://doi.org/10.35940/ijitee.L3585.1081219
3. Bashir, I.: Mastering Blockchain, 2nd edn. Packt Publishing (2018
4. Cai, Z.: Maestro: achieving scalability and coordination in centralized network control plane. Rice University (2011)
5. Dannen, C.: Introducing ethereum and solidity (2017)
6. 10th Planning Commission. Tenth Five Year Plan Report 2002–07. Source, pp. 829–846 (2002). https://niti.gov.in/planningcommission.gov.in/docs/plans/planrel/fiveyr/10th/volume2/v2_ch7_6.pdf
7. Real Estate. https://corporatefinanceinstitute.com/resources/careers/jobs/real-estate/
8. Langaliya, V., Gohil, J.A.G.: A comparative and comprehensive analysis of smart contract enabled blockchain applications. Int. J. Recent Innov. Trends Comput. Commun. **9**(9), 16–26 (2021). https://doi.org/10.17762/ijritcc.v9i9.5489
9. Ullah, F., Al-Turjman, F.: A conceptual framework for blockchain smart contract adoption to manage real estate deals in smart cities. Neural Comput. Appl. (February) (2021). https://doi.org/10.1007/s00521-021-05800-6
10. Kumar, A., Krishnamurthi, R., Nayyar, A., Sharma, K., Grover, V., Hossain, E.: A novel smart healthcare design, simulation, and implementation using healthcare 4.0 processes. IEEE Access **8**, 118433–118471 (2020). https://doi.org/10.1109/ACCESS.2020.3004790
11. Raikwar, M., Mazumdar, S., Ruj, S., Sen Gupta, S., Chattopadhyay, A., Lam, K.-Y.: A blockchain framework for insurance processes. In: 2018 9th IFIP International Conference on New Technologies, Mobility and Security (NTMS), pp. 1–4 (2018). https://doi.org/10.1109/NTMS.2018.8328731
12. Pham, H.L., Tran, T.H., Nakashima, Y.: A secure remote healthcare system for hospital using blockchain smart contract. In: 2018 IEEE Globecom Workshops GC Wkshps 2018 – Proceedings (2019). https://doi.org/10.1109/GLOCOMW.2018.8644164
13. Ali, T., Nadeem, A., Alzahrani, A., Jan, S.: A transparent and trusted property registration system on permissioned blockchain. In: 2019 International Conference on Advances in the Emerging Computing Technologies, AECT 2019 (2020). https://doi.org/10.1109/AECT47998.2020.9194222
14. Daramola, O., Thebus, D.: Architecture-centric evaluation of blockchain-based smart contract e-voting for national elections. Informatics **7**(2), 16 (2020). https://doi.org/10.3390/informatics7020016
15. Gatteschi, V., Lamberti, F., Demartini, C., Pranteda, C., Santamaría, V.: Blockchain and smart insurance contracts: is the technology mature enough? Futur. Internet **10**(2), 8–13 (2018). https://doi.org/10.3390/fi10020020
16. Biswas, S., Sharif, K., Li, F., Mohanty, S.: Blockchain for E-health-care systems: easier said than done. Comput. (Long. Beach. Calif.) **53**(7), 57–67 (2020). https://doi.org/10.1109/MC.2020.2989781
17. Hjalmarsson, F.P., Hreioarsson, G.K., Hamdaqa, M., Hjalmtysson, G.: Blockchain-based E-voting system. In: IEEE International Conference on Cloud Computing, CLOUD, vol. 2018-July, pp. 983–986 (2018). https://doi.org/10.1109/CLOUD.2018.00151
18. Kumar, T., Ramani, V., Ahmad, I., Braeken, A., Harjula, E., Ylianttila, M.: Blockchain utilization in healthcare: key requirements and challenges. In: 2018 IEEE 20th International Conference on e-Health Networking, applications and services (Healthcom 2018) (2018). https://doi.org/10.1109/HealthCom.2018.8531136

19. Karamitsos, I., Papadaki, M., Al Barghuthi, N.B.: Design of the blockchain smart contract: a use case for real estate. J. Inf. Secur. **09**(03), 177–190 (2018). https://doi.org/10.4236/jis.2018.93013

20. Bennett, R., Miller, T., Pickering, M., Kara, A.K.: Hybrid approaches for smart contracts in land administration: Lessons from three blockchain proofs-of-concept. Land **10**(2), 1–23 (2021). https://doi.org/10.3390/land10020220

21. Thakur, V., Doja, M.N., Dwivedi, Y.K., Ahmad, T., Khadanga, G.: Land records on blockchain for implementation of land titling in India. Int. J. Inf. Manage. **52**(March), 1 (2020). https://doi.org/10.1016/j.ijinfomgt.2019.04.013

22. Langaliya, V., Gohil, J.A.: Configuration and Implementation of novel and safe methodology for processing real estate transactions by utilizing hyperledger fabric. SN Comput. Sci. (2023). https://doi.org/10.1007/s42979-023-02099-z

23. Xu, J., et al.: Healthchain: a blockchain-based privacy-preserving scheme for large-scale health data. IEEE Internet Things J. **6**(5), 8770–8781 (2019). https://doi.org/10.1109/JIOT.2019.2923525

24. Waylen, A.: The importance of communication in dentistry. Dent. Update **44**(8), 774–780 (2017). https://doi.org/10.12968/denu.2017.44.8.774

25. Androulaki, E., et al.: Hyperledger fabric: a distributed operating system for permissioned blockchains. In: Proceedings of the 13th EuroSys Conference, EuroSys 2018, vol. 2018-Janua (2018). https://doi.org/10.1145/3190508.3190538

26. Mohanta, B.K., Panda, S.S., Jena, D.: An overview of smart contract and use cases in blockchain technology. In: 2018 9th International Conference on Computer Communication and Networking Technologies, INT 2018, no. October, pp. 1–4 (2018). https://doi.org/10.1109/ICCCNT.2018.8494045

27. Liu, Y., He, D., Obaidat, M.S., Kumar, N., Khan, M.K., Raymond Choo, K.K.: Blockchain-based identity management systems: a review. J. Netw. Comput. Appl. **166**(June), 102731 (2020). https://doi.org/10.1016/j.jnca.2020.102731

28. Endorsement policies. https://hyperledger-fabric.readthedocs.io/en/release-2.2/endorsement-policies.html

29. Sen, S., Mukhopadhyay, S., Karforma, S.: A blockchain-based framework for property registration system in E-governance. Int. J. Inf. Eng. Electron. Bus. **13**(4), 30–46 (2021). https://doi.org/10.5815/ijieeb.2021.04.03

Secure and Immutable Payment Algorithm Using Smart Cards and Hyperledger Blockchain

Ravirajsinh S. Vaghela[1]($\boxtimes$), Kalpesh Popat[2], Vishalsinh Gohil[3], Bansi Chavda[3], and Parag Shukla[1]

[1] School of Cyber Security and Digital Forensic, NFSU, Gandhinagar, India
`ravirajsinh.vaghela@nfsu.ac.in`
[2] FoCA Department, Marwadi University, Rajkot, India
[3] ICT Department, Marwadi University, Rajkot, India

Abstract. By doing digital transactions there is a lot of risk of hacking and also the rising incidence of online fraud. When utilizing the smart cards system, users are concerned about fraud, security problems (hackers), the lack of availability of up-to-date information, and hidden fees. Recent studies clearly show that card-not-present fraud, skimming fraud, and website cloning method has been used more frequently in the smart card system. The frequency of using plastic cards is expected to go up in the upcoming years. Card systems face a variety of issues, including connectivity issues, password forgetfulness, fraud fears, lack of understanding, others technological issues. The scope of the research is limited to the card is particularly used in ATM and online purchase only but by using this proposed system using block chain aggregator we can use any plastic card a to purchase any things transparently and efficiently.

Keywords: Blockchain · sensitive information · smart card · Decentralized Applications

1 Introduction

Initiation of the creation of smart cards began in Germany, France, and Japan in the early 1970s. And in the next few years, numerous suggestions for its use and applications were made, and numerous commercial firms began collaborating on its development [1]. Plastic card – is a personalized payment tool that provides the ability to use your card the face of non-cash payment for goods and services, as well as withdraw cash at bank branches and ATMs. But smart card system is not secure and safe [2]. We currently have different methods of digital payment available in India. Some methods have been in use for more than a decade, some have become recently popular, and others are relatively new. Objective of the paper is to study loopholes in the existing smart card system and develop a cardless system to solve existing issue using block chain. Blockchain is a decentralized distributed ledger system that enables transactions that are safe, transparent, and irreversible. It has the potential to revolutionize many industries by creating a more efficient and trustworthy way to exchange information and assets [3].

S. Rajagopal et al (Eds.): ASCIS 2023, CCIS 2040, pp. 349–356, 2024.
https://doi.org/10.1007/978-3-031-59107-5_23

1.1 Smart Card Payment Problems in Existing System

When utilizing smart cards, users worry about fraud, security concerns, the lack of current information, and hidden fees [4]. By doing digital transactions there is a lot of risk of hacking and also the rising incidence of online fraud [5]. Electronic payment system safety and privacy depends on electronic signature otherwise there will be security risk [6]. If swiping cards at small shops and vendors will not be a risk to caring our cards details and Costly swipe machine is not afforded by every shopkeepers [7]. Recent research has demonstrated that the smart card system has been more commonly exploited by card-not-present fraud, skimming fraud, and website cloning, card cloning, card stalking [8]. The frequency of using plastic cards is expected to go up in the upcoming years. So, expenditure for production of card is more and more day to day. When we withdraw money from ATM then we get fake notes from ATM machine, then bank take higher service charge for further investigation [9]. When we do transaction by plastic card do not know about the money immediate after some time when we get message we come to know about our money. Numerous challenges with the card system exist, including connectivity issues, password forgetfulness, fraud fears, lack of understanding, technological issues [10]. Cards are connected to bank accounts, which are connected to confidential private data that could be dangerous in the hands of any unauthorized individuals. To ensure the security of transactions, a number of steps are being taken, including Password authentication, biometric identifications, Text notifications, and email statements [11]. Additionally, it has been noted that there are some plastic money frauds that can be resolved. These cards are especially popular among consumers who shop online. Money has worth, so we shouldn't become victims of thievery [12]. Some credit card transaction take more time than cash transaction because of some formalities and discounts and rebates can rarely be obtain cardholder is responsible for loss or theft of the card fewer worldwide availability of cards for use in locations where there is a local dispute and fraud involving any credit or debit card copies[13, 14]. The biggest drawbacks of a cashless society are privacy concerns and account hacking. A huge, unorganized sector, persistent poverty, and backwardness make it difficult to transition to a cashless economy [15]. The technology behind the contactless payment system has security flaws [16].

2 Literature Survey of Blockchain and Smart Card Application

In this venture, it gave itemized data about virtual cards and its execution. Share that virtual card to anybody and ensure that they realize how to utilize it. Virtual card is not possible to clone/copy [17]. The bird optimization algorithm is used for solved fraud detection problem in master card [18]. Sending money over a blockchain instead of using a credit card gives security and transparency because blockchain technology allows for nearly cost-free transactions. Additionally, the majority of cross-border expenses can be avoided by eliminating middlemen and connecting the banks at both ends of each transaction directly [19]. The payment transaction is frequently recorded in various ledgers. Both accepting and processing credit and debit cards come with fees for merchants. Blockchain eliminates the need for third-party validators, lowering costs and raising the overall transaction value for the Merchant [20]. Decentralization and the elimination of third parties may be achieved when smart contracts are combined with immutable blockchain technology. This method uses a smart contract between the bank and the consumer to reduce fraud caused by foggy contracts [21]. Financial institutions are constantly improving their fraud detection systems, but fraudsters are also evolving their techniques. To detect deception, many machine learning algorithms can be used [22]. Chargeback fraud is when customers falsely request refunds, keeping the items or services. Blockchain's transparent data sharing enables multiple parties to fight chargeback fraud [23]. By using biometric Credit/Debit Card no need to remember PIN and any other ID to access and reduces the risk of fraud and misuse can be prevented biometric card will work without requiring the major hardware [24]. With the help of multiple Machine Learning-based classifiers, the proposed study categorizes and summarizes the numerous categorization techniques used to categories the transactions. The proposed summary will help researchers, bankers, and people who use credit cards better analyze and stop credit card fraud [25].

In this section we are proposing novel thoughts based to overcome existing problems with blockchain technology.

3   Proposed Blockchain Based Cards Aggregator

Payment cards aggregation system using blockchain is to use a decentralized network of merchants to process transactions. This would eliminate the need for a central payment processor, which would reduce costs and improve efficiency. The system would use blockchain technology to keep track of all transactions and ensure that they are secure and tamper-proof. This means that there would be a very low risk of fraud or theft (Fig. 1).

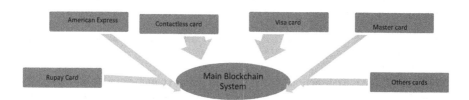

Fig. 1. Smart Card Aggregation System using Blockchain

3.1   Proposed Algorithm

We propose a new algorithm for Multi-Company Smart Card Blockchain Transaction (MCSCBT). This algorithm allows users to make payments between companies using smart cards and blockchain technology. To start, the user generates a private key and public key on their smart card. They then send their public key to the blockchain network. Next, the user creates a transaction request, which includes the recipient company's public key, the amount of money to be transferred, and the company ID of the sender company. The user then signs the transaction request using their private key and broadcasts it to the blockchain network. The blockchain network verifies the signature on the transaction request and the company ID. If the signature is valid and the company ID is correct, the transaction is added to the blockchain. The recipient company can then verify the transaction by checking the blockchain. This algorithm is secure because the user's private key is never shared with anyone. Additionally, the blockchain network ensures that transactions are immutable and cannot be tampered with.

3.2 Selection of Blockchain Technology

In this smart card aggregation concept we select mainly 3 different blockchain concept in which two blockchain having public blockchain and one having private blockchain.

Table 1. Comparison of Blockchain based on feature [26, 27]

Feature	Bitcoin Blockchain	Ethereum Blockchain	Hyperledger Fabric Blockchain
Consensus mechanism	Proof of Work (PoW)	Proof of Stake (PoS)	Byzantine Fault Tolerance (BFT)
Smart contract support	No	Yes	Yes
Programming language	Scripting language	Solidity, Vyper, etc	Go, Node.js, Java, etc
Transactions per second (TPS)	7	15–30	Thousands
Permissioned	No	No	Yes
Scalability	Limited	Good	Excellent
Security	High	High	High

From the Table 1. Transaction per second is important parameter a permissioned also important features need to consider with scalability when we decided any technology. Comparison we can deduce Overall, Hyperledger Fabric is the best blockchain platform for smart card aggregation applications. It is private, permissioned, fast, scalable, and supports smart contracts.

3.3 ALGORITHM: Multi-company Smart Card Blockchain Transaction (MCSCBT)

INPUT:

- User's private key

- User's public key

- Recipient company's public key

- Amount of money to be transferred

- Company ID of the sender company

OUTPUT:

- Transaction ID

BEGIN

// Generate the user's private key and public key on the smart card.

GenerateKeyPair(privateKey, publicKey)

// Send the user's public key to the blockchain network.

SendPublicKey(publicKey)

// Create a transaction request.

TransactionRequest := {

  RecipientCompanyPublicKey: recipientCompanyPublicKey,

  Amount: amount,

  CompanyID: companyID

}

// Sign the transaction request using the user's private key.

Signature := Sign(privateKey, TransactionRequest)

// Broadcast the transaction request to the blockchain network.

BroadcastTransactionRequest(TransactionRequest, Signature)

// Verify the signature on the transaction request and the company ID.

VerifySignature(publicKey, TransactionRequest, Signature)

VerifyCompanyID(companyID)

// If the signature is valid and the company ID is correct, add the transaction to the blockchain.

If SignatureIsValid() and CompanyIDIsValid() then

AddTransactionToBlockchain(TransactionRequest)

// The recipient company can then verify the transaction by checking the blockchain.

RecipientCompany := GetRecipientCompany(TransactionRequest)

RecipientCompany.VerifyTransaction(TransactionRequest)

END

The Pseudocode shows that the process starts with the user generating a private key and public key on their smart card. The user then sends their public key to the blockchain network. Next, the user creates a transaction request, which includes the recipient company's public key, the amount of money to be transferred, and the company ID of the sender company. The user then signs the transaction request using their private key and broadcasts it to the blockchain network. The blockchain network verifies the signature on the transaction request and the company ID. If the signature is valid and the company ID is correct, the transaction is added to the blockchain. The recipient company can then verify the transaction by checking the blockchain.

4   Conclusion

Smart card blockchain transactions between multiple companies offer a number of advantages over traditional payment methods. They are more secure, efficient, and transparent. Smart card blockchain transactions are secure. Additionally, the blockchain network ensures that transactions are immutable and cannot be tampered with. Smart card blockchain transactions are also efficient because they can be processed quickly and without the need for intermediaries. This can save companies time and money. Hyperledger Fabric is a very performant blockchain platform that is capable of processing a large number of transactions per second. However, the performance of a Hyperledger Fabric blockchain depends on a number of factors, including the number of nodes in the network, the hardware and software configuration of each node, and the complexity of the transactions being processed. Finally, smart card blockchain transactions are transparent because all transactions are recorded on the blockchain. This makes it easy for companies to track their spending and ensure that all transactions are legitimate.

5   Future Work

Performance evaluation of proposed algorithm with test environment because performance can be affected by a number of factors, including the hardware, software, and network configuration. For example, using faster hardware or a more reliable network connection can improve performance. Additionally, the type of transaction can also affect performance. Hyper ledger Fabric application testing, we will use the Caliper performance benchmarking tool to test your application and identify any areas where performance can be improved.

References

1. Mahajan, A., Verma, A., Pahuja, D.: Smart card: turning point of technology. Int. J. Comput. Sci. Mob. Comput. Comput. Sci. Mob. Comput. **3**(10), 982–987 (2014)
2. Kumari, A., et al.: ESEAP: ECC based secure and efficient mutual authentication protocol using smart card. J. Inform. Sec. Appl. **51**, 102443 (2020)
3. Adhav, P., et al.: Secure e-wallet system using block chain technology. Int. J. **5**, 12 (2021)
4. Sowmya Praveen, K., Hebbar, C.K.: A study on customer attitude towards the usage and problems of plastic money–with reference to the women customers of SBI bank of Mangalore city. Profession **5**, 20 (2021)
5. Madhav, V.: Cashless economy: a challenging challenge to India; pros and cons. Aut Aut Res. J. **12**, 291–299 (2021)
6. Damodhar, G., Suneetha, T.: E-commerce in India: E-payment methods, trends and challenges
7. Charles, G.: A study on benefits and challenges of digital (cashless) India
8. Singh, A., Jain, A.: An empirical study of AML approach for credit card fraud detection—financial transactions. Int. J. Comput. Commun. Control **14**(6), 670–690 (2019)
9. Antony, J.: A Study on the impact of plastic money on consumer spending pattern. Global J. Manage. and Bus. Res. **18**(3), 29–36 (2018)
10. Sowmya, P.K., Hebbar, C.K.: Impact of digital payment on retail shops-with reference to Mangalore City. EPRA Int. J. Res. Dev. (IJRD), 187–191 (2021)
11. Rana, M.: Transition from paper to plastic: trends and issues of plastic money in India
12. Kiran, D.S.: A study on the people preferences towards plastic money with special reference to Puttur taluk of Dakshina Kannada. EPRA Int. J. Multidiscip. Res. (IJMR) **8**(8), 282–285 (2022)
13. Neelavathi, K., Ramya, C., Uttej, R.: A study on impact of usage of plastic money in India. J. Bus. Manage., 64–69 (2017)
14. Iqbal, S.: The digital economy of India: challenges and prospects (2020)
15. Manoj, G.: The digital economy of India: challenges and prospects
16. Akinyokun, N., Vanessa, T.: Security and privacy implications of NFC-enabled contactless payment systems. In: Proceedings of the 12th International Conference on Availability, Reliability and Security (2017)
17. Ramya, S.T., et al.: Enhanced Features based Private Virtual Card. Ann. Rom. Soc. Cell Biol., 17867–17872 (2021)
18. Shirodkar, N., et al.: Credit card fraud detection techniques–A survey. In: 2020 International Conference on Emerging Trends in Information Technology and Engineering (ic-ETITE). IEEE (2020)
19. Harvey, C.R., Moorman, C., Toledo, M.: How blockchain can help marketers build better relationships with their customers. Harv. Bus. Rev.. Bus. Rev. **9**, 6–13 (2018)
20. Godfrey-Welch, D., et al.: Blockchain in payment card systems. SMU Data Sci. Rev. **1**(1), 3 (2018)
21. Balagolla, E.M.S.W.: et al.: Credit card fraud prevention using blockchain. In: 2021 6th International Conference for Convergence in Technology (I2CT). IEEE (2021)
22. Pandey, K., Piyush, S., Nikam, G.G.: A review of credit card fraud detection techniques. In: 2021 5th International Conference on Computing Methodologies and Communication (ICCMC). IEEE (2021)
23. Liu, D., Lee, J.-H.: CFLedger: preventing chargeback fraud with blockchain. ICT Express **8**(3), 352–356 (2022)
24. Kumar, D., Yeonseung R., Dongseop, K.: A survey on biometric fingerprints: the cardless payment system. In: 2008 International Symposium on Biometrics and Security Technologies. IEEE (2008)

25. Adewumi, A.O., Akinyelu, A.A.: A survey of machine-learning and nature-inspired based credit card fraud detection techniques. Int. J. Syst. Assur. Eng. Manage. **8**, 937–953 (2017)
26. Zhao, Z.: Comparison of hyperledger fabric and ethereum blockchain. In: 2022 IEEE Asia-Pacific Conference on Image Processing, Electronics and Computers (IPEC). IEEE (2022)
27. Gorenflo, C., Lee, S., Golab, L., Keshav, S.: FastFabric: scaling hyperledger fabric to 20 000 transactions per second. Int. J. Netw. Manage. **30**(5), e2099 (2020)

Data Security Complications on Computing Technology in Mobile Cloud

A. Satishkumar and A. Vidhya[✉]

Department of Computer Science, Vels Institute of Science, Technology and Advanced Studies (VISTAS) Pallavaram, Chennai, India
`avidhya.scs@velsuniv.ac.in`

Abstract. Mobile devices resource limitations are a direct result of mobile computing rapid development. Nowadays, the gadget that was primarily used to receive calls and compose messages in earlier decades is capable of handling almost all of the duties currently carried out by computers. On the other hand, the development of mobile computing can be changed by combining mobile and cloud computing techniques, creating a new process known as ^{mobile} cloud computing technology. A mobile handler is now released from the constrained emission of currently available mobile devices as the information is deposited in the cloud's framework and the real implementation shifts to the cloud backdrop. Additionally, in order to utilize cloud services, wireless technology is used to transmit data between clouds and mobile devices. As a result, a few brand-new courses on privacy and security encounters are presented. Even if there are many disagreements, the resulting security elucidations have been projected and acknowledged in the literature by numerous researchers to counteract the experiments. Additionally, compare this effort based on various security and privacy preferences, and as a last point, discuss some open issues. This paper compares the existing RSA and AES algorithm with the proposed algorithm EMSA. The proposed algorithm shows more security than the existing algorithm and this can be used in cloud as well as mobile computing for storing confidential data.

Keywords: Security Issues · Cloud Computing · Virtualization · Mobile computing · Encryption and Decryption

1 Introduction

These days, as the number of mobile users rises daily, Mobile Cloud Computing (MCC) is a technology that is growing rapidly. The adoption of mobile devices raises serious concerns about data security and privacy. MCC can provide any typical smartphone with infrastructure, computational power, software, and platform services. Regarding the security of MCC, there are a number of concerns, including network security, web application security, data access, authentication, authorization, data confidentiality, and data leak. Because of their limited processing and storage capabilities, mobile devices have a lower data storage capacity. Security threats must be researched and evaluated in order to create a secure MCC environment. We provide an algorithm that will improve the mobile cloud's security [1].

Although it is anticipated that the development of sixth-generation (6G) wireless systems will lead to an explosion of user information that is accessible and novel technologies that pose new risks to terrestrial and non-terrestrial networks, privacy and security remain two of the main issues addressed. Reconfigurable Intelligent Surfaces (RISs), which have lately gained attention as potential 6G physical platform support options, have demonstrated the ability to increase the security of next-generation wireless networks. However, because of their low cost and ease of reconfiguration, RISs are susceptible to a number of security risks, and this vulnerability has not yet been fully addressed in prior studies.

The goal is comprehensively assessing the security issues RIS-powered 6G wireless networks are facing in order to close this knowledge gap in the literature [2]. The healthcare industry, smart cities, smart homes, transportation, and smart grid systems are just a few of the industries where Internet of Things (IoT) devices are in use. Through a variety of sensors, actuators, transceivers, or other wearable devices, these gadgets communicate a significant amount of data. There are several hazards, attacks, and threats that might affect data in the IoT ecosystem. A good security system is crucial due to the dangers, weaknesses, security, and privacy issues connected to IoT. A thorough literature evaluation has been done in this study to examine the security of IoT devices and to present mobile computing-based countermeasures to security issues and challenges. IoT security has been thoroughly and thoroughly examined in the context of mobile computing, a revolutionary technique [3].

2 Related Work

Applications of mobile social big data have evolved where mobile social users can use their mobile devices to interchange and share content with one another as the scope of mobile networks and the number of mobile users keeps growing. For the delivery of mobile social big data, the security resource is required. How to allocate the security resource, however, poses a new challenge given the restricted availability of security resources. To deliver mobile social big data, we therefore present in this study a combined match-coalitional game based security-aware resource allocation approach [4]. Through the ideas and practices of virtualization, network slicing, and cloud computing, 5G makes it possible to use many services over the same physical infrastructure. These ideas are used by Mobile Virtual Network Operators (MVNOs), which give different operators the chance to share the same physical infrastructure. Each MVNO may have its own unique support and operating systems. However, the technologies that support such an ecosystem have specific security issues and solutions of their own [5].

A possible method for boosting the security of password-based authenticated key exchange (PAKE) schemes is multi-factor authentication. It is commonly used in numerous everyday mobile applications (such as e-Bank, smart homes, and cloud services) to act as the first line of defence for system security. Despite substantial research, the problem of developing a safe and reliable multi-factor authentication solution remains challenging [6].

Use of the cloud modified the Internet world. Users may share, store, and access their data effortlessly and from any location with the use of cloud computing. The technical foundation for IT-enabled services delivered via the internet, cloud computing is scalable, quick, adaptable, and affordable. Infrastructural storage, software, and hardware are all made available to several users simultaneously through cloud computing. Users of the cloud frequently have no idea where their data is exactly stored or where the data that is stored with it comes from [7]. Due to the widespread use of smartphones, Mobile Cloud Computing (MCC), a concern for cloud computing on mobile devices, has emerged. It involves combining cloud computing and mobile devices to conduct resource-intensive operations online with little impact on cellular resources. Because of their tiny size and user-friendly interface, consumers now rely on mobile devices, but they can no longer rely on internal RAM due to their limited storage capacity. Because of this, there is a pressing need for technology to enable anytime, anywhere access to data for everyone [8].

Large-scale distributed systems, especially cloud and mobile deployments on the cloud, offer top-notch services that boost worker productivity and organizational effectiveness. Peer-to-peer (P2P) cloud systems are brought up as an extension for federated cloud in order to address the risks of P2P computing and match the performance requirements. These cloud implementations can manage resource provisioning for relatively little money. Since they have a decentralized architecture built without any unique central control or monitoring, on independent nodes and resources. There are numerous mobile applications and services as a result, and the number of mobile devices in use might quickly reach billions [9].

There has been a rapid rise in cloud computing over the last few years. The demand for protecting the data of some users using centralized resources has increased as more businesses turn to employing Cloud resources. Securing, protecting, and processing user-owned data are some of the primary issues that cloud computing are now dealing with. Understanding security dangers and identifying the appropriate security techniques used to minimize them in cloud computing are the main objectives of this study [10].

2.1 Data Security in Mobile Cloud and Cloud Computing

Data security describes how data is safely kept, guarded against illegal access, and preserved throughout its existence. Data encryption, tokenization, and key management distribution are all examples. Making sure that cloud networks and connections are secure is a crucial step in protecting data stored in the cloud. Consumers of cloud services need to be mindful of internal network threats such as leakage of confidential information, illegal modification of data, and denial of service. Because of this, it is crucial for users of the cloud to assess the internal network controls of the cloud service provider in light of any needs and security guidelines that may be present. Examining security measures on physical infrastructure and facilities is also one of the main recommendations. Because the infrastructure and facilities are shared in cloud computing, the cloud consumer is responsible for obtaining confirmation from the provider that suitable security controls are taken into consideration [1].

2.2 Cloud Computing Confidentiality

Confidentiality is among the most important security precautions for safeguarding users' data in the cloud. Before the data is saved in the cloud, plaintext encryption using cipher text is included. Even cloud service providers are unable to view or edit the content that is kept in the cloud using this method, which safeguards the users' data. Users' data is protected while it is saved on external drives or other media thanks to the data protection and encryption services provided by Dell [1].

2.3 Cryptographic Algorithm

The procedure Using cryptography, plain text can be changed from being readable and secure to being secure and unreadable, and vice versa. The decoding and encoding processes improve the files' data security. The five main goals of cryptography are: service reliability, privacy, integrity, and non-repudiation. The procedures of verification are included in authentication. By ensuring that the data has not been altered, cryptography assists in establishing the reliability of both the data source and the data itself. Digital certificates, digital signatures, and public key infrastructure (PKI) are used to accomplish this. The secrecy of the data being exchanged is likewise guaranteed by cryptography. To put it another way, the information is secured from assaults and unauthorized users. The integrity of the data is also guaranteed by cryptography. Additionally, cryptography guarantees data integrity, or that the message has not been altered. The sender and recipient cannot deny that the message was sent, which is known as non-repudiation. Finally, since systems are vulnerable to attack, cryptography improves service reliability, ensuring that users receive high-quality service. Figure 1 classification of cryptographic algorithms, public key cryptography and private key cryptography are the two primary subcategories of cryptographic algorithms. The encryption and decryption operations of In addition to being known as private key cryptography, symmetric cryptography, or Secret Key Cryptography (SKC) techniques, require the same key [11].

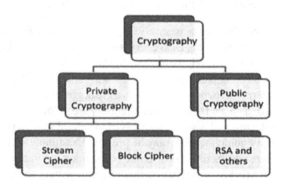

Fig. 1. Classification of the Cryptography Algorithm

The below Fig. 2 describes the private key cryptography algorithm and explains how the plain text is converted to cipher text using encryption technique and the decryption technique used to convert the encrypted text to plain text.

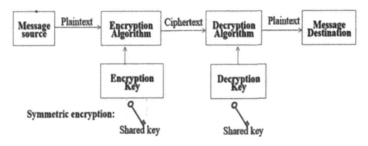

Fig. 2. Private Key Cryptographic Algorithm

2.4 AES (Advance Encryption Standard) Algorithm

AES is frequently used to protect data in the cloud. Data is encrypted using the AES technique when it is saved on the mobile cloud and the user wishes to use any application there. The data is encrypted and sent returned to the user when they request access to it again. AES is used in banking systems, government systems, and high security systems all around the world to secure online or internet banking.

The following are the primary attributes of AES.

i) Symmetric and Parallel Structure: This implementation provides the algorithm with a great deal of flexibility and guards it from crypto analysis assaults.
ii) Modern Processor-Friendly method: This method works well with current CPUs as the Intel Atom, Intel i7, Pentium, etc.
iii) Working well with smart cards [12].

2.5 RSA (Rivest-Shamir-Adleman) Algorithm

A key pair is required for both encryption and decryption in the asymmetric RSA technique. When encrypting data, public keys are used, which are known to all users because they are broadcast private keys, on the other hand, are only utilized when decrypting data by a single user. RSA uses 1024 keys, but 2048 keys are superior for security since 1024 keys have symmetric key lengths of 80 bits, which are easy to crack, whereas 2048 keys are comparable to 112 bits, which are significantly tougher to breach. In order to establish a secure communication channel and to verify the service provider, RSA is used [12].

2.6 Proposed Enhanced Mobile Security Algorithm (EMSA)

The proposed Enhanced Mobile Security Algorithm (EMSA) converts the plain text to QR (Quick Response) code using AES algorithm and with the help of RSA algorithm converting the text encryption with a QR code. In Fig. 3, the proposed algorithm's implementation of the encryption process is shown.

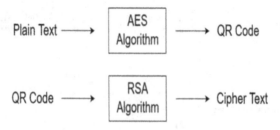

Fig. 3. Encryption Process

The decryption process can be done using RSA algorithm for the conversion of cipher text to QR code and AES algorithm is used to convert QR code to plain text. The diagrammatic representation is shown in Fig. 4.

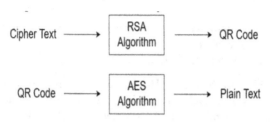

Fig. 4. Process of Decryption

The QR Code generated throughout the encryption and decryption processes must coincide. In order to accomplish this, we will first store the QR code strings in a database and then use a query to match strings. The data has successfully been checked when the strings coincide.

3   Evaluation Parameters

Each encryption method has strengths and weaknesses of its own. Knowing these strong and weak regions is necessary in order to apply the proper approach in a certain application. It is therefore vital to analyse these strategies using a number of features.

3.1   Avalanche Effect

Any encryption technique must have the property that even a little change in the plaintext or the key should result in a noticeable change in the cipher text. However, a slight modification to the plaintext or the key should result in a large alteration to several of the cipher message's bits.

3.2 Memory Needed for Implementation

In order to be implemented, different encryption algorithms need different amounts of memory. Based on how many operations the algorithm needs to do, this memory requirement is necessary. The minimum amount of memory required is optimum.

3.3 Time of Simulation

The simulation time is the length of time the algorithm needs to fully process a given length of data. Processor speed, algorithm complexity, and other factors all have a role. The three algorithms RSA, AES and the proposed algorithm EMSA are evaluated with metrics like avalanche effect, memory management needed for implementation and the duration of the simulation used in the simulators. The results are compared and explained in the below Table 1.

Table 1. Memory requirements and simulation time comparison

Algorithm	Memory(KB)	Simulation Time (Sec)
EMSA	10.2	0.0304
RSA	43.3	0.32
AES	23.4	0.23

The diagrammatic representation presented as a bar chart for the memory requirements in KB with the existing algorithm AES, RSA and the proposed algorithm EMSA are depicted in the Fig. 5. From the diagrammatic representation it is clear that the proposed algorithm EMSA has utilized only less memory. Hence, it is effective when the memory is less in the system, the proposed algorithm will work in an optimized way.

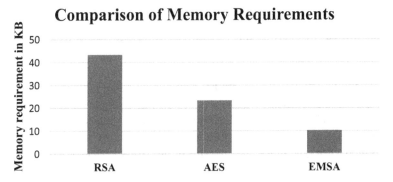

Fig. 5. Comparison of memory requirements with existing and proposed algorithms

The diagrammatic representation using a bar chart to represent the simulation time in sec when it is executed in the simulator with the existing algorithm AES, RSA and the proposed algorithm EMSA are compared depicted in the Fig. 6.

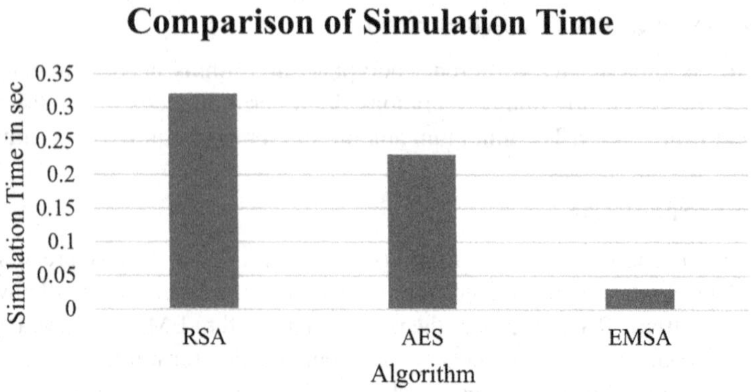

Comparison of Simulation Time

Fig. 6. Time of Simulation Comparison

From the above representation it is clear that the suggested algorithm's simulation time is executed in less time when it is run on the simulator. Based on factors including the avalanche effect and the amount of memory needed to store ciphertext, these algorithms performance is assessed.

This experiment uses two different sets of data:

1) Data1: Consists of alphabetic characters (cryptography is sometimes known as cryptography).
2) Data 2: Alphanumeric characters are present (data4 = deta2).

Table 2. Setting of an algorithm

Algorithm	Key (Bits)	Block size(Bits)
RSA	128	128
AES	128	64
EMSA	512	128

The avalanche effect of cryptographic techniques is seen in Table 2. The findings indicate that AES has a modest avalanche effect, making it simple for anyone to decipher plain text from ciphertext. However, EMSA is more secure because of its high avalanche effect. The graphical representation of the keys in bits is shown in the Fig. 7.

The Fig. 8 shows the block size in terms of bits using avalanche effect for various algorithm is represented.

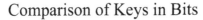

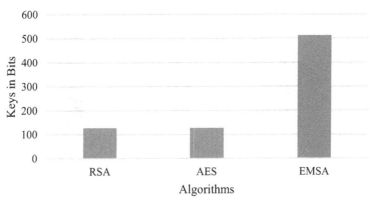

Fig. 7. The comparison of the keys in bits

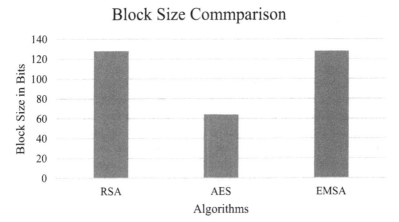

Fig. 8. Comparison of the Block size

The two data sets Data1 and Data2 are compared with the existing and the proposed algorithm and it is represented in the Table 3.

Table 3. Data1 and Data2 Comparison

	Avalanche(RSA)	Avalanche(AES)	Avalanche(EMSA)
Data1	47%	51%	64%
Data2	53%	55%	67%

The diagrammatic representation of avalanche effect among algorithms are shown in the Fig. 9.

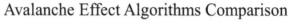

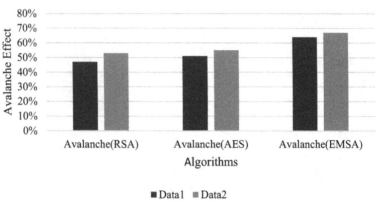

Fig. 9. Comparison of the avalanche effect among algorithms

4   Results and Discussion

The likelihood of a brute force assault is extremely low because it uses two key security methods Key distribution is no longer a problem because the RSA method takes care of it. Cyclic Redundancy Check will be demonstrated (as data integrity is evaluated). The various performance metrics like avalanche effect, memory requirement in terms of KB, block size of the avalanche effect and simulation time in secs are compared with the existing algorithm RSA and AES against the proposed algorithm EMSA. The number of bits and the block size in the avalanche effect will have an effective impact in the cryptography. A slight change made using the proposed algorithm ESMA will be given the more security. From the above results the proposed algorithm are efficient in all the aspects and can be used for storing data with high security.

5   Conclusion and Future Work

To improve mobile cloud computing security, a new technique that combines RSA and AES is presented. The suggested approach uses AES and RSA, which are significantly secure and less vulnerable to threats or viruses of any kind. Data security and application integrity in the mobile cloud are guaranteed by the suggested method. It also confirms user authentication to guarantee that only those with authorization can access the mobile cloud application. An application was developed to assess the results of the provided method and test them can be used.

References

1. Jakimoski, K.: Security techniques for data protection in cloud computing. Int. J. Grid Distrib. Comput. **9**(1), 49–56 (2016)
2. Naeem, F., Ali, M., Kaddoum, G., Huang, C., Yuen, C.: Security and privacy for reconfigurable intelligent surface in 6G: a review of prospective applications and challenges. IEEE Open J. Commun. Soc. **4**, 1196–1217 (2023)
3. Liao, B., Ali, Y., Nazir, S., He, L., Khan, H.U.: Security analysis of IoT devices by using mobile computing: a systematic literature review. IEEE Access **8**, 120331–120350 (2020)
4. Su, Z., Xu, Q.: Security-aware resource allocation for mobile social big data: a matching-coalitional game solution. IEEE Trans. Big Data **7**(4), 632–642 (2021)
5. Ahmad, I., et al.: An overview of the security landscape of virtual mobile networks. IEEE Access **9**, 169014–169030 (2021)
6. Wang, Q., Wang, D.: Understanding failures in security proofs of multi-factor authentication for mobile devices. IEEE Trans. Inf. Forensics Secur. **18**, 597–612 (2023)
7. Sadavarte, R.K., Kurundkar, G.D., Parbhani, D.: Data security and integrity in cloud computing: Threats and Solutions. Int. J. Sci. Res. Comput. Sci. Eng. Inform. Technol. **6**(6), 356–363 (2020)
8. Qayyum, R., Ejaz, H.: Data security in mobile cloud computing: a state of the art review. Int. J. Mod. Educ. Comput. Sci. **12**(2), 30–35 (2020)
9. Tawalbeh, L.A., Saldamli, G.: Reconsidering big data security and privacy in cloud and mobile cloud systems. J. King Saud Univ. – Comput. Inf. Sci. **33**(7), 810–819 (2021)
10. Pradheep, N., Venkatachalam, M., Saroja, M., Sivasooriya, V.: High performance and security techniques for protecting data in cloud computing. Int. J. Creative Res. Thoughts (IJCRT) **8**(10), 1183–1190 (2020)
11. Fatima, S., Rehman, T., Fatima, M., Khan, S., Ali, M.A.: Comparative analysis of AES and RSA algorithms for data security in cloud computing. Eng. Proc. **20**(1), 1–6 (2022)
12. Sarode, R.P., Bhalla, S.: Data security in mobile cloud computing. In: Proceedings of International Conference on Sustainable Computing in Science, Technology and Management (SUSCOM), pp. 491–496. Amity University Rajasthan, Jaipur-India (2019)

An Evaluation of Hybrid RRT* with Anytime RRT* Algorithm for Wheeled Mobile Robot

P. Jai Rajesh[1]([✉]), V. Balambica[2], and M. Achudhan[2]

[1] Department of Mechatronics, Bharath Institute of Higher Education and Research, Selaiyur, Chennai, Tamil Nadu 126, India
jairajesh2008@gmail.com
[2] Department of Mechanical, Bharath Institute of Higher Education and Research, Selaiyur, Chennai, Tamil Nadu 126, India
{balambica.mech,pstoc}@bharathuniv.ac.in

Abstract. In robotics applications, real-time path planning is essential for allowing robots to travel effectively and independently in changing situations. While they offer the best results, traditional path planning algorithms cannot adjust to changing circumstances. This study suggests a hybrid strategy to accomplish effective and anytime-capable path planning for a wheeled mobile robot (WMR) by combining the advantages of the RRT* and Anytime RRT* algorithms. The anytime behaviour of Anytime RRT* is integrated into the RRT* algorithm via the hybrid algorithm known as Hybrid RRT* with Anytime RRT*. This enables the robot to repeatedly improve solution quality and quickly construct an initial viable path using RRT*. It may then adjust this path over time in response to changes in the environment. Real-time tests on a WMR platform and simulations are used to assess the algorithm's performance. Creating a simulation environment with different step sizes and iterations is part of the experimental setup. The algorithm's success is evaluated using performance indicators such as cleaning time, cleaning efficiency, collisions, and near-collisions. The comparison of the outcomes with the conventional RRT* and Anytime RRT* implementations sheds light on the flexibility and efficiency benefits of the hybrid method. Furthermore, the algorithm's performance in dynamic situations is validated by the algorithm's real-time implementation on the WMR. The study advances the area of real-time path planning by introducing a unique hybrid method that integrates the advantages of Anytime RRT* and RRT*. The results demonstrate the flexibility, effectiveness, and high quality of the solution provided by the algorithm.

Keywords: Real-time path planning · Hybrid RRT* · Anytime RRT* · Wheeled Mobile Robot (WMR) · Robotics · Dynamic environments · Performance evaluation · Adaptability · Efficiency · Solution quality

1 Introduction

Path planning is an important challenge in the field of robotics, serving as a cornerstone for enabling autonomous robots to navigate dynamic and complex environments effectively. The ability to generate optimal or near-optimal paths in real-time is paramount

S. Rajagopal et al (Eds.): ASCIS 2023, CCIS 2040, pp. 368–377, 2024.
https://doi.org/10.1007/978-3-031-59107-5_25

for applications such as autonomous vehicles, mobile robots, and drones, where safety, efficiency, and adaptability are critical. Classical path planning algorithms, while capable of delivering optimal solutions in static scenarios, often falter when confronted with the unpredictable and ever-changing nature of the real world. These algorithms typically compute a single optimal path based on initial conditions, assuming a stationary environment—a premise that becomes impractical when facing scenarios replete with environmental dynamics and unanticipated obstacles. Consequently, the exigency arises for path planning algorithms that can swiftly adapt to dynamic settings, continuously update plans, and gracefully navigate through evolving landscapes. In this research, we confront this challenge head-on by proposing a novel hybrid approach that amalgamates the robustness of two distinguished path planning algorithms: Rapidly-exploring Random Trees (RRT*) [3] and Anytime RRT*. Our endeavor revolves around the conception and implementation of the "Hybrid RRT* with Anytime RRT*" algorithm, meticulously tailored for real-time path planning with Wheeled Mobile Robots (WMRs). Our primary objective is to harness the anytime-capable attributes of the Anytime RRT* algorithm and seamlessly integrate them within the RRT* framework, thus fostering the development of an agile, adaptable, and efficient algorithm. The crux of our approach hinges on the ability of our hybrid algorithm to swiftly generate an initial feasible path through RRT* while concurrently embracing Anytime RRT*'s innate propensity to iteratively refine this path. This dynamic interplay allows our algorithm to adapt promptly to shifting environmental dynamics, progressively enhancing solution quality as it operates [4].

The first property is demonstrated by the RRT method, which quickly identifies a first workable solution. Up until recently, it was unclear if the RRT could get a better result as the number of samples rose. It has been demonstrated by Karaman and Frazzoli [7] that there is actually no chance of the RRT algorithm convergent to an optimum solution. A different approach, called RRT*, was presented in the same work. It is a sampling-based algorithm that offers probabilistic completeness guarantees and the asymptotic optimality condition, which is the almost-sure convergence to an optimal solution [5, 6]. Without requiring a significant amount of computing overhead, the RRT* approach attains the asymptotic optimality lacking in the RRT.

We present a comprehensive evaluation of our Hybrid RRT* with Anytime RRT* algorithm, subjecting it to rigorous simulations and real-time experiments. Our assessment entails a comparative analysis against the conventional RRT* and Anytime RRT* algorithms, facilitating insights into our algorithm's efficacy, adaptability, and efficiency in real-time environments. Hence, this research embarks on a journey to not only surmount the limitations of traditional path planning but also to redefine the possibilities of autonomous navigation in a world brimming with uncertainty. Through the ensuing sections of this article, we delve into the methodology, performance evaluation, and insights garnered from our Hybrid RRT* with Anytime RRT* algorithm. We envisage that our findings will illuminate the path toward superior path planning algorithms, fostering more agile and adaptable robotics applications in dynamic real-time scenarios.

2 Literature Review

Gao et al. [1] introduced the BP-RRT* algorithm, which is designed to tackle challenges in motion planning for six-degree-of-freedom manipulators operating in complex 3D environments with multiple obstacles. It combines Back Propagation (BP) neural networks with an improved version of the Rapidly-Exploring Random Tree* (RRT*) algorithm. A significant contribution is the use of a triangular function to evaluate spatial connections between paths and obstacles, identifying collision-free paths in 3D space. The algorithm enhances sampling efficiency through adaptive node sampling probability methods and a stepwise sampling approach, transforming global searches into phased local searches. The BP-RRT* algorithm is valuable for improving path planning efficiency in multi-obstacle spaces, particularly in smart manufacturing. Future research could expand its applicability to various obstacle shapes and explore real-time path planning for dynamic targets, possibly through reinforcement learning integration, offering practical enhancements. In the paper "Multi-AGV's Temporal Memory-based RRT Exploration in Unknown Environment" by Lau et al. [2] an innovative exploration strategy is presented for multiple Autonomous Ground Vehicles (AGVs) in challenging and unknown environments. The study addresses the limitations of traditional frontier-based Rapidly-Exploring Random Tree (RRT) exploration strategies. The proposed Temporal Memory-based RRT (TM-RRT) approach introduces several key enhancements, including adaptive exploration durations for frontiers and a memory system to prevent repeated assignments. It leverages relative AGV positions when calculating frontier revenues for more balanced and efficient exploration. The study validates TM-RRT through simulations and real-world deployments, demonstrating superior performance compared to conventional RRT exploration in terms of exploration duration and distance traveled. Future enhancements may involve deep neural networks for goal assignment, adaptability to various environments, and transitioning to a distributed paradigm. Exploring TM-RRT's integration in heterogeneous robot systems or infrastructure-free environments represents promising research directions, making valuable contributions to multi-robot exploration in unknown environments. Kang et al. [11] presented an enhanced approach to the RRT-Connect algorithm for robot path planning. This improved algorithm incorporates a "Triangular-Rewiring" method based on triangular inequality principles to enhance planning efficiency and optimality compared to the traditional RRT algorithm. Through simulations in various environments, the authors demonstrate that their proposed algorithm outperforms both the traditional RRT algorithm and the original RRT-Connect algorithm, achieving faster planning times and shorter path lengths on average. However, it acknowledges a limitation related to Kino dynamic planning, particularly when intermediate nodes disappear due to the "Triangular-Rewiring" method, potentially causing issues related to the robot's kinematic constraints. In summary, the "Improved RRT-Connect Algorithm Based on Triangular Inequality for Robot Path Planning" introduces an innovative approach to enhance the efficiency and optimality of robot path planning, offering potential improvements over traditional algorithms.

3 Proposed Methodology

3.1 Detailed Description of the Proposed Hybrid RRT* with Anytime RRT* Algorithm

We present a detailed description of the proposed hybrid RRT star with Anytime RRT star algorithm for real-time path planning using a wheeled mobile robot. This algorithm combines the strengths of both RRT* and Anytime RRT* to achieve enhanced performance, adaptivity, and optimality. The algorithm follows the steps outlined below: "HybridRRTstarwithAnytimeRRTstar:Initialize an RRT* tree T with the start configuration. Set an iteration counter iter to 0. If q_new is not null: Rewire the tree T to improve the overall path quality. Check if q_new satisfies the goal condition. If yes, return the optimal path from the start to q_new. Increment iter.

After reaching the maximum iterations, return the best solution found in tree T. NearestNeighbor(q, T): Find the node q_near in tree T that is nearest to configuration q. Return q_near. Extend(q_near, q_rand): Extend the tree T from node q_near towards configuration q_rand using RRT* extend method. Use anytime behavior to iteratively improve the path quality. Return q_new, the newly added node in the tree.

Rewire(T, q_new): Check if there are any nodes in T that can be reached from q_new with a lower cost. Rewire the tree connections to improve the overall path quality. Return the updated tree T. GoalCheck(q): Check if configuration q satisfies the goal condition. Return True if q is a goal configuration, False otherwise. OptimalPath(T, q_goal): Find the optimal path from the start configuration to q_goal in tree T. Return the optimal path as a sequence of configurations. BestSolution(T): Find the best solution (path with the lowest cost-to-go estimate) in tree T. Simplify the path if needed. Return the best solution as a sequence of configurations. This algorithm combines the RRT star algorithm with the anytime behavior of the Anytime RRT star algorithm. By integrating the anytime behaviour into the RRT* algorithm, the hybrid approach offers a balance between exploration and refinement, enabling real-time path planning with improved solution quality [8, 9].

3.2 Experimental Setup on Wheeled Mobile Robot (WMR) Platform

The WMR platform used in the experiments is equipped with the following components: Stepper Motor: The WMR utilizes a Nema 17 stepper motor for its propulsion. The stepper motor provides precise control over the robot's motion by converting electrical pulses into discrete rotational movements. Kinematic Model: The WMR is modeled as a differential drive robot, driven by the Nema 17 stepper motor. The kinematic model determines how the robot moves and turns based on the control signals sent to the stepper motor. Raspberry Pi 4: The Raspberry Pi 4 is used as the main control unit for the WMR. It provides the necessary processing power and I/O capabilities to interface with sensors, control the stepper motor, and execute the hybrid RRT* with Anytime RRT* algorithm. LiDAR Sensor: A LiDAR sensor is utilized for obstacle avoidance. The simulation environment includes the following components: Workspace: The workspace is a 2D or 3D representation of the area in which the WMR operates. It may consist of various terrain types and configurations to simulate real-world scenarios. Obstacles: Static obstacles are positioned within the workspace to test the robot's ability to navigate around them. The obstacles may vary in shape, size, and position to evaluate the algorithm's effectiveness in obstacle avoidance [10].

4 Result and Discussion

4.1 Simulation Findings for the Enhanced Hybrid RRT*Algorithm

Across different iterations and step sizes, the hybrid algorithm demonstrates superior performance. These findings emphasize the hybrid approach's effectiveness in discovering optimal or nearly optimal paths for WMRs.

Table 1. Varying Iteration with varying stepsize, the time taken and path length for different methods

Number of Iteration	Step Size	Existing RRT* Method (Time Taken) (sec)	Existing RRT* Method (Path Length) (cm)	Existing Any time RRT* Method (Time Taken) (sec)	Existing Any time RRT* Method (Path Length) (cm)	Proposed Hybrid Method (Time Taken) (sec)	Proposed Hybrid Method (Path Length) (cm)
500	5	7.42	118.31	3.65	130.25	1.75	119.94
	10	11.4	115.9	3.57	142.29	1.41	115.83
	20	12.26	116.13	3.82	158.1	1.75	119.69
	30	10.32	118.77	3.35	158.1	1.72	119.39
750	5	13.45	123.7	3.45	130.52	10.39	121.58
	10	12.97	114.49	3.5	136.6	4.71	118.11
	20	11.02	119.56	3.57	143.8	4.45	120.69
	30	16.74	120.95	3.71	136.85	3.34	121.44
1000	5	26	119.47	3.03	145.38	17.8	118.89
	10	13	115.72	3.84	133.28	11.86	119.61
	20	14.4	117.9	3.82	148.56	10.55	116.26
	30	12.22	117.17	4.23	152.11	7.31	115.99
1250	5	44	131.2	3.76	140.43	18.97	116.54
	10	32.41	114.67	3.48	140.87	17.45	116.29
	20	22.29	122.48	6.93	148.1	15.98	116.29
	30	37	124.09	3.81	138.37	16.87	116.29

(*continued*)

Table 1. (*continued*)

Number of Iteration	Step Size	Existing RRT* Method (Time Taken) (sec)	Existing RRT* Method (Path Length) (cm)	Existing Any time RRT* Method (Time Taken) (sec)	Existing Any time RRT* Method (Path Length) (cm)	Proposed Hybrid Method (Time Taken) (sec)	Proposed Hybrid Method (Path Length) (cm)
1500	5	45.53	118.88	3.34	134.4	25.11	123.49
	10	47.52	116.92	3.5	134.09	32.8	115.91
	20	35.65	120.75	3.12	143.22	19.44	116.39
	30	74.24	116.74	3.89	122.95	56.23	117.02

The above Table 1 shows the Comparison of different Path Planning Algorithms with varying iterations and step size. We can assess how well the hybrid algorithm performs by looking at both the time it takes and the length of the generated paths.

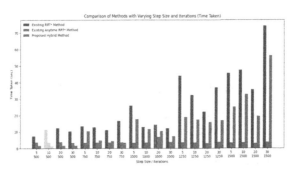

Fig. 1. Comparison of methods with varying step size and iterations (Time Taken)

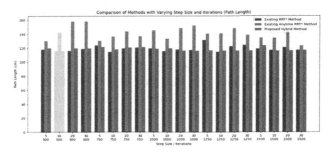

Fig. 2. Comparison of methods with varying step size and iterations (Path length)

From the Figs. 1, 2 and 3 it clearly shows, that, the best method for time taken is Hybrid Method with step size 10 and iterations 500. The best method for path length is Hybrid Method with step size 10 and iterations 500. From the data, we can observe the following: The proposed hybrid method consistently outperforms both the existing RRT* method and the existing anytime RRT* method in terms of time taken. It consistently has the lowest time taken across all tables. Overall, the proposed hybrid method shows promising performance by achieving lower time taken compared to the existing methods, and its path length is comparable or slightly worse in most cases. The proposed hybrid algorithm offers a suitable solution for various real-world scenarios, striking a balance between computation time and solution optimality.

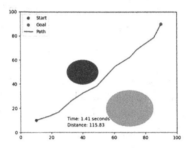

Fig. 3. Best path and Time taken of Hybrid method step size 10 and iteration 500

4.2 Real-Time Implementation for the Proposed Hybrid Algorithm

Description of the hardware and software setup for real-time execution: Hardware: NEMA 17 stepper motor, LIDAR, Raspberry Pi 4, Single-stage gearbox with an output torque of 188 Nm, Power input: 16.8 watts. Software: Operating system: ROS, Programming language: PYTHON, Libraries or frameworks: NUMPY, MATPLOTThe proposed hybrid algorithm was integrated into the WMR platform using the hardware and software setup mentioned above. The algorithm's performance was evaluated in a real-time scenario using the described hardware and software setup. Real-time data, as mentioned earlier, was collected for varying step sizes and iterations. The algorithm's execution time and path length were measured and compared against the existing RRT* method and existing anytime RRT* method. Same result is loop-free paths that tend to be more direct than those of the RRT [15] are shown in Table 2.

From the Figs. 4, 5 and 6 Shows the Best Method for Time Taken: Proposed Hybrid (Step Size: 5, Iterations: 1250) Time Taken: 1.57 s. Best Method for Path Length: Proposed Hybrid (Step Size: 5, Iterations: 1250) Path Length: 116.45 cm.

Table 2. Shows the implementation of WMR Path Planning Algorithms with varying iterations and step size.

Number of Iteration	Step Size	Existing RRT* Method (Time Taken) (sec)	Existing RRT* Method (Path Length) (cm)	Existing Anytime RRT* Method (Time Taken) (sec)	Existing Anytime RRT* Method (Path Length) (cm)	Proposed Hybrid Method (Time Taken) (sec)	Proposed Hybrid Method (Path Length) (cm)
500	5	4.83	121.56	3.67	127.89	2.18	119.72
	10	5.37	120.08	3.74	136.21	1.95	118.41
	20	6.15	118.92	3.85	144.02	1.73	117.32
	30	7.02	117.85	4.02	150.63	1.57	116.45
750	5	12.56	122.41	3.36	128.74	9.48	121.19
	10	13.82	121.32	3.47	137.89	8.64	119.94
	20	15.29	120.23	3.61	145.71	7.89	118.78
	30	16.98	119.14	3.76	152.33	7.21	117.72
1000	5	25.32	123.06	2.94	130.64	16.82	121.48
	10	27.89	121.87	3.09	139.86	15.32	119.95
	20	30.71	120.69	3.28	147.67	13.96	118.52
	30	34.68	119.5	3.49	154.29	12.75	117.19
1250	5	42.57	124.86	3.58	132.52	18.64	121.82
	10	47.13	123.45	3.8	141.79	17.12	120.34
	20	53.02	122.03	4.06	149.61	15.78	118.98
	30	60.23	120.62	4.34	157.23	14.59	117.73
1500	5	50.92	126.3	3.24	134.24	22.97	123.16
	10	56.41	124.75	3.46	143.57	21.01	121.49
	20	62.95	123.2	3.71	151.39	19.21	119.92
	30	70.68	121.65	4.01	159.02	17.55	118.44

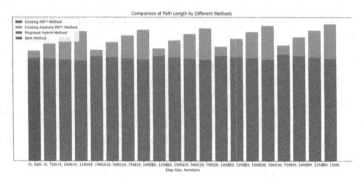

Fig. 4. Comparison of methods with varying step size and iterations (Time Taken)

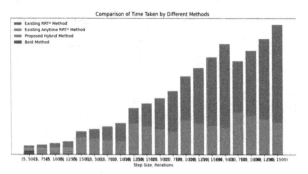

Fig. 5. Comparison of methods with varying step size and iterations (Path length)

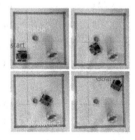

Fig. 6. Step size 5, Iteration 500

5 Conclusion

In conclusion, the research proposed a hybrid algorithm that combines RRT* with Any-time RRT* for improved path planning in robotics. The proposed hybrid method outper-formed existing hybrid algorithms and traditional RRT* and Anytime RRT* methods in terms of time taken and path length. It offers a more efficient and optimal solution for path planning tasks. The findings of this research contribute to the field of robotics by providing an effective approach to enhance path planning algorithms. The proposed hybrid algorithm has the potential to be applied in various robotic applications, including autonomous navigation, motion planning, and robotics systems in dynamic environments. Further advancements and improvements in the hybrid algorithm can lead to even more robust and efficient path planning methods. Continued research in this area will contribute to the development of advanced robotic systems with improved planning capabilities.

References

1. Gao, Q., Yuan, Q., Sun, Y., Xu, L.: Path planning algorithm of robot arm based on improved RRT* and BP neural network algorithm. J. King Saud Univ.-Comput. Inf. Sci. **35**(8), 1–14 (2023)
2. Lau, B.P.L., et al.: Multi-AGV's temporal memory-based RRT exploration in unknown environment. IEEE Rob. Autom. Lett. **7**(4), 9256–9263 (2022)
3. Yang, F., et al.: Obstacle avoidance path planning for UAV based on improved RRT algorithm. Discret. Dyn. Nat. Soc. **2022**(4544499), 1–9 (2022)
4. Chen, L., Yang, Y., Tang, W.S.: Positive-partial-transpose square conjecture for n = 3. Phys. Rev. A **99**(1), 1–6 (2019)
5. Karaman, S., Frazzoli, E.: Sampling-based algorithms for optimal motion planning. Int. J. Rob. Res. **30**(7), 846–894 (2011)
6. Karaman, S., Frazzoli, E.: Incremental sampling-based algorithms for optimal motion planning. Rob. Sci. Syst. **VI 104**(2), 267–274 (2010)
7. Karaman, S., Frazzoli, E.: Anytime motion planning with Gaussian process priors. In: 2011 IEEE International Conference on Robotics and Automation, pp. 687–692. IEEE (2011)
8. Narayanan, V., Phillips, M., Likhachev, M.: Anytime safe interval path planning for dynamic environments. In: 2012 IEEE/RSJ International Conference on Intelligent Robots and Systems, pp. 4708–4715. IEEE, Vilamoura-Algarve, Portugal (2012)
9. Chung, S.Y., Huang, H.P.: Robot motion planning in dynamic uncertain environments. Adv. Robot. **25**(6–7), 849–870 (2011)
10. Yang, H., Kavraki, L.E.: Anytime path planning for autonomous vehicles in uncertain environments. IEEE Trans. Intell. Transp. Syst. **19**(10), 3387–3398 (2018)
11. Kang, J.G., Lim, D.W., Choi, Y.S., Jang, W.J., Jung, J.W.: Improved RRT-connect algorithm based on triangular inequality for robot path planning. Sensors **21**(2), 1–32 (2021)

Identification of Software Design Pattern and Deployment Strategies for AWS RDS Using Pattern for Relational Database

Mini Bhola$^{(\boxtimes)}$ and Sunil Bajeja

Faculty of Computer Applications, Marwadi University, Rajkot, Gujarat, India
bholamini168@gmail.com

Abstract. Cloud computing offerings program and continue services with elasticity, flexibility, broad availability, and minimal expense are all features that entice users to shift their main business processes to the cloud. However, there are various design as well as development issues to address before implementation. For that AWS RDS databases work with design patterns and are considered as a solution for programmers, designers, and developers. The paper introduces the concepts of developing and designing software using relational database patterns, as well as the concept of software deployment approach in the context of AWS. This research paper addresses the requirement of designing software by presenting different design patterns and solutions and discovering deployment strategies. Furthermore, potential design pattern possibilities are discussed based on the research.

Keywords: Cloud computing · Design pattern · AWS database · Deployment strategy

1 Introduction

In recent years, cloud computing has evolved as an innovative technology that offers on demand internet access to a shared pool of computer assets, comprising data storage, servers, and applications. Due to the ever increasing need for computing resources, cloud computing has developed into an essential technology for companies, organizations, and people to maintain and analyze their data, operate programs, and provide services. The idea of cloud computing has upended conventional IT infrastructure by providing reasonably priced, adaptable, scalable, and reliable solutions to the shifting requirements of consumers. According to traditional computing, cloud computing has a number of benefits, including lower prices, greater scalability, flexibility, and accessibility. Due to economical or organizational limitations, it has made it possible for enterprises to take advantage of computational capabilities that were previously inaccessible.

Consumers of cloud computing are able to concentrate on their primary company activities while leaving the administration of the computer systems to the cloud provider. In the cloud computing environment, the fundamental layer is the infrastructure (IaaS), the middle layer is the platform, or framework (PaaS), which acts as the user connection with software and hardware, and the topmost layer is the software (SaaS) [1]. For

S. Rajagopal et al (Eds.): ASCIS 2023, CCIS 2040, pp. 378–390, 2024.
https://doi.org/10.1007/978-3-031-59107-5_26

many firms, SaaS has grown into the standard method for providing services that are cloud-based or apps. The essence of SaaS is multi tenancy; through the integration of organizational groups, multi-tenancy offers consumers (i.e., tenants) and suppliers numerous chances to take advantage of the inherent flexibility provided by cloud infrastructure [2]. Cloud computing has become the go to solution for deploying and managing applications. The ability to provision resources on demand, pay as you go, and scale applications dynamically has made cloud computing the preferred choice for modern application development. There are numerous problems in the cloud environment when developing applications with various cloud models that need to adhere to the criteria for excellent service in terms of architecture, privacy, storage spaces, data integrity, and services. Program developers create successful and extensible approaches to the cloud by leveraging specific design patterns to build economical and adaptable applications. One of the main challenges in applying solutions that were previously designed for multiple diverse, often inconsistent applications to contemporary models is how to reuse data, knowledge, and coding effectively. When selecting a platform that utilizes the cloud to host your application's development, ensure that you take into consideration design patterns that are successful in the cloud environment. For the purpose of creating high-quality software, design patterns are replies to often occurring problems with the software. They were initially presented in the context of architectural engineering by Alexander et al. in 1977. Gamma et al. presented methods for using patterns on cloud-based application deployment in the middle of the 1990s. Gang of four (GoF) patterns, they proposed, are a group of 23 patterns mainly categorized as: structural, creational, and behavioral patterns. Challenges in system module development and execution are addressed by design patterns. Many benefits are allegedly offered by design patterns, including improved decisions regarding design, improved programmer interpersonal interaction, increased or facilitated software reliability and reuse, support in fulfilling the system's non-functional specifications, and expenditures effort, and time savings through reusing tested before solutions.

Design patterns include frequent issues, software deployment, potential influences on the issue or solution, and explanations for the issue. But the main motivating factor behind a software design pattern is a persistent problem, and a systematic approach that broadly generalizes the solution to this issue is an essential component of a good design pattern. The Design patterns are all about the code. You can add new features to your application without breaking the existing code at any time of Software Implementing design patterns which isolate an application's code into reusable components will improve the application's scalability and release, installation, activation, updation etc... Design patterns also enhance the readability of code; if someone wants to extend your application, they will understand the code with little difficulty. Reusability which enables the use of parts and subsystems in various programs and circumstances, maintainability which makes maintenance and development easier and coherence and uniformity in module development and implementation are all examples of good design. Designers may revisit a design pattern after implementing it in order to address a specific designing problem. Design patterns aid in the dissemination of architecture information, the understanding of a new design framework, and the prevention of perils and errors that prospective programmers could have had to discover the hard way [3]. Software design patterns have become an essential tool for creating dependable, expandable, and upgradable software systems. An all-encompassing, reusable solution to a design for software issues that crops up frequently is referred to as a software design pattern. It offers a set of recommendations or best practices for creating software systems that could be used in various situations to address similar challenges.

2 Related Work

Cloud patterns are an extension of conventional look patterns since they provide the finest alternatives for creating applications tailored for cloud settings. It would be possible to develop a plan to make it easier for businesses to move their applications to the cloud, streamlining society and laying the framework for the development of interoperable, portable software [4]. Three of most strongly well-liked cloud computing environments AWS, Azure, and Google Cloud, among others are used to create and execute computational programs in the cloud that use standard, interchangeable services. When developing and launching a software application for a cloud environment, AWS, Microsoft Azure, and other cloud service providers provide a number of design patterns that address common issues. The fact that there are so many more design patterns with cloud providers (AWS, Azure, GCP, etc.) for software deployment indicates that there are many challenges to be overcome when developing and designing applications for the cloud. As researchers reviewed all above 3 design patterns and identified 30 patterns and concluded that they frequently have a positive effect on product quality as well as software development cycles. This Design Patterns (DPS) significantly enhances developer communication. In the process of creating the CDPs (Cloud Design Patterns), researchers examined numerous designs produced by different cloud builders, put them into categories depending upon the kinds of issues they solved, and then developed general design patterns based on such management. Various of these issues may be solved using existing data architecture, so that, first we can work on existing design patterns and throughout experimental analysis finding issues and based on that, provide solutions to address these issues. Based on the identification of design patterns from various platforms, researchers choose the AWS design pattern for deployment because AWS is more economical and effective for cloud storage and infrastructure that actually uses web services. AWS technology for cloud computing uses a variety of techniques and strategies to implement common system design issues in the cloud. It offers blueprints, resources, and thorough guidelines for putting the approach behind the development strategy into action. Before creating a new cloud design pattern, researchers should research existing patterns that may already solve the problem. This will help to avoid reinventing the wheel and ensure that our new pattern provides additional value. Here, researchers have identified all AWS Design Patterns with classification based on their types and usage. Researchers analyze and characterize different design patterns with different types and all the specific patterns with the specific factors and majoring the problems in cloud software deployment to confirm the strength, limitations, and pros of the cloud design patterns which affect software performance (Fig. 1).

Fig. 1. AWS Design Patterns

In AWS Design Pattern there are 8 types of pattern work with cloud environments and among 8 researchers choose Patterns for Relational Database. Because database schema is the platform over which applications are developed and tuning of the physical structure of the data will be performed. In simpler terms, conceptual models are an exceptionally significant design artifact for a database centric communication method's whole existence [6]. The above all cloud database patterns work with databases and are considered as a solution for programmers, designers, and architects since they need to store the information of their applications in an versatile and highly accessible manner from the backside whenever necessary. Decisions made during the design and implementation phase have a huge impact on the performance, quality and the total cost of ownership of cloud hosted applications and services. In order to connect problems with logically conceptualization and execution of databases with corresponding challenges in implementing software, basic software development design patterns are utilized for databases [4]. AWS design patterns have become an essential tool for creating dependable, expandable, and upgradable databases for software systems. An all-encompassing, reusable solution to a design for database issue that crops up frequently is referred to as a software design pattern. It offers a set of 2 recommendations or best Practices for creating software systems databases that could be used in various situations to address similar challenges. Simple DB and Amazon RDS are becoming increasingly recognizable to groups as cloud-based databases since they have opened functioning and emphasized the challenges and drawbacks of currently available cloud databases with respect to functionality, adaptability, and deployment [7]. We are going to analyze and perform AWS database traditional storage options that differ in performance, durability, and cost, as well as in their interfaces [5].

In this research paper we mainly focus and work with AWS RDS database. How to create the necessary level of separation amongst each part when faced with an adjustment in the amount of work being performed represents one for the issues of delivering multi-tenant cloud hosted applications which have been developed to rely on numerous elements. For that researcher focus on the deployment part for that select a database for effective performance of applications [9]. Amazon RDS (Relational Database Service) is a service offered on the internet that runs in the cloud and simplifies the setup, management, and scaling of relational databases. RDS is intended to offer a quick and affordable alternative for maintaining databases. A relational database that's hosted in a cloud environment may be effortlessly set up, run, and scaled using Amazon RDS, a professionally managed databases platform. Amazon RDS eliminates the need to provision and manage hardware, install and configure software, and perform ongoing maintenance tasks such as backups, software updates, and patching. Amazon RDS supports various database engines such as MySQL, PostgreSQL, Oracle, and SQL Server. The choice of database engine depends on the application's requirements, performance, scalability, and security needs. The application should be designed to work with the selected database engine. Amazon RDS database instances should be configured with appropriate parameters such as instance type, storage capacity, and backup retention period. The database instance should be provisioned in a Virtual Private Cloud (VPC) to ensure network isolation and security. The database instance should be configured with appropriate security groups, network settings, and access control policies. The database should be secured using encryption at rest and in transit. The data from the existing database should be migrated to the newly created database instance. Amazon RDS provides various tools and services for migrating data to the cloud. We will create the design pattern which removes the exhausting problems of databases with software deployment systems. This paper presents different types of relational database patterns & different types of deployment strategy In addition how AWS DATABASE used that pattern for recovering solutions for frequent solutions. The remaining part of this paper is organized as follows: Sect. 2 describes the fundamentals of software design pattern. Section 3 presents patterns for relational databases with analysis with respect to AWS databases. Section 4 portrays the different deployment strategy of how AWS deploy software using different approaches with design patterns. Section 5 describes strategy with analysis of the Issues and Challenges deployment with multiple factors and Sect. 6 concludes the paper.

Here, we present a research diagram of how design patterns work with cloud applications and these conventional ideas and consider how they could develop throughout the environment of cloud computing. The way to deploy software in a cloud environment using the suggested design pattern and that pattern allows developers to comprehend cloud environments and create reliable, scalable, secure cloud applications (Fig. 2).

In this diagram, the researcher shows how software developers utilize design patterns to create reusable software solutions for common issues and deploy that software on the cloud. In the cloud environment, researchers initially choose an AWS platform, work with database related patterns, and then deploy the software using a cloud deployment approach. As a consequence, developers identify issues with AWS database services and requirements, analyze those problems, and then solve them using design patterns. Depending on that particular requirement, AWS offers a choice of design patterns that

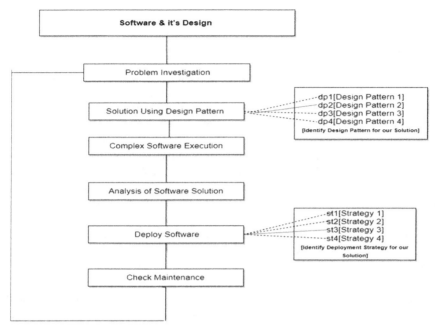

Fig. 2. Design Pattern Working Model

developers can check to see if one suits their model and then choose the one that best suits their requirements. Some patterns are challenging to use in test or staging environments, but they are valuable for deployment in a real world situation. When a researcher has found a problem, they must first analyze the requirements before applying the patterns to a software model and writing the corresponding code. Because there are so many variables that can affect software performance, the researcher presents a logical analysis of relational database pattern results. The way a pattern interacts with a database to resolve problems, how it is used, and its benefits and drawbacks. Now that the software model is finished for deployment, different deployment strategies are being employed for deploying the application in a cloud environment, based on research.

Researchers looked at the four different deployment strategies to find the best one for deploying the program for that purpose. Once the software has been deployed, certain aspects that have an impact on performance should be examined. According to research, there 3 are numerous deployment options available. In order to ensure that we may select the option that best suits our requirements. Some strategies might be costly to use in test or staging environments, but they are effective for deployment in real world situations.

3   Design Pattern Implementation

3.1 Problem Investigation

On an annual basis, countless hours were devoted by programmers to attempting to expand the databases widely in order to keep up with the rapid increase in application outputs as well as data volumes. Designers raised the number of database administration duties by using database shards to deal with the increasing application outputs while handling the expanding database volumes. These pieces' design and implementation required complicated design operations, and the implementation and testing of new pieces took time. Web Services from Amazon Database Infrastructure Upgrade numerous services needed thousands of each of these pieces to provide the necessary performance, creating a hefty administrative pressure on administrators of databases and designers. Select and develop the best AWS database services to update the data in your environment with completely managed, designed specifically databases, which will reduce costs and time, boost performance and production, and speed up development. An experienced AWS trainer will walk it through the advantages and disadvantages of eleven databases, including SQL services like Amazon RDS and Amazon Aurora and NoSQL services like Amazon Neptune, Amazon DynamoDB, Amazon DocumentDB, and more, in addition to the decisions about design which you ought to take into account while through them.

3.2 Solution Using Design Pattern

We suggested a design pattern as a solution for the issue with software deployment in cloud based environments, and for that we proposed a novel design pattern. For that problem we have reviewed many design patterns and concur that they frequently have a positive effect on product quality as well as software development cycles. Design Patterns (DPS) significantly enhances developer communication. The concept of software design patterns was developed after examining the source code of numerous developers from around the globe and observing how many people with no prior contact or 9*-communication solved the same issue in a similar manner. The implementation of software development patterns provides straightforward development for every other cloud which offers cloud administration application programming interfaces (whether open-sourced or commercialized [8]. The fact that there are so many more design patterns with cloud provider (AWS, Azure, GCP, etc.) for software deployment indicates that there are many challenges to be overcome when developing and designing applications for the cloud. Based on the identification of design patterns from various platforms, we chose the AWS design pattern for deployment because AWS is more economical and effective for cloud storage and infrastructure that actually uses web services. In the cloud, AWS cloud computing technologies implement typical system design problems using a group of methods and approaches. It provides designs, tools, and detailed instructions for implementing the methodology for systems design issues. In the process of creating the CDPs, we examined numerous designs produced by different cloud builders, put them into categories depending upon the kinds of issues they solved, and then developed general design patterns based on such management. Various of these issues may be solved using existing data architecture, so that, first we can work on existing design patterns and throughout experimental analysis finding issues and based on that, provide solutions to address these issues. As researchers can say that AWS design pattern for Development and Deployment. There are 8 types of pattern work with AWS. Among 8 we choose Patterns for Relational Database. Because database schema is the platform over which applications are developed and tuning of the physical structure of the database is performed. In other words, logical schemata are the most important design artifact for the full life cycle of a database centric information system. Databases stored in the cloud are currently being viewed as a choice for designers, developers, and engineers who must preserve the contents associated with their apps in a versatile and readily available way from the rear whenever wanted. Cloud forms of databases, Simple DB, and Amazon RDS are becoming increasingly common to the community because these technologies have raised and exposed the challenges and shortcomings of existing relational databases in terms of usability, flexibility, and provisioning [9].

Researchers are going to analyze and perform AWS database traditional storage options that differ in performance, durability, and cost, as well as in their interfaces. In order to do that, we present a Patterns for Relational Database design pattern for interacting with databases. It's growing understanding of fundamental concepts and established design patterns for applications that have been included into numerous effective cloud applications.

Here following present the Patterns for Relational Database [10] **DB Replication Pattern (Replicating Online Databases):** Protecting the information against application collapse, severe weather, and system faults is an extremely crucial and significant part of the recovery process. As time passed, a broad variety of freely available and paid technologies have developed to address the problems and difficulties that arise during the database replication process [15]. Database replication pattern solutions may offer a reliable method for replicating information as well as maintaining copies that might be used to recover in the case of an unexpected event. A pattern that enables reproduction across geographical boundaries. This method allows you to avoid data loss while maintaining access to information reliability. Though this is an old pattern, the implementation of cloud services allows for the economical usage of numerous global sites, allowing this form of distribution a viable alternative [11]. **Read Replica Pattern (Load Distribution through Read Replicas):** A read replica pattern is a copy only duplicate of a database system [12]. Amazon RDS uses the relational database engine's embedded replica functionality to build a read replica using an external Database server. Sending queries to your programs via the read replica may decrease the burden on the original Database server [12]. Users can 4 make any number of read copies from the master Dataset using the Amazon RDS Read Replication capability, either in the identical AWS area or outside of another. These slave or other databases receive an unprocessed copy of information from the master server. For read heavy database tasks, that allows you to elasticity extend out exceeding the memory restrictions of an individual Database server. **In Memory DB Cache Pattern (Caching High Frequency Data):** In databases, memory utilization is not the most important factor for evaluating technique effectiveness; nonetheless, because those databases serve information stored in memory, this utilization is also researched with together the time required to perform every computation to see which procedure uses the storage space optimally [13]. Although the fact that storage utilization shouldn't be a primary factor in determining efficiency, databases explore with how much memory they use and how long it takes to finish every process. As a result, it is vital to determine which one delivers better results for certain data processing to evaluate the operational efficiency of in memory databases pattern in terms of time as well as memory usage [13]. **Sharding Write Pattern (Improving Efficiency in Writing):** Sharding pattern is an approach for dividing the information into portions and distributing it on several physically isolated servers for database storage [16]. Each of the servers is known as a database shard. Describe methods to use Amazon RDS to construct a sharded database design for storage of information that achieves maximum flexibility, high performance, and reliability [14]. While implementing Amazon RDS as a database shard, Will tackle schema design and tracking parameters. To achieve a similar degree of effectiveness, every single one of the database shards typically use the same sort of devices, computer engine, as well as information structure.

According to all above there are so many different kinds of design patterns which specifically offer a different set of capabilities (high availability, scalability, security, performance) and support classes of applications with different characteristics. In the cloud that gives businesses all the tools they need for creating, delivering, and regulating applications avoiding the hassle of setting up, implementing, and maintaining the devices, system software, and application that underpins these offerings. In this scenario, scalability, security, resilience, Performance all represent a crucial necessity, thus suitable technologies must be researched and assessed. For the preceding phase, there are several patterns of analyzing database performance. Business Protection Requirements that aids in resource identification and demonstrates the various types of data which constitute resources in a structure. The pattern involves determining company resources, identifying company elements that have an impact on performance, relating resources with company variables and then determining every piece of property. Design patterns give extensive frameworks that include diagrams and a model for effective software deployment, as well as performance, accuracy, and accessibility for the database. We establish an architecture for design that improves our appreciation of the significant limits and possibilities for strategies deployed across various tiers of the software architecture. We additionally identify the often recurring issues as well as remedies utilized when dealing and managing defects and mistakes. For the purpose of managing dynamic handling of errors between both software and hardware elements, an architecture might be utilized for setting up processes and connectors. In the face of numerous flaws, mistakes, and malfunctions of many kinds, the general objective of this research is to provide a systematic approach allowing the creation and assessment of a right solution in an efficient and inexpensive way. According to this phase, this all design pattern offers the subsequent components like design pattern, Pattern Name/Summary, Solving Issues, Explanation of pattern/Resolution in the cloud, Implementation, Benefits, Notes and Others.

3.3 Analysis of Software Solution

See Table 1.

Table 1. Design Pattern Result Analysis

Pattern Types	Pattern Name	Solving Issues	Implementation	Pros	Cons
AWS pattern for relational database	DB Replication Pattern	Pattern used to prevent data loss and maintain data access availability	Install RDBMS in each of the EC2 instances and set up replication	Recover data without down the system	Downtime
	Read Replica Pattern	Improve performance & distributing reading multiple Read Replica	Create a read-only replica of the master database	Distribute load increase database durability	Disabling the automatic backup
	In Memory Cache Pattern	Improve performance of reading from databases by caching in memory data that is read frequently	Prepare memory cache and use open source memcached in an EC2 instance	Reduce load & use ElastiCache	Require to modify the data
	Sharding Write Pattern	Improving performance of writing with multiple database servers	Prepare multiple RDSs and use as the sharding backend databases	Increase availability improved efficiency	Encryption may be required

3.4 Software Deployment Pattern

According to researchers, there are various deployment patterns used here, and each one has pros and cons of its own. According to research analysis, developers' needs are taken into account while choosing the deployment pattern for cloud based applications [14]. The pattern improves the performance of the software deployment modularity by some specific design pattern framework in which have clearly distinguished functionality: the cloud software deployment design patterns attempts to reduce small flaws which could present 5 difficulties and enhances accessibility to code for designers and architects who are acquainted with programming techniques. Deployment patterns encapsulate the outcome's framework despite being bound to particular service implementations. Components can be designed at various levels of the realm of abstraction, enabling reuse as well as role based continuous building and improvement [18].

Researchers examined the deployment pattern for cloud environments, and found the patterns like Big Bang Deployment, Rolling Deployment, Canary Deployment and Blue-Green Deployment. Big Bang deployment adheres to the classic SDLC approach, and such deployments modify the entire or substantial components of the software in a single stroke. It is more laborious and less appropriate for cutting edge applications since it is a bit more agile for recent organizations [18]. Rolling deployment - in this instance, the freshly released variation on an application gradually takes the place of the old one. The actual deployment happens over a period. During that time, new and old versions coexist without affecting functionality or user experience [17]. Canary deployment Pattern that involves slowly rolling out the new changes to a small subset of users before rolling it out of the entire infrastructure and making it available for everyone [19]. Blue Green deployment - There organizations should have multiple production parameters that are as similar as feasible. Each one of them, to further use an instance of blue, is always living. They do the last round of evaluation for a new version of the application in a green environment [20]. [17] Blue Green deployment approaches must be used if the customers are to experience virtually no downtime and no disruptions throughout the patching process. However, there are still alternative methods to apply the Blue Green deployment pattern.

4   Deployment Pattern Analysis

According to our analysis Cloud based applications are increasing rapidly as hosting and computing resources become more available and efficient with this all design pattern. In order to maximize database scalability and performance of software systems. To determine and remedy any problems with performance, the application as well as its database need to be evaluated on a regular basis. The RDS offered by Amazon has applications for evaluating and optimizing effectiveness (Table 2).

Table 2. Deployment Pattern Analysis

Deployment Strategy	Security	Scalability	Cost	Downtime	Reliability
Blue-Green Deployment	High	Low	High	Low	Medium
Big Bang deployment	Low	Low	High	High	Low
Canary Deployment	High	High	Low	Low	Medium
Rolling deployment	High	Medium	Low	Low	Low

5   Conclusion

In this paper, we go over software deployment in the AWS environment along with software design and development using design patterns. In this study, we analyze and investigate several cloud computing deployment strategies along with different relational database design patterns for managing, organizing, and controlling cloud data challenges. The study on cloud computing software design challenges also looked at the consequences method used in the design pattern and offered some re-architecture choices. Although there are other factors that affect the use of clouds, database-related issues are the primary ones covered in the patterns. Create a novel deployment method based on the findings of the study and planned future research that could allow cloud application programs to fully engage in the cloud without facing significant obstacles.

References

1. Abdul, A., Bass, J., Ghavimi, H., MacRae, N., Adam, P.: Multi-tenancy design patterns in SaaS applications: a performance evaluation case study. Int. J. Digit. Soc. **9**, 1367–1375 (2018). https://doi.org/10.20533/ijds.2040.2570.2018.0168
2. Mu, H., Jiang, S.: Design patterns in software development. In: 2011 IEEE 2nd International Conference on Software Engineering and Service Science, Beijing, China, pp. 322–325 (2011). https://doi.org/10.1109/ICSESS.2011.5982228
3. Ku, C., Marlowe, T., Mantell, N.: Design patterns across software engineering and relational databases, pp. 271–274 (2006)
4. Lakshmi, G.: Database migration on premises to AWS RDS. EAI Endorsed Trans. Cloud Syst. **3**, 154463 (2018). https://doi.org/10.4108/eai.11-4-2018.154463
5. Stathopoulou, E., Vassiliadis, P.: Design patterns for relational databases (2009)
6. Arora, I., Gupta, A.: Cloud databases: a paradigm shift in databases. Int. J. Comput. Sci. Issues **9** (2012)
7. Markoska, E., Ackovska, N., Ristov, S., Gusev, M., Kostoska, M.: Software design patterns to develop an interoperable cloud environment. In: 2015 23rd Telecommunications Forum TEL-FOR (TELFOR), Belgrade, Serbia, pp. 986–989 (2015). https://doi.org/10.1109/TELFOR.2015.7377630
8. Rodin, R., Leet, J., Azua, M., Bygrave, D.: A pattern language for release and deployment management. In: Proceedings of the 18th Conference on Pattern Languages of Programs - PLoP 2011 (2011). https://doi.org/10.1145/2578903.2579147
9. https://en.clouddesignpattern.org
10. Moiz, S.A., Sailaja, P., Venkataswamy, G., Pal, S.: Database replication: a survey of open source and commercial tools. Int. J. Comput. Appl. **13** (2010). https://doi.org/10.5120/1788-2469
11. https://docs.aws.amazon.com/AmazonRDS
12. Kabakus, A.T., Kara, R.: A performance evaluation of in-memory databases. J. King Saud Univ. Comput. Inf. Sci. **29**, 520–525 (2016). https://doi.org/10.1016/j.jksuci.2016.06.007
13. https://aws.amazon.com/blogs/database/sharding-with-amazon-relational-database-ser-vice/
14. Yang, B., Sailer, A., Mohindra, A.: Survey and evaluation of blue-green deployment techniques in cloud native environments (2020). https://doi.org/10.1007/978-3-030-45989-5_6
15. https://hevodata.com/learn/amazon-rds-read-replicas/
16. Chen, L.: Continuous delivery: huge benefits, but challenges too. IEEE Softw. **32**(2), 50–54 (2015). https://doi.org/10.1109/MS.2015.27
17. Rodin, R., Leet, J., Azua, M., Bygrave, D.: A pattern language for release and deployment management. In: Proceedings of the 18th Conference on Pattern Languages of Programs (PLoP 2011), pp. 1–13. Association for Computing Machinery, New York, NY, USA (2011). Article 9. https://doi.org/10.1145/2578903.2579147

18. Rudrabhatla, C.K.: Comparison of zero downtime based deployment techniques in public cloud infrastructure. In: 2020 Fourth International Conference on I-SMAC (IoT in Social, Mobile, Analytics and Cloud) (I-SMAC), Palladam, India, pp. 1082–1086 (2020). https://doi.org/10.1109/I-SMAC49090.2020.9243605

19. Ellenberg, S.S.: The stepped-wedge clinical trial. JAMA **319**(6), 607 (2018). https://doi.org/10.1001/jama.2017.21993

20. https://oda.oslomet.no/oda-xmlui/handle/11250/3016792

21. Arnold, W.C., Eilam, T., Kalantar, M., Konstantinou, A., Totok, A.: Pattern based SOA deployment, pp. 1–12 (2007). https://doi.org/10.1007/978-3-540-74974-5_1

22. Ardagna, C.A., Damiani, E., Frati, F., Rebeccani, D., Ughetti, M.: Scalability patterns for platform-as-a-service. In: 2012 IEEE Fifth International Conference on Cloud Computing, Honolulu, HI, USA, pp. 718–725 (2012). https://doi.org/10.1109/CLOUD.2012.41

Author Index

© The Editor(s) (if applicable) and The Author(s), under exclusive license
to Springer Nature Switzerland AG 2024
S. Rajagopal et al (Eds.): ASCIS 2023, CCIS 2040, pp. 391–392, 2024.
https://doi.org/10.1007/978-3-031-59107-5

Printed in the United States
by Baker & Taylor Publisher Services